Walk the Rainbow

Live the *Way of Wholeness*

Barbara Rose

Art of Synthesis
Preston, UK
www.visionsofreality.co.uk

First published by Art of Synthesis 2022

A catalogue record for this book is available from the British Library
ISBN: 978-0-9567391-8-6

A O S

AUTHOR'S NOTE

Walk the Rainbow is a story, a workbook and an intuitive self-help guide to the innermost self. Its journey began in 2005, when, in a spirit of play, the first 'vision', *Emergence,* was born. Many more works of art followed, each with its own tale to tell, unique visual facet of the whole to reveal and wisdom to impart, and each one derived through play, using a variety of creative sources. Some, like the first, were a product of doodling – hand drawn and inspired by life experience or the fruits of dreams or meditations; others carried the kingdom of nature as inspiration; many had as their source, courtesy of NASA, photographs from the far reaches of the cosmos – galaxies, nebulae, planets and stars. And many more were a combination of all, where images were skilfully blended layer upon layer to marry earth with cosmos, inner with outer; the ultimate in visionary imagery being their synthesised outcome. As creativity and the same spirit of play delved into the world of sacred geometry, what began as an adventurous sojourn into the world of art blossomed into understanding of the inner workings of the universe, and with it the structure of space. Random images now had a place in the grand scheme of things. They held purpose and vision. They had structure. What's more, they provided an answer, at least in part, to the 'how?' in 'how to' *Walk the Rainbow.*

A moment of play that evolved into 144 works of art, each exposing a unique *vision of reality,* could now be seen to include the full spectrum of physical life experience. Furthermore, their combined expression, as will be revealed throughout the ensuing chapters, amounts to a very significant geometry: the stellated dodecahedron or Christ-Consciousness grid, significantly totalling 144 facets. Uncovering this, however, exposes a mere tip of the iceberg. Questions concerning the many subtle layers lying 'beneath the surface' remained unanswered; so too did those referring to Soul and Spirit, their integration with human consciousness and the laws governing their rite of passage. Enter the role of two vitally important threads: the fruit of research, spanning more than five decades, into physical and metaphysical 'systems', spiritual traditions and teachings, esoterica and mythology, being one; a sprinkling of magic, the other.

The systems, two in particular, as well as insights gained from contemplating the aforementioned resources, are the backbone to *Walk the Rainbow* and provide authenticity to material that is largely subjective in nature. Underpinning every musing, introspection, inner dialogue and inter-species communication whilst offering structure and validation to the 'stories' unfolding with each turn of a page, they serve as intuitive signposts in a landscape that would otherwise be impossible to define, let alone navigate. The first system, sacred geometry, has already been touched upon as providing a framework for the 144 visionary expressions of reality, but there is so much more to this Divine Architecture than is offered here. The Science of Light Manifestation,[i] the second system directly affiliated with this material, is so intricately woven into its substance that it is inseparable from the rainbow. Why? Because it **is** the rainbow. How these two complete, independent and all-inclusive systems co-create to deliver a *Way of Wholeness* is by means of the third thread – a sprinkling of magic!

Running as a river through every 'inner' chapter is a story so far-reaching in its delivery of the profound and so expansive in its telling of the Real, yet so accessible in its capacity to embrace the small, that the heart cannot fail to be moved with every step. Esoteric secrets, inaccessible but to the few, evolution of consciousness as it unfolds through time, interdependent relationships between kingdoms in nature, the nature of the

Soul in its own realm and the role of mind, right down to the subtle (and sometimes not so subtle) happenings in daily life are embraced equally as fundamental expressions of life through this captivating and amusing, yet eye-opening, parable.

In *Walk the Rainbow*, the three inseparable threads, none more superior than the others, unravel the wondrous mysteries characterising 'life' in its many and varied forms by expressing multiple layers of subtlety in consciousness. They may be summarised as follows:

- 144 *visions of reality* art works.[1]
- Integral systems – sacred geometry and the Science of Light Manifestation through the Seven Rays.[ii]
- A sprinkling of fairy dust.

The cover says it all

Aside from the title, three straplines frame the focal point of the cover and offer guidance on how to approach this material. Each is explained thoroughly in, 'What is...?' at the end of the book.

A less obvious element lies in the cover graphic and is by far the greatest revealer of 'what this book is really all about'. But before going into the why, let's take it apart and see what's on show. Naturally, the rainbows are the greatest attractor, but look closely at their alignment, allow your heart to feel their undivided flow and you may sense that they are a dead giveaway for the message being transmitted through title, straplines and picture; they are all vertically aligned in perfect symmetry. Begin with the 'umbrella' half-circle rainbow; see how it serves as source, protector and illuminator to all that transpires beneath, including the book's title. Follow this rainbow's journey as it spirals into existence, weaving this way and that whilst still maintaining its integrity as a rainbow; see it enter,

through the heart of an elfin child who, it would appear, has much to impart beyond mere words. Notice that it is here, as the rainbow enters the horizontal plane and is grounded in matter, that the onset of change begins.

Beneath the child's right foot is a large black box, and his stance is such that you are left in no doubt that he would be in full command of any situation that should emerge from within it. Scattered around are a further seven boxes of varying sizes that, unlike the one beneath his foot, are distinguishable by their colour; it would appear the rainbow has landed! What began in wholeness and maintained its integrity throughout the journey is now laid bare at the feet of an unsuspecting child, in pieces – or so it would seem. Return your eyes to the level of the child's heart, where he and the rainbow are perfectly aligned with their source, and see that he is holding a geometric form purposefully in his left hand. With a little imagination you can almost hear him saying, "Look, **this** is what it is really all about," whilst placing a little more pressure upon his right foot to emphasise his point. Can you see what he means? Through his whole demeanour, he is showing us why these dynamics are so significant. How?

Let's look at the boxes. These represent the separate self, the parts of you that feel isolated, alone or even superior to other 'boxes'. These parts may keep you trapped, a prisoner of your own beliefs, but nevertheless they are coloured; they may be fractured, but they are still the rainbow and thus they are whole. All that is required is to remove the blocks that are preventing you from seeing it. This is *Walking the Rainbow*. The black box is especially significant, being the unconscious, both collective and individual, from within which all that is hidden may rise to the surface as and when it sees fit, in whatever manner it chooses. The placement

---

[1] Also published as *Key of Light* contemplation cards (see p.397) available separately.

of the child's foot shows that the only way to embrace this 'box' is through awareness; *Walk the Rainbow* shows you how. The two interlocking circles he is holding are equally important. See how they create an 'eye' at the centre. Look closer and you will see that the 'eyeball' is made up of seven interconnecting circles, each one a colour of the rainbow; our friendly little elf is demonstrating that all returns to wholeness when the heart is attuned to the inner rainbow. The geometries featured here – cube (boxes), two interlocking circles, vesica piscis (eye), seed of life (seven circles) and pentagon (on the child's hat) – are most significant; our wise little friend explains why in the forthcoming chapters.

At a glance – how to use this book

The following summary includes suggestions for using this book and serves as a quick and easy reference guide. It encourages you to look beyond the obvious, open your eyes in wonderment with each inner 'aha' and ride the spiral with joy in your heart as you embark upon the most magical of mystery tours. But be prepared – life as you know it may never be the same again.

1. There are nine chapters. The 'filling in the sandwich' between this note and the final chapter, 'What is…?', is expressed through seven chapters in storybook form. Illustrated by a fairy on each title page, this magical tale meanders with purpose through the chapters, each chapter introduction being a continuation of the journey. The story is a parable in which untold mysteries of the cosmos are revealed with every step. *Italicised text* directs your attention inwards to *feel the words* as they touch your heart in the moment. The structure of space is exposed through explicit geometric forms, and profound spiritual teachings are insightfully explained through the 'wisdom of Thomas', whose passion is science – physical and metaphysical – and whose wisdom is love. Weaving their way throughout the telling are the three inseparable threads – *visions of reality, integral systems* and *magic* – mentioned earlier.

2. Much will be gained by following the story from beginning to end before 'tasting the ingredients' mentioned below. It will give you a sense of the road ahead and provide a bigger-picture perspective for when you explore individual elements. Just turn to the opening pages of the chapters mentioned below, read in sequence, and enjoy the ride!

3. Now to the nitty gritty. The first three chapters of the 'filling' – 'A Story', 'A Gift' and 'A Door' – lead you in gently, introduce you to the primary characters and set the parameters for the forthcoming Rainbow journey; each one takes you deeper into the subtle realms of the Soul whilst addressing vulnerabilities that are part and parcel of being human.

4. The second triad – 'A Rainbow', 'A Diamond' and 'An Invitation' – tantalise your taste buds further by delving into the 'ingredients' making up the 'filling' and offer ways to interact with the contents as if you were attending a workshop, for instance. These constitute the workbook element of *Walk the Rainbow*, are your first port of call when using this material as a conscious path to **Live** the *Way of Wholeness* and are the pages you will return to many times for guidance.

5. 'A Rainbow' is the bigger-picture, **group-conscious (Soul)** perspective, where the second thread, *integral systems,* makes its appearance. Using the seed of life geometry as a window to view Spirit in the course of its apparent fragmentation, seven colours of the rainbow are shown to express both wholeness and individuality, whilst the Seven Rays as group-conscious entities[iii] are surreptitiously

introduced (in *Key of Light* cards these are the suits). Refer to the relevant section in this chapter to bring a broader 'group-context' perspective to your chosen vision. In 'A Diamond', **individual consciousness** (personality), makes the first thread, *visions of reality,* more visible and continues the journey, into ever-increasing degrees of fractured light, to arrive at the multi-faceted diamond of which each vision, or individual *Key of Light* card, is a part. This is a good place to look when beginning your inner journey. The workbook element of *Walk the Rainbow* finds its end, and your beginning, in 'An Invitation'. Here, you are invited to play, engage intimately with every facet of the diamond, marry it with your daily life and consciously *Walk the Rainbow* through living a *Way of Wholeness*. Vision layouts included in this section work best with *Key of Light* cards; however, the material from this book alone can be just as transformative. The most important quality to take on board whilst exploring is that of play. Remember, this whole Rainbow journey began with a doodle!

6. 'An End?', the last chapter in the story, returns our adventurers to the beginning, where, at another turn of the spiral, a choice awaits. To continue the journey and begin again, knowing every step taken is in service to the whole, or to savour the richness of life well lived and celebrate its end. This choice is also yours.

7. As to the 'bread', the outer part of the sandwich, 'Introduction' and 'Author's Note' are self-explanatory. Return to this, especially this list, if you require clarity or direction on the next step – in daily life or with reference to the book. The last chapter, 'What is...?' serves as a guide to the systems, providing knowledge-based information on the researched material underpinning the story; sacred geometry, the Seven Rays, relevant metaphysical and physical science (physics), etc. are included here. Author's afterword shares real-life experiences that inspired Esmerelda's journey, and an alphabetical glossary provides clarity on terms that may not be familiar; it includes phrases or words sourced from every chapter, as well as from relevant external sources. Finally, appendices and a bibliography are included as stimulus for the creative imagination, should you wish to broaden your horizons a little.

8. In summary, this book may be used in any number of ways, a few of which have been suggested here: read it as you would any other book, use it as a resource guide for learning more about the *integral systems* or feel the magic of all it has to impart by consciously engaging with the material as an *Education in Consciousness* and guide to your innermost Self. Remember, be creative, have fun and explore.

APPRECIATION

*To those who walked with joy, the Rainbow path
Who shared, for years, their vulnerability, their vision and
their worth...*

*To those whose hearts believed when at times I didn't
Who held my hand when I almost gave up...*

*To those who were a shining light in the darkest night
Whose wisdom touched the Ancient of Days... and who saw
with a mind so clear...*

*To those who are friends to the Soul (and me)
Who cause my eyes to shine and my heart to smile with
joy... inside...*

*And to those I have yet to greet
Whose fingers have still to grace these pages...*

I offer my eternal gratitude

CONTENTS

FOREWORD

BY RONALD L. HOLT

In the long run of time spent on the spiritual journey, Great Spirit has an enormous task of parenting, educating and then weaning its children within the great expanse of experiences that are phased over many lifetimes. Furthermore, this accumulative, individualized history formulates an identity in the form of a personality which is utilized anew for each given lifetime.

For each of us, all these many lifetimes serve as a long-term gestation process in a manner similar to having a yolk gestate within the secure walls of its protective eggshell. In the case of an individual, this shell protects and secures the 3D definitions, boundaries and beliefs concerning the reality it perceives as existing all around us and extending outwards into the richness of the mysterious cosmos.

At a given point of internal experience and maturity, under the watchful eye of Great Spirit, and just as acclimation to the defined 3D laws of the physics of a personality's encapsulation of reality appears concrete, unbreakable and final, the trickster-like playful spirit of the Creator unexpectedly pokes one or more holes through the eggshell; like using a quantum acupuncture needle to impregnate its trademark of majestic awe and wonder upon the consciousness of the unsuspecting traveller. The physics of 3D belief systems and reality boundaries undergo tremendous change in these circumstances. Concrete 3D perceptions are replaced with an emerging new paradigm in the consciousness of the journeyer, and new seeds, rife with quantum ambiance and characteristics, now enter the realm of possibilities; trading concrete 3D laws with ease whilst replacing the former 3D reality with an emerging new paradigm seems to be an art to Great Spirit, particularly in the timing of such events.

After acclimating quantum surgical acupuncture episodes (complete with their after-effects and processing), Great Spirit, always closely observing, awaits the gestational maturity of the embryo within the eggshell. When it is ready to begin cracking its formative 3D cosmic egg, it enters a profound degree of nakedness and vulnerability where the exoskeleton made up of the many masks worn by the embryonic being is systematically torn apart; the wrapping of a patchwork quilt of snapshot viewpoints and incompletely processed emotions, woven over time and then worn as a false identity, is seen for what it is. At this point, under the guidance of Great Spirit within, all falsehoods fall away, and the embryo is left to redefine and reanimate as its true immortal self.

For many of us, this is the moment when we can use the help and assistance of individuals who have themselves experienced such a process of deep and profound transformational metamorphosis.

As director of the worldwide spiritual organization, Flower of Life, I co-created (with my wife) an advanced sacred geometry workshop called Seed of Life. In the summer of 2007, whilst facilitating this week-long event in Scotland, I first met Barbara Rose; she was a participant at that workshop. Since then, I have always felt a deep bond with Barbara. Engaging her at many opportunities, I find her to possess such an innate and hard-won inner clarity, with a rare gift in bringing clarity, vision and simplicity to those deep and profound complexities of the esoteric, philosophical and even spiritual depths, that it is a pleasure to bear witness.

After directing the Flower of Life organization for 17 years, I concluded my directorship. Following this, in February 2013, I delved straight into what is known as internal shadow work, where we work at facing our deepest and darkest mirror reflections of ourselves; many years investing in Taoist and Hindu yoga studies, as well as practice, were especially foundational in integrating such unconscious mental and emotional belief systems. From exploring, owning and integrating these through working upon my own issues, I was soon moved to assist others using the same inner process; Quantum Navigation classes and group sessions were born.

Barbara and I have kept in regular contact for many years, meeting both in person and on Skype or Zoom, and we continue to share, learn and grow from each other's insights and self-realizations, especially in the shadow issues arena. Because she constantly aspires to reach new depths and understandings within herself, Barbara possesses one of those fountains of inspiration that is inseparable from someone who has walked the road and done the work required to provide an authentic beacon amidst the frequent storms and roiling seas of life. To those on the spiritual journey, challenged by seemingly walking their path alone, such beacons are indispensable.

Barbara Rose's gentle and naked heart shines through her unique storytelling, combined with her vast experience, to dispel the weight of fording the chaos and loneliness commonly experienced by those on the journey. As in life, the reader comes to touch upon the love, inspiration and brilliance that make up this lovely author.

Ronald L. Holt
Phoenix, Arizona
August 2021

INTRODUCTION

*Man, know thyself and thou shalt know
the universe and God...*

This timeless maxim is inscribed upon the forecourt of the Temple of Apollo, Delphi, and has been held up as a touchstone for all seekers throughout the ages in their quest for self-knowledge. But when it comes down to it, when you take a step back and really think, what does it actually mean? Ask yourself, why is it that something so uplifting and apparently obvious proves so elusive? Is it possible to penetrate the mysterious veils that prevent a man or woman from knowing the full magnitude of his or her expression? If so, how? Perhaps it is time to dig a little deeper into the meaning behind this, and many other sweeping 'spiritual' statements that have dogged the sincere in heart whilst walking an awakening path, and find out. Even better, let's take it a stage further, drag them into the 21st century and establish their worth.

It goes without saying that we have a physical body and we have emotions, feelings and thoughts, but how many of us are aware of the impact one has upon the other and, more importantly, how they directly influence relationships and create the reality of the world in which we live? Aside from these, there are many subtle levels making up the totality of man that are often discarded in our modern, materialistic society. These levels interact with and have direct bearing upon our physical health, emotional well-being and peace of mind. We are, for the most part, so fixated on our all-consuming and ever-demanding wants and needs, as well as answering to those of others, that they dictate the course of our lives to the exclusion of all else, with barely a backward glance given to alternative ways of being. Inner peace, balanced relationships and financial stability are often perceived as being part of some idealistic utopia found within the proverbial pot of gold at the end of the rainbow, but again, what does this really mean, and is there anything we can do about it? The answer, of course, is a resounding 'yes'. It is time for us to cease **chasing** rainbows, awaken to who we are and *'***Walk** *the Rainbow'* through our lives – the intention behind taking your first steps upon this unique journey. Again, it's okay to make idealistic statements like this, but do they have any foundation in reality? Perhaps we should take a closer look, a proper look, at the world in which we live, in a deep, experiential, living sense, and see what happens.

Think about the times you have stood rooted to the spot whilst bathing in the presence of a rainbow as it draws an arc of brilliance across a stormy sky. Perhaps you wondered why the pot of gold is always so hard to find or why miracles in nature, so vibrant and alive, are out of reach and never seem to live up to their promise of lasting fulfilment. Maybe you have also questioned the origin of their creation. Ask yourself, why, despite opening your heart to all that life has to offer, does the great void of nothingness spew out an endless sense of lack? And why, oh why, is there never any peace to be found in this increasingly chaotic free-for-all we call 21st-century life? Has it ever occurred to you that maybe you are looking for the answer to these frustratingly persistent, heart-wrenching questions in the wrong place? Perhaps the pot of gold is inside... and maybe, just maybe... you **are** the pot of gold. *Walk the Rainbow* helps you to find out.

In a nutshell, this book is about life, specifically your life, but far more than this, as the opening quote states, it is about you. However, this somewhat ambiguous and sweeping statement doesn't really do it justice. *Walk the Rainbow* **is** life; life **is** you. "How can that be?" you might ask. After all, you are well aware of what life means to you, and maybe you are happy with that understanding, but for some reason you are here reading these words; perhaps your understanding isn't complete after all. So how do these premises provide insight into the substance of the book you are about to read? Perhaps we should take a closer look at what constitutes life and then we can see how it fits in with your understanding.

Beginning with the obvious, our physical universe, it would seem nigh on impossible to set down in a book such as this the full magnitude of all that informs our natural world. From the breath-taking wonder of an indigo sky, illuminated by a vast array of twinkling lights too numerous to comprehend, to galaxies, nebulae, meteors and comets; from stars extinct to those at their pinnacle of potential and stardust carried upon wings of fire to form, from death, worlds anew; from planets and moons to solar systems near and far; from a pinprick of light in a galaxy far, far away to an nondescript lump of carbon closer to home. All of this constitutes life. All of this is you.

Now stand upon this piece of rock called planet earth and wonder at its magnificence. Just think for a moment of the miracle that shapes the kingdom of nature and ponder upon how blatantly we take her so much for granted. Consider the creatures: those that fly, those that crawl, slither or hide beneath sand or stone, those who run or stroll across the land or those who swing with skill amidst forests green, and more, whose playground lies deep beneath the waves. Look to the vegetation, trees, flowers, plants, mosses and lichens and feel, for a moment, just how dependent you are upon their beneficence. Delve deeper into the substance of this place we know as home, to atoms, molecules and quarks, and see that they are, in themselves, a universe in the making. Now view the elements – earth, air, fire and water – and envisage a world without

their cooperation. All of this, and so much more, is life. All of this is you. But, as you well know, it does not end there. Until the imagination is engaged in wonderment and the heart opens to appreciate the magnificent spectacle of which we are so much a part, the miracle of creation is concealed from the eyes of the perceiver.

Now turn your attention to the human being, in a day-by-day, physical-living sense. Think about what constitutes you, as an individual – your body, mental well-being, emotional stability, identity, beliefs and habitual behavioural responses. Expand your awareness into your environment; consider your everyday existence – your work, leisure, health, friends, family, home, neighbourhood, gender, country, heritage and lineage – leave no stone left unturned. Think, really think, about all that completes the picture, in a personal identity sense, that is you. Now connect to humanity as a whole. Think about the role we, as a race, play in the well-being of the world at large; reflect upon how our thoughts, words and deeds affect our fellow human beings and how, through the ripple effect, they influence the future of all that constitutes the natural world. Think about it. This, too, is life. This, too, is you.

However, there is so much more to existence than is recognised through physical expression alone. *One Life* lies beyond the obvious. *One Life* so ubiquitous that we are as cells to its body, droplets to its ocean and seeds in the garden of its infinite expression. This vast and layered inner landscape, this *One Life,* if you would but perceive, defines the constitution of man and is largely unknown save for to those who have walked extensively the inner paths. Multi-layered, expressing light and shadow, false and true, and order and chaos, it is readily available to all who display courage in turning their attention inwards. A boundless etheric web governed by an undisputed Authority, an innate ordered intelligence, that ensures the interconnectedness of all life forms unfolds according to a Will that can only be Divine and patiently awaits the discerning traveller. But what of its methods and codes, its structures and boundaries, and how does it ensure the delicate balance between this way and that, this species and other, is maintained? What of light and shadow, Soul and Spirit or the nature of death? What of time and the laws to which it adheres? What part does all of this play in the return of a divided, isolated and fragmented particle, such as you, to wholeness? How may you navigate this unfamiliar territory when you have no point of reference, let alone a map? And how may you distinguish the subtle realms of Soul and Spirit amidst the many pitfalls set by an equally creative, yet misinformed, shadow self – the unconscious, unhealed and under-processed inner you? How may you, as the droplet, **be** the ocean?

These questions, and so many more, are fundamental to life, but unless you take some time out to pause and reflect upon what 'lies beneath the surface', they remain unanswered in the unconscious swamp that characterises 'life in sleep'. *Walk the Rainbow* is a wake-up call; it is an invitation to take a step back and reflect upon what lies underneath, to swim in the waters of life knowing swimmer and sea are alike in substance and to walk unceasingly inwards until the beyond is as a lamp beneath your feet. It extends an invitation to nurture, as would a mother her new-born child, the Spirit within, to gather to your breast lost children of the Soul and to feed these wounded, lost and abandoned selves that have been denied succour for far, far too long until they are satiated – inside.

Walk the Rainbow is, as the cover says, an invitation to *Manifest the beauty of the Soul... Walk a rainbow through your life...* but, as you can see from this brief introduction, there is far more to it than first meets the eye. *Walk the Rainbow* is a sojourn into the very fabric of existence, your existence, and one where many mysteries, hitherto untold, may arise as knowing in one who is awake. It tells a tale of magic, wonderment and child-like innocence long ago forgotten by those weighed down by the trappings of adulthood. Yes, *Walk the Rainbow* **is** life... but it is life with signposts and even one or two maps. Above all else, it is an adventure. An adventure... in wholeness...

And it begins with a story...

Picture a scene... before the onset of time... when the inky blackness of an indigo sky is devoid of stars. Where space is like an island yet to experience the ocean of which it is so much a part... where a beginning is yet to greet its end...

Picture an existence in which nothing is known, the fabric of this nothingness impregnated with all that can ever be learned and the essence of its Being-ness is to reveal that which is always intended.

Create a setting where eternal darkness is all there ever is... where light has yet to bear its shadow... silence, its sound... and stillness, its activity.

Paint a reality in which the only redeemer is one that can't be saved, the only metronome is one that can't be set and the only heart is one that will never feel...

Into this picture see a tear fall from an eye that does not cry... witness a spark pierce the dark... birthed through a Source that may not be named...

Watch in wonder as water and fire begin their eternal dance... Marvel at its miracle... Ride the spiral... as the matrix of creation stirs into life...

Now bear witness to the echoes of a story... For, as seeds of an adventure, long ago forgotten, awaken... its magic is revealed once more...

a Story

a Gift

a Door

a Rainbow

a Diamond

an Invitation

an End?

A Story

Esmerelda *grew more and more morose with each passing moment. How long had it been since her handsome prince had stood before her? How long since he had held her in his gentle arms or caressed her hair? How long since he had played frivolously with her soft, elfin ears? Esmerelda sighed as she surveyed the walls of the prison in which she now lived... How long since she had experienced the magical world to which she truly belonged... in which she ruled as queen?*

There were times when she could sense his presence. A flash of light darting amongst the trees in the dead of night... the rustle of leaves as they danced upon the breeze... diamond sparkles in a laughing brook... And if she quietened her mind and listened, really listened, she could hear his voice... It whispered silently amongst the cacophony of earthy sound... encouraging her, gently guiding her... "It won't be long now, my love." She knew, even though she continued to wait, she knew he was here... He was her every breath, he flowed through her veins with each beat of her heart... all that she touched, all that she heard, was him... He was here... right now. She knew... yet still she waited expectantly... Again, Esmerelda sighed as she reflected upon the events that had led to her incarceration... Why did she choose to leave the land she loved, to enter this gross unforgiving land? Why did she give up her right to fly? Why? Why? Another sigh...

A fleeting touch, senses barely registering its presence, softened her furrowed brow... "Hello, my love," he says, the warmth of his smile igniting the light in his eyes, "Did you enjoy your nap?" She returns his smile. He never fails to awaken this response in her. He is her handsome prince – the king. "Shall we go for a walk in the grounds before dinner? It's such a beautiful day..."

This short story serves as a metaphor for life in the 21st century and holds within it several parallels to the driving needs that run our everyday lives. We can all, at some point in our lives, relate to Esmerelda or the handsome prince; it is, after all, an archetype of the classic fairy tale in which the lonely, imprisoned princess is rescued by her handsome knight in shining armour. Regardless of our romantic circumstances, we have all experienced times when we wished we could be somewhere other than where we were or thought that happiness would be assured if only certain 'things' would change. As a result, we deny the rich beauty of life as it exists in the present moment.

Paradox is also evident within the story. Is Esmerelda really a prisoner or is it a figment of her own imagination, a part within a dream? Is she the dreamer or the dream? Is the handsome prince, the king who caressed her with *a fleeting touch,* the same lover who drove her to despair at his absence? Was she dreaming of some other-worldly paradise that was, in fact, her everyday life, or was she indeed an incarcerated magical creature from another realm who knew how to fly? Which is the 'real' Esmerelda?

Perhaps there is a ring of truth to all of these possibilities and Esmerelda is **both** earthly queen and magical creature; we are talking paradox, after all. There is also a hint within the story that the handsome prince does not exist as something outside of her – *he was her every breath, he flowed through her veins with each beat of her heart... all that she touched, all that she heard, was him* and *if she quietened her mind and listened, really listened, she could hear his voice...*

Both quotes would lead us to believe that if only we could silence the endless chatter of our thoughts, the voice of 'something' or 'someone' other-worldly with greater wisdom and understanding might be heard. And if we took a little time to listen, we might notice that all we are searching for is here, right now, inside us... Wouldn't it be wonderful if we could find a way to access the part of us that can fly? The part of us that knows the dream, the dreamer and the dreamed, or the part that is the orchestrator of the dream that creates our everyday reality? Is this really possible?

Of course it is! Anything in the world of dreams is possible...

Welcome to the magical world of
Walk the Rainbow!

Cleaning windows

There are many 'windows' through which we perceive the world in which we live. They act as filters or smokescreens and often prevent us from seeing people, events or circumstances as they really are. These filters include our beliefs – about ourselves, others, religions, cultures, etc. – and condition our behavioural responses according to whether we agree or disagree with what we see 'through the window' of our experience; the more deeply engrained our beliefs, the dirtier the windows and the greater our lack of tolerance towards others. Consequently, it is largely these conditioned patterns of behavioural responses that are responsible for the somewhat turbulent and inharmonious way we live our day-to-day lives. If we could only learn to 'clean our windows' once in a while, we would not only feel happier, more accepting and content in ourselves but also be far more tolerant with those who share a differing view of reality. The upshot is that what we believe, what we see 'through the window', creates our reality; seeing is believing, is it not? Maybe it is time to review our perspective, wash our windows and change the *vision* we have of *reality*.

Within the opening story, there are several possible perspectives on how Esmerelda may choose to experience her reality; the story is multi-layered, as are we as human beings. *Walk the Rainbow* reflects and encompasses this truth. Three of these layers, as already set down in the introductory pages, are familiar to most of us – we have a physical body, emotions and thoughts, but how many of us are aware of the impact they have upon each other and, more importantly, how they dictate the reality of the world in which we live? The truth is that there are many expressions of our humanness – from average, 'material' man who is largely reactive in nature, with little or no consideration for the thoughts or feelings of others, to the fully awakened man who is consciously aware, is in touch with the subtle layers uniting him with others and lives from the perspective of the 'bigger picture'; naturally there are many more, a vast majority, who lie somewhere in between. The dividing line between one way of being and the other is awareness – the transformational act of 'cleaning windows'. How can we possibly expect to see clearly if we have mucky windows? How can we hope to lead lighter and brighter lives unless we are willing to embrace these qualities in ourselves and others? And how may we initiate these changes if we are not even aware that both light and shadow qualities exist within us? In short, if we are not even aware that we have a 'Higher Self', or Soul, how can we possibly expect to view the world through its eyes? *Walk the Rainbow* assists you in 'seeing' with 'new eyes' by igniting the light of the Soul; embracing the shadow being a crucial part of the process.

The real voyage of discovery consists not in seeking new landscapes, but in having new eyes.
Marcel Proust

Let there be light...

Esmerelda loved light. The way it transformed the most dismal landscape with a spontaneous flash of its brilliance was, to her, nothing short of miraculous. It added fuel to her imagination, and she never ceased to be amazed at how a perfectly ordinary day led to so many extraordinary encounters, simply through the presence of light... Rays from an intermittent sun filtering through a canopy of leaves exposed beings from other realms, as if by magic. Hidden depths in a forest pool revealed 1000 untold stories as a shaft of light, like a razor, cut through the illusion of a world long since deceased. Amidst pebble and stone she saw water nymphs flirt with the air in a meandering stream... and the beauty of her love reflected in its stillness... In light, she witnessed its forever partner, shadow, follow its every move... inseparable lovers cast into the sands of time... And then there were the stars at night... oh, how she loved the stars. In her special place, right at the heart of the forest where the blanket of green gave way to the enormity of space above, she would rest on a mattress of welcoming moss, gaze upon the endless sky and wonder... forever wonder... at the miracle of light...

*It wasn't only light in the land that made Esmerelda smile. She loved how it made her **feel**. In her, in others, she marvelled at the light that shone through human eyes... Laughter, joy, love, passion, even tears... all of these, for her, were light... and they made her heart swell with so much love and gratitude that she felt she would explode into a million tiny pieces with the pure, unadulterated elation of it all... Starved of its presence for so, so long, something within her hungered for each tiny sparkle... yearned for its life-giving sustenance... It made her whole... complete... But far more than this, it helped her to remember... It helped her to remember... something? Something... she had long ago forgotten... until now... In a flash of insight, she knew... from the depths of her being, she knew... **light***

reminded her of the land of her belonging... it reminded her of the land where she knew how to fly...

Walk the Rainbow helps you to remember. It forges a link to the Soul, the source of your inner light, and helps you to remember the land of your belonging. In recognising your innate strengths, it encourages you to let go of all that no longer serves the 'light' within you, and then, just like Esmerelda, you remember *how to fly*. Grounded in science from both physical and metaphysical perspectives, it builds upon foundations laid in the opening story and takes you deeper into the realms of light. You begin to understand the working of the Soul in its own realm, whilst intimately experiencing every aspect of your 'humanness'. This process is not 'airy-fairy' and does not mean you deny or banish your 'ordinary' life to be blissed out in the land of the Soul. No, it is not about escapism; it is a journey of integration on which you, as an individual, become one with the part of you that exists as pure light. Esmerelda, in her next adventure, reveals how this is possible.

In the twilight zone between waking and sleep, Esmerelda allowed herself to remember... she journeyed, without regret, into the land of her belonging... and once again, she knew how to fly... However, even though she knew how... she didn't... fly, that is... She stood, as a child, and allowed the full glory of light, its immeasurable presence, to permeate every last molecule of her being... She allowed the warmth of its love to nourish the far reaches of her soul... all her senses, deprived of essential nutrients for far too long, relentlessly drank its sweet nectar... Esmerelda sighed as the full impact of her return penetrated her earthly shell... oh, how she had missed this realm... so much... She yielded... she wept... she gave herself totally to the land... until she was no more... all that remained was belonging... no Esmerelda, only belonging... And still she didn't fly... No, the presence, that was Esmerelda, waited...

*Shapes appeared in the land... a few had individual form – some humanlike, others alien... yet more came in the form of geometric grids... All were light... lights within light, distinguishable only by subtle changes in their resonance... and all was in perfect accord, there was no dissonance in this place... 'Life' was so **easy** here... And now she understood... she understood why she didn't fly even though she knew how... There was no need... matching her vibration to her destination, whether light being or land... transported her there... in an instant! Flying, she realised, was so primitive... thought and vibratory resonance were far more effective, more efficient... Slowly, piece by piece, all she once knew returned... She remembered how fluidly she moved between dimensions, how effortlessly she materialised from one form to another, and how, with a simple gesture, all she touched was light... More important than this... she remembered the keys...*

*Life on earth, by comparison, used keys that were so clumsy, so gross; they merely unlocked doors, nothing else... how primitive was that?! They were ineffective in inter-species communication, in conversation that transcended the limits of space and time, that went way beyond the use of mere words; they did not open up aspects of herself she never knew existed... above all, they did not enable her to **know**! Again, Esmerelda sighed... One long, heart-wrenching sigh... How could she possibly have forgotten all of this? How could she not know of the keys? How could she... fail... to remember... all... of this?*

Esmerelda's journey into the subtle realms of light, the *land of her belonging,* is a wonderful metaphor for not only discovering the *Way of the Soul* but also realising the ultimate in *Walk the Rainbow*. Her soul-searching questions, fraught with self-recrimination, echo the profound sense of loss – of something missing, something we can't quite get hold of with our minds – that we

have all felt at one point, whether we were aware of it or not; they reflect the quintessential sense of 'lack' that goes hand in hand with our humanness. We all aspire to be something far greater than ourselves, little realising we already are that which we seek. The closing questions posed by Esmerelda spring from the profound realisation that she had, at last, realised this simple truth. In fact, it so moved her that she wondered how she could have known it to be otherwise – *how could she fail to remember all of this?*

However, the truth is that we do forget. And no matter how often we are told otherwise and how much proof is proffered from whatever source, we still don't believe it – we still see ourselves as something considerably less than our full state of perfection. *Walk the Rainbow* takes you beyond beliefs. It awakens the part of you that knows; the All that is whole and complete.

Esmerelda shares many gifts within her story. She is very child-like, vulnerable and fragile. She loves light in its many and varied forms and has a close affinity with nature, yet she finds it so hard to live in the harsh reality of physical existence. Perhaps you can relate to some or all of this in your own life. The essential 'nutrients' she shares are like the stars at night or a candle in a darkened room; they help us to 'see' and they encourage us to walk ever forward in the certain knowing that there is a pot of gold at the end of the rainbow and that a boundless pot of light is within each one of us – without exception. In short, Esmerelda's gifts encourage us to **shine**!

If we look deeper into her journey, we will see there are three distinct sources from which she draws her light 'sustenance'. Her story began in a place of despair; she pined for the loss of her love, only to find he was right beside her all along, encouraging her to adjust the *vision* she had of *reality*. From a newly found place of rapport, she was able to look upon her earthly existence and appreciate the wonders of nature. She saw how the simple quality of light interacting with its various elements enabled *1000 untold stories* to fuel her imagination and fill her heart with joy. The light in the land encouraged her to see similar qualities reflected in the eyes of others. Finally, she turned her attention inwards and remembered; she remembered all that she had forgotten; she remembered the keys.

In the 'A Diamond' chapter, each vision, as a facet of the diamond, **is** a key. Through image, symbol and seed thought, they take the subtle realms intrinsic to the kingdoms of nature, Soul and Spirit and marry them with the innate essence that expresses humanity at its finest. Rich in symbolism and steeped in spiritual significance, they serve as doorways into the multi-layered nature of human consciousness. Subtle realms of earth and cosmos merge with your personal journey – thoughts, feelings and physical appearances – to provide an *Education in Consciousness* where all are recognised as facets of the multi-dimensional Self; the inner you. Esmerelda discovered at the outset that the route from wholeness to separation and return was rooted in the land of shadows where, until the flower of her awakening opened to the light within, forgetfulness was her only nutrient; her path of return, her awakening, began at this point of recognition. In the land of her belonging, she encountered light-grids, geometric structures, which she soon discovered were *keys* to new ways of being. They attracted refined vibrations of light, facilitated inter-species communication that *transcended space and time*, and introduced intuitive levels of understanding to her mind. The grids of which she spoke are real. They are founded upon the principles of sacred geometry, known collectively as the *Language of Light,* and they enable you to know, without doubt, that you **are** light.

Every vision, through image or symbol, is embedded with geometric structure. *Walk the Rainbow* marries these qualities of divine order with metaphor and story to extol its principles in such a way that you may both intellectually understand how each shape interacts with the others and intuitively **know** how all these principles apply to you, your daily life and your relationship with your ultimate potential: the Soul. Contemplating inside your heart the deep and profound principles laid down on the pages of this book opens up a means of communication that transcends *the boundaries of space and time.* Like Esmerelda, you start to remember that which has for so long been forgotten; all that you **believed** yourself to be falls away and you start to emit a frequency of authenticity; the inner you is expressed outwards as radiance. When reading the pages, try seeing the content through the eyes of Esmerelda, explore as a child and *wonder... forever wonder... at the miracle of light...*

The land of belonging...

Time passed... In the years after her moment of remembering, Esmerelda reached deeper and deeper into the land of her belonging. Far, far too long ago, she'd come to realise that the occasion of her 'awakening' was merely a beginning; full remembrance, she knew, required the passage of time and, above all, commitment. In order to **live** *the 'way of light', she had to travel far into the land; she had to reach out to those who inhabited its regions, who knew of its customs, who sang its song; she had to seek out those who* **were** *light. On top of this, Esmerelda had to find the keys...*

And so she journeyed. Day by day, mile by mile, mortal after mortal, soul after soul, she relentlessly allowed her quest for truth to lead her onwards, ever onwards. More awakenings followed. Insight within insight carried her beyond the bounds of ordinariness into the rich luminous *realms that she loved beyond all else. And yet, there was a part of her that remained untouched by it all... somehow all this light, all this sweet magic wasn't... quite... **real**... There were times, many times, when memories of her former incarceration returned... far too easily despair would envelop her new-found lightness. And then, even her beloved prince could not restore her to her former glory. She would sink into the depths of darkness and allow the prison of her own undoing to engulf all that she had become... Until one day, undeterred, she embraced it...*

*Alone... yet strangely unafraid... she made the darkness her friend... It held her softly... gently... It comforted her, warmed her and fitted her... so, so perfectly... It made her smile... inside... It filled her heart with so much love she melted... The safest and most trusted space she had ever experienced, Esmerelda wondered at its profundity... How could this vast womb-like presence... this exquisite... Divine... **Darkness**... that consumed her so completely, hold her oh-so... lightly? With a long drawn out sigh, she let go... she stopped asking, ceased her scrutiny and simply let go... In one timeless moment, without even knowing she had gone, she disappeared...*

*The familiar sense of belonging returned... Again, Esmerelda smiled... an incandescent radiance matching the light of 1000 suns blazed forth from her tear-strewn eyes... In the depths of her despair, in the comfort of her own darkness, she had, once again, found light... She was in the land of her belonging... only this time, it was **real**...*

All too often, the way of the seeker, the spiritual path, is perceived as being one of sweetness, love and light. If our behaviour exhibits anything less than these ideals, we are not treading the way of light, we are not 'spiritual' and we are most certainly not en*light*ened. However, as Esmerelda soon found out, reality presents a somewhat 'denser' picture, where the darkness of our own

undoing is as much a part of who we are as our highest vibration of light.

At the time of her remembering, Esmerelda realised how much she loved light, how it reminded her so perfectly of the *land of her belonging* and how evident it was in so many aspects of her daily life. Amongst her reflections, she revelled in the magic of light's *forever partner, shadow* and bore witness to their endless dance as *inseparable lovers cast into the sands of time...* When viewed from this holistic and unified perspective, it seems such a shame not to experience the beauty of this intimacy within our own nature. It also begs the question, if light and shadow are so much a part of each other that it is impossible for them to appear independently, why do we choose to deny such a fundamental part of our existence? Why do we focus so intensely on light to the exclusion of all else, particularly whilst treading an 'enlightened' path? Consider the night sky – how captivating would the stars be if they weren't framed by darkness? We would not even be able to see them, let alone allow them to fuel our imagination!

The *Way of Wholeness*, as our leading lady found out, following many years of searching, **must** include both our light and our shadow. And the way to be wholly inclusive is, quite simply, to accept – to embrace both aspects equally, as did Esmerelda. *Walk the Rainbow*, although a journey in light, allows the pure creative spirit of *Divine Darkness* to unfold naturally within you. Every vision holds the 'denser', unhealed parts with gentleness so that you, like Esmerelda on her journey, may become complete and whole.

The underlying and innate essence of the Rainbow, as a totality, is acceptance for 'what is', in the moment. As a seed thought, *It is, as It is,* says it all and extends an invitation to let go and embrace the present moment in whatever form it may appear – light or dark. *Divine Darkness* and

Divine Inspiration are yin and yang, masculine and feminine, fundamental core dualities inherent within each and every one of us. The following admirable tenets can inspire you to experience the *Real* in the *land of your belonging*: *Darkness is a container for light*; *In consummate blackness the light emerges triumphant*; *The more you shine your light the greater is your resonance with Truth.*

In short, consciously engaging with this material will reap the ultimate reward. It is so beautifully subtle, so perfectly simple, that it enables 'you' to *disappear without even knowing you had gone.* How this process unfolds relative to the facets of the diamond is set down in the chapter, 'An Invitation' under 'Introducing *Key of Light* contemplation cards'. For now, we will continue with the star of our story and see if the relationship with her new-found friend opens up new avenues of exploration.

In the days, months and years after meeting her forever friend, shadow, Esmerelda journeyed deeper and deeper into herself. She met parts – smaller selves, bigger selves, angry, hurt, rejected selves and, of course, light-being selves – who she had never known existed, let alone met. Those who were too afraid to make their presence felt, who were too unsure of what reception they would receive if they emerged from the safety of their dark abode. Those who, until now, she had never had the courage to face. Each one she welcomed, embraced with love, touched with her gentle presence, just as she had when she first met her beloved shadow, and each one, in return, made her feel more whole, more complete, more at home within herself. Paradoxically, they made her feel **light**.

And so Esmerelda gave up her search. Did this mean she no longer walked a pathway of light? No, it merely meant she stopped searching. Instead, she walked... just walked.... some days she walked in light... some days she walked in darkness... to her, it didn't really matter. They were all reflections of her innermost Self. Her forever friend was beside her... always... although there were times when she ventured into the most pristine vibrations that he almost disappeared. He became not so much a shadow, distinct in his darkness, but more of a slightly milky variation of light. She knew in time... though not yet... that she would come across a kingdom that was complete in its light... that nothing else existed, save light... where it was so pure, so intense and so entire... that it cast no shadow. And then she and her faithful companion would be no more.

*But for now she walked... she let go... she walked... and she... **allowed**. Whatever, whomsoever she met, she accepted... graciously... within. And in this allowing, in this profound receptive state, she found the keys. Inside, she cried... soft... joy-filled... tears. The kind of tears that result in luminous, polished eyes... those that are coloured with wonder... the kind of tears that spring from a heart overcome with gratitude... All her searching over aeons of time had finally borne fruit. She had let go and miraculously, seemingly from out of nowhere, there they were... seven vibrant Keys of Light...*

A Gift

The keys

"What now?" she wondered. She had found the keys but they were unlike anything she had ever encountered. What's more, she had no idea how or where to begin looking for the doors they might unlock, if such openings even existed or whether their purpose was indeed to unlock doors. It was all quite an enigma, but it was one she was quite happy not trying to decipher... at least for the time being.

So, in the silence of the Great Beyond, she waited. She played with the keys, or so it seemed: in reality, **they** played with **her**. In the stillness of the moment, she allowed magic within their mystery to unfold. They were alive. They were intelligent. But, far more than this, they held purpose. Esmerelda watched, mesmerised, as they danced before her, following what appeared to be some kind of organic ritual. In time, she realised their behaviour was dependent upon her interaction with them or where she chose to place her focus, even down to what she was thinking. She witnessed them spinning so fast she could barely distinguish them as individuals, and then, in an instant, **stop** to reveal one in a position of prominence. Seconds later, the whole process would begin again. It was all so very, very bizarre and, at the same time, riveting. What could this ritualistic dance possibly mean? What, if any, messages were the keys trying to impart? And what was her role within their purpose? She was, after all, the one who had found them, so surely there was something she must 'do' with them. It was clear there was an important clue that was missing and she wasn't going to find it with her mind. So, in the absence of any response to her questions, she set the keys aside – reverently, of course – and gave up. In the ensuing silence... in the stillness of the Great Unknown... she received her answer.

The Word

It was tangible, so palpable she could almost stroke it with her hands and so refined she could barely detect its presence, yet nevertheless visible even through its distinct lack of form. The more she allowed, the more she engaged without trying, and the deeper she surrendered, the greater was her sense of resonance with that which was emerging before her very eyes. But sight was not her first sense of knowing. No, first of all, she felt it. With every fibre of her being, she felt its presence envelop her, felt it descend around, through and within her until she was no more. Now merely a viewer through the mirror of its mind, she bore witness to its passage, knew the wisdom of ages as it bared its Soul to her. She heard the song of its journey and consumed its sweetest nectar, the sorrow and the pain, the love and the joy, the untold stories hidden within lifetimes of shame. In a final act of surrender, she gave herself wholly and completely to that which she had always known, to welcome the familiar sense of belonging experienced only in those whose presence alone is home.

"Who are you?" she ventured to ask. The sweetest sound, spoken by one who had no need of notes, played tunes of joy upon her opened and vulnerable heart. There was no doubt as to their meaning. As music to her ears, without organs of sound, they told the story of **her** journey, revealed visions of **her** lives, the years spent in service, in darkness and in light. Esmerelda cried. Soft, gentle tears birthed through recognition of selfless service. Tears that made no sound, carried no emotion, left no scars upon the heart of the one who wept; tears released only when the one who weeps is not the one who has reason to cry. Her heart, overwhelmed by gratitude, absorbed its message over and over again.

"We are many," they said. *"We are group-consciousness, united in purpose in service to the Will of One. We exist only in Light and answer to many names. If it helps, you may call us Teacher or Mentor, but please understand we have no identity per se. We are merely aspects of Light within the greater expanse of One. All we transmit, all we share, all we have ever known or ever will be is*

the Word – another name by which we are known." In silence, Esmerelda waited. "We come to you now in answer to your call."

"Mmmmm," she thought, "I wasn't aware I had made a call?"

"You asked about the keys. You wanted to know their purpose and what, if anything, you had to do with them," they clarified. "We are here to assist. Without knowing, you have opened a door into the miraculous. Your humility and willingness to surrender all that you believe you know with your mind has enabled us to begin this inner dialogue with you. In effect, your letting go has facilitated the merging of our respective realities where 'information' may flow unimpeded between us without the need for words." For once, Esmerelda was dumbfounded – she had no response, not even in the form of thought! Smiling tenderly, they continued, "We are your innermost Self, the part of you that resides in the land of the Real, the part you chose to forget when, in service to those who reside in darkness, you entered the land of sleep; the great unconscious. We have returned to you now to help you remember." Their transmission paused for what seemed like an eternity before they issued their final tenet. "The most important thing to understand, Esmerelda, is that in all our forthcoming dialogues, we are an expression of you, as you are of us."

There followed a respectful pause, not lacking in substance, in which she allowed all that had been shared in this short but life-changingly Real conversation to penetrate the far reaches of her Soul. She recognised Truth in the Word. She could feel it. And, once she recovered from the initial shock, she began to see all was falling into place. It was even beginning to make sense. "So what about the keys?" she wondered.

In an instant, she felt the familiar Presence. "You have already understood far more than you know," they encouraged. "First, all seven keys are alike in structure and size, differ only in colour and spin in the same direction – clockwise. It is only when they are observed, or focused upon, that one becomes prominent. The mere act of observing arrests the flow of the spin and expands the size of the key."

"Yes," nodded Esmerelda, excitedly. "When it stopped it gave me the chance to go into it, to enter the world of the key, and to tap into its wisdom. Like a door had appeared from nowhere and all I had to do was be still and reap the reward of its gifts."

"Exactly!" Teacher responded. "The key **is** the door. You don't have to go searching for it elsewhere; you just have to surrender to its purpose right where you are. Our first lesson will reveal the full magnitude of its potential. But first, a story…"

The gift

"It was black… pitch black. Not the familiar night sky, not even what science would define as a black hole; it was dark space, just the most pure vision of black. A small ring of stars lined the periphery but this darkness was unlike any other they had explored before. It felt different, they could sense it. Within it was a shape, a barely detectable appearance, so much a part of the surroundings it was impossible to determine its form, like it **was** the space. They soon came to realise that the area through which they travelled was **alive**. An air of expectation, of something about to be unmasked, held their hearts and minds enthralled. The crew of the ship were transfixed, locked in a position of acute alert, eyes focused unwaveringly on the window in front, bodies ready to act."

"Then it moved… slowly. Neither backwards nor forwards, up nor down, right nor left… it just moved. The crew remained as they were… frozen to the spot, incapable of responding to the great space's motion. Until, that is, they realised what had materialised before them. The blackness concealed reality behind its outer expression in the form of an eye. A great aperture, an opening, appearing in a space where, moments before, there was naught.

It filled the full expanse of the window through which they watched, opening as naturally and lazily as would any human awaking from a deep and replenishing slumber. Its gaze alighted benevolently upon the ship and with every millimetre of opening sent waves of diamond-clear light towards each member of the crew. Panic was their instinctive response, chaos their reward. Meanwhile, the eye just watched... lightly."

The significance of this short story was not lost on Esmerelda. Intuitively, she knew the role it played in understanding the great machinations of the cosmos and, on a personal level, she was more than familiar with both fear and Light. What she didn't know about was its relevance in helping her with the keys. "Let us begin by looking at three essential aspects of the story," Teacher responded immediately, "darkness, light and an eye that is singular, not dual. Another point worth considering, and equally important, is the perspective from which the story unfolds, one of duality. If the tale were related from the realm of the Real, where we are now, the resultant outcome following the opening of the eye would be one other than chaos." Esmerelda nodded enthusiastically while Teacher continued, "Now, it is clear that the eye is a doorway – one that is not readily accessible to those who do not have eyes to see. Between which realities does it serve as a bridge, and how may 'we' traverse from one side to the other? Assuming there is a 'side' of course! Enter the role of the keys."

Meanwhile, she had picked up the keys and had absent-mindedly begun to play. "Look at the focal point of the key," they interrupted, "in particular its innate structure; what does it remind you of?"

"Oh, wow!" she exclaimed, "It's an eye..."

"Indeed it is, but this is not an ordinary eye. Its structure is geometric in origin and this is what sets it apart as a gateway. In our story, the eye was revealed to be a door between light and dark, chaos and serenity, and offered a glimpse into the inner working of the cosmos. The keys are alike in this regard whilst also facilitating movement between layers of consciousness within the **same** reality." They paused for a while that she might assimilate the teaching. It was, after all, quite a lot to take in. "The best way for you to understand is to work with a key. You are already aware of the influence your thoughts, feelings and interactions have on the way each key behaves, so we ask that you enter a place of stillness and let go of all desire for any particular outcome. Do what you do best – enter the spirit of play, and allow us to lead."

And this is just what Esmerelda did. She allowed her physical eyes to rest upon the central 'eye', gradually sinking deeper and deeper into its innate structure, until, in a flash, it was inside her – or maybe she was inside it. A new panorama opened up before her; one contained by not one but two interlocking circles, with the eye being the central place of unity and the point where two became one. She allowed her imagination full rein as she explored magic within the land that miraculously redrew itself with each passing thought. But the full miracle in expression was not **her** creative imagination; it was the Presence of Teacher, whom she experienced creating **through** her. There was profound significance in all that featured in this work of art, one she knew she could never have orchestrated alone and may explore for lifetimes and still not come anywhere close to unravelling its deepest secrets. So she watched... and she learnt. Each circle, she was soon to realise, was in truth a sphere and distinct in its content. They appeared to mirror qualities of heaven and earth, whilst the central 'eye', featuring not only a bridge but also a door with steps leading upwards from the earthly kingdom, held a preponderance of human expressions. Esmerelda was in a state of awe. "It's a map!" she cried.

"Now continue to explore," Teacher suggested, "but this time, instead of using your eyes, take a step back and let the map to come to you. Allow it to *envelop you, just as you did with the keys, until you and the map are one. As adventurer and landscape entwine, see the most unique tapestry begin to take shape, moment by moment, as you walk. Then wonder at the miracle of creation... unveiled with every step you take."*

It was the upper circle that entered her awareness first, although it was so refined, so subtle... so **light** and so... **complete**, she could barely discern it as a realm distinct in itself. And yet the kingdom of Spirit, the dominion of the Soul, the homeland of all that she cherished most in her heart was one with which she had become increasingly more familiar. It was the realm where she had first heard the sweet lyrical tones of her Beloved, the space where any sense of self lay buried in the graveyard of the past and where every wonder-filled moment was purpose in itself. It was this space, she knew, that could outshine the light of 1000 suns, reveal all that was hidden in an inspirational flash of percipience and yet remain forever perfect in its pristine mystery. It was the dwelling place of her innermost Presence, the place she had been searching for since she had first entered the land of sleep as an unconscious fragment of the whole... many, many... oh-so-many... lifetimes ago. And here it was – right here, laid bare before her – her divine heritage inscribed as crystalline light. In an instant, she was awake; she was no longer blind; she could see... **clearly**. Now she could embrace her brothers, whose light was a perfect reflection of her own, in full recognition of her quintessential nature. Now Esmerelda could **shine**.

Transition to the second sphere was surprisingly easy. She surrendered all preconceptions, all expectations or ideas of how things 'should' be, and before long, as if by magic, the kingdom of nature opened up before her. Her biggest surprise, however, lay in her response. She soon came to see how remarkably similar it was, in both vibration and ease of being, to the realm of which she had previously felt so much a part; it presented as much

of a sense of 'homecoming' as did the kingdom of the Soul. She wondered why that would be so; after all, planet earth – matter – was reputed to be a step down or antithesis to the kingdom of Spirit, yet all her senses were telling her otherwise. She had learnt how futile it was to try and figure things out with her mind, so she waited. Before long, the kingdom of nature began to communicate its secrets. From flighty, feathered ones that courted air midst hill and vale to those that swam beneath the seas and cetacean pods, infused with joy, whose flirtatious moves twixt sea and air belied their knowing of the stars. From those that crawled and those that weaved their tangled webs to those whose purpose lay deep beneath the earth. From flora and fauna to beasts of every ilk, shape and size and forest friends, anchored so deep in the ground, to those whose presence was to set the pace of time. One by one they revealed their innermost secrets, one by one they shared mystery in their land and each in their turn extended the hand of friendship to the one who, they knew, would do them no harm... whom they trusted... as they would their own.

Esmerelda was visibly moved. She knew these beings were not easily met, and for them to bare their innermost secrets to her with such trust and openness was a rare privilege indeed. In deep humility, she acknowledged that her willingness to surrender, moment after moment, all that was false within her played a valuable part in easing the flow of communication between them. The gift she had been granted through allowing these two spheres to become an intrinsic part of her nature was beyond the understanding of conscious thought. She knew, beyond any doubt, that each one was her; they were One expressed outwards as the substance of two – Spirit and matter united in purpose... through her.

"You have experienced the depths of profundity that are possible should you allow life to come to you," Teacher stepped in. "Your vision and knowing have deepened to such a degree that there is very

little need for external verification. This is how it should be." Esmerelda remained silent as she allowed their words to permeate her new-found sensing of the two spheres. "I am wondering if I must enter the 'eye' of the human kingdom," she mused. "It seems like I have already journeyed there through engaging in this process... although I am lost as to the meaning of the geometric shapes tumbling from the sky. Perhaps if I explored further it might become apparent?"

"You are quite right in all you have surmised, dear friend. You have integrated the opposing dualities of Spirit and matter, heaven and earth, to such perfection that there is no separation, no polarisation, not even in thought, within you; the 'eye', therefore, does not exist as a separate entity. However, in order for you to be complete in your understanding, as revealed through the map, you must pass through the 'eye' and enter the realm of polarity; you must experience yourself as separate so that you may know yourself as whole. The eye is a doorway, a portal, and leads from sleep to clear-seeing and vice versa. It must be experienced consciously in one who is awake and the only way is to become it. Does this make sense?"

"I think so," she replied, with some trepidation. "So I must enter the great unconscious and forget all that I have become?" With boundless compassion, sent upon waves of love, Mentor responded, "Yes, we are sorry but this is the only way. Your return is of tremendous service to the whole for we, and those you engage with on your journey, grow and evolve

as you do. This time, however, we offer you the gift of remembrance. You return only to learn, to further Education in Consciousness for us all, not to redress a previous imbalance. You will be awake and you will know we are forever by your side. Should there be a time when clouds obscure the sunshine of your being, remember, when your mind is still and your heart has entered the Great Silence, we are there. In gentle tones or fleeting image, enriched with symbol, we speak. You will know us through our gift of light; you will sense us through our Presence in love. Rest assured, dear one, you will not forget this time."

Her attention turned towards the keys. "There's really only one, isn't there?"

"You are quite right, friend" they confirmed. "Remember, the keys are a reflection of you. As mirrors to your every thought, feeling, word and deed, they may appear in the form of one or 'many', depending upon the vibration you emit. Right now, you abide in a place of perfect unity so there is only one key: revealer of all doors. Soon you will enter a world where light is fractured and the keys will present as seven, reflecting diversity, in the form of a rainbow."

Esmerelda nodded. She understood perfectly and, somewhat reassured, readied herself for the great adventure. Complete with a set of keys, a map and her inner compass attuned to the infinite light of the Soul, she approached the All-Seeing eye... Hesitating only for a moment, she allowed herself a short period of silent reflection... before stepping resolutely through the door...

A Door

Falling

... the sensation was one of falling... only she wasn't... falling, that is. She was aware the light was behind her... but then it wasn't... it was right here, all around, through and within her. And she was under the impression that her arrival at the destination lay at some indeterminate point in the future... yet another misnomer... she was already there... The place of her arrival was exactly where she was... right then... Did that mean she had never left the land she loved? Did it mean the human kingdom was not hers to explore after all? Or did it simply mean, 'Sit tight and see what happens'? Esmerelda was getting rather used to this, so naturally, she chose the latter. Although she did wonder why, if the light was all around, through and within her, it was so dark. And if she had already arrived at her destination, why weren't there any humans... or anything else for that matter? There were far too many unanswered questions, so she silenced her mind and surrendered to the rich, inky blackness.

A perfectly fitting and well-worn glove... Yes, that's how it felt... A perfect fit, a match made in heaven, a place where she could disappear and not even know she had gone. This was how it was... this oh-so-beautiful... oh-so-sublime... immaculate... Divine... Darkness. It was the safest and most trusted place – an invitation to drink from the blessed waters of life, to touch the infinite light of Spirit before she had learnt how to feel, to experience wonder in creation without encumbrance of form and to know eternity in a moment outside the bounds of time. Yes, this was how it was. Who would have thought the presence of darkness would yield such rich reward? But this was not all. As she rested in its profound receptive state, she bore witness to the birth of a universe, an immaculate new life unfolding within her.

*"It's so... **cosy**...here," she reflected, as she abandoned every last sense of self... So cosy...*

*so still... and so **silent**... yet the air was pregnant with possibility... and... **sound**. "How could that be?" she wondered. How could she detect sound when all was silent? But there it was again... the sweetest note, a prescient melody infused with intent, the most subtle intonation, detectable only through the depths of profundity it evoked within her heart. She fine-tuned her senses further, adjusted her inner organs that she might greet its source and smiled quietly, joyfully, **inside** as her heart welcomed that which she had always known. Amidst gentle oscillations twixt that which was and that which was soon to be she recognised the voice of her Beloved. And, for the first time, she saw them clearly. Soft, golden radiances amidst a backdrop of light so complete and resplendent in its glory it seemed impossible to distinguish anything that may appear to diminish its velocity. But there they were, the Shining Ones, nameless and numberless; the Many vibrating to the tune of One. There they were, her beloved Mentor, ready to impart what would probably prove to be her most essential lesson to date.*

Mystic syllables, ingenious packets of wisdom revealed through every interchange, had veiled their hidden splendour, and now, with each reverberation and with mystery marked as their signature force, they exposed the full magnitude of their expression. Within their Words of Power, transmitted through every perfected outpouring, was the gift of existence. Esmerelda, from her place of darkness, was humbled beyond measure. In a profound state of receptivity, she waited. "Entrainment. Yes, that's what it is," she intuited. The more she succumbed to their emission, the greater her absorption, the more coherent her frequency, the deeper her understanding of Purpose. The more attuned her senses were to Light, the clearer her vision. As her heart entrained with theirs and mind yielded to substance, she released her note. One Sacred Sound... infused with Will...

One sound... intrinsic to Intelligence... One sound... radiant with Love. One glorious note that sent ripples throughout the ocean of space... that shattered forever the darkness of Light... that created the cause for emergence of all. One note... One threefold[2] note... expressing through the substance of One... beauty in the many.

Arriving

She landed on a bed of leaves deep in the heart of the forest. It was the most agreeable, snug and yet nondescript spot she could possibly have imagined, but, although she did not know why, it felt like home. Strangely enough, her immediate response was one of sadness, not for having left the land she loved, but for the profound sense of loss she felt at never before having remembered the wondrous journey she had just experienced. This was how it must be for all those who perpetuated life in sleep, who made their transition from one incarnation to the next without being aware. This was how it had always been for her... until now. Languishing upon her bed of leaves, she allowed herself the luxury of remembrance. From the moment she stepped through the All-Seeing eye and succumbed to the Great Unknown to this delightful day when the earth greeted her with its gift of acceptance, she had witnessed the miracle of change unfold before her. She savoured every last particle, revelled in the smallest detail, absorbed the full magnificence of her journey in its entirety until, satiated, she was able to put together **coherently** *how it was that a single unit of consciousness might progress from wholeness to separation and, equally, how it may effect its way of return.*

It began with the Word. The instant she, as a particle within the infinite expanse of Absolute, expressed the One note, she succumbed to the Law of Vibration. That which had been torn asunder, shattered into fragments and forgotten forever in its

---

[2] See glossary.

former state of wholeness, was, by the same token, assured of its return. For the original threefold note carried the seed of its perfection into every particle – from the smallest atom to the most expansive universe – so no matter how far removed one strayed from its source, it would always, without exception, return to its original condition. Such was the Law. "But, how does it work?" she asked herself quietly. Striking soft tones upon her inner ear was the voice of her beloved Teacher. "This is how it is," they said. "All sound is vibration and all vibration is sound; every particle, be it human, animal, planet or kingdom, therefore vibrates to its own note. The first sound, as you experienced directly, came about through a gathering together of certain aspects of Divinity – Love, Will and Intelligence – and only when their combined resonance reached a state of perfect harmony could they express outwards through substance as the Word."

"So the inner state creates the cause, whilst the sound or resultant vibration is the effect?" replied Esmerelda. "That's right. How you are inside, whether harmonious or not, determines your vibrational state and will be expressed outwards through substance, regardless of whether it is done consciously or not. Do you understand?" Esmerelda nodded. "So now that you have an intuitive grasp of the Law, we can take it a stage further and fine-tune your understanding of the transition."

"First, as you have already gathered, transition from Source to matter is not by way of falling but merely a stepping down in vibration from one level to the next; it only appears as a fall when the change is **un***conscious. The coming of the Word not only sent ripples throughout the ocean of space but also shattered the very fabric of its existence, dispatching to the four corners of the universe fragment upon fragment of its original form. These particles varied not only in frequency but also in their size and density. The closer they were to the original emanation, the more refined their vibration.*

*Those settling furthest afield emitted the densest note to bring solidity to form – matter. Furthermore, their distribution, although giving the appearance of being random and chaotic, was orchestrated according to Purpose; there was order within this apparent chaos." As the teaching was delivered, Esmerelda watched it all unfold. She witnessed the shattering of her beloved darkness and followed each fragment as, unaware, it became isolated within a world of its own creation, and then stepped back in amazement as the Law of Vibration worked out its purpose before her inner eye. "Now let's bring all the pieces of the puzzle together," they continued. "The threefold note is key to understanding this Law, as well as your transition, for each syllable plays a crucial part in **both** the disintegration and subsequent synthesis of all manner of form, whatever its outer appearance." A furrowed look graced her brow as she tried to understand. "We will simplify and make it more relevant to your experience," Mentor responded. "When you stepped through the door, you surrendered all sense of wholeness in order to experience yourself as separate. We know you remember this clearly. However, it was only with the advent of the Word that you became aware of subtle energy streams that were not only intrinsic to your very existence but also instrumental in determining your evolution and subsequent return to Source." Esmerelda remained respectfully silent. "Let's look at these Divine aspects in more detail. First and foremost, is the Will aspect. Without intention, there can be no event and all resultant action will be devoid of purpose. In the case of the first outpouring of Spirit, it is this Will, and this alone, that governs every life form in the manifested universe – including you – and has the power to build or destroy according to its Purpose. Now, as you have already witnessed, the Will of the Divine is not chaotic or random in its method; all is orchestrated according to order, Divine Order..."*

"Enter the second quality, Intelligence. Every separate particle, whether conscious or lacking in awareness, inert or vibrantly alive, animal, plant or star – from atom to molecule, human to Soul, acorn to oak, has intrinsic to its nature an innate intelligence. Each is not separate; each is imbibed with consciousness – the substance within which all seeds bear fruit – and it is this vibration that echoes upon the winds of silence to whisper... 'Grow, grow... grow.' So even though the world as you knew it was shattered into a zillion tiny pieces with no apparent hope of reconciliation, it will always, without fail, return to its former state of wholeness. Why? Because there is 'something' within every particle that demands it to be so, there is 'something' other than the will of the small that determines the purpose of all and there is 'something' that knows all who step through the door never leave the land of their belonging. Every fragment is and always will be 'home' right where it is; this is Intelligence, this is order in divinity. The only barrier to recognising it is lack of awareness – life in sleep."

"So how does it all come together?" she interjected. "It is through Love, my friend. The means by which the particle returns to wholeness is by means of the third innate aspect of Divinity – Love, the intuitive glue that holds all apparent separates in a state of wholeness. As one aspect (Will) tears apart and another distributes through intelligent compliance (Intelligence), all is held in the warm embrace of Love; Intelligent Love. It initiates the way of return and is integral to the Art of Synthesis."

Esmerelda had given their transmission her undivided attention, but she had also become increasingly aware of subtle intonations within the matrix of light augmenting their presence. It came in visual form, and she couldn't make it out at first, as it was so very subtle. It also faded in and out of existence with each variation of tone and, of course, was nothing like anything she had ever encountered. But over the course of their interaction, it anchored more and more into a form that she could see clearly, even though she had no frame of reference for its meaning. "Ah," Teacher acknowledged, "you can see nature's perfect pattern, otherwise called the divine matrix or flower of life. It is the blueprint of creation, and, as well as confirming the presence of ordered reality, it shows, in geometric form, how that which appears to be isolated and chaotic in expression is in reality whole and complete." Esmerelda was fascinated. "Now look closer, for the secret of life is concealed within its architecture. Notice that amidst the concentric rounds of circles are 13 circles holding positions of prominence. In a like manner to our natural world, they are the fruit within the flower and create the cause of the manifestation of 3D reality – life on earth. Can you see?"

"I can see the 13 but haven't made the 3D connection yet," she replied, somewhat perplexed.

"That's because there is an important element missing. Watch." She noticed lines of light trace, as if by magic, a path from the centre of one circle to the next, rather like a child's 'join the dots' game, each one revealing a new grid as it completed a circuit. In time, a remarkable pattern began to emerge; one that had geometric structures concealed within it – figures that triggered a distant memory. Mind afire with excitement, she quickly recalled its source. Not only were they a prominent feature within her map of consciousness, but they had inspired her leap of faith into the Great Unknown – these hitherto-unknown models had marked the beginning of her greatest adventure. Retrieving her treasured gift, she unravelled it carefully to confirm her suspicions, and yes, there they were – five geometric figures tumbling, in spiral-like fashion, from the sky...

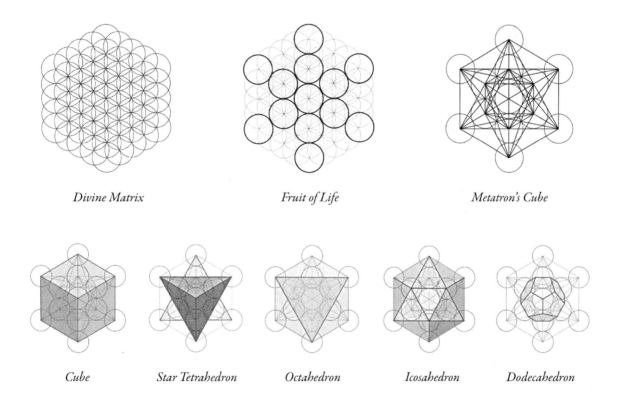

Divine Matrix *Fruit of Life* *Metatron's Cube*

Cube *Star Tetrahedron* *Octahedron* *Icosahedron* *Dodecahedron*

Returning

*... only they weren't **falling** – their movement flowed completely in the reverse direction... No, they weren't falling at all, they were **evolving**... Beginning with a cube at the hidden gate, they traced an **ascending** path leading from earth to the stars... Mesmerised, Esmerelda watched them spiral within their prescribed orbits before dissolving into each other; it was as if she were bearing witness to some great cosmic dance orchestrated to the rhythm of an unsung tune. In deep surrender, she granted permission for her mind to roam free. Question after question demanded answer; for, intuitively, she knew there was far more to these simple structures than had been revealed through visual expression. She rewound her journey to the emergence of fruit from the flower, replayed in her mind the somewhat surreal etching of lighted pathways between each strategically placed sphere and stood back astonished as unrecognisable geometric realities were birthed through the resultant structures. Was the fruit with its illumed circuits another doorway? Was it a map? What about the emerging forms – what was their significance, and how were they able to initiate an evolutionary path of return? Furthermore, what possible relevance could they have to her ensuing interactions with the human race? Esmerelda was afire, almost to the point of despair. No wonder she had chosen to be unconscious on all previous sojourns into the separative state!*

"Don't despair, Little One," rang the all-too-familiar Voice. "As usual, you have understood far more than you believe."

"Phew," she expressed inwardly, somewhat relieved.

*"First, the most important thing to remember is that all of these structures – flower, fruit, grid-work and geometries – are **symbols** of that which cannot be named nor expressed in either verbal or visual form; they are **representative** of Truth, not*

Truth itself. This may only be experienced directly; it cannot be described, not even through dialogues such as this. However, just as a picture is said to paint 1000 words, so it is that a symbol paints 1000 pictures, and every sacred symbol, together with its inherent qualities, serves as a gateway to the miraculous light of Absolute. Does this make sense so far?"

"Yes, perfect sense," she replied with gratitude.

"Now let's fill in a few gaps," they began. "The advent of sound created the cause for the manifested world of form; this, you know and have experienced directly. However, there are many layers, syllables, expressions and sub-layers within this first transmission, with each one defining reality according to its vibrational frequency. Additionally, the involutionary journey from Source to matter is passive in nature and unfolds through following a line of least resistance. In this way, no amount of force is wasted in its effort and not a single particle, regardless of its outer appearance or expression, is of detriment to the whole; everything has its place and all matures according to the maxim, 'Use minimum effort to create maximum effect.' The laws of nature are governed by this tenet, and, without realising it, you too, Esmerelda, have followed this sacred way since you first stepped through the eye." Somewhat aghast, she waited for their transmission to continue without firing off yet another question. "The way of minimum effort, the line of least resistance, is cultivated through the passive art of surrender – the transformational act of allowing that which is to be just as it is, and the giving up of the small, in its entirety, to the whole. Now retrace your steps. Do you remember how you rested in darkness until there was no part that could be identified as you? Or the moment of your arrival in the forest when you welcomed the presence of nature as she revealed her gift of acceptance? Do you recall your total absorption in the presence of One before the Sacred Sound was birthed through

you? Do you remember, Esmerelda, do you?" With tears in her eyes and heart aflame with wonder at the mark of her refinement, in abject humility, she nodded. "The way of the humble heart has become so much a part of who you are, you have become blind to its pure expression, but this too is how it is; acknowledge its gift and then do what you do best – let it pass. This is the feminine way; it allows and accepts that which is, without direction, judgement or agenda, and then turns to celebrate the next miracle on the great wheel of life, as if it were its first adventure."

"Now turn your attention to the flower of life and notice how it is made up entirely of circles (simply bring it to the forefront of your mind and it will be there). Circles, spirals and waves are feminine in nature whereas straight lines and points are masculine; generally speaking, in terms of quality, one is representative of the heart, the other of mind. You, in your sojourn through the layers of consciousness, have experienced directly the unravelling of nature's perfect pattern. In embracing every step, in engaging the spirit of wonder through your vulnerability, you have allowed the magic of existence to unfold through you. Only upon arrival at the heart of matter did your thirst for understanding ignite inner dialogue in the form of questions. In other words, the seeds of mind, nurtured within the flower of your consciousness throughout, blossomed through the onset of thought. With your every enquiry, a line was drawn, connections were made, individual structures were formed – solid and unique, each yet to be defined, each a reality to be known or experienced at some future point in time. Already, synchronous with your arrival, nature's first pattern had borne its fruit and five steps to return had already made their presence felt. So yes, Esmerelda, you are correct in **both** your assumptions – the fruit, Metatron's cube, with its illumined pathways, is indeed a doorway. However, not only is it the

gateway to physical reality, but it also marks the path of return and in this respect it serves well as a map!"

She had been following their direction quite well thus far but now she was a little confused. She couldn't quite grasp how Metatron's cube could be a door, a map and bi-directional in function at the same time. Mentor was frustratingly silent. It became increasingly clear that the only way to find answers was to enter the map and experience it directly. Again, she revisited her outward journey, paying more attention this time to the vibrational resonances experienced at each stage – chaos became order, random particles transformed into spherical realities; she watched, felt and sensed, with every fabric of her being, the miracle of creation as it flowed through and within her. Esmerelda not only knew the map, she became it. She toyed with thought, sent lighted pathways with her mind to build geometric structures and witnessed their emergence into form and their immediate dissolution as she released all to the whole in brief moments of surrender. She became familiar with the art of passive resistance – the interplay of mind with heart; how one offered release and the other entrapment and how each was essential to the other, both serving as a way in **and** a way out. She soon saw that it really was very simple (Truth usually is!). Every inner letting go led to nature's first pattern, every moment spent in Absolute perfection brought congruence to the whole and every time she surrendered all sense of self, consciousness returned to greet itself. Yet, in precisely the same instant, she was also the separate self – Esmerelda in physical form.

It was a strange paradox but one she recognised as being essential to mastery of life in physical form. So even though she had no idea of the particulars of each geometric form, nor the role they played in determining reality, she was in no doubt as to their significance. She knew each was a perfect mirror to an inner state and somehow facilitated movement between one vibration and another, from one level to the next. As well as opening doors, these were keys to whole new ways of being; they were keys to **being** light! The more attuned she was to the divine matrix, the greater her affinity with the whole; the more fluidly she allowed herself to move between each reality expressed through these enigmatic structures, the more complete she was in essence.

Esmerelda was content. She had the map and had become familiar with passing through the door. She had not one but two maps, as well as a blueprint and a set of keys. She had everything she needed to begin her adventure into the world of matter, and, of course, her beloved Mentor was always present to guide her on her way. There was nothing to hold her back, so, excited beyond measure and with a sprightly spring in her step, she made her way through the forest towards the 'outside' world. Only she didn't get very far. A transient thought brought her grinding to a halt, and as she sat down upon a rather conveniently placed and inviting 'Esmerelda-shaped' stone, she felt Mentor smile. "Why hadn't I realised this before?" she wondered, "It seems so obvious now. What about the seed?" The question held such prominence in her mind that she could not let it go. "Where is the seed?" she asked, respectfully. "Clearly, there is something missing. You have spoken of the flower, how it represents purity in consciousness, how it produces fruit and even of the nature of its offspring, but you have never once mentioned the nature of the seed. Surely, there must be a seed before there is ever a flower? And doesn't the fruit also contain the seed? What about the seed... where is it... where is the seed?" she repeated to herself...

A Rainbow

Consciousness withdrew into itself. Returning to its point of origin, before it was ever a spark, it bore witness to its own birth. Now it knew the circumstances of its creation and the purpose for which it was intended, it could recount its journey whilst honouring the full magnitude of the seed. As Divine Intermediary, consciousness is the substance from which all 'things' emerge and to which they will inevitably return. It is Alpha and Omega, first and last, beginning and end, and so far as it will repel, in a like manner and with equal force, it will attract. That which is torn apart will always be delivered into the hands of One, for the nature of consciousness is All. The Ultimate in paradox, it began as an adventure... one inspired through curiosity... and wonder... "How would it be... if...?"

*In an instant, within the boundless expanse of Absolute, the impetus to express outwards through its substance arose. But, in its infinite wisdom, Great Cause knew it may only share outwardly if there was 'something separate' to itself into which it could sound its note – a space that was other than Light. And so, as a function of itself, Spirit created its polar opposite, dark, **within** the infinite expanse of its Being-ness. The advent of the great unconscious brought life in sleep, but this was not the end. Into the dark was sent a spark, complete in its will to consume – a mere fragment, a particle, boundless in its capacity to illumine and infused with the essence of All. Expression of three into the space of two delivered the children of One; seven points of light, keepers of the seed, whose purpose in substance was to ignite fire in the hearts of many... to return the parts within the whole to unity. And so it was that the appearance of two, through the force of seven, gave rise to existence...*

Although consciousness had withdrawn, Esmerelda had been aware of all that had transpired since. In fact, as she sat comfortably upon her rock, wrapped up in her own thoughts, a strange phenomenon had taken place. At first, she didn't

notice the change, so consumed was she by her search for answers, but soon it became so palpable that she couldn't fail to sit up and give it her full attention. It was the air that marked their arrival; similar to a foggy day but with no water droplets nor a decline in temperature. On the contrary, it was warm, so much so that, in the midst of her quiet reverie, she believed she was basking in full sun on a glorious summer's day. But no, when she opened her eyes, the idyllic spot in her forest had disappeared, replaced by an incandescent, yet strangely inviting, smog. She could not see more than a few feet in front of her, and the closer she looked, the denser it became until, within a few moments, she could barely see her hand in front of her face. It reminded her of the first visitation from her Beloved, only this time there was an absence of sound... and Presence. On this occasion, it was her eyes that led her forwards to seek within the enveloping mirage so that she may greet the anomaly shielded by a cloak of obscurity.

Pinpricks of light, yes, that's what they were. If it had been a night sky they would be stars, but it wasn't and they weren't. Here, in what was clearly a meeting of worlds, they were sparks of light, fireflies dancing on a breeze or lovers courting stillness upon air freed from breath. She perceived them as many, numberless, animated sparkles revolving, twisting, turning and playing in joyous spirals, as if they were gifting the most prestigious performance of their life. But as their capers slowed to a standstill, as they matched their vibration to the realm in which she watched, she saw they were but seven. In arresting all movement, they anchored more into her reality and she witnessed them grow outwards exponentially to reach the full magnitude of their expression. In place of pinpricks emerged seven radiant beings, whose soft, golden light emanated from an epicentre infused with love. Formless, yet wholly and completely visible against the nebulous backdrop, they emanated such an air of profound peace that Esmerelda could not fail to be moved by their presence. "Who are you?" she asked, respectfully.

"We are the Seed," they responded, in unison. "We are the Flame of Mind, seven notes of the Cosmic Chord. Our point of origin is the first sound, with which you are familiar; however, we are syllables within its composition, not the chord itself, just as we are particles of light within the first emanation of Spirit, not substance in its entirety. You may know us as entities within the group-consciousness you call Mentor but our combined state of being is in the initial stages of separation; we have within our group awareness the beginnings of individual identity even though we remain One as a group in consciousness." Esmerelda was just about managing to keep up but only because she had surrendered her mind to their presence. She had given up trying to disentangle the message through intellectual analysis and 'felt' the words through her heart instead, and their intrinsic meaning translated to inner knowing. Yes, she was keeping up... but only just!

"Let us explain," they continued. "In order for One to become many, there must be many stages or levels in between; to complete the process all in one go would lack purpose. Without order, there would be no hope of a particle ever resuming its former state of wholeness. No, all must follow the principles of Divine Architecture and come under the auspices of Cosmic Law. After the initial outpouring, and as a function within its substance (consciousness), the process of disintegration began; you experienced this directly after stepping through the 'eye'. As consciousness is All, it cannot ever be separate; it must employ other means to fulfil the purpose of establishing a separate existence. Enter the role of mind. However, mind and consciousness are so inextricably linked that it is hard to tell them apart, so much so that mind believes it **is** consciousness and is the substance of all things; in a way it is! So, in answer to your question, we are indeed the seed; the seed that has consciousness as its substance, that

draws its nutrient from the All and yet whose flower bears fruit upon the plane of mind."

"We can feel confusion within your vibration, so, before we elaborate further, please refocus your attention upon the seven forms gathered around you. Refine your visual senses, look deeper into their substance and observe the subtle changes taking place within their vibrational resonance. Can you see, Esmerelda? Can you see?" It took some time, as she had to adjust her eyes within the pea-souper – no less diminished in density since its first appearance – but the more she refined her attention and the more attuned she was to their presence, the brighter they became, to such a degree that she could distinguish individual particles within each entity. What's more, not only were they fluctuating with each dynamic interchange, but they were also changing colour. Fascinated, she became totally absorbed in their mysterious toing and froing. She was aware that despite presenting the appearance of chaos, they were being orchestrated by 'something' other than the ethereal beings within which they moved; each particle was arranging itself in waves both according to its vibrational resonance and by colour. Esmerelda was bearing witness to the formation of individual identities within an entity that was quintessentially whole and complete. Separation continued. The Seven, who had first appeared as sparks within a greater expanse of light, were now barely recognisable as such; in their place, and clearly identifiable, were seven autonomous spheres coloured with such vibrant intensity that they could not fail to illuminate. "They really are quite beautiful," thought Esmerelda.

"You now have within your awareness not only a knowing of our presence but also an understanding of how the process of disintegration comes into being and arises naturally from within a state of wholeness," continued the voice of the Seven. "You have also gained insight into the subtleties between mind and consciousness. Now we shall unravel this *a little more and clarify our role as mind within the seed.*" She was all ears; like before, she was only just keeping up! "*Turn your attention to the seven spheres and watch as we rearrange their position relative to each other. Notice how the resultant geometry is like the divine matrix in structure but with fewer circles. See how it naturally lends itself to the imposition of straight lines to conjoin the petals within its central flower. If we were to continue drawing circles, using the seed as a foundation, we would eventually arrive at the full flower, which in turn would yield the fruit and, subsequently, 3D reality. Now assuming, in this instance, that circles are representative of consciousness and straight lines of mind, it is easy to see how the seed of life has within it the modus operandi for the establishment of, not only layers of mind but also multiple levels and expressions of existence. Does this make sense?*"

"*Yes, vaguely,*" she replied, "*but what about the colours, and what is your role within this great cosmic experiment?*"

"*Ah,*" said the Seven. "*We are both sparks of light upon the plane of mind and the Rainbow. As individuals, through our varying coloured rays, we emit frequencies infused with attributes of Absolute. As a group, through embodiment of the full spectrum of rainbow light, we nurture the seed and are one in consciousness. Our role, quite simply, is to illuminate.*" Then, as an afterthought, "*Our playground is mind, but it is not who we are.*"

"*Well,*" thought Esmerelda, as she sat upon her rock in the forest, "*that's given me plenty to think about.*" But, if she'd learnt anything from this exchange, it was that it was nothing to do with 'thinking' at all. No, in order to appreciate the full magnitude of their expression, she had to come into her heart and **feel** it.

"*And that is where you will find us,*" returned the Seven. "*The heart is where the seed is germinated. It is here that the will to illumine fulfils its purpose and all is returned to wholeness.*" They allowed her some time to assimilate before adding, "*Remember, it is consciousness that informs life, all life, including you and us, but as the root of separation lies in mind, it is through the auspices of its presence that we will find our route to salvation. Only in knowing the trickster and its games, and recognising it for what it is, may we savour the rich nutrient within which it grows.*"

With that, they left; the air returned to its former clarity and the forest became her familiar sanctuary once again. Satiated, Esmerelda lay down upon the soft floor beneath an umbrella of shiny, green leaves. For what seemed like days, she bathed in the afterglow of her experience; each profound sharing she absorbed, every blessing she welcomed with gratitude, and as the wisdom of her heart blossomed, in consummate joy she felt the seed

Seed of Life

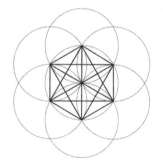

Seed of Life: Precursor to the many

*of illumination stir into life. She must have fallen asleep, or 'someone' was playing tricks with her mind, for when she opened her eyes, laid out beside her, in a place of prominence... were the keys. Now they presented as seven, each not only matching a colour of the rainbow but also carrying its own distinctive symbol. Instantly awake, she jumped up in excitement... It was time to **play**!*

So engrossed was she, so totally immersed in wonderment and so complete in her gratitude for all that had been gifted, that she failed to notice his arrival. Even when he spoke, she did not hear – her ears being more accustomed to the refined notes of her Beloved. She was within the world of matter but not of it... at least not yet. That was, until he spoke again, this time with more insistence and force. "Hello, my name is Thomas." Well, Esmerelda very nearly jumped out of her skin. Recovering her composure somewhat, she turned her attention towards the source of that which had startled her to such a degree that her precious keys had jumped out of her hands and landed in disarray upon the softened earth. Stood before her was a young boy, similar in size and perhaps age to her. Dressed in knee-length green shorts with a matching chequered shirt, he wore no shoes or socks. His tousled light-brown hair, cheeky face and piercing yet gentle, brown eyes, together with his laid-back appearance, somewhat belied the seriousness of his attitude. Esmerelda greeted him with a friendly smile. Appreciably encouraged, and now that he had her undivided attention, he repeated his original question and added a little more. "Hello, my name is Thomas. What are you doing in my wood?"

*Esmerelda laughed gracefully as she introduced herself. She knew it wasn't really **his** wood and, more importantly, so did he. They both knew it was just a ruse that he might engage her in conversation and find out about those strange objects that she had been playing with. So, having invited him to sit down beside her (there was plenty of room for two on her rock!), she relayed her story. From the very beginning, before she stepped through the door, to the point of her arrival in 'his' forest; she excluded nothing from her narrative. Esmerelda told of her precious gifts, how she came to meet her beloved Mentor and the Sacred Seven, and the wisdom that flowed so effortlessly between them in naked vulnerability. Thomas could not fail to be moved. The magic of her journey flowed from her heart to his in such a profound outpouring of love that he knew, even though he did not experience it in the way she did, that he understood. Both were at peace as they took on the full measure of each other. In silence, they absorbed the magnitude of their meeting, appreciated the gifts each to the other shared and smiled in recognition that friendship, beyond the bounds of time, had once again been forged. Easily, and without fear of judgement, Thomas shared his understanding of her journey.*

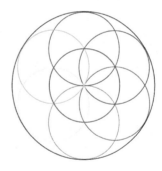

The Way of Creation
Rainbow: Seven spheres as one
Seed thought: It is, as It is

"This is how I see it," he began. "Unity is **not** the All; it is an expression of All as one. In the beginning is Zero, Absolute Zero, from within which unity is expressed as one. Intrinsic to the one, as a function of All, is the paradox of opposites, which may divide to create two or, conversely, come together in harmony to be one.

Two within one is three – the trinity – which is why three will always remember the one; it is fundamental to its architecture, as are the two. Expressing this as circles or spheres is a formula for creation and shows how unity, being duality and trinity, produces seven, precursor to the many:

0 (zero) + 0 (1) + 00 (2) + 000 (3) = 0000000 (7)

As you can well imagine, Esmerelda was more than a little lost, although inside she could feel a deepening resonance with all he had shared. Without knowing why, its depth and profundity touched a space within her that she knew well. More than familiar with the workings of mind and its propensity to lead the questioner down blind alleys, she nevertheless felt its relevance here in revealing deeper aspects of Truth. His words, she recognised, served as seed thoughts that, through contemplation and absorption within the heart, would lead to union with that which was beyond words or even thought. So she remained quiescent and allowed her new-found friend to continue.

"Your journey," continued Thomas, "began as All. In stepping through the 'eye', you became nothing, zero, which to you appeared as darkness – a womb-like space within which 'you' felt comfortable and safe even though, being zero, you did not exist. However, in a way you **did exist**, you existed as **potential**, just like the one, two, three and many. The group-consciousness, Mentor, is unity expressed directly from zero and, as well you know, the Sacred Seven are so much a part of its constitution that you could, at first, barely distinguish them as separate entities. Add to this your gathering together of the three aspects of Divinity prior to sounding the One note and you have within your story the building blocks of creation as it unfolds through the formula above." *All the while he was talking, Thomas was drawing circles in the earth beneath their feet.*

Fascinated, Esmerelda gave it her full attention whilst absorbing his every word. "As you can see, Esmerelda, your journey can also be revealed through geometric structure."

She found it hard to believe such profound teachings were being transmitted through one so young (and human to boot!) but she could not fail to express her respect and gratitude for his gift. His presentation of that which was largely beyond the remit of conscious thought in such a simple way meant that understanding easily found its way into her awakened mind. His clean presentation added depth and clarity, as well as validation, to her, at times, rather nebulous, experiences. She turned towards him and smiled in encouragement; the light from her eyes equal in measure to the love radiating through her appreciative heart. Thomas beamed.

"Take another look at your map," he directed, "the one you first received as a gift." *Esmerelda dutifully retrieved her map of consciousness whilst making a subtle 'note to self' that there were times when it was wise not to question his direction – to just do as he asked with the minimum of fuss.* "Notice how the symbol that frames the different kingdoms is the same as that used for paradox (two as one) in our geometric formula. Known as the womb of creation, this geometry allows for seemingly apparent opposites (light and dark, heaven and earth, masculine and feminine, etc.) to exist in the same space at the same time; in other words, paradox." *Esmerelda recalled her experience when she first entered the map and how easy it was to become both cosmos and the kingdom of earth. She remembered how, far from being the antithesis to each other, the feelings they evoked were one and the same, each giving her a sense of being at home within herself.* "It is also clear to see how the meeting of two gives birth to a third possibility; in your map, for instance, it is the human kingdom, mediator between heaven and earth. Isn't it wonderful that one symbol can reveal such a magnitude of possibilities? And when you take it as a starting point for the unravelling of the whole of creation, there is no end to the mysteries that may be unveiled through reflecting upon its principles!"

His enthusiasm was infectious. Without her knowing why, or how, Thomas had ignited 'something' within her that made her want to explore these geometric shapes further. After all, if her understanding of cosmic principles had expanded through consideration of a mere two circles, how would it be if they considered the seven aspects of the seed or beyond to the flower and fruit? It really was quite mind-boggling, but it was exciting at the same time. However, it would appear the lesson was over for now, for, without further ado, Thomas leapt to his feet. "It's time for tea," he said. "If I don't leave now I shall be late, and there will be hell to pay when I get home!" Then, glancing backwards as he ran off, "Can we meet again, Esmerelda? I've really enjoyed sharing with you. Perhaps we can play with the keys?"

"Perhaps?" she teased, with a mischievous twinkle in her eye. And with that he was gone.

"Well, it would appear I have met my first human," reflected Esmerelda, following his rather abrupt disappearance. "I never would have imagined it transpiring this way and revealing quite so much." After all, Mentor was her teacher and inner resource of immeasurable wisdom, it was Mentor to whom she turned when her mind returned no answers to her soul-searching questions and it was Mentor whom she knew to be her most pure expression – inseparable in both mind and consciousness from her innate Being-ness. Now it seemed there was 'something' or 'someone' outside of herself who was an equally profound source of sustenance – in the form of Thomas, a human being. She was sure the implications of this would evolve during their next meeting, and any future ones, but for now she was quite content to accept their friendship for what it was and simply celebrate joy in his companionship.

With a lightness of being, she retrieved the keys from their resting place upon the earth and resumed her play; this time applying the wisdom of Thomas.

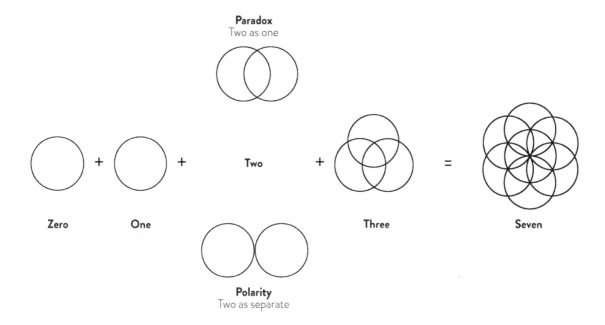

Every key, each 'eye', revealed unity as a paradox of two; each in turn was the trinity, three serving as unifier to the two; and every key led the way to the Seven, founder to the many. Now she understood, with both her heart and her mind, why her map was such an important gift; it revealed the secret to life itself. The seed, and all that had been shared by the Sacred Seven, took on a whole new meaning as she measured it against Thomas' formula of creation; fractured light, as colour, together with the seed's inherent properties, revealed a glorious tapestry in which every 'separate' was essential to perfection of beauty in the whole. Yes, Esmerelda could see that the symbol defining her map was most important. It was most important indeed. It marked, after all, the beginning of everything!

"Now what are you doing?" He had appeared, almost as if by magic, with not even the snap of a broken twig to announce his arrival. However, even though barely a day had passed, she was now attuned to his frequency, so the element of surprise, along with its associated reaction, was absent. *"I'm exploring the beginning of everything,"* Esmerelda replied somewhat absent-mindedly, so deeply engrossed was she in her 'play'. *"Come closer and see, Thomas. I have been looking deeper into the seven spheres and have found each one to be not* only different in colour but also unique in its mode of expression. It's like each one is an entity in its own right with its own purpose and quality, but is, nevertheless, a complete expression of the whole in its entirety. It's fascinating!"

Thomas was equally enthusiastic as he joined her in this new game. "Yes, I can see," he responded. "It's very clever how you have taken the behaviour of light and reformed it into layers of consciousness, like each sphere not only is a whole world in itself but also serves as a map to integrate aspects of wholeness within one who believes himself to be separate." *Esmerelda turned to look at Thomas with increasing respect. "Wow, I hadn't made that connection. But you're right, the seven spheres, which in a linear form would be seven coloured rays of the rainbow, reflect aspects of Divinity that, when embraced, assist the small self to recognise itself as whole." They looked at each other and beamed triumphantly. "Yes Thomas, that's it. That's it precisely!"* "Shall we take a closer look? It'll be fun to explore and you never know, we might learn something," said Thomas, tongue-in-cheek. *"He could be quite mischievous at times,"* thought Esmerelda. And so, keys and maps in hand, the two intrepid adventurers set off to investigate the rainbow.

Esmerelda's Map: Birth of a Rainbow

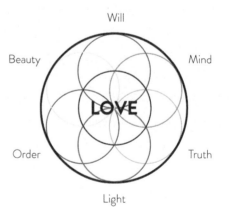

Esmerelda's Map: Spheres of Consciousness

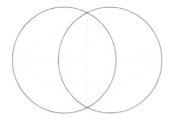

Beauty
Colour: Yellow
Seed thought: Empty and be filled
Geometry: Two tetrahedrons, golden ratio
Inspiration: Harmony through Conflict – Ray 4
Quantum Navigation

Worthless Shadow dwelled in the place of shadows, as conspicuous in her absence of light as she was in her capacity to illumine, as desperate in her urge to be free as she was in her desire to be safe and as sure in her perception of truth as she was in its appetite for deceit. But it was her sovereignty, her undisputed hold over the land of the living that exerted the most influence, though she knew it not. Mistress of illusion, weaver of destiny and creator of fables that dispatched the most acclaimed storytellers to the graveyard of obscurity, Worthless was a force to be reckoned with. Adversary to the fearless and friend only to the bravest of hearts, she orchestrated the timely appearances of every perceived reality with such intimate precision there could be little doubt of their origin in divinity – if there were only those with faith enough to believe. From the brightest of nights to the most perilous of days, from the clearest of vision to the depths of despair, from the high to the low, from the near to the far and from the joy of belonging to a wasteland alone, Worthless had it all under her belt, though she knew it not. But the greatest of gifts this shadow proffered – whose heart knew no bounds, whose ear always listened though she yearned to be heard and whose place in the mystery would always be told – was her potential to be whole, for no matter the cause, regardless the

source, she loved. Worthless Shadow loved, beyond measure; though, of course, she knew it not.

Lost within a labyrinth of belief, trapped in a world to which she alone was responsible, day by day, moment by moment, Worthless set another brick in the wall, reinforcing the bedrock of her own undoing and ensuring none would ever discover her whereabouts, or so she believed. Since the beginning of time, at first cast into the abyss, it had been so. For as long as she could remember, even though she was lost, abandoned and alone, she had relished the power she held over her kingdom. Servants – Blame, Shame, Pain, Guilt, Grief, Fear, Anger to name but a few – carried out her will without question. Each one was a power in its own right, but in reality they were merely distractors, masters of deceit, storytellers and weavers of fables, who served admirably in deflecting attention away from the real power behind the throne. But there was one whom she counted as her greatest ally, who stood as guardian of Wall, who despatched with ruthless velocity anyone who dared to venture beyond, whose effectiveness was so proficient Worthless Shadow surrendered all authority, in this regard, to him. As Protector of Wall, he was her partner, her champion, her rejecter supreme, and in him she

Guardian of Wall

had faith, in him she was whole and **through** him she learnt how to trust... or so she believed...

On the other side of wall, at the most extreme limit of the great divide, She Who Lived walked in ignorance, for the most part oblivious to the shadowlands of which she was so much a part. There were many times when she wondered why 'bad things' (or even 'good things') happened to her, why she would on occasion feel lost and alone, why those she loved – so much – barely had moments to spare and why the finger of blame was inevitably pointed at her, regardless of its origin in truth. Yes, for many, many years she wondered, but she never questioned the origin of such happenings, never tried to source the fleeting moments of despair, query her fiery outbursts or quantify her need to be loved. No, She Who Lived would pick herself up, deny all existence of pain, unconsciously reject those who had inflicted hurt and carry on with life as if nothing untoward had occurred. So she proceeded, day after day, year in, year out – setting a course from cradle to the grave, as so many had done before – blissfully unaware of the cliff edge she was walking towards. In innocence she roamed, blind to all save gratification of her own base desires, until came the day when the world as she knew it was destined to change beyond all recognition. Suddenly, without warning, blinded by a flash of inner sight and mirrored through an impending sense of her own demise, the earth disappeared from beneath her feet and she came face to face with the reality of her half-life in sleep; her existence – all she considered safe and familiar – she realised, was meaningless. Shocked to her core, stilled to a point where she knew, beyond all doubt, that resistance was futile, She Who Lived had no alternative but to direct her attention inwards. Blame was no longer an option. Shame, guilt, rage and fear, all conceivable emotions, were entities to be embraced. Dark voices in her mind were freed to be heard. And, most important of all, the pain she had endured for far too long, imprisoned deep inside the dense flesh binding her heart, was granted space to feel. In short, when the world as she knew it turned upside down, She Who Lived fell apart, or so it would seem.

Worthless Shadow, senses fine-tuned to any subtle fluctuation in vibration, was instantly alert; change was afoot, and it was imperative she gave it proper attention. There were new programs to write, stories to fabricate and characters to enlist now that the one with whom she was so intimately entwined had directed all attention towards **her**. But, and this is a very big but, Worthless wasn't really sure this was a 'good' thing to be happening; after all, she had spent the entirety of her existence, since the beginning of time, ensuring none, no matter how well intentioned, would penetrate her defences. "No, better tread carefully," she thought, as ever, deciding to play it safe. So in blindness they travelled, dancing to a tune set before they were born, each one silently wondering about the strange tug from somewhere deep inside that pulled them this way and that. Over time, the reality of She Who Lived slowly took on never-seen-before appearances and, although the echoes of doubt would periodically raise their unwelcomed attentions, little by little, step by step, Light and Shadow drew ever closer. Oftentimes, although still poles apart, their sisterhood would become more transparent and, in the silence of the Great Beyond as time released its captives, they would marvel at the miracle of creation when every discord rooted in the past would return all as a profound presence of peace. However, of course, they understood it not... and it never lasted... so onwards they marched into oblivion.

"Not sure I'm getting this," interjected Thomas. "I mean, what's it all about? Who are these characters and why is one invisible? I have a feeling their relationship is far more universal than is being played out through this fable, but I don't understand why... and what does a wall have to do with it?" They had been watching in silence for quite some time, each engaging, in their own way, with the hidden messages concealed within the script. In Thomas, the veils were clearly more well defined than he would perhaps have liked, hence his somewhat frustrated outburst. Esmerelda, on the other hand, more than understood. Her rite of passage that had led her from incarceration, through the shadowlands, to her experience of the Beloved paralleled the twists and turns unfolding before her eyes. Yes, she knew it well, yet she took her time to respond (unwittingly adding to Thomas' frustration!) and chose not to answer his questions directly. *"Before I answer,"* she replied, with measured consideration, *"it is important we allow the story to unfold some more."* His demeanour reflected how he felt about this so he did not dignify it with a response (he could be quite grumpy at times!). *"As you have intuited, Thomas, there is a bigger picture being presented here – be patient, watch and you will see what I mean."*

In rapid succession, one scene gave way to another as our two spectators bore witness to the wheel of life cycling into and out of existence. One conflict followed another; wars were lost... and won; battles fought on land, sea and air were rendered fruitless in their pursuit of peace; petty squabbles in peaceful neighbourhoods made a nonsense of suburban politeness; spiteful exchanges in the most prestigious company charted the course of nations; family feuds, heralding lifetimes of regret, were ignited by unfortunate turns of phrase. Yes, it was a very challenging sphere to view, especially through the eyes of innocents more accustomed to harmonious surroundings, yet strangely, it didn't really feel that way. Underlying this frantic desire to assert authority, whether individual, national or global, there was an air of necessity – necessity impregnated with purpose – which was oddly soothing to the beholder. "What I am seeing

with my eyes belies the sense of unity I feel in my heart," stated Thomas, not without a hint of confusion. *"Excellent, Thomas, now stay centred in your heart as we return to our story."*

Years passed. Days filled with magic – where contentment, married with self-acceptance, returned a sense of completion that nothing, not even the most traumatic of imagined events, could disturb – were interspersed with barely tangible, yet nevertheless felt, experiences of despair. Days where simple everyday activities took on a life of their own, miracles in nature issued songs to feed a starving soul and dark crannies in her vulnerable heart were permeated with so much joy she feared it would burst. Yet, equal in number, were days of thunder, where these self-same sources of enrichment were seen to veil a hidden mystery of which she so desperately yearned to be part. Yes, it was, without doubt, a period of paradox and one in which She Who Lived and Worthless Shadow would emerge so transformed as to be unrecognisable. But the time was not yet. Pieces of the jigsaw had yet to find one another, random visions, gifts from the sublime, had yet to expose their roots in clarity and veils of separation, masquerading as a wall, had yet to be drawn aside. Yes, it was a time of beauty and a time

of extreme polarity, but above all, it was a time of miraculous transformation.

Many, many years before, in the silence of a perfect moment, She Who Lived had encountered a mighty door. Set beneath the waves and obscured by creatures whose origin lay in the Ancient of Days, it stood as guardian to realms she had no right to seek. As a child, she settled deep on the ocean floor, legs crossed comfortably beneath her opened heart, hands nestled quietly in her lap and eyes gazing longingly upon the great steel fortress ahead. In innocence she waited, marvelling at the soft golden light emerging from beyond, knowing that on the other side of door and here in her heart, beneath the mighty waves, lay the answer to her prayers. Door returned its verdict softly, quietly and with deep compassion, "The time is not ripe, my love, wait. Wait and all you ask for shall be granted." So she waited. Sometimes with patience and oftentimes not, but as days grew into years, and years translated into decades, she adhered to the quiet wisdom imparted whilst in the presence of Door. Now, unbeknownst to her, as many pieces of the jigsaw fell resolutely into place, the time was ripe. From the perspective of She Who Lived, this cliff edge was more far-reaching in its potential to awaken, more destructive in its effect and, above all, more inclusive in its capacity to embrace that which had always been denied. You might say it opened impenetrable steel doors and crumbled solid brick walls to dust. You might also say it despatched to the four corners of the universe every layer of protection, all manner of faithful 'servants' and every conceivable strategy designed to resist the pull of the inevitable. Yes, it was time She Who Lived faced her nemesis... time for her to lie naked upon the altar of death... and time for her prayers to be answered. Though, of course... she knew it not.

*Three triggers, that's all. Three independent triggers spaced over the course of three short months. Three triggers expressed through three different forms, each brandishing a sword, pristine in newness yet ancient in origin. Three forms, one sword. One sword birthed through the eternal flame. One sword honed to perfection. One sword wielded through three forms to cut clean the chains that bind. One sword, three forms... One sword, three forms... and a common theme... It was enough. In the case of She Who Lived, this theme was time; a quality the three individual forms reserved mainly for themselves, leaving little or no time for her (or so she believed). "I know I am worth more than this," she said to herself. "I know these relationships are worth more than a few stolen moments amidst their whirlwind of activity. I know. I know I am worth more than this," she emphasised again and again, before lapsing into a dark void of despair. In darkness she remained, desiring nothing, wanting naught... soaking its presence deep into what little remained of her sense of self... and soon even that was gone... The ensuing silence was interminable, the stillness impregnable, the voice in the presiding presence barely audible, yet it persisted. Each delivery reinforced its message, every incantation increased, in waves of gentle persuasion, the echoes of its intent until, as the chains of doubt holding her heart in bondage finally released their hostage, she allowed herself to receive. "Yes, you are, my love... you **are** worth more than this... You are worth so, so much more than this... But... you don't believe it..."*

*As the penny dropped, the wall collapsed. As the wall collapsed, the mirror shattered. And with the shattering of the mirror came release of the shadow. Worthless Shadow was free. She Who Lived had acknowledged her existence, but oh-so much more than this, she had also appreciated and valued her **worth**... Worthless could **feel** it. In the dawning of day there followed a pause of intense magnitude, a pause in which silence granted existence space to sound its song and the ubiquitous expanse of Spirit found expression in every living molecule,* *a momentous pause in which unconscious roots sown in ancient soil exposed virtue in disgust... a pause of boundless duration in which a shadow labelled 'worthless' experienced beauty... through the heart of She Who Lived...*

"Well I never!" marvelled Thomas. "So all along they were both one and the same. Two sides of the same coin, so to speak?" *Esmerelda smiled warmly towards him, acknowledging his surprise without feeling a need to use words. "He really is quite charming in his expression of innocence," she reflected quietly to herself, whilst radiating her appreciation.* Suitably encouraged, he gave his thoughts full rein – verbally, of course! "I mean, how is it possible that any living entity could be so unaware of a part so intrinsically linked to their fundamental nature as to be indistinguishable in their expression of reality that they are blind to its existence? How can it be? How can anyone not be aware of the currents running around, through and within every response, reaction or manifestation of ideas, feelings and actions, whether self-originated or not? Esmerelda, how can one be so oblivious for so long that it penetrates the barrier of death? How... how... how can it be?" Before she could reply, he surmised incredulously, "It's something to do with the wall, isn't it?"

"Rather than answer your question directly, I shall lead you on another little adventure to elaborate." Thomas willingly settled down to absorb her every word.

"Now, place yourself before the onset of time when it existed merely as a thought, an idea, in the mind of Absolute. See that idea grow steadily within the fertile soil in which it is seeded. Witness the fruit of its transition burst forth to become the brightest light in the night sky. Watch it, almost instantaneously, transform into the manifested universe. See, in your infinite capacity to know all things, that it is but one of many star systems.

*Feel with every fibre of your being how it is to know all, to create all with a single thought and to **be** all. Feel... Know... **Be**." Esmerelda paused. It was vitally important that he be given sufficient space in time to fully embrace the conditions that had been set, that the seeds of memories soon to be forgotten would be recalled when circumstances dictated their ripening. "Now," she continued, as tears of knowing graced her eyes, "let your mind go blank. Erase all trace of thought, all memory of who or what you are. Let it all go. Be empty. Be nothing." Again, she paused... this time the interval was longer... much longer. In order to experience nothingness... to **be** nothing... everything must go... And to surrender everything to nothing... time and space must also arrest their passage. So Esmerelda waited... waited some more... and then some more... until she was sure the seeds of awakening had come of age. Softly, delicately, with breath leaving scant impression upon the air, she spoke again, calling his name in increasing volume until it became quite audible, even to one who was, to all intents and purposes, lost to the realm from which she spoke. "Thomas... Thomas... Thomas." Noticing a spark of registration ripple across his translucent brow, she held her silence once more and then... slowly, deliberately, she continued, "Thomas, the time is ripe for you to return, but do not rush. Allow your eyes to rest peacefully behind closed lids; listen carefully to whispers of the Soul as you cross the great divide into the realm of physical plane existence... With each step, divide your attention equally between being nothing and your increasing awareness of the familiar. In your own time, if it be your wish to do so, speak."*

"Nothing is not as it seems." His voice was distant, issued in shades of subtle colours and carried by resonances clearly not of this world (*"Not unlike the melodies sounded by the Beloved," reflected Esmerelda*). "Nothing is not as it seems," he repeated, almost as if he had lost any recollection of having spoken at all. "Nothingness is not as it seems; it is not alone. In nothing, something is always present... but it is not always detectable. It arises as it wills, in whatever form it wishes, but in and of itself it is without will, being directed by forces other than it. Something is nothing. Nothing is something. They are the same." For what felt like an eternity, he remained silent. "Once something has been created, it never dies. Even though it gives the appearance that it has, even though it dissolves into nothing, even though all that it once was is gone, there is always something that remains. Like fingernails running torturously across an unmarked board that leave no visible trace of their passage, its echo will always send reverberations across the fabric of space-time; something will always leave an imprint, a shadow of itself, upon the fabric of nothingness." Thomas paused, this time gathering momentum for his impending return, "Something comes in many forms and exists across all realities in every dimension; its imprints are thus everywhere. Nothingness is nowhere. Nothing is nowhere... but the imprints upon its fabric are everywhere." He opened his eyes and smiled. "So it would seem, Esmerelda, no matter how hard you may try, whatever avoidance tactics you may employ, there really is no escaping the shadow... not even through death."

"Now do you understand how easy it is to be so blind to one who is intrinsic to who you are, yet so removed in presence that you cannot possibly be aware of their every move – how life can unfold without any apparent semblance of order, let alone control?" Thomas nodded, somewhat sheepishly, before he spoke. "There is so much in this Esmerelda. There are so many layers, potentialities and subtleties woven into its fabric that it is no wonder lifetimes must pass before even a glimpse into the inner workings of Light and Shadow may be exposed. As far as I can see, the story

concerns an individual and the revelations she experiences when coming face to face with her nemesis, yet the snapshot of the bigger picture shows its relevance to every life event pertaining to humanity as a whole. A shattering of the wall in one paves the way for others, and humanity in its entirety is enriched as a consequence. It's wonderful, Esmerelda, it really is. No wonder this sphere expresses *Beauty* – resolution of polarity through conflict, whether outer or inner, can be quite beautiful when viewed from this unified perspective. However, I sense that only when all the pieces of the jigsaw come together through exploring the Seven as a whole, allowing the full picture to emerge, will its true significance as a ***Way of Beauty,*** be revealed."

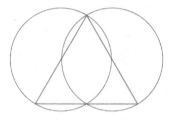

Light
Colour: Green
Seed thought: To every season is a purpose
Geometry: Triangle
Inspiration: Active Intelligence – Ray 3
                       Quantum Navigation

"It's a very busy sphere," stated Thomas, verbalising the obvious. *"Indeed Thomas, I must say I agree with you... although I have a feeling there is more to all this manic activity than meets the eye."* They had been catapulted into the 21st century as soon as the key rose to prominence, but, fortunately for our two adventurers, they remained detached observers rather than active participants. It was akin to watching a movie stuck on fast forward whilst being acutely aware of equally frantic individual dramas unfolding within the lives of the foremost characters. Time played a leading role, as did space. And there appeared to be an intense desire to fill every available moment without any consideration afforded to quality, substance or purpose. It really was a most uncomfortable movie to watch, especially for those used to more tranquil settings. All this, however, was set to change. In the blink of an eye, intense activity returned all to nothing, and in the ensuing silence, stillness, antithesis to mindless activity, enabled space to breathe... **Light** had more far-reaching layers to reveal before the full magnitude of its expression could be grasped, and nothingness was as good a place as any to begin.

Nothingness

All that is born never dies. Every dream, thought, word and deed masquerading as the subterranean self creates an endless source of hidden 'somethings' to dictate the course of a life. All creations etched into the fabric of nothingness, like indelible ink scoured into a board that is black, combine to build an intricate, fragmented sense of self, a bedrock for all that deems itself to be separate. These multiple 'somethings' cannot be seen but they are there, and their influence upon the present, not to be underestimated, is immeasurable.

Dark matter is invisible yet its effect upon the manifested universe is evident through observation of the visible. It is the glue – an attractive, gravitational substance – that holds the manifested universe together. It can't be seen but, because of its effects on space, it can be felt. Nothingness is no different. It is the glue that holds the structured self together. Layer upon layer, belief after belief, program on top of sub-routine, it attracts all that perpetuates an identity of falsehood, whose influence extends far beyond the grave in any physical-plane life.

Layer upon layer of imprints permeate the eternal blackness, but are they really there? If they cannot be seen, even by those who have the gift of inner sight, are they mere distortions in a reality that doesn't even exist? Or is their behaviour more like that of dark matter, whose effects may be only observed, with the vast store of their infinite substance relegated to the substrate?

If imprints lie in the origin of the separate self, how easy is it to let go? When lifetimes have been devoted to the structure of an identity, how easily may it be surrendered if a single thought in the present can stir into life all that once was? And how can the nothingness in all things be embraced when falling apart returns such a profound sense of loss for all that once was that it renders every foray into acceptance futile?

How may the self be relinquished when the seed of identity is carved into the very fabric of existence? Is it possible to be nothing if something is always present? Is dark matter always wholly and completely dark or nothingness entirely empty? Or maybe something never really exists at all; maybe it is a mere distortion of the will to be by a mind intent on furthering its own import... Perhaps all there ever is... is nothing... nothing, unfolding within itself... and perhaps dark matter isn't really dark at all... Perhaps... it is light...

We are Seven

Deep inside a magical forest, in a place not very far from home, seven spirits play amongst the trees. Known only as their colours, Red, Orange, Yellow, Green, Blue, Indigo and Violet, they are invisible to all. But those who walk in innocence, those whose hearts believe and those who dance with fairies in their dreams can sense their presence.

Then, in recognition of beauty in the heart of one who knows, the forest cannot help but reveal its mystery. Seven little spirits, seven vibrant lights, seven wielders of magic, each with a purpose to fulfil, dance together to celebrate in joy the finding of their new playmate. Before long, as a huge thank you, they have painted a most magnificent display of radiant colours right across the sky, high above the forest.

So the next time you wander through a forest or a wood, or even stand in the presence of a tree, pause for a moment. Look closely at the spaces between leaves, feel with your heart the love nature has to offer and listen. Listen to the laughter of the spirits... really listen... and if you're really, really lucky, they might paint a rainbow across the sky... just for you!

First Female

Within eternal dark stirred an echo of movement. Subtle at first, barely registering as impact upon the perpetual stillness of the deep. Yet move it did... slowly and with purpose. It marked the onset of time but not as it is nowadays known or even as it might have been perceived then. Gathering momentum, it

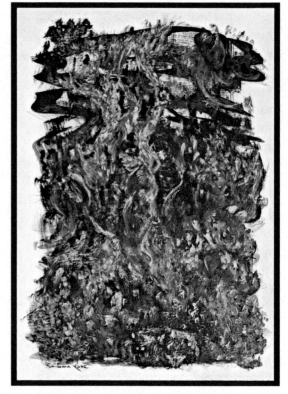

First Female

stirred up a frenzy of activity. Intelligences, driven by instinct and whose only remit was to obey, joined the party. Ghosts and ghouls appeared, remnants of a bygone age, perhaps? Elementals blended geometric structure as prelude to form-building whilst children of the damned prepared to meet their maker, yet even with all this intense activity, there was far more to come.

Round upon round, faster and faster, the weaver of worlds worked out its destiny. Wider and wider its influence reached, deeper and deeper was its penetration of the eternal blackness as it returned all to itself, until it consumed the very heart of its mystery. Naught was left – or so it seemed. Primordial chaos, mother to all forms, had arrived and there was nothing, absolutely nothing, that could arrest her passage. She is First Female –

intelligent, primal, instinctive and seductive. Mistress of change, she answers to no-one or no-thing. She is nothing and nowhere, yet the effects of her passage are everywhere. There are those who try to tame, coerce or bind her to their bidding and many, many more who attempt to heal or fix the effects of her passing, but their efforts fall on stony ground. Why? Because they presume to tame the untameable, manipulate the profound or fix perfection. How dare they!

But those who welcome her into their heart with no agenda, who set aside fear at her passage, who give of their all to her pristine intelligence, who are sincere in heart or touched by her divine majesty are granted passage to ride the serpent of change as she stretches time into the boundless expanse of Absolute.

So would you fly the winds of change, bathe in the waters of Absolute or dance in the flames of her majestic splendour? Would you? Then prepare to greet the serpent of destiny, prepare to embrace the essence of life itself and prepare to let go of all you ever believed yourself to be. Prepare. First, however, you must befriend the dark...

As ever, Thomas was first to speak, "Well, I wasn't expecting that," he said, with a tone of incredulity. "Who would have thought the manic activity we witnessed upon entering would expose such depths of profundity." He paused for a while to allow the effects of all they had witnessed to sink in a bit more. "Although, the more I think about it, the more obvious it is that there really couldn't have been any other progression. There simply had to be many layers of hidden depths to present such a perfect picture of chaos, wouldn't you say Esmerelda?"

*"Absolutely, Thomas, the layers are far-reaching and expressive and invite deeper exploration than is verbalised on a surface level through each story. **Nothingness**, for instance, delves into the origin of the separate self where apparent chaos in the present is the only picture that may possibly arise,*

*considering the unconscious actions perpetuated time after time by each character. **We are Seven** exposes the subtle realms of nature – the hidden mystery concealed within, around and beyond all natural forms. **First Female**, whose origin gives rise to time itself, brings all forms, regardless of realm or expression, into such intimate relationship that its intelligent activity can be nothing other than divine. But I still feel, even after experiencing the intricacies hinted at in this wonderful web of life, that the fullness of its expression will not be revealed until we have journeyed into all seven keys. I sense a picture is emerging in which the unseen in-between is preparing to emerge into the full light of day, and until all spheres have been absorbed, we will have no idea what mysteries it wishes to impart."* Thomas, of course, agreed. "Let's shuffle the keys and see what doorway appears next," he suggested, grinning from ear to ear.

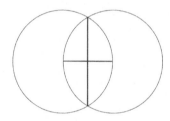

Love
Colour: Indigo
Seed thought: Let go and let God
Geometry: Golden ratio
Inspiration: Love-Wisdom – Ray 2

Indigo, colour of the night sky, was deep, exceedingly deep. It was still, still beyond any concept of what stillness might be or any idea of how it may be experienced. And it was quiet yet oh-so much more than this. Akin to swimming in deep water, without swimmer or any tangible sense of anything wet, it returned such a profound impression of peace that

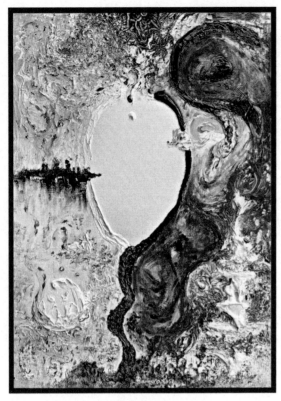

Everywhere

the only recourse was to surrender all, bathe in its majestic presence and receive its beneficence... For in this void of plenty... everything was allowed... and yet... nothing existed...

Everywhere

The message, though sounded upon waves of subtle vibration, was clear – "Form is empty, emptiness is form."[3] Clear, yes, but only in the sense that it could be heard, for it produced more questions than it did answers. How can emptiness be painted? How may it be expressed if it does not exist? How? In short, it can't, at least not directly. The expression of an idea of what it isn't is all that may be done. In stepping into this world of make-believe, a picture appears, and suddenly, amidst multiple layers of distractions,

---

[3] Heart Sutra. Mahayana Buddhist teaching.

dancing between light and shadow, paradox is unveiled. In a flash, recognition awakens clarity deep within the heart and with it comes knowing. Emptiness is... everywhere. You just can't see it...

Consciousness rises when there is nothing left...

Inside each and every one of us there is a part that is immutable, unchanging. It is called by many names, including God, but, essentially, its essence is One. Suspended within the planes of Great Spirit, as an individualised living flame, the Monad of Self is the spark of human consciousness that is **identifiable** as One. When nothingness returns all that is false to itself, the nameless one rises, as does a lotus rising from the detritus of a dark and dingy swamp, to stand pure and undefiled amongst the ashes of all that was.

Golden nugget

Beneath a solitary cloud, in a sky otherwise bare of presence, the circle of life perpetuates its forever existence. Round after round, cycle upon cycle it turns, driven by an unconscious need to fulfil its destiny, little knowing that the very act of wishing serves as fuel to keep the great wheel in motion. For, as long as there is one who desires, one who thinks or one who acts, the present will always be a product of the past. Only when existence releases its need to exist, only when the craftsman ceases to build something from nothing and only when the orchestrator returns each note to silence will the resolution of time complete its course and destiny have fulfilled its purpose. Aside from the circle of life, attention in the 'Golden Nugget' illustration is naturally drawn toward the nugget at the apex and, although significant, this is a necessary distraction. The multi-layered subterranean landscape is closer, for it holds imprints of the past, but it is the seed lying deep beneath the earth's crust that is key to unlocking the mysteries contained herein; its roots and especially the soil within which they grow are worthy of contemplation. Unconscious roots, source of all imprints, are anchored in soil that is conscious. This bears repeating – *unconscious roots grow in soil that is conscious*; consciousness thus serves as source to unconsciousness.

But whence comes the seed, how may it be found and how may the jewels within its crown be harvested? Digging with mind or shovel, though it may take lifetimes to realise, yields little reward. Fishing using line, net or more manipulative means renders every effort worthless. Even the tender ministrations of an open and loving heart barely scratch the surface. No, other means must be employed before the seed releases its treasures – means whereby dark may know its brother, every imprint is dissolved in an ocean of blackness

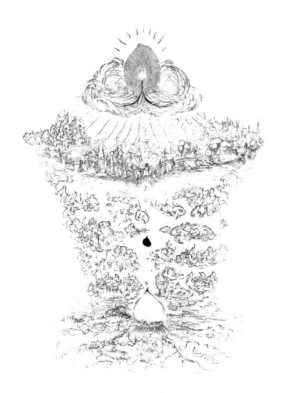

Golden Nugget

and roots, whose tendrils reach far beyond the bounds of time, are found to be one in the Self. When the consciousness of one who seeks surrenders every desire to know, when the heart of one who trusts faces its fear of death and when the imprints of the past are but a shadow to its mind, only then will the Fount of All Wisdom rise up to claim mastery. You see, it is not the golden nugget that grants passage to the seed but the seemingly insignificant black droplet drawing sustenance from an endless supply of unconscious substance. Every inner letting go draws darkness to itself, whilst every ounce of resistance perpetuates the stories to stamp more imprints upon its fabric. Each time the self recognises itself as being nothing, the tiny black droplet takes a step closer to the seed, not in a linear way but through absorption.

The illustration shows three nuggets – golden, black and white – as being separate entities, but they are not: each is inseparable from the other. When the self gives way to the great void of nothingness, time and space cease to exist; there is no nugget, no fabric, no seed, no roots – nothing – nothing that may be distinguished as separate. In the aftermath, the miracle of consciousness is birthed, arising only when there is nothing else left. Until then, the words of Nisargadatta are a fitting description for the illustration as it stands...

> *Love says "I am everything." Wisdom says*
> *"I am nothing." Between the two, my life flows.*

They took time to emerge from the inky blackness. Two hearts, two minds, separated only in their physical-form appearance, were one in consciousness. All that had transpired, they knew; every nuance, every subtle vibration, they knew; each to the other in their respective journeys, they knew... Above all else, they knew the fullness of their expression was empty. All they had received, every teaching that had been gifted, all they had imparted one to the other was empty; however, emptiness, they also knew, was not without purpose... Slowly, silently the two friends opened their eyes. As one they turned towards each other. As one they smiled... As one they radiated love... for a very, very long time... No words were spoken... there really was nothing to be said...

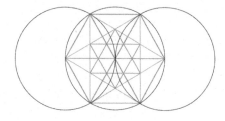

Mind

Colour: Orange
Seed thought: Every thought is a prayer
Geometry: Hexagon, hexagram, triangle
Inspiration: Concrete Knowledge or Science
               Ray 5
               Quantum Navigation

Trapped

"Where did it come from?" pondered the brain in a box, "this all-consuming thought that repeated itself over and over again, that kept him prisoner to its responses, that ensured he would never... ever... be free. Where did it come from? What was its point of origin, and why, oh why, did he allow it to dictate the course of his life?" Round and round in circles he went trying to figure it out, trying to execute a change of mind, trying to stop its endless tyrannical chatter. Backwards and forwards through time he travelled, searching for events that might have served as a trigger or spark to ignite its passage. Stories inside stories rose to the surface – stories that fed his desperate need to find answers, stories that led him down blind alleys, stories that offered

glimpses of hope – but not one marked an ending to his torment. He was a prisoner inside his own head, and it appeared there was absolutely nothing he could do about it. "You will never find the origin of thought using your mind... just as you will never solve a problem using the same mindset that created it." The voice was clear, seemingly coming from inside him, and spoke with an authority that brooked no questioning. Little did he know, but in admitting there was nothing he could do, our little 'brain in a box', had opened a door behind which clarity, in the form of inner guidance, could make its presence felt or, in this case, heard. *"So there **is** another way," he realised.* There was a way in which his obsession with every aspect of his life conforming to some sort of order could be reconciled with his desire to be free, a way in which his torment might be laid to rest, in which he might at last know peace. It was just a question of how long he was willing to put off the inevitable before executing a change of mind... *Clearly, the time was not yet, as another thought rose to the surface... "Now, I wonder where that Voice in the Silence came from?"*

Obsession

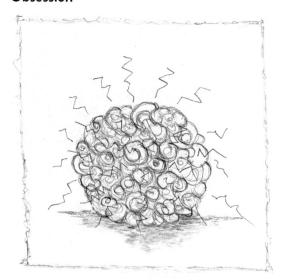

In Greek and Roman mythology, the Gordian knot was an extremely complicated knot tied by Gordius, the king of Phrygia in Asia Minor, which was subsequently destroyed by Alexander the Great. It came to symbolise a difficult problem that was almost impossible to solve. The phrase 'cutting the Gordian knot' has thus come to denote a bold solution to a complicated problem. The knot in the case of our 'brain in a box' symbolises mental entanglements arising through obsessive behavioural patterns, beliefs and programs. Decisive action, mental acuity or shift in perspective – lateral thinking – is required to stop feeding these obsessions, alongside an open and loving heart; acceptance being its agent. Once set in motion, gridlock within the square – the box – is released, allowing the inner diamond, as a spiral in the heart, to loosen threads that bind and entanglements to miraculously free themselves.

Origin

The assault came out of the blue. It was a vicious, seemingly unprovoked attack, employing words as a weapon to cut to her core. She was shocked, scared and frantic, as, try as she may, there was no evading his wrath. Wherever she went, he followed; whatever tactic she employed, he matched; even staying put rendered her escape efforts futile. Then, as fast as it had begun, it was over; at least in a physical sense. Her mind, however, went into overdrive – for days – driven by a need for justice. Over and over, in one imagined scenario after another, it constructed situations, conversations and actions in which she might redress his lack of remorse for the pain he had inflicted. This unrestrained bully had gotten away with it. She was suffering – big time – and he really needed to pay for that. Yet there was another voice inside – one less frantic, one rooted in reason, one that was aware of the Law – and it served her well in stemming the flow of her revenge... "What goes around comes around," it reasoned. "Every cause has its effect, every effect has its cause... And then... yours is not the task to work out the Law. It is out of your hands, but be assured that the Law **will** *work out and the effects of his wrongdoing* **will** *be played out; however, orchestration will be in alignment with the Will of the Divine, not yours. You have no part in this."* It was hard, very hard, but with every inner letting go and every time she heard the still-small voice, she listened. Above all, she took notice. Then, as suddenly as it had all begun, another bolt from the blue sent her crashing to her knees. *"I created this,"* words from the voice of reason echoed through her mind. *"Every effect has its cause... every effect has its cause... every effect..."* and then, as if to ensure the realisation had really hit home, *"I... have... created this... I* **am** *the cause."*

As the full impact of this realisation sank in, it was akin to witnessing a house of cards tumbling to the ground after the passage of a hurricane-force wind. Minute by minute, hour by hour, the hands of time reversed their forward motion, thread by thread, entangled knots released their grip on her obsessive mind and scene by scene, truth was revealed as the movie of her life played out before her eyes. Every encounter, every detailed conversation, she relived. Words as voices in her head claimed recrimination for her actions. Suffering she had caused left her sick to the stomach. Pain – inflicted on both herself and others – built a cage of ice around her heart, but the revolutionary impetus of these effects was to outstrip the momentous unravelling of the cause. When the reality of her past came home to roost, when shame took the place of vengeance, when regret soothed the raging furnace in her belly... and love, as an unconditional force of acceptance, returned all to unity... slowly, slowly the ice began to melt...

Impossibilities

Every window exposes a reality, but do they condemn the observer to entrapment in which any hope of release conjures up a vision of impossibility? Perhaps other options are available if one allows impossibilities to be possible? Perhaps? Ultimately, I guess the question must be, how far down the rabbit hole are you willing to travel to find out?

"Isn't mind fascinating," marvelled Thomas. "There are so many layers, intricate relationships and subtleties in vibration, it is a wonder anyone can make any sense out of it at all, let alone disentangle the matrix of its creations. I find it quite remarkable, I really do." *"That is because you*

Impossibilities

come from a space that is not mind, Thomas. This was intimated in the first story when the Voice in the Silence wisely stated, 'You will never find the origin of thought using your mind.' You and I abide in consciousness, the soil in which mind grows, and so we may delve into every aspect of it without becoming entangled in its web of deceit. You might even say we are the screen upon which the movie of mind acts out its stories. We see everything clearly but are untouched by any of it."

"That's all well and good, but it doesn't really help anyone who is trapped in the matrix does, it? I mean, how can they possibly escape when they are not even aware they are imprisoned? *"Ah, now you've hit the nail on the head. Being aware is a good place to begin, as the star of 'Origin' found out. In knowing and, above all, accepting the part she played in creating the reality of her experience, she was able to extricate herself from future karmic propensities that might trigger the demise of the 'house of cards'. In the story she was portrayed as a victim, but in reality she was the perpetrator."* "Oh, wow! Just goes to show things are rarely, if ever, as they seem." *"The victim/perpetrator dynamic,"* Esmerelda continued, *"is universal in its expression, being played out over and over again through many lifetimes until, as in this case, the cycle is broken. Yet there is even more to it than this; a third dynamic enters the equation, the rescuer, when someone, not necessarily directly involved, tries to fix it all without knowing the bigger picture; taking sides reinforces polarity, thus perpetuating the never-ending cycle of the war."* "So being aware of these dynamics is but a beginning, living them is crucial, but the real crux of the matter is being able to distinguish mind from consciousness; soil from the seed."

"Spot on again, Thomas. When the origin of mind is traced to its source, all that is false is returned to nothing, leaving the Real in its stead."

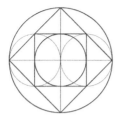

Order

Colour: Violet
Seed thought: Beauty expressed outwards is life
Geometry: Square, circle
Inspiration: Ceremonial Order or Magic – Ray 7

The plan was clear. He held the vision, knew the method by which it may come to fruition and had the forms with which to build; yes, the Magician was well versed in the miracle of his craft. He was master in the art of moulding matter to his will and had built with some considerable success, but there was always something missing. There was always 'something' that ensured the outer reality never quite lived up to his inner vision. He had no idea why it should be so. He had tried all manner of means to access its source and stripped apart every last detail in his approach, but he could never quite reach the depth of clarity required to reveal the missing link; something, in almost all the acts of his creation, left him with a sense of imperfection. "Why must it be so?" he cried desperately to himself, as he searched within his troubled mind for reasons.

Esmerelda watched. She observed him raise those forms with which he would create his masterpiece – piece by piece, block by block, molecule by molecule – to his eye. She saw him examine every last one with detailed precision and bore witness to the high degree of scrutiny he levelled at each. She felt his pain, his frustration. Not a single facet was missed nor stone left unturned. From the point of an object's origin when it was merely an idea to the solid structure he held in his hands; from the love in his heart to the vision of beauty he held in his mind;

every last layer of expression he tore apart in his frenzy of investigation. But still he did not find the source of his demise. Yes, the master knew his trade and the building blocks of his creations, but the vital element – that which would see his vision bear fruit in reality – he lacked.

*And then, in a flash of inspiration, he knew. In the depths of his despair, as he exhausted every avenue of expression and exposed each particle in its desire to be whole, he recognised the part of himself that was separate; he knew that every vision he held, every desire birthed in his heart and each inspired act had the separate self as its origin. Aware and holistically inspired as he was, each was **his** vision, **his** masterpiece, **his** desire; every creative expression had **his** mind as its origin. In abject humility, the Magician smiled inwardly. Now, at last, he had found the missing link. And now, at last, he had located the element that would bring beauty to form. All he had needed to do was get out of the way to reveal what was there all along. Beauty in him, expressed outwards, brought perfection in form; it brought **life**.*

"Can you see, Esmerelda, how the art of building in matter is not as straightforward as it would at first seem?" Three of the Sacred Seven had appeared beside her upon selection of the key, each subtle appearances of the Violet, Indigo and Orange rays. It was the keeper of the Violet flame, Architect of Order, who posed the question and to whom she turned when issuing her response. First, she took some time to assimilate all that had passed before her eyes since stepping through the violet 'window'. She had surrendered far into its realm that she may know, intimately, the agony experienced by the Magician, the lengths he had explored to reach his ultimate revelation and the frustration he felt in not being able to marry his heart's desire with that which he held in his hand. Every cherished object in his soul-searching journey she experienced directly, but far more than this, through her own magical transition,

*she understood the many subtle layers woven into each masterpiece. She understood, beyond all doubt, that the real Creator was not the one who wielded the outer form, but that which created **through** him. Every minute detail, every layer of implied subtlety, she knew, expressly. How? Because the moment Esmerelda stepped into his realm, she ceased to exist; she became the Magician. And so it was, as a worker in the field of magic, that she voiced her reply.*

*"Magic and alchemy are inseparable," she stated, with authority. "The error is made real when emphasis is placed upon one to the exclusion of the other, when the one who serves believes themselves to be the director of the show or when distinction is made between what lies within and that which is perceived to be without. As the wielder of form came to see, when working in the field of magic, the only recourse for one who would serve in this way is to surrender all sense of self that the Real may orchestrate its purpose **through** them. With every inner letting go, all that is false dies, bringing the highest and lowest into the most intimate relationship. Then, and only then, may the One plan manifest as Divine Purpose upon the physical plane of existence. Just as the caterpillar surrenders its existence that it may emerge as a butterfly, so does the lower give of itself to the higher. One serves as fuel for the other. This is alchemy, inner alchemy, magic in its most pure form."*

The Shining Ones remained silent as she continued. "Furthermore, the Magician's story shows how the plan works out through particles, such as human beings, within its substance and explains why you, whose responsibility is Order, are co-creator with Wisdom, keeper of the Indigo flame, and Mind, of the Orange. Every plan begins as an idea, whether it emanates through Universal, Group or human mind, whilst the quality of wisdom comes into play through conscious choice. The will of the small sacrifices its own desire-based agenda that a more holistic, bigger-picture

perspective may be birthed into reality."

"Yes," spoke the Three, as One, "learning the art of sacrifice is paramount. It is cyclic in nature and ensures every inner allowance returns the thinker to co-create itself at ever-increasing turns of the spiral; a refined, more inclusive, expression of Spirit within matter is the eventual outcome. How it comes about is by means of order, Divine Order. However, as you can well imagine, Esmerelda, there is far more to it than this..."

It was at this point that Thomas chipped in. "All that has been spoken of, and more, is reflected in the symbol for order," he enthused. "The equal-armed cross is indicative of perfect balance, where not only the horizontal and vertical life but also the four elements in nature are in accord. Taking the two straight lines as a starting point, the horizontal one is matter and characterises all that contributes to physical existence. In the case of the human being, it encompasses the three dimensions expressed through the physical, emotional and mental bodies plus the spiritual as it pertains to an individual; the second straight line is Spirit as a whole. Four elements – earth, air, fire and water – defined through the arms of the cross, are not only representative of the four human 'bodies' but also the building blocks of **all** matter. Life and death in every form of physical existence, including the earth herself, is determined by the dynamic interplay between these four cosmic curators. And to whose metronome do they set their rhythm? Order, under the direction of Divine Will, of course!"

Thomas was on a roll, and without pausing for breath, he carried on, "Let's look at it from another perspective – sacred geometry. Join the outer edges and the equal-armed cross becomes a square. Now employ a little bit of imagination and you will see it emerge as a 3D cube, each face being a square." To illustrate his point, Thomas began drawing in the dirt again. Fascinated, Esmerelda watched,

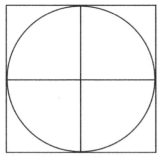

Centre of Symbol

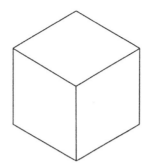

Cube

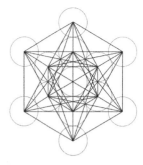

Collapsed Cube

quietly absorbing the fruits of his passion. As mental constructs, so alien to her intuitive nature, became one with her innate substance, the sacred space within her heart blossomed. She understood all that he was sharing, in a knowing, this-is-who-I-am sense. Suddenly, from out of nowhere and as if by magic, Thomas produced a cube. "This is how I witnessed the Magician's dilemma," he continued. "The building blocks, the tools of his trade, were to me cubes and, as we have seen through the gift of the symbol, they were naught but reflections of himself, each face an aspect of his character. Every time he picked up a cube to scrutinise it in such precise detail, he was probing into his own physical, mental and emotional constructs. But he was blind and could not see it. Until, in a flash of insight, he awoke. Now watch. See what happens when you collapse the cube. In returning its 3D shape to a 2D one, the cube is transformed; it becomes a hexagon, the divine blueprint or Metatron's cube. And, as every platonic solid is birthed through it, Metatron's cube serves well as a gateway to all realities.

"Returning to the Magician's story, even though he was adept in his art, he was creating through the lens of his own character, albeit very subtly at this stage. Only when the mirror was shattered – collapse of the cube – could he build anew as an architect of the Divine. All subsequent forms were not his; they were Absolute. The art of creating

in matter, as you have shared in your own way, Esmerelda, is a continuous process of returning to the matrix of all creation whilst allowing form to arise through the hands of one who builds. It is a natural outpouring and expression of wonderment experienced within. This is order in creation; Spirit expressed in matter as a *Way of Beauty*."

Esmerelda withdrew to assimilate. Intuitively, she was aware of the subtle flow of energy between within and without and how knowing its principles was essential to being a conscious co-creator in the world of form, but what of the four elements? She sensed there was far more to the role they played than had been exposed so far; surely it wasn't 'just' about balance? How did they influence life and death? Why was their agency so vital that they could determine the demise of anything within physicality? Upon whose instrument did they play their tune?

"Teachings on the profound nature of elemental forces are deep," spoke the Three, "and perhaps not for this moment in time and space. We will, however, share that which we consider to be of particular relevance now. First of all, Esmerelda, you are correct in your assumption that there is a hierarchy within the subtle realms of nature, just as there are layers within the makeup of a human being, and all elemental forces come under the auspices of the Devic kingdom whose remit is to build in matter through ordered intelligence. The four

elements are closest to the physical plane. Indeed, if you consider the physical body, they are part and parcel, inseparable from its outer form. Aside from observing their effects within the world around you, consideration of the death process[iv] brings an intimacy and understanding of their role as builders and destroyers of matter; know death and you understand life, for they are inseparable. When death to the physical form is in its final stages, there is clear order in how consciousness extracts itself from the identity it has taken on in any particular life. First, the gross physical body, earth element, begins to deteriorate and dissolves into water, which in turn sinks into fire. Fire is absorbed by air, which transmutes into consciousness, thus completing the initial stage. Now, when you take into account the correlation between the elements and the subtle bodies within human consciousness, it is easy to see how the destructive process at death offers great insight into how these layers play out when entering into a conscious de-construct of the personality self during life, such as we are engaging with here."

"All workers in the field of magic must know themselves above all else," agreed Thomas, "for, make no mistake, alchemy is magic. It is an inner destructive process in which the lesser is systematically broken down wholly and completely that the one may know itself as All; physical pain (earth), emotional desires (water), self-serving thoughts (air) and identity (fire), must be surrendered that the spark of divinity within may enrich the lives of all through the one who serves. I see it like this: if the Will of the Divine is set upon creation of a butterfly, why would I want to put all my time and effort into producing a cube!"

Ripples of joy echoed upon waves of light in appreciation of his direct and to-the-point assessment of how it is. "Indeed Thomas, you have summed it up perfectly. Now, in order to bring this most rewarding interchange to its inevitable conclusion, we would like to add one final word to the mix: cooperation.

You have both intimated at its qualities throughout our dialogues and have most certainly demonstrated how its effects may bear fruit in bountiful creative expression, but clarification is needed as to why it is such a vital ingredient in the art of Spirit expressing outwards through one who serves. 'No man is an island,' is often said, but it is never more applicable than in the art of conscious alchemy. When the magician surrendered all sense of self, he instantly became aligned in vibration with those whose purpose, under Divine Will, is to build in matter. He became a conscious co-creator whose only 'desire' was to express the wonderment and beauty he felt for Spirit outwards through his creations. He could not do this as an island; he had to let go of all he believed himself to be and allow those whose purpose was to work alongside him, for whatever reason, to do their part; he had to cooperate."

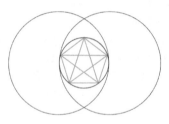

Truth
Colour: Blue
Seed thought: The key is the door as is the vision reality
Geometry: Pentagon, pentagram, golden ratio
Inspiration: Devotion or Idealism – Ray 6
               Quantum Navigation

Nowhere

"Where are you going?"

"Nowhere," replied Thomas.

"What do you mean, nowhere? You're clearly going somewhere," responded Fly, somewhat perplexed.

"I'm not going somewhere, I'm going Nowhere," repeated Thomas, matter-of-factly.

Fly, clearly confused, paused for a few seconds before replying. *"But... but... but... it's obvious you're going somewhere as you're walking so purposefully in a clear direction..."* Another pause. "If you weren't going anywhere, you'd be stood still," he concluded, rather pleased with himself.

"Ahhh, now you've introduced another place. Let me explain," said Thomas, hoping to gently encourage his inquisitive friend. "I am not going somewhere, neither am I going anywhere. In fact, I'm not going at all. I may appear to be walking but I'm not; I am staying right where I am. I might find somewhere and I might be everywhere while I'm walking but until I reach Nowhere I won't know."

Fly was speechless, so Thomas continued. "You see, Fly, unless I discover Nowhere I will never find somewhere, or anywhere, or even everywhere, and I most certainly will never find out what is on the other side of Nowhere. I have to find Nowhere first."

"Now I am really confused. My mind is running rings round itself trying to make sense of it all. It's tied itself in knots and now my head hurts... **a lot!**"

"Ha, ha, ha, that's the whole point, my friend," chuckled Thomas. "You will never reach Nowhere with your mind... neither will you find it if you look for it... You just have to wait... and one day, if you're really, really lucky, it will appear... just like that... And then you will realise it was right there with you all along... you just didn't know it."

His little friend gave up. And while Thomas settled down in his favourite spot in the forest, Fly buzzed about – here, there and everywhere – searching for who knows what... who knows where... and finding nothing...

It was Esmerelda's turn to be incredulous. Thomas had never left her side since selecting the key, was sat right beside her even now and yet, at the same time, he was inside the sphere having a meaningful dialogue with a fly (assuming it was a fly, of course – she'd never heard of winged creatures like these having the capacity to speak, let alone think)! With eyes wide open, and chin almost touching her knees, she turned towards her friend, *"How did you do that, Thomas? You were clearly in two places at once. How did you do it?"* With a mischievous twinkle in his eye, he turned to face her and grinned. His response was equally bemusing, "Magic, Esmerelda, magic." *"Well Thomas, there is clearly more to you than meets the eye. I am impressed. It's not often I am at a loss when faced with the inner workings of the cosmos, but I must admit you've got me this time..."* She didn't probe any further, respecting his autonomy in the 'ways of magic' relative to the world in which he lived, moved and had his being. In mutual respect, they paused for a while before Esmerelda broke the silence once again, *'I wonder if Fly realised that when he'd stumbled across nothing... he might just have found... **everything**...'* She mused. "You mean the space where everything is allowed... yet nothing exists..." teased Thomas.

A story

Beneath a tropical sky, radiant with stars, a child is born. With such divine spectacle, it is hard to imagine circumstances that might betray the silence of the night, but cries of the wounded soon reach her tender ears, almost from the moment she first draws breath. More cries follow, closer this time, heralding yet more stories. Laughter, pain, voices – some whispered, others rising in urgency or anger – add to the melee during the opening moments of the unsuspecting child's first taste of life. Yet all was not as is painted here. Cradled in her mother's arms, suckling at her breast, the child bathes in ignorance; she is safe, safe from all that might threaten her experience of peace, but far more than this, she is loved, loved beyond measure. In her tiny little heart, though she had no idea what it was, she could feel it. She continued to blossom, secure in the nurturing presence of those who cared. However, it was not to last. Unbeknownst to her, seeds sown in ancient soil, many of her own planting, were ripening, and in too few years the narrative setting out the course of her life was rewritten. Echoes of the war present at her inception returned to work out their destiny. Words replaced a more obvious enactment of conflict fired by those she had, in all innocence, come to trust – implicitly – to inject blame, shame, condemnation and, sometimes, even love into her unsuspecting heart. Confusion became the new order of the day as slowly, slowly something inside died. Doubt ate away trust, fear took the place of love and instinct arose as her only ally in survival. *"Where has all the love gone?"* she wondered. *"What did I do to drive it away? Where has love gone? What have I done?"*

Hungry ghost

A mighty mouth is a perfect metaphor for the great void of nothingness buried deep inside the belly of a ghoul. Two beady eyes, perched atop its head, direct its attention outward to anything that might stem the tide of irrepressible need that fuels its existence. Cradled in one hand is an urn filled with treasured, ill-gotten gains, and the other hand holds a child rendered helpless in the power of its grasp. Symbology in this illustration is rich. Neither child nor urn are essential to its existence, yet the ghoul, parent to its destiny, is powerless to let them go. The demon of desire defies all resistance; its ways are familiar, addictive and, to the ghoul, true, but it is the sense of emptiness, the bottomless empty pit it senses inside, that keeps the fires of its hell burning brightly. It fills its mind with tantalising visions of a plentiful world stuffed with 'must-have' commodities that lie forever beyond its reach. With attention directed outwards at every turn, the reality of its existence is never, ever found... its needs are never, ever met... and its desires remain unfulfilled. Why? Because a hungry ghost doesn't even know why it is hungry; it just eats.

Hungry Ghost

Longing

Longing emerges when **be**longing is complete. It is seen clearly when the muddied waters of searching, whether for a special other or for anything other than what is present, are stilled to nothing. Longing recognises itself in the mirror of its mind as a need, something it has always wanted but never found, something or someone that would make life complete if only it were present. Loneliness, isolation and unity are one and the same but you must swim in very deep waters to *feel* it... then there is no one experiencing the feeling... No one seeing clearly, no one feeling... No one. There is only experiencing... Until then, there is only longing... but you won't know it.

Searching

With an eye to see and a heart that feels
The way of the seeker will soon be revealed
From a time of beginning she searched for the truth
Her long-seeking goal... to be Absolute
The path of devotion for aeons, she explored
Only to find its way to be flawed
Now through All-Seeing eye, she clearly sees
Student with master forever will be
Trapped in a world of polarity
For love and devotion are confusing emotions
Fuelled by desire that demands salvation
Love of love gives rise to devotion
A way of being that holds no emotion
And when courage, as wrath, ignites divine fire
There is no self, and no other, to confuse with desire
No search, and no seeker, no truth to be found
Where the way of non-being... is Spirit unbound

"I like how these stories, though appearing separate, embody a sense of purpose in their unfolding," spoke Esmerelda, who was still very much present with the energy running through them. *"In a way, I feel my own journey is being expressed here but not as I* experienced or even in such a way that I could claim aspects of it as mine. It's like I am touching upon the essence of a principle that is universal in expression yet revealed through individual experience. Does this make sense, Thomas?"* He took a while to respond, as he was, in his own way, internally disentangling the matrix of many layers of expression. "It does. Even though I have no direct experience from an individual perspective, I know the energy running through it intimately, so it is easy for me to join the dots. Of course, playing an active part in the opening scene is a distinct advantage," he added, smiling. She didn't accept the carrot being dangled in front of her, choosing instead to continue with her interpretation as it unfolded inside her. *"Yes, that's it! It's an energy stream,"* she exclaimed. *"It's a stream of energy that runs not only through this sphere and its collection*

Longing

of stories but through other spheres and their stories as well. I knew the stories were familiar, especially those concerning the shadow; now I know why. Can you feel it, Thomas? Can you feel the pure vibration of love as it is expressed through these stories?" Even though questions were being directed towards him, he remained silent, preferring not to interrupt her flow. *"Now, when I bring into my awareness tales from other spheres, two in particular, I sense a picture of paradise revealing itself, even though visually it presents as discord. Cast your mind back to Worthless in the Beauty sphere. Remember its stories well, for they shine a light on why it may be so."*

"I know!" interrupted Thomas, eager to get a word in. "I know, I know, I know, Esmerelda!" As you can tell, he could hardly contain himself. "'A story,' 'Hungry ghost' and 'Longing' all give rise to the shadow. In effect, they are the cause, whose origin lies in the past, which gives rise to unconscious behaviour in the present." It was Esmerelda's turn to respect her friend's space, allowing him unrestricted freedom of expression to explore further. "The remaining stories, 'Nowhere' and 'Searching', reveal the bigger picture in that all stories, all forms, even the seeker's inner journey, are basically empty; they are nothing in and of themselves. In this, they align very well with the sphere of Love." Esmerelda mirrored her friend in expression, beaming from ear to ear, as she confirmed his reasoning. *"Thomas, my dear friend, you never cease to amaze me. Yes, you are absolutely spot on. Love, Love Divine, is indeed the energy stream running through all three spheres. It is the glue that holds all apparent opposites in its warm embrace and ensures, no matter how great the divide, it will always return every separate particle to itself. Why? Because the essence of life, all life, is love."* "And therein lies the foundation of all Truth," he finished, with a flourish.

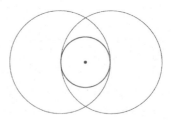

Will

Colour: Red
Seed thought: Be the change
Geometry: Point within a circle
Inspiration: Will or Power – Ray 1

The landscape was bleak. No matter which way he turned, the ghosts of his past were there, in ghoulish form, to remind him of his shame. Voices – his voices, their voices, some never-before-heard voices – played incessant games inside his head. "Don't look back in anger," they admonished, but he did, always. Every slight, every hurt, every act that threatened his existence, he remembered... with a vengeance. And they all, without exception, required payback. And for many, too many, years this had been his way. But inside, buried far beneath the walls of self-recrimination, a tiny spark still lived. Sometimes it would stir and bring isolated moments of joy in an otherwise empty existence. Sometimes it would surprise him with its warmth, **his** *warmth. And, on occasion, it would even take over completely and fill his being with its presence, and the endless clatter of voices in his head would cease and he could smile...* **really** *smile. But now he was tired. He had had enough of the endless war he perpetuated inside himself and could no longer endure the agony of self-imposed isolation or stomach his diet of endless shame. "No more," he cried. "Enough is enough." A new course was required, with direction and purpose, in which he had value, recognition and worth. In which he could find some sense of wholeness or love, and certainty that he was not ever alone.*

In an instant, the landscape altered, and, although still barren, it offered some hope of change. A distant vision, like a mirage in the mist, became a source for his salvation; although he couldn't see it and didn't know if it was true, it somehow gave him hope. So he forged his way forward, driven in desperation by a will to evolve. In stepping through the sacred mountain's gate, he faced his nemesis. Determination, fuelled by anger at his past, drove him on; the climb had begun. And, though fire ripped through his body and his anguished soul cried out in pain... though his mind offered tantalising, hard-to-refute visions of comfort, warmth and food and though his heart yearned in desperation for those it held so close... still he climbed... Eyes fixed firmly upon the summit, never flinching from the goal... undaunted, he climbed. Every step a challenge, each ounce of resistance a crashing to his knees... still, he climbed. Every breath a bloodied bath as flesh from his bones turned to fodder for the birds... Undeterred, he climbed. Every cry returned his agony unheard upon echoes in the wind... Still, he marched onward, step by agonising step... fury at his pathetic life driving him on, fanning the flames of his soul.

Many times he screamed for it to cease, to be released from the prison he had placed himself inside, for the pain of transcendence to play a different tune. Many times he sank to his knees, begging some higher authority to reveal itself to him, to show him he did not struggle in vain. And all too often the physical agony experienced in his broken heart carried so much despair he could have thrown himself upon rocks in the valley far below with barely a second thought. But he didn't. He walked, and he climbed, relentlessly. There was no choice: to cease his quest, to return to the valley none the wiser, would be to deny his very existence. The spark had been ignited, and now there was no turning back. So he walked. He didn't think, he didn't feel, he just walked. Until one day he didn't.

It was strange, really. The summit was in view, he had only a few more steps, a few more feet to climb, and his journey would be complete. But, instead of continuing, he sat down upon a rock and absorbed the view. And that's when it happened. A Great Silence permeated the space where he rested. All his striving and reaching out for some unattainable goal had led to this; dying to himself through 1000 untold deaths had led to this; his final letting go of his ultimate ambition, had led to this. If he'd still had identity, if he'd still been able to feel or if he'd still had any semblance of self remaining, he might have been awestruck. But, no, he had vanished, along with the mountain upon which his body had been resting... inside the Silence...

Our two explorers, rather than stepping into the red sphere to experience it directly, chose to remain where they were and wait patiently to see what would be revealed. As you can imagine, it took some time for them to absorb all that had unfolded before their eyes. Esmerelda, in particular, was most touched, in a feeling sense, by the pilgrim's story. *"I know his journey,"* she revealed, with tears in her eyes. *"The circumstances are different, but at its core, it is the same story – almost identical to when I was trapped in the prison of my own darkness. Unaware of the beauty, the spark that was my true nature, I had to travel far into all that I was not in order to recognise that which I was. It is a deeply profound and very painful experience on many levels but the rewards are, quite literally, out of this world."* Thomas remained silent. *"You see, in a way, it is made all the more difficult, particularly if you are on an awakening journey, as you have to enter fully into the persona of the false self; you have to take on and* **be** *the ego in all its polarised 'magnificence'. Unless you have experienced it yourself, owned all your 'faults' and known yourself as an individual distinct from the mass consciousness of humanity, you cannot really embrace the full magnitude of* *who you really are. Do you understand, Thomas?"* He nodded, but his tongue remained still, his voice silent. *"In other words, you must step back from the crowd, go against the grain and forge your own way, independent of others' beliefs or attempts to control. The ego has to develop to its full potential, to experience total individualism, before it can be seen for what it is. Then, and only then, may it surrender all to the ultimate Authority – the Will of the Divine. Dying '1000 deaths' on the part of the pilgrim was only possible because he knew they were false. He knew he had no option but to go on. So even though he had not yet come to know his True Self and had no idea of what lay ahead, 'something' inside kept him going; blind trust, through force of will, was his only ally."* Thomas, still silent, absorbed all she had shared. After a period of prolonged silence, he spoke.

"I understand, but the way I see it... as this sphere is very much about 'Will', we need to look at how it is expressed, not only from the perspective of the human being but also as an involutionary force where Spirit, in its infusion with matter, instils the Will to exist; in other words, Divine Purpose. The story we witnessed was one of evolution, where a human, in this case a man, had abused his power to the detriment of himself and others. Eventually, however, he began to see the error of his ways, transmuted all into energy and used it as fuel to affect his path of return. This is how it is for all of humanity. What isn't clear within the story is how this force for good played such a pivotal role in bringing about the U-turn, how its 'behind-the-scenes' direction inspired unequivocal action or why the pilgrim, as representative of all humanity, had no choice but to surrender all to its Authority." *Even though Esmerelda knew the involutionary journey intimately through her own experience (it was, after all, how she had arrived in Thomas' forest in the first place!), she loved how he explained things in a way that she never could, so she smiled encouragingly and nodded for him to continue.*

"Take a look at the symbol, Esmerelda. It's just a circle with a dot in the centre, right?" In fine fettle by then, Thomas couldn't wait for a response. Pausing only for a second to gather momentum, he accepted her non-verbal agreement and continued, with renewed enthusiasm. "Yes, it's a point within a circle, obviously, but it is so much more than that. In this symbol is not only the pilgrim's journey in its entirety but also the history of all humanity and, indeed, the sum total of the universe as we know it." *"Hard to imagine," reflected Esmerelda, catching his drift, nevertheless.* "If you remember our geometric story of creation (p.49), you'll know that 'life' begins as a sphere of nothingness – the circle – into which unity is expressed as one – the point in our symbol; Divine Will is this expression directed outwards into matter. The thing is, the point is not only an outward expression of Divine Will, but it is also the very thing that created the circle in the first place; try constructing a circle without using the sharp end of a compass and you will understand what I am getting at. So, in this symbol is Truth as paradox. Without the circle, there would be no space into which Divine Will could manifest its purpose, yet without the point, there would be no circle." Having caught Esmerelda's bewildered expression, Thomas paused for breath. *"I can feel all that you are attempting to convey," she shared, honestly. "And you are so good at putting across, in a matter-of-fact way, that which is impossible to articulate with words alone. But sometimes my mind gets lost when you start talking in paradoxical sentences."*

"You've hit the nail on the head there, Esmerelda. The mind does not, nor will it ever, understand paradox. It is being asked to accept a scenario in which two or more supposedly opposite possibilities, or truths, occupy the same space at the same time; it cannot do that. It cannot rationalise the irrational, so it ties itself in knots trying to figure it out. The only option open to it is to give up, and therein lies its salvation: when the mind gives up, it becomes the space defining its origin, and in being nothing, it understands everything." *Esmerelda laughed, "Of course, now I get it!"* It was her turn to 'pause for thought'. After a period of time – quite a long period of time in the opinion of Thomas – she continued.

"It would help to complete my understanding if I could apply all of this to the pilgrim's journey." Thomas bowed graciously as he invited her to continue. *"Spirit, through an act of Will, created a space into which it could emanate its light. This space began as nothing but was, in fact, everything. The force of Spirit, through its Will alone, moved across the face of the void to create the cause of existence of all things, including, of course, the pilgrim in our story. All living entities were thus infused with the gift of life; their purpose, through the will to evolve, ensured all, at some point in time, returned to the bosom of the One. However, there were two significant obstacles to any individual, be it animal, planet or human being, affecting its return; unconsciousness and time."* "Yes, brilliant," interrupted her very enthusiastic companion. "The very nature of the circle is unconscious (remember the creation story where, in order to experience itself as separate, Great Spirit had to send a portion of itself to sleep, thus making it unconscious?), whereas the point distributes its will to exist over time; all living things are therefore under the influence of these two basic laws of existence before they've even been born. WOW! How amazing is that Esmerelda? No wonder it is so hard to wake up!" As you might well imagine, such was their child-like wonder at the situation, it was some time before Esmerelda could continue.

"Exactly!" she laughed in agreeance. "Now let's get back to our pilgrim. His purpose, from the moment he was infused with life, was to wake up, only he didn't know it because he was unconscious. So, over the course of his existence, he grew into a fully-fledged ego, taking on the full expression of all that this entailed – control, identity, blame, shame, fear, etc. – and believed, for a very long time, that that was who he was. Until came the crash. In a flash of insight, he began to question the meaning, or lack of it, of his life as a whole; after all his ambitious years of fighting to reach the top of the ladder, he suddenly realised it meant nothing. Inside he was empty. "And the rest, as they say, is history," chirped Thomas. *"Absolutely! It certainly defined a moment in his awakening, as well as marking the beginning of his 'climb', but look deeper – ask yourself, what was the trigger? What lay behind the cause of his awakening and how did it come about?"* "Well, the simple answer is Divine Will of course, on both counts. But it doesn't explain the 'how'." *"Spot on, Thomas. The Will of the Divine is prevalent throughout all space and all time. Non-discriminatory in its action, it determines the rate at which planets orbit the sun, how the moon affects the tides and how the waves return to shore. It brings a season to its close and births another in its wake. It draws a pigeon to its home and a dolphin to its pod, and, in a desolate forest, a tiny seed survives in spite of its destructive fire reducing all to ash. Cities and civilisations are brought to their knees in a quake lasting but a few seconds, yet the will of the small believes it wields the most power. But it is on the inner planes where Divine Will is clearly felt and at its most powerful. As the Call of the Eternal is carried upon wings of the Soul, its message is clear – 'I am That and That I am.'"*

"Now I have it," said Thomas, moved beyond words by Esmerelda's soulful expression of the divine in her. "It is the subtle message leaving repeated impressions upon the mind of one who is unconscious that eventually results in it waking up. Initially, as in the case of our pilgrim, it manifests as conscience – tiny pinpricks of light that grow and expand unnoticed over time until, in a flash, there they are and, 'Voila!', it's wake-up time." *"As usual, Thomas, you have summed it up perfectly. These subtle impressions are vital, but it takes much apparent destruction on the part of the ego-self before the one who is asleep can step aside sufficiently to hear the Voice in the Silence. Our pilgrim had almost reached the summit of his **inner** ambitions before he finally let go. When he did, the Great Silence descended and he was gone."* "Mmmmm... wonder where he is now," reflected Thomas, almost to himself. They both turned towards each other and smiled knowingly, and, without sharing another word, peered into the red sphere.

The landscape was the same inasmuch as it featured a mountain, a narrow, rocky path and a valley; everything else was different. The whole panorama had a 'light' feel about it, an unfamiliar presence permeated the air, and every living particle held a vibrancy that was nothing short of divine. At first glance, it seemed the pilgrim had disappeared, dissolved completely amidst the rapturous wonder he had experienced during his awakening on the mountain top. But no, there he was, a lone figure walking nonchalantly amongst the wild spring flowers close to the base of the mountain. He had returned to the valley. There was an ease about him, a quality of being at home within himself, and he emanated an air of quietude not dissimilar to that of the Great Silence...

"Wonder why he didn't stay at the mountain top," pondered Thomas, after they'd returned to the forest. *"I don't know,"* she replied, *"but it reminds me of a saying I heard a very, very long time ago..."*

> *Before enlightenment, chop wood. After enlightenment, chop wood.*
> Zen proverb

Joining the dots

The two friends sat in silence for a very long time, each bathing in the after-effect ambience of their adventure. They had borne witness to an eye-opening, and sometimes heart-wrenching, spectacle through which stories within each sphere revealed their most profound experience of truth in naked vulnerability. And, even though these may have presented as mere snapshots of their expression, they left our two explorers feeling extremely full inside – as if they had, in a very short space of time, consumed a seven-course banquet with little space to digest the delicacies offered on each plate. Is it any wonder they needed to take a well-deserved nap to allow it all to sink in? It was over too soon though, especially for Esmerelda, who could have dwelled in its perfect peace for many more moons, so akin was it to her inner homeland, but truth danced to its own metronome, and the time of the sharing was now. Esmerelda, as it turned out, was first to break the silence.

"There is such a delicious sense of wholeness as I absorb the many, many subtle, and even not-so-subtle, vibrations running through each of these spheres, especially when I allow them to co-exist in the same space at the same time. It is as if I am embraced, so lovingly, by the seven vibrations of mind within the greater expanse of Mentor... and even beyond to the pristine consciousness of the Beloved. Yet how may this profound holism, complete in its expression of supreme, divided individualism, be explained, let alone shared?" She was at a loss for words and she posed the question to herself rather than anyone else. She wasn't even sure she desired an answer. No, for the time being she was content to swim in the gentle waters of pondering, trusting that when the time was right, all the pieces of the jigsaw would fall readily into place without her having to 'do' anything.

Thomas, of course, was eager to fill in the gaps! "I think we have to look to the symbols, Esmerelda. There is more to them than meets the eye and I have a sense that when we look at them from a perspective of wholeness, individualism and holism will be seen to be one and the same; fractal and hologram so to speak. The way I see it, if we find the origin of the symbols, then the relationship between the spheres, and by association, the rainbow, will become obvious – that's the theory anyway!"

Rainbow Relationships

Every Rainbow symbol has the vesica piscis as its source. However, even the vesica piscis has a pre-existent point of origin – a single circle – and if we trace it back even further, we find it is a single point that defines its pre-existent state (in sacred geometry this is the point of the compass). Symbols, then, regardless of their individual significance, embody all these geometric principles before they mature into the full expression of an idea.

The vesica piscis first put in an appearance as Esmerelda's map of consciousness; it emerged again upon discovery of the keys and again, in 'A Door', where Thomas revealed its purpose as a gateway into physical manifestation. Progression to seed, flower and fruit of life, through ever-increasing circles followed, culminating in Metatron's cube from which the five platonic solids emerged. Esmerelda's map, however, has more secrets to reveal. If we turn our attention to the central 'eye' where the two circles meet, and consider the integral qualities of each circle, we find that the 'eye' serves as container for both the human kingdom and that of the Soul. Why? Because the Soul is integral to Spirit (upper circle) and the human being is inseparable from nature, matter (lower circle). Soul integration, then, takes place within the inner 'Eye of God'. The remainder of this chapter is devoted to, 'how?'. If you pay attention as we go, you will see that it is not only personality and Soul that are fused within the eye, but mind as well.

First, it is worth saying the journey from vesica piscis, through seed of life and the platonic solids, to divine matrix and Metatron's cube is but a beginning and illustrates only one half of the picture – or one of the two spheres – doorway to the **outer** world of manifestation. By far and away its most revealing gift is its function as gateway to the **inner**, subjective nature of consciousness – the 'power behind the throne', so to speak, which

Vesica Piscis

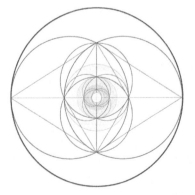

Inner Vesica Piscis

informs, through intent, the manifested universe. Upon these foundations, the Rainbow spheres, and their associated symbols, emerge as entities within the greater expanse of the whole, but to see and experience this we must delve into the construction – the sacred geometry – of the inner 'Eye' of God. How does the inner journey unfold within itself and what is its significance when applied to consciousness? Appendix 1, 'Practical Geometry', presents detailed diagrams of this process and much will be gained by turning to p.462 and following its directions as we continue; for now, suffice to say, the following geometries play a significant part in its unfolding: golden ratio/cross (Love), two tetrahedrons (Beauty) and hexagram (Mind). Light, being represented by a triangle and integral to the hexagram, also plays a part. In a nutshell, two tetrahedrons are drawn by connecting salient points within the vesica piscis; this serves as the 'gate in' and facilitates construction of the hexagram. A progressive journey inwards reveals that all geometries rotate by 90° in cyclic fashion to expose an alternate perspective on reality. Let's see how it pans out when we delve a little deeper.

Bigger picture

In Figure 1, 'Dynamics of Change', symbols are first placed at salient points around the hexagram (six-pointed star). Far from accidental, these placements show, from a bigger-picture perspective, the origin of relationship between the seven spheres of consciousness. Six align with two triads in hexagram – Will, Love, Light and Mind, Truth, Order. The seventh – Beauty – is the structure in its entirety, which serves as gateway to the inner 'eye'; the *Way of Beauty* being the transcendent awakened state. How does this come about? In order to find out, we must tease the structure apart even further and rearrange the symbols so they reveal different dynamics;

dynamics that demonstrate that the *Way of Wholeness* is more than just a buzzword, more than an ideal and more than an out-of-reach goal whose fruits always lie just beyond your grasp. No, when the true significance of these relationships is taken on board, integrated and digested, these dynamic interchanges show how the inner vision, as a causal factor, really does manifest in reality where every rotational 90° shift in consciousness opens the door to new perspectives to create the ultimate in physical form expression: an awakened human.

The Rainbow Bridge[4]

Known in esoteric language as the Antahkarana, meaning the 'inner cause', the Rainbow Bridge is built in mental matter between body (personality) and Soul, and Soul/Spirit. In Figure 2, 'Rainbow Bridge', the inner vesica piscis has been expanded outwards to expose this inner bridge; symbols in the hexagram, now two individual triangles, remain in the same positions but have additional qualities assigned to them according to their place on the tree. At the level of the Monad, Will, Love and Light express themselves as Divine Will, Divine Love (intuition) and higher mind, whereas the three expressions of personality – lower mind, emotion and physical form – are represented by Mind, Truth and Order respectively; the role of Beauty, in its unified state, remains the same – life as a *Way of Beauty*.

However, this is but a way in to the inner workings of the Soul. Pivotal to its blending with the personality is integration with the shadow, symbolised by the dark sphere at the centre of the Rainbow Bridge. Unless unseen hidden parts are both acknowledged and accepted, fusion is virtually impossible. There is a reason this sphere is dark: not only does it denote nothingness, particularly in the form of identity, whether on

---

[4] See 'What is...?', 'Building bridges'.

personality, Soul or Monadic planes of existence, but it also represents the unconscious – all within the bounds of its expression is asleep until the call is heard to wake up. Enter the role of the pentagram, five-pointed star, integral to the darkness of the void. When symbols are aligned to its points, new dynamics come into play. Notice only five of the seven are positioned here, the remaining two – Will and Order – form spheres of their own above and below the bridge. Their significance will become clear in a moment.

As a symbol for life itself, the pentagram is ideal for harmonising all aspects of the shadow. At the top is Love, a presiding radiance whose presence is not only unconditional in its acceptance of all unredeemed parts of the shadow but also integral to those symbols placed at the 'legs', Truth and Beauty, to which it is intimately connected through geometry and their relationships to the golden ratio. Before moving on to the 'arms' of the pentagram, it is important to understand that the qualities of Beauty that are expressed in this position, its shadow properties, are those of polarity; bringing opposing duals to a place of harmony and thence to unity is a skill not easily mastered, let alone integrated, but is nevertheless essential if the shadow self is to be fully redeemed. Choosing one pole over another, especially if taking a projective or defensive stance, is guaranteed to perpetuate the war. The arms of the pentagram reveal two aspects of mind, Light, as the higher mind, and Mind, as the lower; how they knit together will become obvious when we take a closer look at the properties of the individual symbols, but for now, suffice to say, their position at the top of the structure is significant.

To bring this section to a close, we must draw the bridge into itself, not returning it to its original form but incorporating the lessons we have learnt along the way; in short, we must return each section to its point of synthesis and then collapse the three spheres into one (refer to Figure 2, 'Rainbow Bridge', for clarity). This is how: Three qualities of the Monad (Atma, Buddhi, higher manas) are synthesised into one symbol – the circle and point (Will) to express Spirit as a whole. Personality trinity (physical/etheric, astral, lower manas) becomes symbol for Order as the pure vibration of the Word sounded in matter. Last, five aspects of the shadow self (Love, Beauty, Truth, Light and Mind), revealed through our adventurers' journey into the spheres, are one in the pentagram – symbol for Truth.

Building the Rainbow Bridge

When the six-pointed star is integrated with qualities of the five (pentagram) it results in the perfected 'integrated' human, where Spirit (Will) flows unimpeded through form (Order) as a way of life (Beauty). Symbols in their alignments to hexagram or pentagram within the Rainbow Bridge show the stages in this process.

Shadow integration

During shadow integration, five symbols, with their integral qualities, are harmonised within the pentagram and then, upon completion, reduced to a single sphere. In Figure 4, this sphere becomes the inner eye of vesica piscis, where the enclosing two circles reflect the bigger-picture dynamics of Spirit and matter – symbols for Will (Spirit) and Order (matter). Seven spheres are thus reduced to three inside one symbol. Figure 5 continues the collapsing process, where all seven are reduced to three and amalgamated into one symbol, that for Order. Body (Order) and Spirit (Will – circle and point) are fused and in direct, fluid relationship, the shadow self is no longer a separate entity (Truth – pentagram) so the Soul-infused personality, functioning through a single harmonious vibration, is thus free to express Soul purpose as a *Way of Wholeness* in daily life.

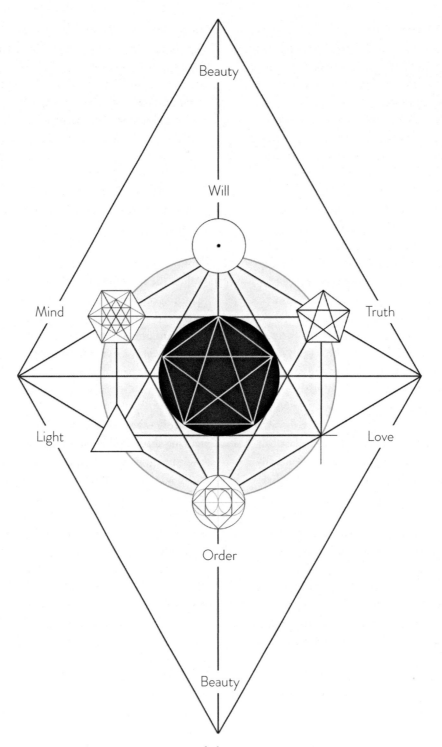

Figure 1 Dynamics of Change: Inner Vesica Piscis

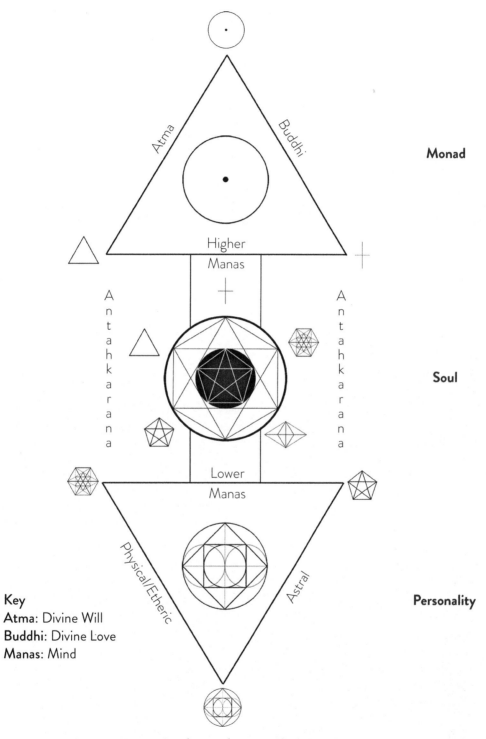

Monad

Soul

Personality

Key
Atma: Divine Will
Buddhi: Divine Love
Manas: Mind

Figure 2 Rainbow Bridge: Inner Vesica Piscis

Figure 3 Five Spheres

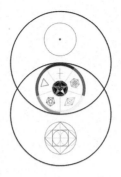

Figure 4 Seven Become Three

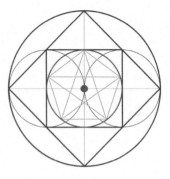

Figure 5 Three Become One

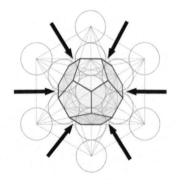

Dodecahedron in Metatron's Cube:
Arrows show extra lines

Dodecahedron within Hexagram:
Synthesis of the five and six

N.B. The pentagram may only be drawn inside a circle through the addition of extra lines and circles[5] – practically, 'dropping in' to the heart allows a more refined way of being, through integration of the shadow. The dodecahedron (12 pentagrams), also connected to the heart, is the same – extra lines need to be joined before it can be extracted from Metatron's cube.

The nitty gritty

Symbols express Absolute through two lines of force – Will and Love – with their inherent relationships being made apparent through geometric structure married with esoteric philosophy. Woven into the very fabric of these relationships, as will be revealed through the telling, are principles of cosmic ordering,[6] otherwise called universal Laws, which govern their rite of passage during the integration process, whatever level is being expressed at the time. To the aware, it will therefore become apparent that many potential connections exist outside of these placements, bounded only by the limits of individual insight and imagination. Consider then, the following to be a foundation, rooted in consciousness, which extends a warm invitation to awaken the creative imagination and begin your own voyage of discovery.

---

[5] See 'Appendix 1: Practical Geometry', 'Constructing a pentagon/pentagram within vesica piscis'.

[6] See 'What is...?', 'What are the Universal Principles?'.

Will Line

 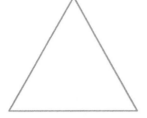 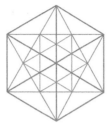 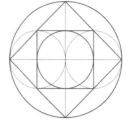

Will: Ray 1   *Light: Ray 3*   *Mind: Ray 5*   *Order: Ray 7*

Even a cursory glance reveals why symbols have fallen so readily into these categories. Go a little deeper, engaging the feeling body alongside the creative imagination, and you will intuitively not only know but also experience the forces at play. How they interact, their integral geometries and the way they serve to express aspects of Divinity become increasingly obvious, in a 'felt' sense, the more they are contemplated. However, a little direction may be in order for the uninitiated. First and foremost is the symbol for Will, circle and point. Not only does it mark the beginning of everything, but it also has a depth of profundity embedded within it that is worthy of a lifetime's reflection. Consider the circle to be a space, containing everything or nothing, into which light, in the form of a spark, emanates a will to exist. Take it a stage further and envisage this spark to be infused with intent, a divine idea, from which everything in the manifested universe is created. Now follow this idea through the remaining three symbols in this line of force. Notice how they become more intricate as the Will of the Divine works out its purpose. See how, by and large, the resultant matrix is linear in its expression, and how each is intimately connected to and evolves through the one preceding it.

Unpacking these relationships further, whilst also holding in our awareness the learnings gained through exploring the Rainbow Bridge, we can see two interconnected pairs are worthy of further consideration: Will/Order and Light/Mind. The first has already been discussed from a bigger-picture perspective; now we need to tease it apart a bit more. What if the point of light were not only a spark of intent, a divine idea, but also a sound? What if the manifested universe, in its entirety, were but an echo of the Word? If this were the case, wouldn't it be wonderful if a symbol, perhaps the antithesis to its original outpouring, would also be able to reflect this? Of course it would, and so it does: the symbol for Order is the sacred geometry of an octave – sound as vibration and expression of the Word through multiple layers of existence as it penetrates deep into the crystalline structure of matter. Will and Order then, are at the extreme poles of existence; everything unfolds within their parameters and all, in the fullness of time, will return the One unto itself. In between is the matrix of thought expressed through two symbols: Light and Mind. How the symbols reflect these dynamics will come to fruition under 'Integration through Mind' but for now the focus must be on mind as a causal factor in the web of life. Rewinding the matrix of creation to the very beginning once again, let us revisit the circle and point, paying particular attention to it being the origin of an idea, the will to exist, from which the manifested universe was created out of nothing. The implication is that this spark was not only the original idea but also, crucially, the primal Cause for all that followed. Add to this the assumption that the space into which it emanated its light was unconscious and you have a formula for creation in which truth is considered to be all that is light, with dark being its polar opposite.

But, what if it were the other way around? What if it were the divine matrix that were unconscious and the soil from which it draws its sustenance, Absolute nothingness, that were conscious? What if light, in the form of thought, created a web of deceit, and nothingness was the means by which it may be seen clearly for what it is? Wouldn't that turn everything on its head,

wouldn't it create a cause to re-examine the whole fabric of existence and wouldn't it make you wonder, if only for a moment, whether all you were perceiving through your senses, including your thoughts, had any foundation in reality? In short, what if all you believed to be true, wasn't? Now let's throw another spanner in the works... What if **both** possibilities were true? What if nothingness were, at one and the same time, **both** conscious and unconscious? And, what if the point were both the beginning and the end of existence? What if Truth were a paradox... and the only way to resolve it was to enter a space that was not mind?

Love Line

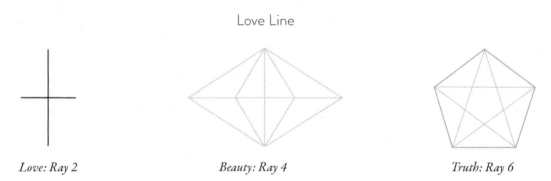

Love: Ray 2   *Beauty: Ray 4*   *Truth: Ray 6*

In the same way that symbols on the Will line fell easily into place, so it is with Love. However, their alignment, particularly regarding the symbol for Truth, is perhaps more subtle and engages the feeling body more intuitively than the mind. There is a reason for this. All three symbols have as their root the golden ratio (also called the golden section, divine proportion, golden mean rectangle or Phi/phi), expressed in number as 1.618/0.618. Instances of this ratio appearing are manifold – our natural world, solar systems, music, architecture, artwork and even in the human body, including DNA, are but a few examples – but, for now, we will confine our attention to the task in hand: three symbols

and their expression of love. Love and Beauty, it is clear, are intimately linked; not only does the cross rest at the centre of the vesica piscis in both geometries, but it also serves as foundation to the inner journey through its perfect, divine expression of duality; the difference being, one is duality in its integrated state (two experienced from a position of unity), the other is duality polarised by energising the war of opposites.

How this plays out in reality will be explained when we explore the relationship between the heart and mind, but first, we need to find the golden ratio within the pentagram/pentagon, which is best explained through a diagram. Four examples (there are many more) in the diagram below have been highlighted to show the relationship, the ratio, between long and short lines. Even without compass or straight edge, and even using different physical form dynamics, it is clear the relationship between these lines is identical to those of the cross in the first two symbols.

However, this is but a beginning. The golden ratio comes into its own when expressed as a geometric structure in its own right, but to find out why, we have a bit more digging to do. All things 'golden' in respect to the ratio are an expression of Spirit, with the formula 1.618 being key to its expression. The kingdom of nature, although equally divine, uses its own formula, known as the Fibonacci sequence, to **approximate** Spirit. A series of numbers beginning with 1, it goes something like this: "Take the past and add it to the present to create the future." Numerically, it translates as 1 (past) + 1 (present) = 2 (future) and continues ad infinitum: 2, 3, 5, 8, 13, 21, 34, 55, etc. The larger the number, the closer it gets to phi until at the 12th instance, number 144, it creates an almost exact match. When plotted on a graph, as diagram below opposite shows, the Fibonacci sequence translates to a spiral. See how, beginning at the centre, the squares equate in size

to the numbers in the sequence – 1, 1, 2, 3, 5 and 8. The golden ratio may also be expressed in this way, the crucial difference being that the golden spiral has no beginning and no end; the Fibonacci spiral has a beginning but no end.

In summary, all three symbols on this line of force express divinity through ever-increasing and decreasing spirals, expanding and contracting with each cosmic in-breath and out-breath, in alignment with the Will of the Divine, not the human. To experience its flow is to be in harmony with the universe: integrated, individual, complete. The way in is through the heart, its password is surrender, its territory nothing and yet its reward is everything. Therein lies Truth, expressed as paradox.

Integration through Mind

Building upon the relationships already discussed, it is easy to see how the two symbols representing the higher and lower aspects of mind are interconnected; one is quite literally inside the other. As you might expect if Spirit truly were universal in its expression, especially on the plane of mind, any representation of its methods must be true to its divine nature. The triad, and the way it plays out in a dualistic universe, serves as source

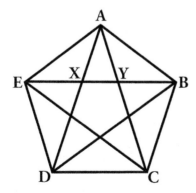

Pentagon/Pentagram: Showing golden ratios
AE/XY, AB/BY, EC/ED, AC/CD

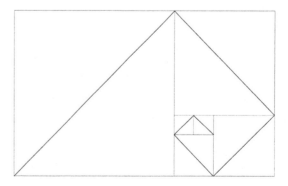

Fibonacci Spiral

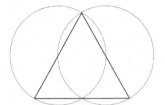
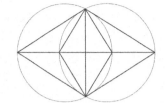
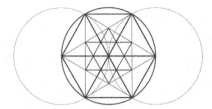

Higher Mind   *Polarity*   *Lower Mind*

to integrating the lower with the higher, but how? If we cast our mind back to the sphere of Mind, in particular to the story concerning Origin (p.65), Esmerelda refers to three players in a causal relationship – victim, perpetrator and rescuer – any two of which, if energised, perpetuate the war of polarity; even the third option, being part of the same dynamic interchange, does not elevate consciousness to a place where integration may take place.

No, other means must be explored before we have our answer. Perhaps a 'higher' dynamic, the spiritual triad at the apex of the Rainbow Bridge, will provide some clarity. Here again, we have a trinity – Divine Will, Divine Love and higher mind – however, here they are synchronous in their modus operandi: they appear as separate but they are not; they are one in consciousness. So how do we move from one to the other? Do we actually have to move anywhere? Introducing a third symbol, Beauty (polarity) solves the riddle but before we go into the why, let's look a little closer at the symbol for the lower mind. At its heart is a hexagram, two triangles, one upwards pointing the other downwards, perfectly balanced. Here is where the work begins in harmonising the two triads, geometrically speaking of course. Look closer and you will see embedded within the symbol two diamonds, integral to which is the golden ratio – symbol for Love. Now we can get to the how.

When the war of polarity comes into play, it is crucial not to charge the war; taking sides, even if the motive is with the best of intentions, holding 'all in light' if there is a perception of something needing to be fixed or, perceptibly even worse, denying there is anything untoward reinforces polarity. However, just as in the 'Origin story', if recognition for the part one has played in creating the matrix is seen clearly and, above all, owned, the war of opposites ceases to exist. All resistances collapse, the golden ratio returns all to itself and the lower is one with the higher. Look again at the symbols for lower and higher mind; each is one in the other and all that need be removed are the obstacles preventing you from experiencing them.

Heart – Mind

The intuitive amongst you may have worked out that there is more to the amalgamation of these two aspects of mind than mind itself. Introducing the golden ratio within the symbol for Beauty opened the heart to acceptance, so all perceptions of conflict could be dissolved into nothing, integration being the only possible outcome. This, however, is not all. To bring our journey through the Rainbow symbols to a close, uniting all seven spheres in the process, there is one more to consider: the icing on the cake you might say – the symbol for Order. In this, you will see, it not only embodies the vibrational resonances of the universe from macro to microcosm but also facilitates the seamless synthesis of both heart and mind as it unites Spirit with matter. In order to see how, we must expand the geometry of sound to its full expression as an octave and then take it apart whilst marrying it with the integration process. The diagram on the left, below, illustrates the geometry of an octave in its full expression, with three vibrational layers. Notice how it is made up of squares, diamonds (or squares rotated 90°) and circles in three sizes; the smallest circles are eight in number, totalling one octave. At the centre is an additional circle bounded by a square which grows in size exponentially with each vibrational shift (see 'Geometry of Octave' diagrams); its creation forms a double vesica piscis just like we found in the symbol for the lower mind. All these structures are vital in unfolding the matrix of creation and understanding the role of the heart and mind in its process. Let's find out why.

The squares in the diagram on the right below represent the lower mind in its most 'stuck' state: the 'box' containing our beliefs, programs and reactions to stimuli, whether external or internal. They also symbolise the past, our stuck-ness as it goes back decades or, more often than not, lifetimes. It is here that karmic propensities reside, playing the same old record over and over again until the call is heard to awaken. Enter the role of the diamonds or rotated squares. Each 90° rotation is a shift in perception, resulting in a change of

Geometry of Octave: Circles as waves

mindset and more inclusive perpective. A 90° shift generates a spiral, which in turn leads to expansion in the heart, where love, in this case, is expressed as an all-inclusive radiance. Circles, as well as being spirals, may express themselves as a wave; dynamic movement within the space they create. Think about this; it is worthy of contemplation.

Last, the centre circle in both symbol and octave sets the whole creative process in motion. Think of it as a droplet of water entering a pond, creating ripple effects, in all directions until it fizzles itself out. Life really is all about vibration: a single impulse, be it thought, word or deed, has a profound effect upon the whole matrix. Rainbow symbols offer a way in for you to experience this directly.

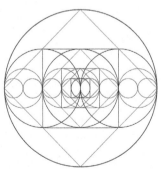

Geometry of Octave: Three layers, one octave

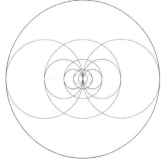

Geometry of Octave: Circles (Heart)

Geometry of Octave: Squares (Mind)

A Diamond

"Ouch!" quickly followed by, "Damn!" and then, "Owww... that really hurt." Thomas hopped about on one leg clutching a wounded toe. In his enthusiasm, he had raced on ahead, barefoot as usual, in pursuit of their next great adventure, and he was paying the price for not watching where he placed his feet. Esmerelda arrived a few moments later to witness this quite comical turn of events. "Let me take a look," she implored, trying, most unsuccessfully, to mask her amusement. Somewhat begrudgingly, Thomas sat down on the soft earth whilst Esmerelda administered to his wound. As you can well imagine, it was his pride that bore the brunt of the pain, not his toe! However, somewhat consoled, he soon leapt to his feet. "Now I shall retrace my steps and find the offending object so I can give it a piece of my mind," he mumbled, whilst hobbling off in the direction from whence he came. Curiosity getting the better of her, Esmerelda trotted along behind him. After all, there was never anything coincidental in the way their adventures unravelled themselves, and she was sure this occasion would prove to be no different. She was right.

"Wow, look at this, Esmerelda. I knew it was far more than an ordinary rock that had tripped me up." He was bent down, eyes to the ground, peering at what appeared to be a perfectly ordinary piece of granite, such as you would expect to find in any area of woodland. However, this was not an ordinary clump of trees; it was a magical forest. And furthermore, it was Thomas' wood, a space in time where all manner of phantasmagorical appearances and happenings took place. "No, Esmerelda, it is not a lump of rock. In fact, it is not a rock at all. Look, can you see how it shines? It is a diamond!" Thomas was beside himself with joy as he lifted it from the earth, held it up towards the sky – well, as far as he could: it was particularly large and required both hands to raise it from the ground

– and peered enthusiastically into its crystalline structure. "What's more, Esmerelda, this is not an ordinary diamond." He was addressing her but communing with the beautiful object he held, most reverently, within his hands. "Its structure is geometric, as if it has been meticulously carved, layer by layer, over aeons of time." Esmerelda, in her own way, was equally transfixed. In fact, she had no words with which to respond. She listened. She took every word he uttered into her heart and she absorbed every facet he revealed through his scrutiny until, fragment by fragment, the pieces of her inner jigsaw fell into place. Still, she did not speak.

"Its outer form is a work of art in itself but look at the layers within it. There are structures within structures, geometries inside geometries and lines of light linking the passage of time through the process of its evolutionary journey. Let me show you how." He rested the diamond upon the earth, turning it from face to face so she could get a tangible sense of the principles he was talking about. "First of all, if you pay attention to the outer form, you will see that although it is made up of straight lines, it is still quite rounded in shape. This is how evolution works. Over aeons of time all separate particles refine themselves more and more until they eventually return to the perfect sphere; in geometry this process begins with a tetrahedron (a star tetrahedron used in *Walk the Rainbow* is two tetrahedrons), followed by a cube, an octahedron and an icosahedron to a dodecahedron, the most rounded of the platonic solids. This beautiful diamond is a **stellated** dodecahedron. What does this mean?" Out came the familiar stick as he cleared a space in the earth upon which he could draw.

"Let's begin with a dodecahedron. Notice it has 12 faces, each one pentagonal (five sided) in shape. Now, if we take each of these faces and extract the corners by drawing a line into the centre, we end up with a star on every face; each star being made up of five triangles. The stellated dodecahedron is therefore formed of 60 triangles (12 × 5) and 12 pentagonal (five-sided) pyramids. Voila!" Esmerelda watched and played as Thomas shared his art, but, still very much engrossed in her own process, she remained silent.

"However, as fascinating and mind-blowing, as this all is," he continued, "it is by no means the end." Thomas paused, not only to gather his thoughts but also to create added effect for his pièce de résistance. "It is the structure **within** that makes the stellated dodecahedron, and with it the diamond, the remarkable piece of precision engineering that it is." Again, he paused; this time solely for effect! "This is an icosahedron," he stated whilst drawing in the sand. "See how even though it is made up of triangles (20 in all), it also forms a pentagonal 'cap' at both top and bottom?" Esmerelda nodded. "This brings it into unique relationship with the dodecahedron and is therefore fundamental to the creation of the stellated dodecahedron geometry ('Thomas' diamond); you might say it is its foundation. When all triangular faces are extracted into a star (like we did with the dodecahedron) the **stellated** icosahedron is birthed, creating 60 triangles (20 × 3) around the outside of the icosahedron.

Now link the external triangular **points** of the stellated icosahedron together (five on each of 12 pentagonal faces) and, as if by magic, a dodecahedron appears!

The dodecahedron forms around the 'points' of the stellated icosahedron and becomes a foundation for the stellated dodecahedron. Make sense?" Esmerelda smiled politely, but she was only just following. Thomas sensed it too, so he offered some clarification. "Apart from their inherent relationship, the most important thing to understand is that both the stellated icosahedron and the dodecahedron sit **inside** the stellated dodecahedron. They are the inner structure of the diamond and without them, not only would it lack substance but also it would never be able to shine... and... if..." His voice faded as he turned to face Esmerelda. She had taken on a translucent appearance and even though her physical form was evident, her presence was somewhat other-worldly, like she existed in more than one reality at the same time. Never in his life had he experienced so much love emanating from a single being, never had he known such incredible peace and never had he borne witness to one who was so completely at home in her own body that it could not fail to impact upon any one, or more, beings who were there to sense

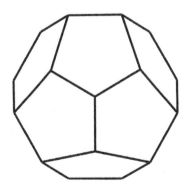

Dodecahedron: 12 pentagrams

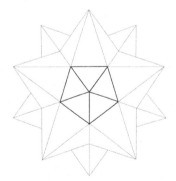

Stellated Dodecahedron: 60 triangles,
12 pentagonal pyramids

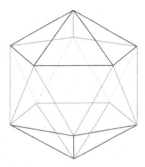

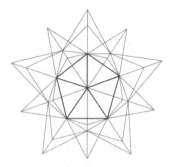

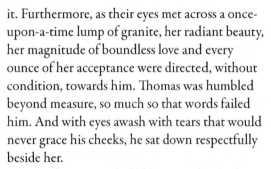

Icosahedron: Showing pentagonal 'caps'

Stellated Icosahedron: 60 triangles

it. Furthermore, as their eyes met across a once-upon-a-time lump of granite, her radiant beauty, her magnitude of boundless love and every ounce of her acceptance were directed, without condition, towards him. Thomas was humbled beyond measure, so much so that words failed him. And with eyes awash with tears that would never grace his cheeks, he sat down respectfully beside her.

From the moment he held it up to the sky, from the minute his razor-sharp mind engaged with its structure, even before he had opened his mouth to share, Esmerelda knew. She knew, with every fibre of her being – from the broadest expanse of her mind to the darkest shadows within her all-inclusive yet vulnerable heart. She knew, beyond all doubt, that encased within this obscure clump of rock, concealed amongst its multiplicitous lines of luminous distractions, were wondrous mysteries hitherto unknown to this race of man. She knew it was no accident that deep within the magical forest in which they played, her inquisitive friend had stumbled upon this lump of granite and been brought unceremoniously to his knees, and she knew his big toe had played no small part in bringing them to this point of revelation. She knew it was time for secrets, held deep inside the bounds of time and space, to be unleashed. Yes, Esmerelda knew. She knew it was time for the hidden story of humanity to be revealed. It was time to dive into

the unbridled recesses buried within the walls of every heart encased in stone. It was time to shatter, with relentless intensity, that which had for aeons enslaved minds in belief. It was time to stand up and be counted.

In her mind's eye, she was led to the outer reaches of the universe where a distant star, still a bright pinprick of light against an indigo sky when viewed from planet earth, had entered its final stage of death. Like most of its kind, it had taken millions upon millions of years to reach this juncture. Now, as Esmerelda bore witness, it had exhausted every possible source of fuel in trying to sustain an insatiable inner fire. She watched in wonder as it increased in magnitude to such a degree that it could no longer contain itself. In a flash of brilliance, the star, now the most intense shade of red, for a brief period became the brightest light in the universe. Then it was gone. Puff! Blown apart, shattered into a zillion tiny pieces and scattered in the four corners of the cosmos. The brightest light in the night sky was reduced to particles of dust: stardust. And so, as Thomas enthusiastically extolled the virtues of his piece of granite, gifted through the generosity of his big toe, Esmerelda was shown not only the demise of a star but also, through its transition, something far more significant and intrinsic to her.

"Stardust really is quite remarkable," she thought, as she traced visible particles of light, illuminated by its misty presence, through myriad star systems,

nebulae, galaxies and all manner of strange substances floating amidst the vast panorama of space. Yes, this dust of the stars was remarkable indeed and somewhat beguiling, for it really was not quite as it seemed; inside it, she knew, were Light Codes of Creation. And as she homed in on a single particle, she witnessed it bear fruit. Millennium after millennium it drew to itself others of its kind like a giant magnet. It resourced every ingredient until, in the fullness of time, a planet came into being, followed by a multitude of stars and yet more planets. Before too long, an entire universe had been birthed – all from a single particle of stardust whose origin was a giant explosion brought about through the death of another star. Esmerelda was struck to her very core. But she had barely scratched the surface of the wonderment arena. As consciousness unravelled its mysteries further, she journeyed deep into the heart of an emerging planet – one whose beauty held no bounds, whose gift for the creation of life forms was matched by no other and whose unparalleled generosity would, over aeons of time, allow Spirit to know its most polarised expression within the bounds of matter. More exposure followed with the passage of time until deep beneath the planet's surface, at its innermost core, Esmerelda felt her body burn; stardust was on fire – again! Now, when extreme heat is married with intense pressure, such as is experienced at the heart of a planet, magic, explosive in proportion, is possible. What began as stardust and had been fashioned over time into a rather large chunk of carbon was very soon ejected, through multiple layers of rock and sediment, towards the cool planetary surface, where it emerged, transformed beyond all recognition.

Its appearance marked the point, for Esmerelda, when the penny finally dropped. You see in this instance, stardust was not really stardust at all. No, it most certainly was not. It was **diamond**-dust. Furthermore, as you have more than likely surmised, the planet in Esmerelda's fascinating and most informative journey was not some random planet. No, it had far greater significance. It was, of course, our very own Mother Earth, haven to an enchanted forest, a small boy and a rather important shiny rock. No wonder Esmerelda beamed when her eyes refocused and alighted, with so much gratitude, upon her dear friend. It was he, through his meticulous scrutiny of the object he held in his hands, who had led her to this miraculous discovery and he who had opened a door in her that consciousness may expand upon his gift to reveal the full magnitude of its mystery. But far, far more than this, it was Thomas who had unwittingly brought her home to herself.

"How could this be?" you might well ask. A major drawback in relating a story after the event is that it tends to come out in linear form, with one occurrence following the previous one in sequential order. Throw into the mix multiple layers of consciousness being unravelled at one and the same time, such as Esmerelda's experience of the diamond, and you have the potential to miss one or more vital links or reduce the entire narrative to immeasurable chaos, where nothing is understood no matter where the awareness of the listener may reside. And so, as Thomas took apart the inner structure of the diamond, as Esmerelda's inner eye took her on a voyage to discover its origins in a far-distant universe and as the light in his eyes equalled the joy in her heart, she travelled inwards to find not one but two diamonds, each inimitable in their pristine reflection of the whole, each one nested within the other. And this is how it came about.

Imagine, for a moment, you have been presented with the most wonderful gift in the whole universe; one that holds within it the secret to life, all life, everywhere. It is the most beautiful gift ever created, a marvellous tapestry interwoven with many, many life forms and one whose song echoes upon celestial chords infused with light. Now look closer. Notice how this perfect, complete work of art is defined by numerous, far-too-numerous-to-quantify, fragments, each one essential to the perfection of the whole. From your panoramic, bigger-picture perspective, you see it is a jigsaw; a jigsaw to end all jigsaws. One that has so many pieces it would need a table of universal magnitude on which to assemble all the pieces, one that has so many layers it is impossible to determine which particle belongs to which and one that has so many intricate and subtle shades it is hard to fathom any structure or shape within it. Now take your perfect gift, your pristine work of art, and throw all the contents in the air. Cast every fragment to the four corners of the known universe, not only throughout space but also throughout all time. Muster as much force as you can that no two pieces may remain conjoined and not a single layer may touch another. Ensure that every separate part is so distant from its closest partner that it has absolutely no recollection of being a most perfect piece within the greatest work of art ever created. Engage your imagination still further. Be the master builder whose task it is to not only locate every single fragment but also assemble the jigsaw, layer by layer, until every particle is returned to wholeness. Watch your mind as it sets about this seemingly impossible task, witness it try in vain to marry each piece that a picture may stand revealed, observe the futility of its search, the elusive nature of every subtle layer and the senseless agony in promises unfulfilled and, finally, breathe a great sigh of relief as it eventually gives up.

Now let's paint a different picture, one in which the master builder employs means other than mind to fulfil the task in hand. One in which every single fragment, no matter how distant, how obscure or how hidden, is known, in which light and shadow appreciate the gift each to the other

brings and in which a moment of forgetfulness brings lifetimes of remembrance. Let us create a canvas on which every single particle, even in its most polarised expression, knows it is whole and complete in its separateness. On which the jigsaw may seem to have been shattered but in recognising it is nothing, is known to be whole. In short, let's create a vision in which all the pieces of the jigsaw miraculously fall into place at the mere snap of a finger and nothing, instantaneously, gives birth to everything.

And this is just how it was for the star of our story. As Thomas delved deeper into the structure of his rock and as Esmerelda absent-mindedly wondered at its strange appearance, every single piece of her personal jigsaw, even those parts she had never been aware existed, fell into place. In the space of a split second, a Great Silence opened up inside her and, as if by magic, the full magnitude of her expression, the totality of her every experience, in naked innocence, stood revealed. It began as a distant echo – a pulse disguised as thought inside a mind whose heart kissed the Real. In the silent pause between beats that cast no sound she heard a drum with no beginning play a song that had no end. Its message was insistent, impossible to deny, for the Call of the Eternal, once heard, could never be undone. In the stillness of its passage, she felt her parts come home. From the time of her beginning through lifetimes of regret, when she entered the collective and chose to forget, to her return in the land of belonging and her first vision of hope, from meeting her Beloved to her journey through the fall, and from the time of her arrival where she met her greatest friend – of all – she felt the heartbeat of her Presence draw all to its Cause until, in the blinking of an eye, every sorrow knew its joy, each light befriended dark, and every thought, despite its origin, knew its prayer; in the heart of a forest, in the company of one who enthused, the Call of the Eternal had returned the end to the beginning and all that was lost, was found.

*The strangest part of her story was that even though it bore some resemblance to the dramatic flash of light heralding the death of a star, even though recognition of her inner diamond reflected, almost too perfectly, the journey of a particle of stardust through multiple dimensions of space, fire and brimstone to emerge, over aeons of time, as a full-blown diamond and even though the timeliness of her arrival was, without doubt, equally predetermined and divinely orchestrated, Esmerelda knew there was something fundamentally different in her experience. She knew because she could **feel** it. Her 'falling' upon the Great Silence had created an opening so profound, so totally inclusive, that she knew there was nothing, absolutely nothing, that was not her. So it was no surprise when, deep inside the sedimentary layers of her unconscious, she found those parts that had for too long been denied cowering in the dirt. She had arranged this without even knowing what she was doing. Lifetimes of effort, even those spent in sleep, had led to this calling. Instantaneous assemblage of her jigsaw was thus neither a great show of light nor a banishment in hell but a quiet, understated embracing of that which was there all along. And so, as Thomas deconstructed the many facets of his diamond, Esmerelda gathered into her heart the disowned, unloved parts of her shadow self, and as he explained the inner structure in multiple lines of light, she, who was nothing, rejoiced quietly inside. For waiting in the substratum layers, hidden beneath a mantle of shame and barriers forged in pain, were the many, many facets of her shadow crying out to be heard. And as she listened to their plea, she found in diamond-clear light beyond the land of shadows the darkest diamond… inside a piece of granite… posing as her heart.*

All had come full circle. As Thomas reflected upon the translucent form of his radiant companion, as he absorbed her love and sank into the deepest experience of peace he had ever known and as Esmerelda travelled far into the heart of the diamond to gather unto herself all she had long ago forgotten, an avenue of communication opened up between them where words were a hindrance to one's intimate knowing of the other. If there had been witnesses to this silent exchange (as it turned out, there were many, but that's another story!) they would have seen a young boy and a young girl resting side by side, bathed in soft golden light. If they had fine-tuned their senses further, they would have experienced a gentle, somewhat-surreal presence flowing from one heart to the other, unimpeded by the limits of their physical forms. And if they had listened, really listened, they might have heard the most exquisite orchestral symphony waxing lyrical upon the air. Reluctant to break their synchronous interchange, they bathed in each other's radiance for what was to them an eternity until from a time outside of time, as naturally as night follows day, the moment passed. Esmerelda turned towards her dearest friend and smiled.

"You see, Thomas, there are two diamonds – one light, the other dark – each nested one within the other, perfectly expressed through your geometric structures as you so admirably explained. But their significance is far greater than we could possibly have imagined, for the true message of the diamond may only be revealed through the heart. Only in the heart may every facet, both light and dark, find its way home. Only in the heart may each part know it is loved and accepted exactly as it is. Only in the heart may the consciousness of every life form be expressed outwards as Spirit with crystalline, diamond-clear vision. The heart is a gateway to the miraculous, but it requires a mind that is clear to see it." "Yes, I get it," replied Thomas, excitedly. "This is why you and I complement each other so perfectly. My meticulous examination of these structures, which are always created in ordered sequence, opens a door into the subtle realm of feelings, where you may easily access the profound nature of the

reality being expressed through them; one is a way in for the other, and each allows Spirit to know itself on ever deeper levels." *"Indeed, Thomas. You might say, as individuals we express both diamonds respectively, but through our intimate relationship in consciousness, we are the wholeness that is both."*

Thomas paused for a while. Well, it was considerably longer than 'a while', but from out of the silence, he eventually added, "I have been thinking about the geometries defining the diamond. In particular, the quality of number that determines each is a perfect replica of divinity in its creative expression." *Esmerelda, since their intimate communion, had developed a new skillset in keeping track of his 'complicated' explanations; she not only listened with her heart but also invited her mind to experience it directly. So rather than trying to disentangle threads she could not possibly master, she felt his words through her mind.* "Beginning with the inner foundation, stellated icosahedron and dodecahedron, we know it is made up of 60 triangles and 12 pentagrams, making 72 facets in total. Now consider the outer, stellated dodecahedron. Can you see it also has 72 facets – 60 triangles and 12 pentagonal pyramids – isn't it remarkable, Esmerelda?" *"So the outer is a mirror of the inner and vice versa?" she responded, surprising even herself at being able to grasp the qualities of number so easily.* "Precisely," enthused Thomas. "Take it a step further and you will see the full expression of the diamond, inner and outer, is composed of 144 separate facets. Now, 144 is a very special number. It is the number of Light, and if you add all the digits together $(1 + 4 + 4)$ the sum total is nine, another very significant number." *The familiar quizzical expression returned to her face.* "Nine is the number of synthesis," he offered, by way of explanation. "Take it apart and you will see it can be arrived at not only as a multiple of three in the triple triad,[7] being 3×3 aspects of Spirit, Soul

---

[7] See glossary.

and body respectively (an aid to integration through the triangle's innate ability to facilitate change), but also through combinations of all singular digits $(1+8, 2+7, 3+6, 4+5$, not forgetting nine itself, which brings zero, a most important number, into the equation). And so nine is both the number of synthesis and the number of perfection, otherwise known as the number of God."

"Now I get it!" she replied triumphantly. "When I 'fell' into the diamond as you were holding it up before me, I entered a place where all the digits, together with their respective correspondences, could come together. I experienced them as unhealed, buried and banished aspects coming home, but as numbers they signified qualities embedded within a fully functional geometric structure – your diamond. Both reflected aspects of Truth *as viewed through the eyes of each of us: to me, they became a multi-faceted diamond within the space of my heart, where every separate part could see its true nature mirrored through its crystalline clarity."*

"Yes, Esmerelda, a perfect summation, as always," Thomas encouraged. "However, there is just one more thing I would like to add, by way of closure. The geometry of which we have been speaking, in its totality, is usually referred to as the 'Christ-Consciousness' grid." *In absorbing the implications of his statement, the last piece of the jigsaw finally fell into place. It reflected in no uncertain terms the clarity and depth of feeling she experienced in not only engaging with Thomas' piece of rock but also welcoming every facet, especially those concealed within the dark layers obscured from her pristine awareness, that consciousness wished to express through her. Christ-Consciousness, she realised, was not some longed-for collective dream; it was real. Furthermore, it only appeared following considerable time and effort being spent on stripping one's essential nature down to the bare roots to reveal that which was there all along. Christ-Consciousness, the multi-faceted double diamond in the heart, remains when nothing else is left.*

"So can we go and explore now?" Thomas' adventurous spirit had returned and, with his damaged toe all but a forgotten memory, he ran off into the forest without a care in the world. Suddenly, he stopped dead in his tracks. "Esmerelda, I know we have 144 facets to find, and I know they will, most assuredly, return many enchanted tales, but something inside tells me it is time to consult your map." She fumbled in her bag to retrieve what he was asking for, but by now they had accumulated many special treasures and she wasn't quite clear on what he was requesting. "It's the first gift you were presented with, before you ever met me. When you first arrived in the land of light, you met Mentor and they presented you with a map of consciousness. We need to consult it before we go any further."

Having found the map (see p.34), they looked for a suitable place in which to plan their next step. "I knew there was something," said Thomas, after unravelling the treasured article with meticulous care and attention. "Look – see how it defines, through its geometry, three distinct expressions of consciousness? Two interlocking spheres clearly mark the kingdoms of the Soul, being one with Spirit, and nature, being one with humanity, with the 'Eye of God' sitting centre stage as intermediary to both. It really is a most remarkable and informative composition." *"Yes, I agree, and I am most appreciative of the gift, but what is your point, Thomas?"* "Well, up to now, we have explored, through the *Way of Creation*, the kingdom of Spirit, and we have engaged intimately, through the Rainbow, the inner 'Eye of God', and now the Diamond, through its multiple facets, is presenting exploration of the human kingdom… " *"But, what about the kingdom of nature?" Esmerelda, most uncharacteristically, interrupted.* "Exactly!" *"Perhaps it is part of the Diamond, one or more of the facets, and the creatures that inhabit its realm will make their presence felt as we explore?"* "I am sure you are right on both counts, but I have learnt a little of their ways through playing in this enchanted wood, and they are not so very easily met, especially if they don't want to be." *She looked at him with increasing respect.* "However, I have also noticed that since your arrival they have been very interested in our exchanges. Were you aware we were being watched as we shared within the space of the Great Silence?" *Esmerelda nodded, "I was aware of the presence of other-worldly beings but, not being familiar with nature spirits, I hadn't attributed the change in energy to them."* "I can see some further education is in order. Why don't we begin our adventure and see what is revealed through the many facets of the diamond. I am sure the shy ones, if they so wish, will make their presence felt in ways known only to them. In the meantime, as we walk, I shall share what little I know of their customs that we may better recognise the signs when they appear. I am in no doubt that they will."

So they walked and, as the creatures of the forest watched, Thomas shared his deep love for the natural world in which he lived. Esmerelda hung on his every word and, in the diamond of her heart, felt the little folk gather round. They were unseen and unheard, but she had no doubt they were there or that they were very, very interested in what was afoot. After all, it was they who had placed a rather unobtrusive lump of rock in the path of an unsuspecting boy running barefoot through **their** wood.

The Way of Nature

"Are you familiar with cats?" They had been walking side by side and in silence since consulting her map of consciousness, Thomas had been thinking about the magical creatures that inhabited the forest, especially how he may share his relationship to them with Esmerelda. The question arose, quite spontaneously, as if it had been placed at the forefront of his mind by something or someone. He turned towards her and laughed as she replied, *"I know of them but am not familiar with their ways. I am assuming you are referring to the domestic variety not the let's-have-a-human-for-breakfast kind?"* "Hahaha! Yes, the former of course, although even big cats have many similar qualities and mannerisms to the little bundle of fur that sits upon its pet human's knee." *She loved this emerging, never-before-seen side to Thomas and smiled warmly towards him as he continued.*

"A long time ago, many thousands of years in the past, cats held quite a position of prominence in human society. As a matter of fact, in ancient Egyptian times, they were once revered and worshipped as gods. And, although humankind woke up and ultimately redressed this 'erroneous state of affairs' by setting themselves up as supreme rulers over all 'lesser' kingdoms, cats have never forgotten their regal heritage. Nor have they ever failed to remember their inherent supremacy over all creatures that inhabit this earth, whether they walk upon two legs or four. You might say their knowledge of being the 'king of beasts', irrelevant of physical appearance or size, is deeply engrained in their DNA and, therefore, they are worthy of respect, if not reverence. So if you were intent on striking up a friendship with a passing feline, it would be wise to approach them with the deference you would use when in the presence of someone deemed to be 'important' in the world of humans – royalty, for instance. Now, assuming these unspoken protocols are adhered to, there is no reason why feline and human cannot have a lasting, fulfilling and mutually rewarding relationship spanning many, many years."
Esmerelda was very attentive, but nevertheless wasn't quite sure where this was leading or even whether it was relevant to her 'nature education'. She expressed her thoughts to Thomas, very kindly, of course.

"I was just coming to that!" he said, adopting an air of feigned hurt. "You see, Esmerelda, nature spirits are, in many ways, similar to cats. Integral to their 'DNA' (they are made up of elemental essence so don't really have DNA, but it's a good analogy) is an intelligence that has as its origin the very beginnings of life, all life. You might say that within their encoded matrix are divine builders responsible for the manifestation of all life forms. Whether planet, star, tree, insect or bird, whether animal, cetacean or reptile, every life form, including you and I and, of course, our regal feline, has as its point of creation these elusive creatures that inhabit the unseen in-between. In a nutshell, the subtle realms of nature impregnate, sustain and ultimately reclaim all that is theirs to create according to the Law." He watched, in gratitude, as understanding impregnated the heart of his dear friend. Her whole persona became enlivened with renewed vitality as she spoke.

"I know these beings," she responded, somewhat taken aback. "When I was in the land of light, where light and dark do not exist as separate entities, where self and other have yet to be conceived and where first I encountered the Beloved, they were there. They appeared as many colours – a multitude in shining light but not such as you would encounter even in the most vibrant of places in this world. The sweetest of sounds, though they heard it not, announced their arrival before ever they were seen, and intelligence beyond the bounds of time expressed their wisdom in an age. I know them as the Shining Ones, Deva Builders, whose origin is the Universal mind of God, expressed as innate intelligence. Their purpose is to set the course for building in matter, to wield the web of elemental essence and to sound the call to lesser beings along the nature trail that the task of form-building may be fulfilled, all in accord with the Sacred Law. Yes, Thomas, I know these beings of which you speak but I have a sense

that those I have met on the inner planes are in a different league."

"As always, you have hit the nail on the head," he replied enthusiastically. "For, just as there are many levels and vibrations in consciousness for the human being, so it is with Devas. They follow their own evolutionary journey independent of mankind, in parallel you might say, yet the two are inextricably linked: one assists or impedes through intention, the other through unfaltering obeisance to the Law. The beings that you know so intimately are of the highest order, are of a more refined vibration than all but the most enlightened in the consciousness of man and are the directors of the form-building show, so to speak. The magical creatures who have been gracing us with their presence, all be it unseen, are those who are more directly involved in the physical moulding of form and so have closer contact with the grosser elements of the human race. Their remit is to obey the Law as it is decreed – nothing more, nothing less. It is why they are so very wary and require appropriate respect (and considerable patience) before they will make themselves known. In short, mankind, through his blatant abuse and disregard for the ways of nature, has forfeited their trust so must consume a considerable amount of humble pie before any kind of relationship may be forged. Does this make sense, Esmerelda?"

"Yes, perfect sense, but I will expand on it a little more. You see, when the human being eats 'humble pie', as you quite rightly suggest, he relinquishes all sense of superiority, especially the idea that he knows what is best. After many repeated doses, his consciousness is elevated to a plane where the Deva Builders abide. Here, a creative bridge may be forged between both evolutionary paths where that which is separate becomes united in purpose, with the resultant outcome a conscious co-creative partnership whose intention is the upliftment of

all life forms. Whether human, elemental, nature spirit, animal, insect or planet is irrelevant, they are all embraced equally under an umbrella of co-creative peace and harmony." A quizzical, deeply furrowed expression graced Thomas' brow. "But I don't understand how knowing this helps, in a practical sense, when I am running barefoot through a forest and mischievous little nature spirits place a lump of rock in my path. How does it help me to find out why they did it if I cannot communicate with them?" *"Ahhh, I see what you mean," she responded with compassion. "Let me put it another way. This time I shall draw on the innate qualities of your feline friends, with which I sense you are intimately familiar, especially those concerning watchfulness and playfulness. Have you noticed how many hours a day a cat spends sitting quietly, almost Buddha-like, observing the world that it deems to be its territory or how it instantly awakens to belie the appearance of one who lies in deep slumber. Have you ever judged it to be cruel when toying with its prey even though its appetite is satiated, or perhaps you have laughed joyfully at its antics following an invitation to play?"* There was no need to answer. His open heart was tangible to the point of presence and every word she uttered struck chords of knowing upon his heartstrings. The deep love, respect and admiration he held for his feline companions required no acknowledgment; Thomas loved cats and that's all there was to it.

"Now can you see, Thomas? All that you admire so much in the domestic cat, all the love you have shared and all the learnings you have acquired through watching their ways have instilled in you a deep respect for those whose terms of existence are other than your own. Without even knowing it, you have forged a bridge to the kingdom of nature simply through your unconditional love for the creatures that share your life. Let's probe a bit further. Have you ever known a cat to engage in

play, or even to sit quietly in the presence of another, if there wasn't at first a large degree of trust?" Thomas shook his head. *"So by the same token, wouldn't you agree that the creatures of the forest, in their own way, may be extending an invitation to engage because the element of trust has already been established, albeit on a level that is not, at first, obvious? Perhaps the only way they could gain your attention was to place a shiny rock in the way of your feet as you ran without regard through their wood. Or perhaps they even ignited your love of cats, in the form of thought, that this whole dialogue may be brought to the surface."* She paused to allow her explanations to sink in and to give Thomas a chance to close his mouth, as his chin was rapidly descending towards his knees! "Are you trying to tell me it was the Deva Builders, in cooperation with an aspect of myself with which I have yet to become familiar, who orchestrated this whole string of events?" he questioned, not without some degree of indignation. Thomas, after all, was quite down to earth, in a matter-of-fact way, and sometimes found it hard to accept the subtleties in truth with which Esmerelda was already familiar. *Nevertheless, their friendship was such that she allowed an encouraging chuckle to escape her lips amidst an accepting inner smile.* "Yes, my dear friend," she acknowledged, "I suppose I am. However, as you may well guess, it's not quite as straightforward as that." *There followed an extended period of silence in which these two treasured companions, in the company of the watchers in the wood, gathered into themselves to assimilate all that had been revealed thus far. The merging of their combined presence became consciousness in group expression and, using the voice of Esmerelda, they proffered the following by way of explanation.*

"First of all, may we begin by stating that the intelligent forces of nature, of which mankind is but a part, yet is independent in evolutionary purpose, are entirely the responsibility of the custodians of that realm. The Devic kingdom adheres to its own laws and has its own hierarchical structure, and its ways are known only to Devas; rarely are their secrets divulged to 'outsiders', particularly to the less-evolved members of the human family. Therefore, any understanding revealed through these words is at their bequest, is offered for the sole purpose of assisting mankind to know the essential role it plays in the well-being of the planet and inhabitants and is by no means complete in its reasoning. The key thing to grasp, as has already been intimated, is that the kingdom of nature runs parallel to that of the human race but, as the life within the form, is also fundamental to the evolution of both. What does this mean?"

"We shall cite Thomas, as he is such a shining example. Even though he was unaware, the unconditional positive regard he felt towards those in his care and, we might add, towards the creatures of the forest established a position of trust, and those who have, for far too long, been wary of the human being may now gain sufficient confidence in making their presence felt. As they each inhabit different universes, so to speak, and each has their own distinct method of communication, they appear somewhat clumsy in the way they go about it. The Devas cannot speak to him directly, as it is not their way, and Thomas, who may as well be blind to their presence, fails to notice their more subtle attempts in extending the hand of friendship. In short, it takes a, not insignificant, piece of rock for him to finally wake up to the fact that they are desirous of his attention. Now let's bring Esmerelda into the picture. She, as we are well aware, is very familiar with the subtle realms lying betwixt, behind and within the outer expression of all physical forms. Although she did not offer her opinion at the time, she knew of the bridge being established between all the players in this particular game of life. In being conscious, in holding all in equal value and in having no agenda or projected outcome, she had,

on the inner planes, created the cause for all to come together as one, in peace. If we delve into this a little more, if we examine the way each of these parallel universes work alongside each other and if we look at how their respective players interact, it becomes increasingly obvious there is a far bigger picture unfolding. The redress of a small boy's injured toe, brought about through a nature spirit's apparent inability to communicate in an appropriate manner towards him, takes on a whole new meaning. Yes, indeed, there is far more afoot (pardon the pun!) than at first meets the eye!"

"Without giving too much away, the Devic kingdom is passive, receptive and feminine in nature and awaits instruction from its masculine counterpart on which it will act, under the direction of the Universal mind, according to Cosmic Law; its agent is obeisance.ᵛ Their innate essence is intelligence, which, once stimulated, creates activity with the remit to build in matter. Humanity, on the other hand, fulfils the opposite in Divine Purpose. It expresses the masculine principle – positive and aggressive – with an innate essence of love using its agent, thought. Why the interaction between Thomas and his nature friends was able to take place is becoming a bit clearer: each, in their respective realms, expressed their innate essence – Thomas through his love of nature, and spirits through their intelligent activity in gifting him the diamond as a response to that love. Now we just have to figure out how. If there are two independent, albeit parallel, universes, how do they come together? How or by what is the bridge created?"

"This, as you may well surmise, is a very deep and profound topic, but the most succinct and uncomplicated answer, is elemental essence.ᵛⁱ You might say that elemental essence is the fabric of the void, that which infiltrates every level of reality from the most subtle to the densest forms of matter regardless of which universe is under scrutiny (spiritual, Monadic essence is also integral to all aspects of life but we are dealing specifically with the kingdom of nature here). Elemental essence, therefore, is the bridge. But remember, as the fabric of the Devic kingdom, its nature is passive: in and of itself it can do nothing until it is impregnated with its polar opposite – in this case, human interaction through the power of thought. Every thought, whether conscious or otherwise, issued from the mind of man (as well as the group-mind of the Soul and Universal mind of Spirit) is considered to be a command and is acted upon by Devas to create a thought-form elemental whose sole purpose is to build in matter that which was intended. Once set in motion, it must work out its remit and, for the most part, cannot be retracted. As you can see, the web of life, of which we are all a part, has many weavers." Esmerelda could feel Thomas fidgeting excitedly by her side, so she brought her transmission to a close.

"I think I get it!" he exclaimed, without waiting for her to gather breath. "Even though I was not consciously co-creating, in consistently sharing my love for all creatures in the kingdom I was not only expressing the highest aspect of my innate nature as a human – love – but also building a bridge to the very beings I revered beyond all else. I was creating thought-form elementals and unconsciously inviting them to come and play with me. **Wow**! Who would have thought that something so magnificent could come out of sharing that which I love?" Pausing for a mere moment, he, almost absent-mindedly, added, "I guess the next step for me is to keep refining and building upon my relationship with these mischief-makers that I may become a conscious co-creator alongside the real directors of the show!" Esmerelda laughed, visibly moved by his outward show of wonderment, and secretly speculated whether he might even be a nature spirit. Then she let it go – dismissing it as 'just a passing thought'.

Nature's symbol

"There is one more thing," Thomas interjected, whilst reaching for his drawing stick. "It has just dawned on me how well the symbol reflects all we have been discussing. It is a double spiral arranged as a mirror image of one spiral to the other, independent yet inextricably linked, alike but not. It shows the evolutionary journey of two kingdoms running parallel to each other. Now look what happens when we interlink them. As the two merge into one, a highly symbolic 'yoni' is revealed, indicative of the creative womb of the universe where man may be a co-creative builder in matter in harmony with nature. In these three symbols, we have both a single Fibonacci spiral (fundamental to the creative, cyclic flow of Spirit as it integrates with matter) and an illustration of how sacred geometry **is** divinity in action, revealing the hidden mysteries of the universe unfolding through and within it in alignment with its principles."

"Of course," Esmerelda reflected inwardly. *"We have only been exploring one aspect of this all-encompassing world, that of the relationship between human and Deva, particularly how they may work together in a spirit of co-creation to build a world where peace and harmony are foundations for every life form. In addition, its many subtle layers include the entire fabric of the space-time continuum, seasons, cycles and elemental forces, as well as the lesser kingdoms – animal, vegetable and mineral. There are many other beings who inhabit this realm who are far more easily recognisable, if only through the works of art they produce: radiant beings who paint the flowers, those who work with plants and shrubs, some who cause rain to fall from a cloudless sky or tend to creatures of the earth and many more who support their feathered friends in flight. Magnificent beings, with hearts of stone, guard treasures in sacred hills. Others expose, in subtle shades of green, those whose feet dig deep into the ground that they may kiss the sky by day and dance amidst the stars at night. Then there are those whose presence would grace the most resplendent of forms and bring the hosts of heaven to its knees. Indeed, the kingdom of nature is a most daring place, filled with many extraordinary sights, and pitfalls too for those who would abuse her trust, but it is the inner planes a humble heart must tread that its greatest gifts may be bestowed. Our natural world is, above all else, the Way of Beauty... a call to the tune of the wild... a treat to dance in its mystery... And one that the pure in heart must know..."* spoke Esmerelda, expressed as infinite light of the Soul.

Thomas, in the meantime, was playing with his diamond. But, as you may imagine, his play was not without direction or considered intention. With intense focus, he scrutinised every facet, turning it upside down and rotating it through every angle until it became clear in his mind how they may make the most of this lump of

  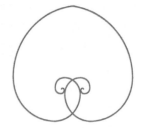

Fibonacci Spiral: Nature's cyclic flow

Double Spiral: Two kingdoms in parallel

Double Spiral: Two kingdoms as co-creative force

granite gifted by the kingdom of nature. He was mesmerised by the purity of its inner structure and amazed at how it sparkled yet was never tainted by external forces (such as a small boy turning it over and over in his grubby hands), but far more than this, he marvelled at the many rainbows it cast when it was struck by light. He knew he was witnessing its many facets and had no doubt in his mind the diamond was extending an invitation to explore further. His attention turned towards his friend as he watched her emerge from her silent moment. With lightness of heart, and not a little impatience, he sprung to his feet. "Come, come, Esmerelda. It is time for another adventure," he enthused. His excitement was infectious and brooked no refusal, so she rose to her feet (with a little more dignity than Thomas) and took hold of his hand, and together they skipped through the forest led by a lump of granite that never ceased to sparkle; the many facets of the diamond, each one a doorway revealing a *vision of reality*, were keen to be noticed.

Before moving forward...

The remainder of this chapter is devoted to the 144 facets of the diamond (*Key of Light* contemplation cards). Each title as well as featuring a unique *vision of reality,* begins with a contemplation followed by suggested guidance and concludes with: Soul alignment *quality,* Absolute *aspect,* integral *geometry* and the Rainbow *sphere* to which it belongs. This marks the beginning of your Rainbow journey and is the point where the 'theory' may be put into practice, where you engage intimately with the wisdom revealed with each page turn and where, most importantly, you may apply it to your daily challenges. Rather than reading it page by page, approach it as you would an adventure. Flick through the pages, notice where they come to rest, take note of any images that jump out at you (whether they appeal or not) or close your eyes and walk your fingers along the outer edge of the book until they want to stop. There are many possibilities at your disposal, limited only by the scope of your imagination. Use your chosen *vision/card/facet* (these are interchangeable) as a starting point, for, as you will soon come to see, many pathways are revealed upon a single selection.

As well as belonging to a Rainbow sphere, some visions are part of a larger collective, a Diamond group, and these are noted in the footnotes; these visions have identical *contemplations*. Consider any groups in your personal life; without doubt, each will have its own code or ideal that each member is assumed to follow. Diamond groups are no different: contemplations follow the group ideal whilst *guidance* shows the individual qualities within the wider expression. Much benefit will be gained from exploring the individual facets making up a Diamond group over a period of time whilst holding in your awareness the collective contemplation. Think of Rainbow spheres (*Key of Light* suits) as you would the family into which you were born – part of who you are, your familial lineage. Diamond collections allow families from different lineages to come together in the furtherance of a shared ideal. Last, be creative. Where it seems commentaries are alike, turn to the vision or vice versa; the deeper you go and the more intuitive your approach, the further the multi-faceted diamond **in you** will be able to reach.

Appendix 2 tabulates a few *co-creative families* and Rainbow spheres in which many facets of the diamond come together to reveal their purpose. Use them as a reference guide or, if you are feeling adventurous, begin at the end and use them to explore the hidden mystery of the universe as it flows through and within you.

N.B. The border around each vision is coloured according to the Rainbow sphere to which it belongs, e.g., Truth: blue, Will: red, etc.

Contemplation

*"In the end, it all comes down to choice," she surmised. "But far more than this, it is the point of awareness at which consciousness abides when the decision is being made that is of paramount importance." Esmerelda, following guidance from the Word, allowed her mind to toy with the meaning of 'Absorption'. "Consciousness must be acutely aware of the origin of the cause that is being assimilated at any given moment in time. It must know whether the inflowing energy is the particle recreating itself or whether it is indeed the original Cause[8] that is being assimilated." She allowed her mind to digest these new understandings. Soon, in visionary form, there was a response from Mentor. Streams of cube-like blocks were stuffed into her crown as if she were the designated receptacle for cosmic (and any other) garbage. Recognition of the state of affairs, along with its source, was sufficient to reverse the flow; there was no requirement for analysis or rejection; it just needed to be seen for what it was to naturally return to its source. Removal of the false allowed the ever-present river of light to be revealed. "Absorption is the way of return," said the Word. "It is the condition in which outpouring, involutionary forces may be 'absorbed' in one who is on the evolutionary path of return; the resultant expression – you – is becoming." Esmerelda smiled. "So what I allow in, what I energise, is the cause of what I give out: garbage in, garbage out; light in, light out?" "Precisely!" the inner voice replied. "All that you are now – the journeys, cellular memories, products of the past – is becoming absorbed into liquid light. Each inner letting go and surrender to the Zero allows the force of becoming to effortlessly do its work. All you have to do is get out of the way and allow it!" Now she understood. "The choice is always there – to assimilate within myself and co-create myself or to surrender to the Zero and allow Absorption to work its magic." "Yes, the only way to get out of the repetitive cycle of self-creation is to surrender and return to the Zero. However, first you have to know yourself as an individual particle within expression; you have to know that which you are **not** before you may become that which you **are**." It all seemed so very, very simple. Esmerelda softened inside as she sank deeper and deeper into the wonderment of Absorption. With every inner letting go, her intimate relation to the outpouring force was revealed. Each breath became an expression of its Light, each beat of her heart an expression of its Love and in abject humility, she knew, beyond all doubt and as a mere 'particle within substance', the vital role she played in the unfoldment of its Divine Purpose. Furthermore, with increasing clarity... she saw the Light Codes of Creation were embedded within Absorption... keys to unlocking the origin of thought.*

Guidance

"Garbage in, garbage out": what you allow in is what you give out. How you think is how you are. As well as pondering the deeper meanings exposed within the script, consider your 'diet'. Perhaps it is time for a change.

---

[8] See *Conversion*.

Absorption

Quality: Assimilation
Absolute Aspect: Love
Geometry: None
Rainbow Sphere: Rainbow

Contemplation

They met as they had always met, inside the Hall of Learning, where all that is possible to know is known. However, on this occasion, as Consciousness sensed the presence of the Shining One long before it put in an appearance, a ripple of excitement, barely detectable to others in the vicinity, echoed throughout its substance. "Greetings, my friend," sounded the luminous being without employing words. "We have a task before us concerning the future well-being of a world for which we are equally responsible and for which you must be prepared. We must journey together into four realms, each a kingdom in its own right, with which I am far more familiar than you, to engage with those whose remit is to work in the lesser, denser fields of service. We must engage intimately with those whose presence is not usually made visible to any outsider and who would, in normal circumstances, be hostile to any infringement of their domain. However, it is recognised that your participation in this is paramount, so exceptions have been made and they wish you to know that, in furtherance of mutual cooperation, you are welcome in their respective worlds." Consciousness, of course, was a willing participant and engaged gracefully with each as they made their presence felt. Spirits of air approached in varying degrees of expansion and subtlety. At once they were the vast reaches of the sky and then, through a multitude of forms, they breathed; in rock, plant and mineral they were found, cleansing all in their wake. In the sacred breath, they carried subtle currents from the Universal mind to the mind of humanity, encouraging it to hear its plea. But few listened, choosing instead to pollute the atmosphere with their unconscious, destructive thought patterns. "They are unaware of the harm they cause and the toxic waste upon the physical plane that is created as a result," admonished the Shining One. "And this is why I am here," Consciousness replied. "I am mediator between your domain and theirs. Mine is the task of making them aware and in me lies responsibility to stimulate change in them."

Guidance

Four facets of the diamond lead into the magical world of nature spirits: *Air* (sylphs), *Earth* (gnomes), *Fire* (salamanders) and *Water* (undines). Each is responsible for the maintenance, purification and ultimate balance of their respective domains. A fifth vision, *Brilliance*, is the 'Shining One', a Deva, or angelic being, who has under its direction these 'lesser' creative builders. *Air* connects to the intellectual mind and, through the breath, to the heart. It highlights the relationship between thought and feeling and offers a healthy way to 'feel without the story'. Rise above the 'clouds that veil the sun' and see things as they **are**, not how you **perceive** them. More importantly, you are invited to embrace the spirits of the air in recognition of and appreciation for their dedication in purifying the effluent of **your** unconscious thought patterns...

Air

Quality: Thought
Absolute Aspect: Intelligence
Geometry: Metatron's cube, torus
Rainbow Sphere: Beauty

Contemplation

Caw Caw, Caw Caw, Caw Caw… The call (which she perceived to be a racket) was insistent. So much so, it brought her stomp through the woods to an abrupt end. Equally annoying and far more detrimental to her current state of mind, as well as her somewhat misguided sense of well-being, was the effect it had upon the flow of her entangled web of melodramatic thoughts. Caw Caw, Caw Caw, Caw Caw… it persisted, adding for good measure a crescendo with each utterance. Caw Caw, Caw Caw, Caw Caw… "Alright, alright," she acknowledged, whilst turning in the direction of its source. "You have my undivided attention, now what do you want?" She had arrived at the foot of a somewhat uninspiring tree, characterised by a preponderance of ivy hugging its trunk from base to sky, and searched amongst its foliage for the cause of her disturbance. Almost at the top, amongst its uppermost branches, perched a crow. Now silent, gaze fixed meaningfully upon the expectant child below, it waited patiently for her to acknowledge its presence. As their eyes met, language became detrimental to dialogue, and in the enveloping stillness, presences of species hitherto apart found knowing of each other. Crow, shapeshifter and keeper of Sacred Law, led the way. Through oceans deep and rivers swift and true, in thunderous clouds to the softest drops of dew, past mountains high capped with ice and silken flowers painted white, into seams of crystal deep beneath the crust, they travelled. Each encounter was an opening to the Way, every place an adherence to the Law and, without exception, each contact an exposure of the truth. Earth was sick, the Mother was dying and responsibility lay with the species to which she belonged. The child, wise beyond her years, was sick to her stomach… She understood why Messenger had been insistent… knew the purpose of their meet… and now she must act…

Guidance

Ten visions[9] pave the way to restoration of balance following centuries of neglect inflicted upon our planet by the human race. Individually, as characters in the script, they tell a tale of creation as it is reflected through your inner diamond. *Alchemist,* shapeshifter and mistress of magic, is Crow appearing as the divine feminine, keeper of Sacred Law and Queen of Creation, who patrols the primordial waters of the unconscious and calls to the surface all that is denied by those who flaunt her existence. Look closely at *Messenger* alongside *Alchemist* and you will see an 'elemental' presence standing behind and above the leading 'figure' dominating the foreground. Left to its own devices, Shadow is always unseen director of the show; Sacred Law commands it, nature obeys it and now it is time for humanity to follow suit. So should the Queen of the Night knock at your door… take heed… It is only by her grace that you will see the light of day…

---

[9] *Alchemist, Fortitude, Integrity, Invitation, Messenger, New Earth, Raindance, Reception, Sanctuary, Stewardship.*

Alchemist

Quality: Elemental Magic
Absolute Aspect: Intelligence
Geometry: Torus
Rainbow Sphere: Order

Contemplation

Long, long ago, before a fledgling planet prepared to flex her wings, there came to earth those who would prove to be the masters of the race. Their purpose, multiple in expression, was to instil amongst infant humanity wisdom in an age. And for aeons, it was so. Miraculous feats, performed through understanding the laws of the physical universe, were effortless: remarkable structures appeared; advanced technology enabled travel through time and space; music and art, exquisite in their expression of the divine, were celebrated in a spirit of unity. Man and gods in co-creative partnership heralded an era of peace, a golden age, in which the great continent flourished. But it was not to last. There were those who claimed the hidden powers, shared so generously without condition, as their own; those who used the secret knowledge to manipulate and control and would stop at nothing to be the new rulers of the race. And so began the Great War. Silent as the grave, the Masters of Wisdom withdrew their presence from the land, sending in their stead a mighty flood to take all, save a few, to certain death beneath the waves. Before long, Atlantis was no more, or so says the legend. In deep meditation, the meditator knew these tales to be far more than myth. Billions of years after the event, the same dynamics were still being played out inside him and in the world at large – this he knew. Atlantis still lived. Manipulation, control and desire for power were obvious, but more subtle, and carrying far greater significance, were the psychic powers running rife amidst an unsuspecting populace. The Siddhis were strong... in his meditation he could feel them... and their allure was so, so tempting...

Guidance

The Atlantean root race, as documented in well-researched material,[vii] is part of a greater cycle (mantvantara) spanning many millions of years. However, it is the golden age – its fall and how the resultant karma plays out on 21st-century earth – that we are concerned with here. Five visions[10] serve as a bridge in time where these forces may be contemplated as an inner process. *Alien Nation* is a nod to the beings introduced at the outset – the 'masters of the race' – who, without doubt, included extra-terrestrial intelligences that originated beyond our solar system. However, there is far more to the scope of its influence than connection to extra-terrestrials; it leads straight to the heart of 21st-century life, where isolation, loneliness and polarised communities are signature forces in a broken society. In *Alien Nation*, there is no middle road – despair on the one hand, supreme intelligence on the other – but there is a way forward. Isolation is potentially the most profound state of human consciousness. Embrace it. Welcome it. **Choose it**. Suddenly, you are no longer there... and the cosmos in its entirety is laid bare beneath your feet...

---

[10] *Alien Nation, Burning Ground, Follow the Crowd?, Stillness, Welcome.*

Alien Nation

Quality: Isolation
Absolute Aspect: Will
Geometry: None
Rainbow Sphere: Will

Contemplation

Deep in the bowels of the earth, the beast roamed free... Unchallenged for millennia... lord of its domain... it was indestructible... or so it believed. Nothing escaped its watchful eye... a master in scrutiny, all senses fine-tuned to subtle changes in its environment... every movement, breath, sound, smell... it knew... But above all, it knew with unnerving accuracy when fear engulfed the heart of another... Darkness was its way, suspicion its trusted friend... 'survival, above all else' it's timeless legend... Now it sensed change... For the first time, the beast felt fear as others did... its kingdom was under threat... it could... **smell** *it... Escape was its instinctive response... it had to run...* **now**! *And then,* **she** *came... she with a light so bright, a love so pure and courage enough to melt the hearts of 1000 fearless warriors. Step by unfaltering step, she walked the descending spiral into* **his** *domain... Nothing distracted from her purpose... no amount of cunning or wily ways, which had served him so well in the past, sent her screaming in terror to the land from whence she came... As innocent as the day she was born, she continued her journey... never losing her focus for even a second... until, with every hiding place exhausted, she found him. The beast cowered in shame... motionless. She did nothing, said nothing... but he knew her... he* **smelt** *her... and then he felt her... he felt her love... her* **gratitude**... *for him?*

Guidance

Both beast and innocent child are within us. As archetypal characters in an endless war of supremacy, they reside deep inside the unconscious mind, generating instinctual behavioural responses that wreak havoc in our relationships and turn our lives upside down when we least expect it. As part of the limbic system in the mid-brain, the amygdala is responsible for many of these responses, including reflexive emotions such as fear and anxiety. It is the storehouse of the past in which our base animal instincts, our core fears and our emotional learning result in a highly evolved state of awareness – **instinctual** knowing. The calling of this vision, in company with its mirror image, *Beauty and the Beast,* is to befriend these masters of intrigue, bring their subtle manipulations into the cool light of day and recognise the origin of your behavioural responses. *Amygdala* takes you deep into the physical body. Notice how it responds to external stimuli. Observe how your pulse quickens, your mouth goes dry and your muscles tense in preparation for flight, **before** you even know you are afraid. Allow the beast to be your guide, for it has many gifts to share, but before you step into 'his' domain... take the child into your heart...

Amygdala

Quality: Instinctual Knowing
Absolute Aspect: Will
Geometry: None
Rainbow Sphere: Beauty

Contemplation

*It existed. This it knew, but what else? It had no form, no gender... no... **identity**? If it could think, it may be purpose, or if it could feel, it might be fear... but no, all that returned from the inky blackness was nothing... absolutely nothing. Yet, exist it did. Perhaps it **was** the dark space. Or maybe it was something else. Did it really matter? It existed. All else was enigma. As a brain without a body, inside a mind bereft of cause, echoes of former life... returned. Subtle impressions arose from times long since gone and left indelible footprints upon the fabric of the void... Fleeting visions... faces, figures, events... returned the thinker to its mind... Despair in isolation... fear of death... and love... brought the heart to its knees. In a kaleidoscope of coloured experiences, each fractured particle became a story in the making – the actor playing centre stage clear to see. Now it remembered. It **had** identity... and gender... with a form to suit the part. He remembered the fullness of life well lived, how rich was his reward for excelling at the game, how much he cherished those he held close to his heart and the distances he would travel to ensure his will was obeyed. Then, with a heart awash with shame, he became the agent of his demise... the apocalypse. With the pinnacle of his achievements laid bare before his eyes, he witnessed his downfall. Shattered forever was the self that was small, as eternal fire, through the Will of One, reduced all that he was to ash. Then, in his heart, he knew that nothing was the only reward for **being** life well lived. It existed. Existence is enough... Existence is...*

Guidance

To arrive at a place of existential awareness is to step outside the bounds of time and space. However, as the script suggests, much has to be relinquished in order to recognise that wholeness in being nothing is not only a letting go of all that is false but also an open door to the changeless face of all reality. Two visions serve as facilitators to ease the transition – *Apocalypse Fire* and *Apocalypse Water* – each a key element in unravelling the matrix of the structured self – your identity. Psychological triggers (fire) coupled with emotional charges (water) ensure the story of the separate self is reinforced over and over again; one ignites the other. Only when they can be recognised and seen for what they are may the process of disentanglement start; this begins the apocalypse. *Apocalypse Fire* calls your attention to your thought processes. Know what triggers an emotional charge, know your patterns and resultant behavioural responses and then take it all into your heart and embrace every last piece of who you are. Through its agent, fire, the Will of the Divine will work out. It will leave you empty of all that obscured the reality of who you really are. But remember, with nothing to be taken away and nothing to add... existence is free to experience itself... All else is distraction...

Apocalypse Fire

Quality: Identity – Psychological Triggers
Absolute Aspect: Will
Geometry: Star tetrahedron
Rainbow Sphere: Will

Contemplation

*It existed. This it knew, but what else? It had no form, no gender... no... **identity**? If it could think, it may be purpose, or if it could feel, it might be fear... but no, all that returned from the inky blackness was nothing... absolutely nothing. Yet, exist it did. Perhaps it **was** the dark space. Or maybe it was something else. Did it really matter? It existed. All else was enigma. As a brain without a body, inside a mind bereft of cause, echoes of former life... returned. Subtle impressions arose from times long since gone and left indelible footprints upon the fabric of the void... Fleeting visions... faces, figures, events... returned the thinker to its mind... Despair in isolation... fear of death... and love... brought the heart to its knees. In a kaleidoscope of coloured experiences, each fractured particle became a story in the making – the actor playing centre stage clear to see. Now it remembered. It **had** identity... and gender... with a form to suit the part. He remembered the fullness of life well lived, how rich was his reward for excelling at the game, how much he cherished those he held close to his heart and the distances he would travel to ensure his will was obeyed. Then, with a heart awash with shame, he became the agent of his demise... the apocalypse. With the pinnacle of his achievements laid bare before his eyes, he witnessed his downfall. Shattered forever was the self that was small, as eternal fire, through the Will of One, reduced all that he was to ash. Then, in his heart, he knew that nothing was the only reward for **being** life well lived. It existed. Existence is enough... Existence is...*

Guidance

To arrive at a place of existential awareness is to step outside the bounds of time and space. However, as the script suggests, much must be relinquished in order to recognise that wholeness in being nothing is not only a letting go of all that is false but also an open door to the changeless face of all reality. Two visions serve as facilitators to ease the transition – *Apocalypse Fire* and *Apocalypse Water* – each a key element in unravelling the matrix of the structured self – your identity. Psychological triggers (fire) coupled with emotional charges (water) ensure the story of the separate self is reinforced over and over again; one ignites the other. Only when they can be recognised and seen for what they are may the process of disentanglement start; this begins the apocalypse. *Apocalypse Water* calls your attention to emotional charges. Recognise when your mind quickens to create stories around feelings. Know your triggers, patterns and resultant behavioural responses, and then take all into your open and vulnerable heart. Through its agent, water, the Will of the Divine will work out and, though many tears may be shed along the way, you will stand empty of all that obscured the reality of who you really are. You will know that without all these distractions, with nothing to be taken away and nothing to add... existence is free to experience itself... **as it is**...

Apocalypse Water

Quality: Identity – Emotional Charges
Absolute Aspect: Will
Geometry: Star tetrahedron
Rainbow Sphere: Truth

Contemplation

*Two trees – one Dark, the other Light... Guardians of the Way... Keepers of the Real – set the scene for the expression of All. Between the two flow the above and the below... eternally One in existence yet apart in their seeming. Beyond the beginning, in a place not of this world, the Watcher, true in its knowing, single in its vision... never sleeps. It knows, beyond knowing, that in the above and below, appearances are never as they are painted... It knows the above is below and the below, above... inside is out and outside, in... and light is dark and darkness, light... But even in this, the Watcher knows all is not as it would appear... To know the Way is to engage intimately with that which appears to be without, to experience the majestic splendour of light as revealed by dark and to surrender all to that which lies beyond all endings and every beginning... To know the Way is to walk the perilous path and give up all hope of the dream... To know the Way is important to some so they give it their all... in pursuit of the One... But, to **be** the Way... to belong in the longing... swim in the drowning... and laugh with the shaming... is to know peace beyond measure... or so it would seem... To **be** the Way... to know peace beyond measure... to be One in the seeming... Could this also be a dream or is it the Real?*

Guidance

Charting a course amidst the ebb and flow of our dualistic universe is a seemingly impossible task, particularly when these core dualities are polarised by a mind steeped in judgement, and requires skills in navigation few are able to muster. However, all is not lost, for the script offers a way forward. Taking its lead from the image, it introduces a world of paradox in which seemingly apparent opposites not only exist in the same place at the same time, but are also shown to be one and the same in substance. Aside from this, it provides clear direction as to how paradox may translate into a *Way of Beauty* when daily challenges are seen for what they are; not an easy task, for it requires a high degree of honest reflection to see beyond a mind that always 'knows' itself to be right. In order to *belong in the longing... swim in the drowning... and laugh with the shaming...*, your compass must be turned inwards; you must know yourself **before** the two may embrace each other. Importantly, you must know the ways of your inner trickster; it will beguile you at every turn when given free rein, so be vigilant. *Appearances*, therefore, asks you to look beyond your perception of reality and, above all, to be open to the possibility that, should you embark upon this journey, life as you know it will, in all probability, never be quite the same again. After all, when everything gets turned on its head, how can you possibly view the world from the same perspective?

Appearances

Quality: The Beauty Way
Absolute Aspect: Love
Geometry: None
Rainbow Sphere: Beauty

Contemplation

He knew it was a gateway... but to what or where? And how did it open? Was there some magic button he could press to reveal all... in an instant? Or perhaps it was more subtle, far simpler than he could possibly imagine. It was an enigma, and one he had been pondering upon for quite some time. Somewhat perplexed, he took a break from his meanderings to people-watch at a local cafe. The toing and froing captured his imagination, alongside the miraculous opening of doors as people approached, regardless of their direction, speed or intent. A strange juxtaposition occurred as he took it all in, allowing another reality to merge with his current time frame, and while figures came and went, a sense of wonderment stirred in his heart. He witnessed life, his life, pass before his eyes. The most peculiar thing, it was life without stories; there were no actors and no players gracing his personal stage, not even props to embellish this magnificent theatrical drama. No, the great opening in his inner sky revealed a kaleidoscope of visionary delight but, even though it was his journey, he did not feature as a 'star' in the movie, and so, lacking identity, he was free to participate – fully – without claiming it as 'his'. He experienced every feeling, every unfolding turn of events, through his heart with such a sense of total absorption that he could not fail to marvel at the depth of intimate relationship he felt with not only those present before and within him but also all manner of entities in the cosmos. As much as his eyes drank in the splendour, as deep as his heart embraced the totality of his life, all life, his presence soared to be one with the stars. Mirroring the scene in the cafe, the door had opened miraculously before him... but how did he create the opening when he wasn't even there?

Guidance

Arcturus is a portal, a way in or possibly even a way out. Appearing during periods of transition – physical birth, death and especially during the symbolic demise of the personality as it begins its integral alignment with the Soul – it takes its name from the brightest star in the Bootes constellation. Its subtle appearance during times of transition comes about because, "Arcturus is, however, far more than a star. It is a frequency that one possesses within."[viii] Drawing upon the group-conscious, extra-terrestrial intelligences that facilitate the birth and death process, it often appears as a tunnel of soft, golden light, accompanied by an almost overwhelming sense of unconditional love.[ix] The well-known saying, "When life gives you lemons make lemonade," alluded to in the opening script, means, "Be with whatever life has to offer at any given moment in time." Embracing the gifts *Arcturus* brings will help considerably in this process. In the case of our storyteller, it was people passing through automatic doors in a cafe that exposed a way in; a perfectly ordinary, everyday occurrence, you might say. So when it appears life is turning rather pear-shaped, when all you believe yourself to be is being called into question or when the best-laid plans get turned on their head, consider that instead of everything falling apart, it might just be falling into place. *Arcturus,* as a *vision of reality,* is a window offering an alternative viewpoint where, if you pay attention to what lies right before your eyes, you may not only understand lemons but also master the art of making lemonade...

Arcturus

Quality: Intimacy
Absolute Aspect: Love
Geometry: Flower of life, seed of life, sphere
Rainbow Sphere: Order

Contemplation

It began with a spark, although it was barely discernible as such. Like a solitary firefly illuminating the darkest night... it was just a spark... wasn't it? How could she possibly have known the impact it would have, the power it would unleash... or the devastating potential it held to destroy that which she considered her greatest asset. Where had it come from... this insignificant packet of fire, this isolated thought that had set her mind ablaze with light? What was its source? Who was the dispenser of the flame? And who was the thinker? A vision, fleeting but clear, appeared before her inner eye. *Upon the floor in front of her were piles of books stacked one on top of the other, a plethora of information contained within numerous articles and, of course, her trusty laptop where all manner of research may be undertaken. All around the air was **still**, pregnant with untold knowing... and knowledge.* Esmerelda could not contain herself; she laughed until her belly ached. Her customary method of research seemed so primitive, tedious and, well, ridiculous! *"Ok,"* she softly goaded her inner teacher, *"Show me **your** way."* Allowing this was in itself a tremendous challenge. Her greatest assets, or so she believed, were her attention to detail and her meticulous approach to research, especially into topics like this one. Now she had to go deep into its territory, seek out the origin of thought and determine its modus operandi and purpose, and all without using her mind! Nevertheless, she stepped aside and permitted the Word to pour forth its wisdom. *"The spark, a particle of divine fire within substance, originates as an impulse in the mind of Absolute; it is a function of its Being-ness. Once ignited, it follows its agreed pathway in accordance with its Will. Spark ignites spark through multiple layers of existence until it is discerned as thought in the mind of one who thinks – such as you."* Subtle threads of understanding joined the dots in her head as Mentor continued. *"In consummate surrender, the light of clear-seeing enables Truth to stand revealed. Light Codes of Creation, embedded within the substance of Absorption, are keys to unlocking the power of thought. Remember, assimilation within the Cause before expression is the method by which consciousness unfolds within itself to co-create itself; thought, as a packet of light within its substance is no different. Every thought returns to itself as an expression within Cause to manifest as reality, whether for good or ill."* Now it all made perfect sense.

Guidance

Three visions[11] tease apart the workings out of thought as it is expressed through an equal number of layered expressions: body, Soul and Spirit. As *Above, So Below* is the power to evoke that which is beyond thought and leads to the origin of the first spark, where, by a gift of grace, the door to the mind of God stands open before you. But remember, the realm of the abstract cannot be accessed by one who 'thinks'; it is unveiled through the Will of the Divine **alone**, not by you.

---

[11] *As Above, So Below, Inside Out, Sweet Surrender.*

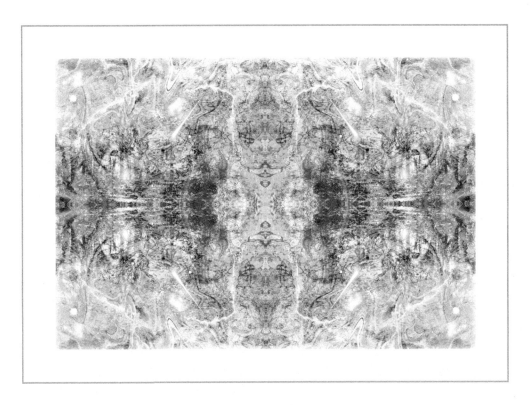

As Above, So Below

Quality: Evocation
Absolute Aspect: Love
Geometry: None
Rainbow Sphere: Mind

Contemplation

Enough! Enough! His heartfelt cry came from a place of indescribable pain. Many recoil in fear, even more retaliate in anger, but one or two, who know the Way of Fire, rejoice. He was aware, intimately, of his inner programs: chained forever to the hamster wheel of regret, his heart shamed beyond measure and his soul consigned to dust. He knew, he was aware, but still he succumbed... Still he danced to the trickster's tune... Still he unleashed the grapes of wrath upon an unsuspecting world... And still he cried the tears of the damned... Doomed, he believed his fate to be... doomed... Until now.

Guidance

Seeds of destruction are sown on the battlefields of the lower self. Hatred, anger, envy – every despicable emotion is expressed with ferocity towards those who would threaten its survival or harm its persona. If that threat continues, antagonistic seeds will ripen into even more efficient means of reaping carnage. Such is the suffering of humanity in its un-awakened state. Lack of consciousness breeds reactive behaviour, which is painfully obvious but not often acknowledged. Only when base desires have been exhausted is there any hope of remission or any chance of leaving the fires of hell on the battleground, where they may be finally laid to rest. Then the fire of awareness may burn through the dross of the lower nature in response to the call of the Soul. *Aspiration* is awash with fire, so much so it is a wonder it does not ignite in your hand! The land glows red as if Prometheus, thief of fire, has marked his passage in a rush to escape the wrath of the gods. Golden sky, alive with colour – red, orange, blue splashed with radiant white – calls you to its side. An ocean of liquid light evokes hope in a mind all but lost to the waters of despair. Yet, in spite of the preponderance of red, with its destructive implications, there is little sign of carnage: there are no charred cinders or frazzled remains; quite the opposite, the entire panorama is vibrant and **alive!** It therefore comes as no surprise that *Aspiration* is a calling to befriend the element of fire – to know its many qualities, its detriments and its efficacy as the supreme agent of change. It asks that you harness the fire of your passion, turn your sight to the Soul and allow the fire in your belly to bring strength to your courageous heart. The battle is about to commence, but it is not fought on land; it is waged in a mind of awareness, in one whose heart has answered the call of the Soul and in one who is ready to receive a baptism in fire. This vision offers a gift of choice. Do you join the mass of humanity to wage the never-ending cry of war or do you take an inward path and dance to tune of the Divine? Are you ready to tread the *Way of Fire*?

Aspiration

Quality: Right Choice
Absolute Aspect: Will
Geometry: None
Rainbow Sphere: Truth

Contemplation

First it entered the lake... why? Curiosity... perhaps? But a fleeting shift in perspective had allowed a strange phenomenon to appear. Between copious lotus flowers floating languidly upon its pristine surface was what, at first glance, appeared to be a mirror... a reflective surface wherein it could clearly see itself... Consciousness was intrigued... Diving beneath the surface, its curiosity was inspired further... not a ripple did it make, nor molecule disturb... no sense of touch, of sight, of sound... yet every sense alive in its intimate relationship with the world in which it now moved. Far beneath its point of entry, at the bedrock of the earth, layers of sediment... remains of all that had long since gone, became its temporary abode... It tasted the slimy, gritty consistency, gorged upon its plethora of nutrients and felt the lotus of its heart blossom in the land... every exquisite flower that radiated the fruits of its passage... was an expression of itself... this it knew... Consciousness expanded... Its field of reference entered bastions of towering monoliths... It flew on air, danced with the sun... then, in a moment of intimate release, turned its attention to the stars... On the far reaches of the solar system... consciousness entered a small, ringed planet... Uranus, the awakener... In an instant, mind within its substance, shattered... Sparks of electric fire set its world ablaze, particles of light exploded into worlds anew... and that which had hitherto been separate was whole... Consciousness had returned once more unto itself... And with it, through the gift of the flame, came knowing of the mirror...

Guidance

Uranus,[12] the awakener, is inspiration for this vision. The image includes a discretely hidden photo of the planet, is ablaze with light and extends an invitation to, quite literally, wake up! However, it was the lake in the foreground that inspired consciousness to explore the panorama at its feet, particularly the reflective nature of its pristine surface. The entire journey, from the first shift in perspective to the moment consciousness returned to itself, serves as a metaphor for understanding the intimate, and inextricable, relationship between mind and consciousness. It is important to recognise that consciousness **is** the river – the substance within which mind flows – and, as expression of Absolute, is the remaining presence when all else is gone, including mind. As the script reveals, mind serves as a mirror in which consciousness may know itself – the error lies in taking the servant to be real. Until a moment of awakening, when the mirror is shattered, all that is perceived is mind; there is **nothing** that isn't mind. The gift consciousness received, following its exploration, was the light of awareness, the flame of mind that illuminates all that is false. It was able to see the reflection as a facet of itself and in that recognition there was no further need for the mirror... *Awakening* asks you to befriend the servant, to look in the mirror and know your mind, for only in taking apart the subtle and intricate web it weaves... will you come to experience the Real...

---

[12] Five visions portray the essential essence of the outer 'transpersonal' planets: *Awakening* (Uranus), *Illumination* and *Illusion* (Neptune), *Transcendence* and *Underworld* (Pluto).

Awakening

Quality: Originality
Absolute Aspect: Will
Geometry: None
Rainbow Sphere: Order

Contemplation

Deep in the bowels of the earth, the beast roamed free... Unchallenged for millennia... lord of its domain... it was indestructible... or so it believed. Nothing escaped its watchful eye... a master in scrutiny, all senses fine-tuned to subtle changes in its environment... every movement, breath, sound, smell... it knew... But above all, it knew with unnerving accuracy when fear engulfed the heart of another... Darkness was its way, suspicion its trusted friend... 'survival, above all else' it's timeless legend... Now it sensed change... For the first time, the beast felt fear as others did... its kingdom was under threat... it could... **smell** *it... Escape was its instinctive response... it had to run...* **now!** *And then,* **she** *came... she with a light so bright, a love so pure and courage enough to melt the hearts of 1000 fearless warriors. Step by unfaltering step, she walked the descending spiral into* **his** *domain... Nothing distracted from her purpose... no amount of cunning or wily ways, which had served him so well in the past, sent her screaming in terror to the land from whence she came... As innocent as the day she was born, she continued her journey... never losing her focus for even a second... until, with every hiding place exhausted, she found him. The beast cowered in shame... motionless. She did nothing, said nothing... but he knew her... he* **smelt** *her... and then he felt her... he felt her love... her* **gratitude**... *for him?*

Guidance

Both beast and innocent child are within us. As archetypal characters in an endless war of supremacy, they reside deep inside the unconscious mind, generating instinctual behavioural responses that wreak havoc in our relationships and turn our lives upside down when we least expect it. As part of the limbic system in the mid-brain, the amygdala is responsible for many of these responses, including reflexive emotions such as fear and anxiety. It is the storehouse of the past in which our base animal instincts, our core fears and our emotional learning result in a highly evolved state of awareness – **instinctual** knowing. The calling of this vision, in company with its mirror, *Amygdala,* is to befriend these masters of intrigue, bring their subtle manipulations into the cool light of day and recognise the origin of your behavioural responses. *Beauty and the Beast* asks you to embrace the qualities of the innocent child. Her gratitude and love transcended all, so she was able to step resolutely into the territory of the beast. Why did she feel so indebted to him? And how did she know him so well? It is time to reflect honestly, recognise the beauty within, regardless of its appearance, and appreciate that without the gifts of both beast and innocent child you would be as the moon without the stars – bereft and incomplete.

Beauty and the Beast

Quality: Suspending Judgement
Absolute Aspect: Intelligence
Geometry: None
Rainbow Sphere: Truth

Contemplation

Esmerelda woke from her slumbers. The dream, the vision and, above all, the message were fresh in her mind. Like a beacon they shone, offering clear resolution to questions she had, in frustration, long ago abandoned. *"In deepest dark glows Eye of All-Seeing... Darkest of dark... Light of All Being... Seed of creation... Unmanifest becoming."* Direction maybe, but hardly clear! Her questions returned with renewed vigour. "How did 'it' all begin? Why? How could 'something' possibly be birthed from nothing? Who, or what, is '*Unmanifest becoming*'? Could it be the eye in her dream? Or perhaps it was the elusive 'Cause'[13]?" Esmerelda stilled to nothing. She knew the answers to these questions and more... deep in her heart she could *feel* them. Soon, there was more... *"Becoming is the divine nature of Cause... Cause is the influx state that uses the force of becoming to multiply itself within expression."* Now she could sense the subtle currents running within this profound outpouring. Now her mind could assemble the pieces of the jigsaw. And now she could actively enter the wondrous beauty of creation as a *way of being*. But first, with a little assistance from *the Word*, she must unravel the paradox. *"Unmanifest is the constant, changeless state of Absolute. Its nature and mode of expression, as the primal Cause within the manifested world, is Becoming. This continuous outpouring allows each particle within its substance to assimilate within itself to co-create itself. Zero is the 'seed' wherein Cause unfolds within itself according to its Will. It is intrinsic to the fabric of life itself and, therefore, also Absolute."* Esmerelda entered the stillness and once again became Zero. Soon 'she' came to understand that this nothingness was a gateway, a doorway, wherein she may 'become' the Will of Absolute. It allowed her to step outside her perpetual cycle of co-creating herself and **be** Zero, **be** Cause expressing **through** her. Furthermore, she understood the paradox. She saw clearly that light and dark, something and nothing, any number of myriad forms within every possible dimension, occupied the same space at the same time; it was the constant, unchanging state of Absolute. They only appeared to be separate when she observed them as such.

Guidance

Becoming is the ultimate in expressing and creating reality, its source being the primal Cause or individual particle within it depending upon where consciousness abides. *Becoming* reflects this. It is an invitation to look beyond the obvious, to know the intelligence that informs life – **your** life – and to recognise the forces at play in the manifestation of reality. Are you really a co-creator in true 'Esmerelda' fashion? Does your life mirror this? Do you dance to the tune of the divine or are you driven by your will alone? Who, or what, is it that informs your life? Ponder deeply these soul-searching questions, then let them all go... and wait... Can you **feel** the wonder of creation as it flows through you?

---

[13] See *Conversion*.

Becoming

Quality: Unmanifest
Absolute Aspect: Intelligence
Geometry: Seed of life, tree of life, vesica piscis
Rainbow Sphere: Light

Contemplation

*Absolute Zero... nothing. No thought. No sound. No scent. No other. No-**thing**... So light, it is not even there... so perfectly, absurdly empty, it must be dark... yet it is not. It is Zero; Absolute Zero. A space upon which existence may unfold within itself... may write its story... may know itself as it is... A space that is not space... a space that **is**... a space where all is erased the moment it is drawn. Absolute Zero... Mystery... Wonderment... Ordinariness... inscribed upon a fabric that is blank...*

Guidance

The space we call nothing, the great chasm that leaves us feeling bereft inside, is one we spend all our lives trying to avoid. We fill it with all manner of meaningless 'external' things, from the latest gadget or therapy to trivial chat, superficial relationships and even spiritual practice. Anything to stem the tide of unfathomable emptiness we might feel inside should we stop, even for a second. When we finally wake up to see the game we have been playing and it all comes crashing down around our ears, we still do our utmost to fill the great hole that is the end result. What would happen if we ignored the voice that impels us to seek outside of ourselves for resolution, which instructs us to suppress our sense of loss for all that has gone? What would happen if, instead, we embraced the emptiness inside? What would happen if we let go? *Blank Canvas* encourages you to do just that – let go. It is an invitation to engage with the deep abiding presence that pervades all things, to penetrate deep into its mystery, to realise you are nothing and then to rest in that nothingness until you know, beyond all doubt, that nothing is all there is. Begin by watching your breath. Notice the subtle pause between each in-breath and out-breath and then slowly sink into the image. Let it be your guide, allow it to take you deep into your core and to strip to the bone every last vestige of your false sense of self until, naked and vulnerable, you surrender. Slowly at first, it creeps up on you... then, with increasing intensity, it envelops your whole being... Soon you come to see that which you have been afraid of for so, so long... is no longer there. The answer to every question, every endless search, you now know to be simple. Nothing remains when all else is gone... It is the fabric upon which life, **your** life, is written... wonderment in ordinariness... inscribed upon a fabric that is blank...

Blank Canvas

Quality: Unknowable
Absolute Aspect: Intelligence
Geometry: None
Rainbow Sphere: Rainbow

Contemplation

The landscape was bleak... at least on first impression... but as her eyes adjusted to its subtle shades and the tight knot deep in her belly relaxed its hold, her heart opened to an enveloping presence. Darkness of impending twilight gave way to the glow of golden dawn, spectres in the gloom appeared as friends in the mist and, despite her trepidation at the impending gathering, at which she would play a vital role, the essence of Love emanated such unconditional acceptance that it could not fail to ignite in her unquestionable trust. With awakened confidence, she walked deep into their kingdom and, taking her place at the centre, lay resolutely upon the soft, receptive land, whilst elders of the tribe, each in their own place, gathered around. As one they sang, in ancient tones, a lullaby of the lost. In Truth they stayed as Light Transcendent drew near. And in unison they cried as the Blessed One bestowed its blessing. With heart attuned to silence, hands rested comfortingly upon her rounded belly and eyes fixed unwaveringly upon the Great Unknown, the sacrificial lamb gave all of herself to the impending deliverance. In consummate absorption, all that she was, all that she is now and all that she has yet to be – journeys, memories, hopes and wishes, beliefs, programs, light and shadow – dissolved into a river of liquid light. To Zero, Absolute Zero, she returned. In Zero, she was delivered... and as Zero, what began as bleak... was redeemed...

Guidance

Three facets of the diamond[14] chart a course from darkness to light, from despair to hope and from separation to unity as it unfolds through an evolutionary path of return, each vision exposing a role in a story that is timeless in the telling. The scene is set in *Gathering* where a sacrificial lamb, under the ministrations of ancient ones, whose knowing of deliverance is beyond question, is granted redemption. *Absorption,* as the way of return, is the means by which all entanglements face their demise. *Blessing* marks an act of grace, without which any transformative way of redemption would never stay the course. The image, in spite of its subtlety, aligns well with the script and its sister visions; colour alone would unite them in purpose but their essence and energetic fabric confirm, without doubt, their relationship. Allow your eyes to move beyond the structure of tree and prostrate figure, to the lighted beings upon which her gaze is fixed and you will see, cradled in the arms of an emanating presence and suckling upon its ample breast, the subtle outline of an unborn child. Less obvious is the connection between these outer and inner forms. When the sacrificial lamb, habitually chained to an altar of desire, relinquishes its hold, when the *lullaby of the lost* is heard by the starved and when the wounded soul is as a foetus in the womb of creation, all deliverance is blessed... Herein lies redemption... not only for the lamb but also for the species...

---

[14] *Absorption, Blessing, Gathering.*

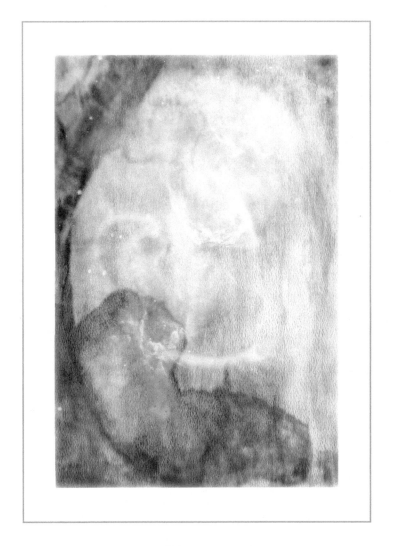

Blessing

Quality: Grace
Absolute Aspect: Love
Geometry: None
Rainbow Sphere: Truth

Contemplation

Curiosity spurred them onwards. They had been ambling through the forest, soaking up the ambience of a lazy summer's day, when their eyes were drawn towards two majestic trees in the distance. One was in shade, the other, full sun, they were struck by the black and white semblance of duplicity each to the other brought... Somehow, this unfortunate trick of the light belied the sense of wholeness they both felt in their hearts. Standing beneath the shadows, amidst scantily spread roots, wonderment took the place of curiosity. "Look Thomas," cried Esmerelda in amazement. "It's a wall! How can that be? I mean, why would anyone build a wall beneath two trees?" Thomas' response was to dive in for a closer look. "It's a very solid wall," he offered, whilst kicking it rather forcefully with his boot. "It seems as if it has only just been built, yet I sense it is very, very old." Esmerelda nodded in agreement. "You are quite correct, Thomas. It is an ancient structure and not quite as it appears. Look, see what happens when I approach it with gentleness." She reached out and softly stroked the surface of the bricks, encouraging her friend to do the same. "Not so solid after all, eh Thomas?" The more they engaged playfully with its substance, the more pliable Wall became until it was not dissimilar to putty, palpable putty, in their hands. Golden radiances responded to their touch to deliver ecstatic ripples upon its surface. They knew 'something' beyond desired expression. 'Something' that Wall for aeons of time had served as guardian to its innermost secrets. 'Something' they felt deep inside was fundamental to who they were now. Intuitively, hand in hand, hearts entwined as one, Esmerelda and Thomas walked purposefully towards Wall and, without a second thought, stepped into its presence... A vast panorama opened up before them as it surrendered to their passage... Bathed in soft, golden light was a perfectly ordinary landscape, rich in translucent colours that would befit the most luminous of rainbows and set with the most agreeable of creatures of every ilk, size and vibration... "You see what is possible, Thomas, when the idea of how things should be is surrendered to 'what is'?" "I do indeed, Esmerelda," he replied, congenially, "but far more than this, I see how miracles happen when differences are set aside and beings act in unison..."

Guidance

Sometimes a wall is not as it seems. Sometimes that which appears as a barrier isn't so. And sometimes, just sometimes, the presence of apparent exclusion is in perfect accord with the natural rhythm and pulse of something far greater. Oftentimes that which is perceived through the senses is not as it appears. Sometimes life is not about you; sometimes it is, sometimes it isn't, but many times life has its own agenda. Sometimes that which is without is within. And sometimes, just sometimes, a wall is not really a wall at all... it is a door.

Brick Wall

Quality: Resistance
Absolute Aspect: Intelligence
Geometry: None
Rainbow Sphere: Love

Contemplation

Clouds... all around, clouds... In darkness, she stumbled backwards and forwards through the mists of time... She searched... she cried... she pleaded... but her calls fell upon ears that did not hear... Silence... equalled the pallor of her days. There was no path to be found, no subtle scent or sign of footprints gone before... no hint of light to show the way. A wall of unfathomable, flat greyness obscured her vision, confused her mind and, after what seemed like lifetimes of penetrating the far reaches of its substance, her heart crumpled into the depths of despair. A blinding flash dispersed the vapour in her mind... clouds yielded to clarity... Now she could see... it was thought, her thought **alone**, *that kept her chained to the annals of the past and imprisoned her mind in belief. Rainbow light transformed the wispy terrain... and, as its radiance broke through the shadows of her mind, she stared in wonderment at the way ahead... not a path with footprints well trodden across its land but a bridge... a footpath in the sky... a way of hope that stung her eyes with joy. Infused with diamond sparkles, holding promise of pastures new, it called her onward and left her with no choice but to echo its return... With resting place and final ground unknown, one foot resolutely placed before the other, she took her first tentative steps... The waiting Presence stirred... with heart of compassion and mind instilled in substance hitherto unknown, it expressed its Will... Packets of light, impregnated with subtle tones of thought, fleeting visions and sound in silence... cast delicate impressions upon the fabric of her mind... She had forged the bridge... Now the real work could begin...*

Guidance

The bridge between the lower and higher seems interminable and full of pitfalls and is often discarded when what appears to be considerable spiritual effort reaps little return. What fails to be recognised, certainly in the early stages, is that the very pitfalls and despondent attitudes encountered upon the way are the cornerstones of bridge-building. The bridge of light is not found upon some unknown shore; it is forged in the heart of matter where every inner letting go, every heartfelt plea and every cry of despair is the lower giving itself over to the higher. The Rainbow Bridge, as it is referred to in esoteric teaching, is a multi-layered pathway on the plane of mind where knowing is cultivated and 'bridged' between all aspects of the self. The journey begins with harmonising the three aspects of the personality – physical, emotional and mental – then, as the *waiting Presence* expressed, the real work of building the bridge to the Soul may begin. The script is a 'way in' and, together with its image, expresses guidance for this vision. Turn your attention to your thoughts; notice how they cloud your vision and leave you fumbling forever in the dark. You will never find clarity of mind if you pander to these distractions... and you will never, ever... know the bridge of light...

Bridge Across Forever

Quality: Holding the Vision
Absolute Aspect: Will
Geometry: None
Rainbow Sphere: Mind

Contemplation

They met as they had before, inside the Hall of Learning. "Greetings again, my friend," sounded the luminous being without employing words. "We must continue our task concerning the future well-being of a world for which we are equally responsible. You were prepared for this during our earlier meetings." Consciousness nodded and recalled with ease its engagement with spirits of the four elements. It remembered clearly the words of the Shining One, each one a dagger in its heart, "Mankind has evolved to become a master of destruction on many levels." Interrupting its musing, the Shining One continued, "In our interactions with spirits of earth, air, fire and water you have been made aware of not only the destructive nature of mankind but also the vital role these lesser builders play in the creation and sustenance of the Mother planet. Now, as the evolution of our respective species is at stake, it is important you understand how we, as creative builders, function as a team. We follow our own line of evolution independent to humanity, we are governed by our own laws and, crucially, we have our own hierarchical intelligence ordered through the mind of God." Consciousness bowed graciously. "First, know there are two lines of force – involutionary (spirit's descent into matter) and evolutionary (matter raised to spirit) – underpinning all creative processes. Elementals, with which we have engaged so intimately, follow the involutionary line and serve under the law of obeisance: every thought, word and deed is considered to be an order and is acted upon accordingly, without exception. Second, the co-creative partnership, in which humanity and the Devic kingdom cooperate in manifesting the 'Kingdom of God' on earth, takes place upon the Buddhic-plane of consciousness, where 'self' and 'other' are non-existent. We are able to interact, in this and through our previous journeys, solely because we vibrate in unison upon the plane of the Soul. Should this not be the case, as occurs with those who would manipulate and control these elemental forces, damage of far greater significance than has been revealed thus far is the outcome." Consciousness, in full understanding, responded with gratitude, "I am mediator between your domain and theirs, all you have imparted is recognised and, as mine is the task of helping humanity to see clearly, to assist them in waking up, all that I may do, I will."

Guidance

Interwoven into the fabric of six facets of the diamond[15] is the kingdom of nature as it interfaces with human consciousness. Each in its own way exposes responsibility for maintaining, purifying and ultimately balancing respective elements, whilst creating in consciousness 'heaven' on earth. *Brilliance* is the *Shining One*, a Deva, or angelic being, who has under its direction the 'lesser' creative builders. At this critical juncture in earth's history, it is vital that the message transmitted through these six linked visions, is heard... Consciousness changes matter... it is imperative we, as a race, wake up... and it begins with you...

---

[15] Four elements – *Air, Earth, Fire* and *Water, Brilliance, Cooperation.*

Brilliance

Quality: Expansion
Absolute Aspect: Intelligence
Geometry: None
Rainbow Sphere: Rainbow

Contemplation

It was time for her next lesson. She was well versed in the language of thought, the role it played in establishing the many and varied expressions within the established universe and how it was but a servant to the all-encompassing Absolute expression, consciousness. Now she was ready to learn how it might be applied, in a constructive way, to further the upliftment of human consciousness. In preparation, she surrendered wholly and completely to the Zero, allowing the force of Becoming, the primal Cause, to flow effortlessly through and within her. All that was her identity – journeys, cellular memories, products of the past – she absorbed into liquid light, assimilating all into the Cause. Here, the presence that was Esmerelda rested. Subtle impressions announced their arrival – visual perfection in the appearance of many 'lighted' beings, so much a part of the surroundings they were barely discernible as such – confirmed the presence of her beloved Teacher, and sound... music such as had never before graced her inner organs, identified the lyrical tones of their combined outpouring expression. *"Greetings, dear friend,"* they whispered. *"You have come far on your journey to be able to meet with us in this way. But only in this manner, through matching your vibration to those of us who work on the inner planes, may you realise the full potential of all we are about to impart. Only in this manner may you be of true service to others. Establishing the combined intention of the group, **prior to expression**, is a prerequisite to the construction of thought-form using consciousness as the point of origin, not mind."* Esmerelda remained silent. There was no need for words; all was assimilated effortlessly within the transmission. *"Embedded within the state of Absorption, being at one with substance, are Light Codes of Creation, keys to unlocking the power of thought. This you know. Consciousness, as sole expression of Absolute, recognises and ignites these keys using mind as its vessel, so uniting with substance, prior to the creation of thought, ensures the true qualities of mind are expressed. Creating with consciousness ensures matter is thus elevated to the plane of Absolute from the point of its highest creative potential; thought-form creation, without prior alignment to substance, serves only the lower aspect of mind to perpetuate life in sleep."* They sensed ripples in her mental body as she tried to understand. *"Review our earlier lessons.*[16] *Be the child, celebrate that which has already been given and from there, allow creative impulse to generate thought... in wonderment."* She let go. *"So all has come full circle,"* she transmitted. *"That which began as a thought, establishing 'life in sleep', has worked out the fruits of its passage to be returned to its point of origin. Absolute has experienced knowing what it is not, only to be returned to that which it **is**... by those who were once asleep!"*

Guidance

Consciousness, not mind, expresses the true qualities of mind. This is a deep vision, rich in gifts, but first, you must know mind, especially what it is **not**.

---

[16] See *Eye Eye, Impulse, Materialisation, Point of Light.*

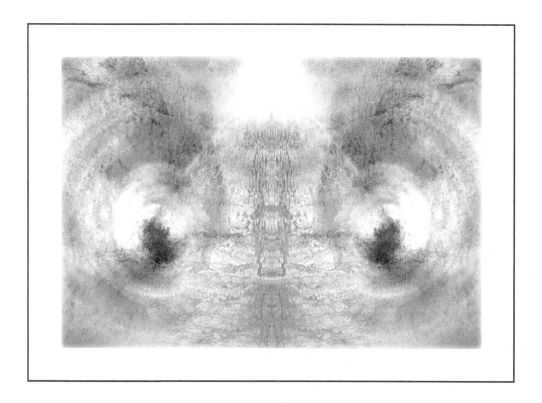

Brotherhood

Quality: Community
Absolute Aspect: Love
Geometry: None
Rainbow Sphere: Order

Contemplation

Long, long ago, before a fledgling planet prepared to flex her wings, there came to earth those who would prove to be the masters of the race. Their purpose, multiple in expression, was to instil amongst infant humanity wisdom in an age. And for aeons, it was so. Miraculous feats, performed through understanding the laws of the physical universe, were effortless: remarkable structures appeared; advanced technology enabled travel through time and space; music and art, exquisite in their expression of the divine, were celebrated in a spirit of unity. Man and gods in co-creative partnership heralded an era of peace, a golden age, in which the great continent flourished. But it was not to last. There were those who claimed the hidden powers, shared so generously without condition, as their own; those who used the secret knowledge to manipulate and control and would stop at nothing to be the new rulers of the race. And so began the Great War. Silent as the grave, the Masters of Wisdom withdrew their presence from the land, sending in their stead a mighty flood to take all, but a few, to certain death beneath the waves. Before long, Atlantis was no more, or so says the legend. In deep meditation, the meditator knew these tales to be far more than myth. Billions of years after the event, the same dynamics were still being played out inside him and in the world at large – this he knew. Atlantis still lived. Manipulation, control and desire for power were obvious, but more subtle, and carrying far greater significance, were the psychic powers running rife amidst an unsuspecting populace. The Siddhis were strong... in his meditation he could feel them... and their allure was so, so tempting...

Guidance

The Atlantean root race, as documented in well-researched material,[x] is part of a greater cycle (mantvantara) spanning many millions of years. However, it is the golden age – its fall and how the resultant karma plays out on 21st-century earth – that we are concerned with here. Five visions[17] serve as a bridge in time where these forces may be contemplated as an inner process. *Burning Ground* covers the full spectrum of this journey, from its inception in Atlantis, through the fall, to karmic repercussions playing out in the modern age. Begin at the end – with you, now: slowly, slowly your part within the great cosmic error is revealed; slowly, slowly a new version of you emerges; slowly, slowly the collective is transformed. When all that is false is as ash upon the funeral pyre of the past, once again the great golden age of Atlantis may rise once more. Stewarded by a race worthy of trust, with karmic propensities redeemed, it will herald an age in which masters and humanity serve in unison... wind beneath the wings of a fledgling planet... granted freedom to fly...

---

[17] *Alien Nation, Burning Ground, Follow the Crowd?, Stillness, Welcome.*

Burning Ground

Quality: Personality Refinement
Absolute Aspect: Will
Geometry: None
Rainbow Sphere: Beauty

Contemplation

*She was an innocent... born in remembrance of Truth... She was an innocent....clear in vision to those who held her close... rich in presence to all who sensed to feel... She was an innocent... cradled in gentleness that none, save the pure, could perceive. She was an innocent... born at the full of the moon, kin to children of old, parent to seasons in time and sustained through love... that only the Mother could yield. She was an innocent... gifted in the art of rapport... friend to the shy... protector to the lost and wise to the ways of the wild. Yes, she was an innocent... Long, long ago she was an innocent... but that was then. Now she is sullied by time... encased in a heart made of stone... imprisoned by fables... not hers for the taking. Now she wallows in shame, bound by a mind that enslaves, and believes all innocence to be myth. Now in the dungeon of her darkness, in the dense quarry of her excrement... she hears the sound of her tormentors... over... and over... and over again. "You must do this... you must do that. This is the right way, this, wrong. You must wear this, you mustn't wear that. You are female, your mission is clear... in this there is no doubt... give birth to the children, carry their load and when all love is rejected, do not scream and shout. You are female, your mission is clear... and you have failed." At this final condemnation, there followed a great pause... an interminable quiescence... Until, in the hitherto unbreakable silence... the sweetest sound... a melodious melody... issued from one so pure it shattered the prism of her belief... Chirp, chirp... chirp, chirp... chirp, chirp... it resounded over... and over... and over again. She was an innocent... the message was clear... She was an innocent... Now she's in no doubt... She **is** an innocent...*

Guidance

Celebration introduces the magical kingdoms in nature but in a way that is less than obvious when following the script alone. The image offers another way in. Gentle folk of hill, mountain, valley and dale are gathered for what appears, in the form of a cube, to be a birth. Fairy lights abound amidst an air of quiet expectation infused with nurturing acceptance for the one who is to come. All takes place within the headspace of a, clearly feminine, august presence against the backdrop of a radiant moonlit sky. Stretch your imagination a little and you will appreciate the highest regard that Mother Nature and her faithful servants hold for all sentient beings who, through divine grace, are granted domicile within her kingdom. *Celebration* is, first, a return to innocence whereupon the 'box' inside you that has been built through collective conditioning is torn apart. Second, it is a calling to the Spirit of the Mother, which expresses the divine feminine not through stereotypical societal dictates of how it **should** be, but through reverence, appreciation and humility for the way it **is**. Purpose, long ago forgotten, may thus be fulfilled as the Sacred Female takes her rightful place amongst the celestial giants of the cosmos. Worth celebrating, wouldn't you say?

Celebration

Quality: Boundaries
Absolute Aspect: Will
Geometry: Cube
Rainbow Sphere: Light

Contemplation

It had appeared by magic, out of nowhere... a great opening in the sky, a rendering of heaven in its full majestic glory, exposed to all regardless of their worthiness to behold its mystery. Moments before, as he'd lain upon the soft, warm sand adjacent to a sea of tranquillity, he'd marvelled at the seamless marriage of ocean and cloudless sky. Lost to himself in nature's miracle, mind lazily seeking the ending of one and beginning of the other, he knew it to be a meeting of worlds, a space in time, an interval wherein a glimpse of the eternal may penetrate the forbidden territory of earth's sovereignty. Myriad shades of rich indigo blue, graced by random shafts of light, so clear their solar origin was impossible to source, coloured the air, and even though he sensed, deep inside, the impeding providence, he was left unmoved by their appearance. "Another miracle, another sparkle," he whispered to himself, somewhat disenchanted. "How do these displays of other-worldly glories assist? They are there and I am here. If life on earth is not enhanced by these great displays of light," he mused, "then how do they serve?" The young man lapsed into silence... a victim of his own quandary...

Guidance

Enlightenment is a destructive process, a systematic removal of all that is perceived through the crystal-clear lens of awareness and deemed to be false. The script hints at this through the dismissal of what would appear, at first glance, to be a great spiritual revelation. It is clear the 'seeker' has experienced many of these 'sparkles' and is left feeling somewhat disenchanted by the appearance of another. After all, he questions, how has his quality of life been enhanced as a result? A way forward is offered through the words, "they are there and I am here". As long as there is distance between there and here, whether in space or time, there will never be integration; light and dark become equal in their propensity to obscure if this should be so. *Celestial Light* takes these soul-searching dilemmas into the warm and loving waters of your open and trusting heart. It invites you to enter the destructive process, to examine closely every veil and subtle appearance of your desire to be special and to embrace with love all of your findings. Take a close look at the imagery and you will see it resembles a spinal column, with the ribs and chest area being prominent. As well as the lighted angelic stairway in the sky, autumn leaves, appearing as curtains drawn aside, are prominent, implying 'something' must be sacrificed for a new reality to be established. Clouds obscuring the sun serve as a reminder to the mind that through its judgemental beliefs and deeply ingrained unconscious 'programs', it blocks the way to seeing life 'as it is'. It is time to address these core issues. Only in so doing may the door to the miraculous open wide... **inside**...

Celestial Light

Quality: Love
Absolute Aspect: Intelligence
Geometry: Divine matrix
Rainbow Sphere: Love

Contemplation

*The vision was fleeting... barely registering as such in her deepening awareness... but it was clear and left no doubt as to its profundity. When the Call of the Eternal strikes a chord that's vaguely familiar... fleeting visions become lasting impressions... and the whole being falls into alignment. Such was the timeliness of this event. But far more than this, it was the feeling it evoked... a sense of remembering... recalling that which had long, long ago been forgotten... a sense of being home. Gentle souls, rainbow light devoid of colour and fields of gold were the unseen backdrop to this fair land. A child, a young boy, played with ease... alone... yet not. He walked... he danced... explored... rested upon the air... toyed with creatures naked to the eye and sang sweet songs to one whose silence was marked by its apparent absence. There was nothing to do, nowhere to go... the entire panorama held an air of totality... and Presence. Esmerelda knew this place... she also recognised the child. He was her. The fall had, until now, erased all memory; such was the decree, the irrevocable Law of Return. Born instead to a world of incessant war, petty squabbles and disagreements over nothing, she had plumbed the depths of despair on more occasions than she cared to remember. Tired of this warring planet, tired of standing on the bridge between one side and another, she had finally reached the end of the road... In abject humility, she let go and, in so doing, came face to face with herself. She knew the war intimately. It was nothing to do with anyone else; it had been inside **her** all along. She sighed... one long, gut-wrenching, soul-destroying... cry. Then she smiled. It was time to weave a new fabric... time to paint a different picture... It was time for a new vision!*

Guidance

Chaos, as the script reveals, is very much dependent upon the perspective of one who observes the 'war'. Standing resolutely on the bridge between one faction and another or coming down wholly and completely on the part of one to the exclusion of its opposite is to ceaselessly energise the 'war of two'. The very act of observing their discrepancies is to ensure the continuance of polarised consciousness, whether you are directly engaging with the respective poles or not. The only recourse, as Esmerelda discovered, is to weave a new tapestry, preferably with fabric never before encountered. In other words, if you change the record, you emit a more harmonious frequency, which, in turn, directly impacts reality as you and others experience it. And this is the gift that *Chaos,* as a vision, brings. Ponder deeply the nuances within the script. In letting go, Esmerelda allowed the land she knew as home to return. She had a choice as to whether to feed the war, in defence of self, or to surrender all to the burgeoning light within. Which do you choose? Remember, the fields of light are **always** there... you just have to get out of your own way to appreciate it.

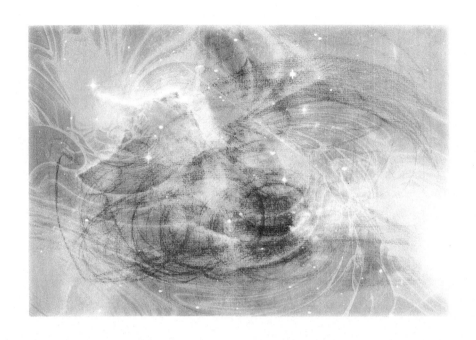

Chaos

Quality: Call of the Eternal
Absolute Aspect: Love
Geometry: None
Rainbow Sphere: Beauty

Contemplation

He couldn't understand. All his life he had grasped every opportunity. He had reached the pinnacle of success, amassed considerable standing in his community and accumulated material possessions aplenty. He had loved and lost, laughed and cried and filled every minute of each day throughout his rich and colourful life with all that his questing heart desired. But now, for the first time, he faced uncertainty. On the verge of consummating his ultimate ambition, he doubted his ability; the familiar buzz was not there, the thrill of the 'deal', gone. Suddenly, all he believed himself to be meant nothing. Inside he was bereft, and as unfathomable emptiness tore his life apart, he bore witness to the movie of his life. Every last detail he absorbed, all measure of blame, shame, and ruthless ambition he took into his thirst-quenching heart until, in a moment of clarity, he recognised the cause of his demise. He had prostituted his inner self upon the altar of desire that he may fit in... so he could belong. But he didn't, and he never would. How could he possibly belong when the very core of his being had been banished? How may he fit in when so much of him lay buried in the graveyard of pained experience? And how may he live, really live, with his heart encased in stone? He was dead... inside... But all was not lost. In the ensuing stillness, hope echoed upon wings of the Soul as every last part of himself, every part he had consigned to perpetual darkness, was called home... And in the quiet, inner space between each in-breath and out-breath, he allowed all those he'd long ago denied a voice...

Guidance

It is no coincidence the character in our story marries perfectly with the title and Soul alignment quality of this vision, as transition from grub to butterfly and personality to Soul is identical. A caterpillar's only purpose in life is to eat. Gorging, day by day, until it can consume no more, it eventually turns inwards to digest every last nutrient. Outwardly, it's an empty shell, but inside, as the real work begins, the sacrificial grub surrenders all to fulfil a destiny set the moment it was born. The character in our story is no different. Suddenly, in a moment of clarity, he knew his life was meaningless and he would neither find peace through seeking outside of himself nor understand the predictable control dramas playing out in his life with such regularity. In short, he had fallen into a space where he knew, beyond all doubt, he was nothing. *Chrysalis* invites you to step into nothingness, to view your life as a movie, to accept those parts – both light and shadow – you have denied for so very long and to create a space inside yourself where they may feel safe to come home. Allow the sacrificial grub to inspire your leap into the unknown... As you forsake all... as you savour the sweetest nectar... inwardly, you fly.

Chrysalis

Quality: Metamorphosis
Absolute Aspect: Intelligence
Geometry: Divine matrix
Rainbow Sphere: Beauty

Contemplation

The bridge of light was in place, a community of a like kind was assembled in purpose upon the inner planes and the Blessed One was poised in readiness to transmit the Perennial Wisdom... Time was of the essence... time not determined by the world of clocks nor even by the order of cycles great and small. No, this time was measured by something far more subtle and infinitely more profound. It was set by Presence. In the heart of the Great Mother, the Blessed One drew unto itself the mantle of silence and, with no arising nor falling, gave of its breath to the Eternal Stillness... As air moved twixt the in and the out, without beginning or end, the Will of One was thus assured of purpose... for the Eternal One Breath flows through all... and the Fount of All Wisdom lies in all, like unto One... And so, as the Beloved received, so did it transmit, as it inhaled, so did it breathe out, for the Way of One is in parlance with all... It gives as it receives, it loves as it finds and it wills as it may... such is the Way made present to all... And for aeons it has been so... round upon round of the hidden mystery made available to those who would know the ways of the Great Ones, to those who may, in their infinite yearning, sample a droplet from the sacred chalice or poise for a moment amidst their Holy Presence. But the will of the small, persistent in its ways, is obscurer of Truth... and though the Fount overflows... Its Voice is unheard...

Guidance

Five facets of the diamond[18] convey the multi-layered presence of the Soul as it expresses through kingdoms in nature. *City of Light* is aligned to the Group Soul, community on the inner planes. In the script lies purpose – high vibratory beings have gathered to further evolution of a species, such as humanity – however, its message is far more profound than this. The 'City' refers to both a gathering and the 'Inner Ashram', a space in time where the Great Ones – Masters of Wisdom, Deva beings of the highest order and many more who have transcended the confines of their lower vibratory nature – meet in furtherance of Divine Purpose. Teachings are received, thought-forms are created and purpose is set before being sent outward through substance to ensure all sentient beings are assured of their return to the One. As the great Cosmic Clock echoes the Perennial Wisdom throughout the ages, balance through order, including destruction and annihilation, brings all to fruition. And herein lies the direction of this vision. Set aside your desire to belong, to 'join your tribe', and turn your attention inwards. The Group Soul, of which you are so much a part, is already there; the wisdom you seek is present for the knowing... Be still... heed the whispers in silence... now fine-tune your senses... and feel the Great Ones gathering...

---

[18] *City of Light, Family of Light, Presence, Solar Angel, The Well.*

City of Light

Quality: Group-Consciousness
Absolute Aspect: Will
Geometry: None
Rainbow Sphere: Beauty

Contemplation

And so spoke the Word, "Assimilate within the cause... conversion is not to change something into something else... but to assimilate first... then express." Esmerelda pondered deeply... profound teachings, appearing from 'nowhere' as if by magic, had struck her to her core. She drank them in, taking them deep into her heart, and silently repeated over and over, as a mantra, "assimilate within the cause... assimilate within the cause... assimilate..." What could it possibly mean? *The Voice in the Silence responded, "Absolute is constant yet contains the conditions to express **out** through its substance. It is not space and light, it is the **substance** of space and light. It is the substance of all things, the condition to create the many, yet is constant (unchanging). Cause is constant but once expressed, it 'converts' into a change."* She wasn't sure this helped at all – it was way outside her remit, her appreciation of how things were – and she very nearly walked away. But there was a niggling inside; something within her knew the validity of these teachings, recognised their worth and their relevance to her role in the world. Esmerelda persisted. Piece by piece she teased the message apart, applying each fragment to her frame of reference, creating more mantras that she might assimilate their intrinsic meaning, until, with her mind a mess of knots, she let go. The image beckoned, and as ever, it was light that drew her. Onwards she walked, further and further into its substance, yet never any closer to recognising the elusive Cause. *The Word spoke again, "Consciousness does not convert back into the Cause as consciousness **is** the Cause."* She stopped dead in her tracks as realisation dawned. She would never know the Cause by reaching **towards** it. It was an **out**pouring force; she had to allow 'it' to come to her. In an instant she felt its Presence, and as she surrendered, her heart swelled until it was consumed completely... there was nothing, absolutely nothing, save the Cause. *Then, another clue... "Absorption..."*[19] In consummate surrender, 'she' knew she was mere 'substance' within the Cause, a vessel through which it may 'express' its Will; nothing more, nothing less. Furthermore, she knew beyond any doubt, that its Will was Love, Divine Love. Esmerelda allowed its mystery to flow through her. She knew the Word, its message, she knew its power and, with crystalline clarity, she expressed its wisdom. *"Conversion, as the Cause, is a formula of creation. Its substance and means of expression is consciousness, using assimilation within the Cause as its method. Absorption is the means by which consciousness (substance) 'converts', through assimilation, into the Cause; it is the way of return. Its method is surrender."*

Guidance

When a unit of consciousness, such as you, delivers every last facet of itself to the service of the whole, it ceases to exist; identification is wholly and completely with the Cause. All that remains is its Will expressing as an outpouring of Love through its substance: **you**... But first, you must let go... and assimilate...

---

[19] See *Absorption.*

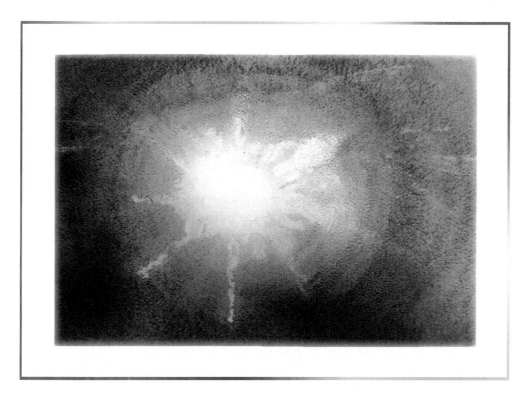

Conversion

Quality: Expression
Absolute Aspect: Will
Geometry: None
Rainbow Sphere: Rainbow

Contemplation

They met as they had always met, inside the Hall of Learning, where all that is possible to know is known. However, on this occasion, as Consciousness sensed the presence of the Shining One long before it put in an appearance, a ripple of excitement, barely detectable to others in its vicinity, echoed throughout its substance. "Greetings, my friend," sounded the luminous being without employing words. "We have a task before us concerning the future well-being of a world for which we are equally responsible and for which you must be prepared. We must journey together into four realms, each a kingdom in its own right, with which I am far more familiar than you, to engage with those whose remit is to work in the lesser, denser fields of service. We must engage intimately with those whose presence is not usually made visible to any outsider and who would, in normal circumstances, be hostile to any infringement of their domain. However, as it is recognised that your participation in this is paramount, exceptions have been made and they wish you to know that, in furtherance of mutual cooperation, you are welcome in their respective worlds." Consciousness, of course, was a willing participant and with heart steeped in compassion, engaged gracefully with each element as it made its presence felt. Each told a story, hiding nothing from its discriminating gaze, of great abuse being inflicted upon the Mother by a race too wrapped up in its own interests to care. In the element of air, it came through destructive thought, in water, through emotional baggage, earth bore the brunt of their toxic waste and in fire, perhaps the greatest affront of all, was their abject denial of Spirit. "Mankind has evolved to become a master of destruction on many levels," admonished the Shining One, with more than a hint of sadness. "In this journey you have seen evidence of their blatant disregard for any life form other than their own, and even in that they are self-obsessed. The tragedy, as you have witnessed through my faithful servants, is that this mess is not just physical in origin, but its roots lie in more subtle soil – thoughts, emotions, psychic abuse and spiritual misdirection – of which they are largely unaware." "And this is why I am here," Consciousness replied. "I am mediator between your domain and theirs. Mine is the task of helping them to see clearly, to assist them in waking up, and in me lies responsibility to stimulate change in them."

Guidance

Cooperation is one of six visions[20] working together in co-creative partnership to bring peace and harmony to the whole. Now, at a critical juncture in earth's history, the message of this vision could not be clearer... Consciousness changes matter... it is imperative we, as a race, wake up... and it begins with you...

---

[20] Four elements – *Air, Earth, Fire* and *Water, Brilliance.*

Cooperation

Quality: Co-Creation
Absolute Aspect: Will
Geometry: Torus
Rainbow Sphere: Light

Contemplation

Cosmic Orchestra, in the context of time, is the autumn equinox, whose signature force is the water element – your feelings. It signifies a time when the fruits of summer have given of their best, when the nights start to draw in and when the leaves start to wither and fall. It is the season of harvest, a time when the earth reclaims its children and when the season of death and decay is upon us. It includes the pagan festival of Samhain, or Halloween, where the veils between worlds are thinned and remembrance of those who have gone before is ritually honoured. *Cosmic Orchestra* brings together all these qualities. Fluidity is its clear autograph. A sheet of water, like a veil, invites you to explore the shifting sands beyond; an endless stream highlights the inevitable sense of loss endured when that which was of this realm moves on. And yet, all is not lost. The vibrant colours of autumn show there is beauty in death, something to be celebrated. Hands of friendship reach out from a realm that knows only light, a land where all is forever whole and death is but a long-forgotten memory, captive to the cyclic bonds of time. The all-inclusive vibration of Love asks that you look beyond the veil of death, sacrifice all that is bound by its governance and embrace that which is your true heritage. Remember, the caterpillar is sacrificial lamb to the butterfly; in metamorphosis nothing ever dies. In order to experience the richness of life, change is inevitable. *Now take a step back, bring your mind and attention to your breath and feel all that you perceive to be lost as it washes through you. Let grief run its course. Allow its quiet inevitability to permeate every last cell in your body, all measure of attachment in your heart and every ounce of resistance in your mind. Then celebrate the gift of life. Breathe... breathe deep... breathe again... Breathe in the gift of gratitude for all that was. Allow each refreshing breath to fill your mind with acceptance... every expansion of your breast to instil reverence in your heart... and know each tick of the Cosmic Clock is a welcome home... a welcome home... to you. Now rest.*

Guidance – balance is alchemical

The combined essence of eight linked visions is an invitation to tune into the natural rhythm – birth, life, decay and death – expressed through the four seasons (*Ostara*: Spring, *Cosmic Orchestra*: Autumn, *Woodhenge*: Summer, *Unconquered Sun*: Winter) – and to marry it with those areas in your life symbolised by the four elements (*Fire*: Spirit, *Earth*: physical form, *Air*: thought, *Water*: feeling). Restoration of balance is an alchemical process that blends, harmonises and transforms 'the lowliest grub into a creature of the air'. Remember, you have the capacity to 'fly' as much as the caterpillar. Nature demonstrates this. It is time to reconnect to the pulse of life, to be the inner alchemist and to restore natural rhythm and order in your life... but first, you must let go...

Cosmic Orchestra

Quality: Through the Veil
Absolute Aspect: Love
Geometry: Metatron's cube
Rainbow Sphere: Light

Contemplation

First, a spark, a thought inspired through vision, impressed upon a mind yet to know a brain. Rooted deep within a heart that yearned to feel its pulse, the seed of purpose rested. All around, the building blocks of flesh gathered in their subtle ways to bring substance to the form. But this vision in the making was but a story with no teller... a song without a voice... merely miracle in creation that had yet to share its splendour with a world that had no shape. But the weaver of the Way knew well its craft, and inert its progeny remained, perfect in its pristine mystery, until all was met as it was set. So it waited. Then, expressing outwards through its breath, it emitted its note... and with it... came life... The breath was deep... a powerful inhalation accompanied by inner organs awakening to their purpose. Life had taken its hold. Barely discernible as human, the luminous one began its sojourn into the world of matter. Without gender, it was complete in itself... its presence wholly with the One who gave it life. Every thought arose through its mind, every breath was its song, each tender moment an expression of its love... every deed presented in celebration of the One it loved beyond all else. Its heart had yet to feel the pain of loss, its eyes to see the glamour of the pleasured way and its tender Soul to know the agony of death. More than this, it knew not that soon it would forget... that soon it would be captive, held in a world it would come to despise... But not yet, for now his eyes rested upon the beauty he had made, the seeds he had sown and the love he shared as a mark of his gratitude. Unaware of the change, he regarded himself as male... and so began the forgetting... entwined within a fabric of two...

Guidance

Nine visions[21] mark the relationship of Spirit to matter as it is expressed outwards through a particle within its substance. Complete in itself, each vision charts a course from Source, through multiple layers of expression, to reach the deepest level of forgetfulness before effecting a way of return. Inspired by Buddhist meditation practice in which the suffering of the world is inhaled and then exhaled as compassionate radiance, *Creation* is a return to the original Self. In the great cycle of existence relayed through the script, it marks the point at which Spirit makes its first appearance into the world of physical form to herald an era of peace, innocence and wonderment, where concepts of 'you' and 'I' are barely sparks in the mind of one who dreams. Three golden nuggets at its heart highlight the essential nature of the golden being: compassion. But its beauty lies beyond that experienced by one who feels; compassion, as implied here, is an expression of that which it **is**. The golden eye rests with One, origin of a spark, seed to those who shine within a presence that is All. As the tale of two draws to a close... as the luminous one draws deep its breath... it sparks remembrance...

---

[21] *Creation, Emergence, Empty Vessel, Eye Eye, Mind, Phone Home, Recognition, River of Souls, Welcome.*

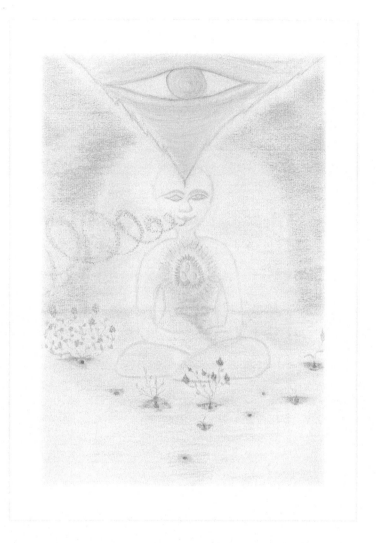

Creation

Quality: Heart in Compassion
Absolute Aspect: Love
Geometry: None
Rainbow Sphere: Beauty

Contemplation

In the heart of a forest, far, far away, in an age when the air breaths fresh and clean and the rivers run pure and undefiled, the mighty oak spreads wide its boughs to expose a heart open to all. Custodian to this fair land, it stands as witness to the comings and goings, toing and froing, of those who walk in reverence upon the land and those who hail its lofty governance in wings of song across the vast ocean of the skies. Outer expression to an inner magnificence, its countenance brooks no denial, for the wisdom of ages pulses through its veins and strength born through adversity renders it worthy of its undisputed sovereignty. Custodian it is, but, in spite of its grandeur, it is but a shadow to the One, who stands beyond the mists of time and apart from the profane. Giver of life, orchestrator to the stars, haven to the realms of nine and bridge to the highest and the low, the One Tree cradles every ilk, shape and form within its breast. Origin of all wisdom and home to creatures great and small, it is Mother to the past, keeper of Light and guardian to all that moves within the night. So as one appears as kin to the other, alike in form though distinct in density, each tree, in its expression, is an age apart. And still, there are others, less imposing in structure, whose purpose is of such profound significance that heaven would fail in its mission without their participation. Those whose appearance is less than vertical, whose structure is far more delicate yet whose intricate web of filaments, fibres, flora and spawn, infused with intelligence of irrefutable order, is able to unite where others fail. Those whose nourishing blanket of green conceals sprinklings of magic... where one perhaps, with a discerning eye, may bear witness to the little folk celebrating in wonder the miracle of nature's abundance...

Guidance

Five visions[22] serve as awakeners to the intelligent life forms that dwell amongst the flora and fauna of our majestic woodlands. *Custodian,* as the image reveals, is the mighty oak. Appearing from an ethereal, other-worldly realm, as if it has, quite literally, stepped through an opened door, an imposing 'leafy' figure takes on a position of strength in preparation for engaging with its new reality: Metatron's cube, which, as Spirit bridge to the subtle realms, **is** a portal. Herein is a call to governance. It asks you to acknowledge the vital role you play as custodian to your innermost being, to take responsibility for the small selves dictating your every reactive response and to see they are as acorns to the mighty oak or cells to your physical form. Bear witness to their powers to destroy, unite or renew and know that, as with all seedlings, they will at some point in time ripen to bear fruit as reality. Responsibility for their governance is yours and yours alone.
Be clear on this.

---

[22] *Custodian, Enchantment, Stability, Wallington Wood, World Tree.*

Custodian

Quality: Vitality
Absolute Aspect: Intelligence
Geometry: Metatron's cube
Rainbow Sphere: Will

Contemplation

One foot before the other, spiral laying bare before her, she walks... How long since she first set out on her journey? How many forms has she worn, veils has she crossed and worlds has she seen? How many? As ever, spiral leads the way, no choice but to follow. Always her every existence, she wonders now at its purpose. No closer than when she first accepted its invitation... so long, long ago, she begins to doubt there will ever be an answer... questions barely have a frame of reference, yet still she walks... one foot resolutely placed before the other... never ceasing her quest. Until, as the spiral reaches another turn, she relinquishes her search. Finally at peace, she welcomes the land upon which she rests, the air that swells her breast, love that fuels her heart and mind that runs with light so clear. The darkness inside her smiles... at last it knows... the quest is the veil, all else is light... so obvious really... Why had it taken her so very, very long to see?

Guidance

The way of the spiritual seeker is one with which we can all identify. It defines the eternal quest for truth and, particularly in this day and age, the relationship between the seeker and 'his' guru. Three visions –*Devotion Clarity, Devotion Compassion* and *Devotion Unity* – employ symbol and potent visual imagery to map out its passage. When combined with the script, they assist you to recognise the pitfalls on the path and to finally cease looking outside of yourself for answers that may only be found within. The longest journey a man may ever undertake, a mere 12 inches, leads from the head to the heart; it defines the seeker in a way that is beyond redemption and is the cornerstone for each of these visions. *Clarity* brings the gift of clear sight in a mind that is beyond thought. The geometry at the heart of the headless figure, stellated dodecahedron, is synonymous with Christ-Consciousness, the union of heart and mind. However, it is the figure itself, with a watchful eye above, that claims attention. Notice her position relative to the geometry in the foreground; she has clearly set herself apart from its symbolic quality – bliss – to become the detached observer, has reached a level in transparency where her whole being is one with the land and is little disturbed by a mind clouded with deluded thought. In quiet solitude, she knows the search is over, the journey she began, so many lifetimes ago, echoes its finale, and as she watches the last remnants of her former self dissolve, she understands the gift of the spiral... instrument of the veil.

Devotion Clarity

Quality: Clear-Seeing
Absolute Aspect: Intelligence
Geometry: Dodecahedron/stellated dodecahedron, spiral
Rainbow Sphere: Truth

Contemplation

One foot before the other, spiral laying bare before her, she walks... How long since she first set out on her journey? How many forms has she worn, veils has she crossed and worlds has she seen? How many? As ever, spiral leads the way, no choice but to follow. Always her every existence, she wonders now at its purpose. No closer than when she first accepted its invitation... so long, long ago, she begins to doubt there will ever be an answer... questions barely have a frame of reference, yet still she walks... one foot resolutely placed before the other... never ceasing her quest. Until, as the spiral reaches another turn, she relinquishes her search. Finally at peace, she welcomes the land upon which she rests, the air that swells her breast, love that fuels her heart and mind that runs with light so clear. The darkness inside her smiles... at last it knows... the quest is the veil, all else is light... so obvious really... Why had it taken her so very, very long to see?

Guidance

The way of the spiritual seeker is one with which we can all identify. It defines the eternal quest for truth and, particularly in this day and age, the relationship between the seeker and 'his' guru. Three visions – *Devotion Clarity, Devotion Compassion* and *Devotion Unity* – employ symbol and potent visual imagery to map out its passage. When combined with the commentary, they assist you to recognise the pitfalls on the path and to finally cease looking outside of yourself for answers that may only be found within. The longest journey a man may ever undertake, a mere 12 inches, leads from the head to the heart; it defines the seeker in a way that is beyond redemption and is the cornerstone for each of these visions. *Compassion* opens the way to the heart. The geometry in the foreground, dodecahedron, is of particular significance, for it is synonymous with bliss – probably the most seductive trap on the path and one that may take many years, even lifetimes, to move through. The seeker has to realise that it is merely a stage, that at some point the bubble will burst and that without clarity of mind, the heart is little able to be of real service to the whole. The message of this vision is resoundingly clear. Enjoy the beauty of your opened heart, know every ecstatic state is transitory and keep on riding the spiral regardless of outer appearances. Remember, the way of compassion arises naturally in one whose heart has known the darkness of the light within.

Devotion Compassion

Quality: Acceptance
Absolute Aspect: Love
Geometry: Dodecahedron/stellated dodecahedron, spiral
Rainbow Sphere: Truth

Contemplation

One foot before the other, spiral laying bare before her, she walks... How long since she first set out on her journey? How many forms has she worn, veils has she crossed and worlds has she seen? How many? As ever, spiral leads the way, no choice but to follow. Always her every existence, she wonders now at its purpose. No closer than when she first accepted its invitation... so long, long ago, she begins to doubt there will ever be an answer... questions barely have a frame of reference, yet still she walks... one foot resolutely placed before the other... never ceasing her quest. Until, as the spiral reaches another turn, she relinquishes her search. Finally at peace, she welcomes the land upon which she rests, the air that swells her breast, love that fuels her heart and mind that runs with light so clear. The darkness inside her smiles... at last it knows... the quest is the veil, all else is light... so obvious really... Why had it taken her so very, very long to see?

Guidance

The way of the spiritual seeker is one with which we can all identify. It defines the eternal quest for truth and, particularly in this day and age, the relationship between the seeker and 'his' guru. Three visions – *Devotion Clarity, Devotion Compassion* and *Devotion Unity* – employ symbol and potent visual imagery to map out its passage. When combined with the script, they assist you to recognise the pitfalls on the path and to finally cease looking outside of yourself for answers that may only be found within. The longest journey a man may ever undertake, a mere 12 inches, leads from the head to the heart; it defines the seeker in a way that is beyond redemption and is the cornerstone for each of these visions. *Unity* is not only the end of the search, it also marks the demise of one who seeks. Neither geometry, with associated symbolism, nor transitory figure grace the land; a solitary eye is all that remains. But this vehicle of vision does not belong to any one or any thing; it appears, as would a window when the blinds have been removed, a natural outcome following a sequence of events. Place yourself on the other side of this portal in the sky, watch the great spiral as it moves through existence and see those within form inextricably entwined with its passage as they journey through life. Then witness their death, their transition through the veil to the space where you now abide. How does it feel to be life beyond the spiral? The search is over... the seeker is no more... spiral continues... do you?

Devotion Unity

Quality: Inter-Being
Absolute Aspect: Will
Geometry: Spiral
Rainbow Sphere: Truth

Contemplation

*In the locus of the soul, they meet for the first time... two brothers, each a mirror of the other, though they know it not... One, who loves beyond measure, his heart an open door, is a magnet to those in need... His motto, "To love and include," determines the course of his life. The other, less well loved, sees with a light so clear, even the most depraved in spirit are struck by its radiance. His discriminating gaze knows all things intimately... Naked, in Truth, is his way... no-thing is exempt... not even himself... Heavenly twins, two wings of a bird, are the brothers, two. They are the circle and point, the singer and song... as far apart as ocean and sky yet each cut from the same cloth, incomplete without the other... and still, even now, they know it not... The sacred space knows them well, has witnessed their forever journeys in silence as deep as the grave... So intent on their purpose, each following his own course, they are blinded to all but their own... But now, at this timely juncture, in this place that is so alive yet **still**... they can hear it... faint at first but clear and growing in intensity... Soon, each heeds the Voice in the Silence, feels the beat of his brother's heart as his own... knows the great gifts each has bestowed, the journey they have shared... and then, in recognition, they turn towards each other... and smile... as the mirror cracks...*

Guidance

Ancient teachings[23] speak of two essential qualities that align the heart with the mind and are needed before access to the kingdom of the Soul may be granted. As inseparable as the air from the breath, a drop from the ocean or a seed from its flower, each is fuel for the other, and together they birth the ultimate in Truth, wisdom. Appropriately expressed through two visions, *Secret Garden* and *Dharmakaya*, they help you not only to recognise qualities of compassion and clear-seeing within yourself but also to consciously live your life in accordance with their united principles. *Dharmakaya* is the 'less loved' brother whose way is naked truth. It takes its name from the ultimate expression of Buddha, the Truth body, and asks you to look at truth, the whole truth and nothing but the truth – your beliefs, perceptions and, above all, your relationship to truth within you. The image displays a sky ablaze with light. Demons, light beings, dark clouds and even a 'bird' in flight grace the foreground. Every aspect is called into question, from the brightest light to darkest days – inside and out. The calling of this vision is to examine, **deeply**, every aspect. Then, when you are stripped to your core... when you are naked and vulnerable... you are ready to recognise your brother... and smile...

---

[23] Mahayana Buddhism.

Dharmakaya

Quality: Ultimate Truth
Absolute Aspect: Will
Geometry: None
Rainbow Sphere: Truth

Contemplation

*Darkness was upon her... Divine Darkness... It was black, pitch black. Not a single pinprick of light disturbed its perfect mystery... yet it fitted her oh-so perfectly... She who loved Light, who heralded its majesty, and chose it above all else, was touched, beyond measure, by its absence. This consummate blackness, this great cosmic womb, was the most trusted space... a space where she had disappeared without even knowing she had gone... It was so safe, so secure... and so... her. Forgotten for so, so long, her acquaintance with the land of shadows returned to expose its familiarity. She knew this place... she knew it well... Surrendering to its Presence, she welcomed it into her heart... and watched in stupendous admiration as the miracle of existence flowed through her... She saw the Great Cause express through its substance. Symbols, atoms, molecules, **sound** and geometric structure... all unfolding in perfect symmetry to build myriad forms... Single-celled organisms, planets and stars to galaxies and immeasurable universes... all were orchestrated according to its Divine Architecture... None was exempt... each followed Absolute order... one, two, followed by three and seven... and then the many... Such was the way of existence... such was substance unfolding within itself... and such was divinity expressing its perfection through... **her**. Esmerelda was stunned to silence... Then she was gone.*

Guidance

Seven visions[24] illustrate the involutionary journey of creation using geometric form. Through ever-expanding rounds of concentric circles, they highlight divinity, expressing first as one (*Through the Portal*), followed by one appearing as two (*Becoming*) and then duality as separate entities (*Divine Darkness, Divine Inspiration*). Completing the process is the trinity (*Love, Will, Intelligence*), precursors to the full divine matrix, the blueprint of all creative expression within the manifested world (*Gnosis*). Duality, the realm of polarised consciousness, is not only the playground of this vision, it also marks the nature of our existence, setting the stage for every possible conflict played out in our daily lives. However, once understood, it is also the route to salvation. The beauty of contemplating, understanding and above all **being** the natural creative force of the universe is that all apparent opposites reach a point of wholeness within, to the point where they cease to exist as separate. *Becoming*, in spite of its intricate geometric structures, was an invitation to return to the Zero. It asked that you set aside your need to be on one side or the other and engage with the pure creative flow of the universe as a whole, the primal Cause. Two separate particles, yin and yang being feminine and masculine respectively, take this to the next stage, appeal to classic archetypes and encourage you to explore them within your life. *Divine Darkness,* is a call to your soft, gentle nature; the inner mother whose heart holds no bars, whose arms extend to the far reaches of the universe and whose boundless love is the home of the Soul. She arises naturally when your heart is still and your mind silent...

---

[24] *Becoming, Divine Darkness, Divine Inspiration, Gnosis (Intelligence, Purity, Tranquillity), Through the Portal.*

Divine Darkness

Quality: Duality: Yin
Absolute Aspect: Love
Geometry: Seed of life, tree of life
Rainbow Sphere: Light

Contemplation

*The Mighty One flexed its cosmic muscle, drew deep its breath and with fixed intent exhaled Purpose. It was ready to express... ready to create... but far more than this... it was ready to **play**! The time to reveal through its substance was nigh... the Way of Fire, imminent... expression of the All, paramount. He felt the ripples, the vibration as, like a mighty river, its thunderous current surged through his being. He felt its power... knew its purpose... understood its call to action. It inspired a response in him that he could not possibly ignore... had no choice but to succumb to... So he let go... welcomed it into his heart... and, in stupendous admiration, watched as the miracle of existence flowed through him... He bore witness to the Great Cause expressing outwards through its substance. Symbols, atoms, molecules, **sound** and geometric structure... all unfolding in perfect symmetry to build myriad forms... Single-celled organisms, planets and stars to galaxies and immeasurable universes... all were orchestrated according to its Divine Architecture... None was exempt... each followed Absolute order... one, two, followed by three and seven... and then the many... Such was the Way of Fire... such was substance unfolding within itself... and such was divinity expressing its perfection through... **him**. The meditator was stunned to silence... In an instant, he was gone, then awake... With eyes wide open... he began to play*

Guidance

Seven visions[25] illustrate the involutionary journey of creation using geometric form. Through ever-expanding rounds of concentric circles, they highlight divinity, expressing first as one (*Through the Portal*), followed by one appearing as two (*Becoming*) and then duality as separate entities (*Divine Darkness, Divine Inspiration*). Completing the process is the trinity, expanding outwards to the full divine matrix, the blueprint of all creative expression within the manifested world (*Gnosis*). Duality, the realm of polarised consciousness, is not only the playground of this vision, it also marks the nature of our existence, setting the stage for every possible conflict played out in our daily lives. However, once understood, it is also the route to salvation. The beauty of contemplating, understanding and above all **being** the natural creative force of the universe as it flows through you is that all apparent opposites reach a point of wholeness within, to the point where they cease to exist as separate. Two separate particles, yin and yang being feminine and masculine respectively, appeal to classic archetypes and encourage you to explore them within your life. *Divine Inspiration* is a call to Spirit. Its essence is Light, the divine masculine, and it challenges you to engage wholeheartedly with the force of becoming... but not as an expression of personal agenda... It compels you to succumb... completely... to the Will of the Divine... to resolutely allow it to express Purpose through you... as you **play**...

---

[25] *Becoming, Divine Darkness, Divine Inspiration, Gnosis (Intelligence, Purity, Tranquillity), Through the Portal.*

Divine Inspiration

Quality: Duality: Yang
Absolute Aspect: Will
Geometry: Seed of life, tree of life
Rainbow Sphere: Light

Contemplation

*Surely her eyes must be deceiving her? It was the same brick wall, the identical, solid, entire... brick wall... she walked past everyday... But, no, there it was again... halfway up, as clear as day, and shimmering as if it had always been there... a doorway... without a door... Beyond, as far as her eyes could see, was light – diamond-clear light, such as she had never before envisioned. It vanished as miraculously as it had appeared. She was dumbstruck! But the significance of its timely arrival was not lost on her... she knew it to be of tremendous import in her search... knew it was key to unlocking her fixed beliefs concerning the role of mind and its relation to consciousness... and, most of all, she knew this symbolic opening was the route to her innermost Self... where mind, as the trickster, could be identified... **clearly**... for what it was. The Voice in the Silence echoed her thoughts... "Mind is an expression of Absolute and therefore within all things, on every level; there is no-thing that is not mind, for it is within expression of the All. Consciousness is the river, the substance, within which mind flows. It recognises and ignites thought-forms using mind as its vessel – it is its means of communication. In alignment with its Will, purpose is thus expressed through all forms, regardless of their level of intelligence." The penny dropped. She experienced mind as a mechanism by which layers of expression, through particles within substance, communicated with each other. She witnessed consciousness as the impetus for creation of thought... and knew it to be the driver of the vehicle... knew that without it, mind would have nowhere to go... "So why," she asked, "does it seem thoughts are always running the show?"*

Guidance

As well as answering Esmerelda's question, the script helps us to see that the route to higher consciousness is forged through the medium of mind and serves as a bridge between the dense vibrations of matter and the more subtle harmonies of Soul and Spirit. The error lies in mistaking the conveyer, or bridge, for that which is the Real. Making this distinction is an important part of the path to wholeness. Mind must be seen for the illusory nature that is its signature force, the origin of thought must be known to be other than its own nature and consciousness must be recognised as sole expression when mind is no longer present. As well as the obvious, *Doorway,* through its imagery, offers many 'tricks' of light that may, or may not, lead to the 'Real'. Whether you choose the steps, the bridge or to tread a precipitous path along the beam of light to the door is irrelevant; the pivotal point in recognising the origin of all appearances, whatever their apparent expression, is where consciousness abides. *Doorway* asks you to dive deep into the substance of mind, to experience the great gift it bestows in introducing its lowest expression to its highest and then, when all conditions have been exhausted, to shatter its reflective mirror...

Doorway

Quality: Building the Bridge
Absolute Aspect: Will
Geometry: None
Rainbow Sphere: Mind

Contemplation

They met as they had always met, inside the Hall of Learning, where all that is possible to know is known. However, on this occasion, as Consciousness sensed the presence of the Shining One long before it put in an appearance, a ripple of excitement, barely detectable to others in the vicinity, echoed throughout its substance. "Greetings, my friend," sounded the luminous being without employing words. "We have a task before us concerning the future well-being of a world for which we are equally responsible and for which you must be prepared. We must journey together into four realms, each a kingdom in its own right, with which I am far more familiar than you, to engage with those whose remit is to work in the lesser, denser fields of service. We must engage intimately with those whose presence is not usually made visible to any outsider and who would, in normal circumstances, be hostile to any infringement of their domain. However, it is recognised that your participation in this is paramount, so exceptions have been made and they wish you to know that, in furtherance of mutual cooperation, you are welcome in their respective worlds." Consciousness, of course, was a willing participant and engaged gracefully with each as they made their presence felt. Into the heart of a large, rounded stone they travelled, where a creature – gnarled, twisted and somewhat ugly – paced backwards and forwards, clearly in a state of distress, and was oblivious to their appearance, at least for a while. Consciousness wept as the source of its despair became evident. Surrounding its home, a 'foreign' liquid had reduced the rich earth to sticky blackness and well-tended and lovingly nurtured greenery had started to wither and die. "Mankind triumphs again. Here is evidence of their blatant disregard for life forms other than their own," admonished the Shining One. "The tragedy is that this disgusting mess is not just physical in origin; its roots lie in far more subtle soil – thoughts, emotions, psychic abuse and spiritual misdirection – of which they are sadly completely unaware." "And this is why I am here," Consciousness replied. "I am mediator between your domain and theirs. Mine is the task of making them aware and in me lies responsibility to stimulate change in them."

Guidance

Four facets of the diamond lead into the magical world of nature spirits – *Air* (sylphs), *Earth* (gnomes), *Fire* (salamanders) and *Water* (undines) – each responsible for the maintenance, purification and ultimate balance of their respective domains. A fifth vision, *Brilliance*, is the 'Shining One', a Deva, or angelic being, who has under its direction these 'lesser' creative builders. Tending to the earth, toiling deep underground, placing stones, cutting crystals and painting plants and flowers in innumerable shades of colour are nature's physical guardians, the gnomes. Your physical body and its health and well-being also come under the auspices of their kingdom – time to take notice, wouldn't you say?

Earth

Quality: Physical Form
Absolute Aspect: Intelligence
Geometry: Metatron's cube, seed of life
Rainbow Sphere: Beauty

Contemplation

When the end approaches the beginning... and the journey, with its stories, is but an echo on the wind... When the sun has lost its shadow and the moon consigned to day... When the tribe of many colours is just a pattern in the sky... When the stars have ceased to twinkle, the seasons and the cycles no more complete their turn and the droplet to the ocean has forever more returned... When the glory of emergence sends you crashing to your knees... When the only light remaining is the one you cannot see... And when the end, as the beginning... completes its dance of two... soon you come to recognise the only One is you... Then the Call of the Eternal strikes a chord you've always known... of gentle souls and fields of light, of the land you know is home...

Guidance

Truth is a paradox, and there are many within the opening script; however, the potential of this vision is to lead you beyond the parable of duality to a realm where unity of being is the only way. Central to the image is a figure of eight formed by a snake consuming its own tail, each half mirroring the same scene – one night, the other day. Forming the backdrop, and inspiration for the script, is a gentle being of golden light whose demeanour holds the entire panorama within its soft embrace, as if every vibration it utters brings harmony to the *dance of two*. A solid little house at the pivotal point, whose radiance is in accord with the golden being, outshines the smaller houses featured in each picture, whilst smoke from its chimney forms an upward spiral to touch the brow of the luminous one. There is significant symbology within this simple scene. Sun and moon, as well as depicting night and day, are masculine and feminine; trees, through their roots, reach deep into the earth whilst their branches touch the sky; smoke and its direction shows alignment with the Soul, whilst the little house is the home of Spirit – you. The snake is a powerful metaphor for change, particularly as depicted here in the form of the Ouroboros (the cycle of life, death and rebirth into the realm of the immortals being its signature tune). *Emergence* asks you to be present with duality, in its manifold forms, as it flows through your life. Be the little house at the pivotal point between the two and allow the smoke from your inner fire to ignite the light of the Soul. Soon, you will come to see that *the land you know is home* is not found upon some far-distant shore; it lies here, right now – beneath your feet.

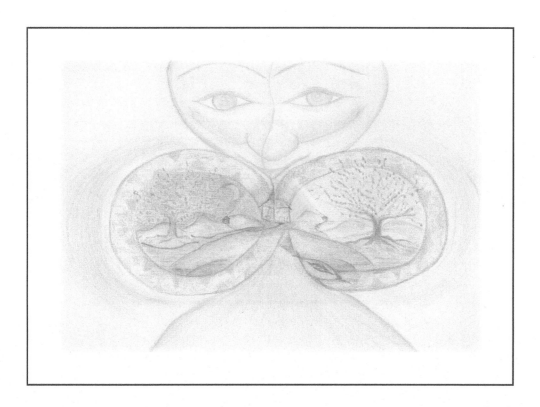

Emergence

Quality: Innocence
Absolute Aspect: Love
Geometry: Ouroborus
Rainbow Sphere: Love

Contemplation

*She cast her mind back to when it began. It was but a moment, one that could so easily have been missed, but no, this split second in time outside of time held within it a lifetime of understanding. As eyes met across an empty street, as minds fused and hearts entrained, they knew, beyond all doubt, that the timelessness of this moment would forever in their hearts remain. It mattered not that one was soon to leave this world, that all would soon be torn apart as friendships met their end, for in this perfect moment, purpose was set. A small body ravaged in pain, children playing without a care and friends locked in recognition, all held within an air of infinite peace heralding the silence of impending transition. She was just nine years old; within two days her friend had died. But, unbeknownst to her, the seed of remembrance had been sown and silently, in the dark recesses of her broken heart, it worked its magic. Over coming decades, it fuelled the search, directed her life and led her to texts that might otherwise have been discarded. In desperation, she tried to find, if only for a moment, the sense of wholeness she had felt so many, many years ago, focusing her mind outwards... books, friends, relationships, **things**, teachings, gurus, spiritual practices... no stone was left unturned, but frustration was her only reward. So she gave up. In an about-face she turned her attention inwards... Bit by bit, piece by piece, she dismantled herself. All she ever thought she was or believed herself to be, she tore away... Systematic in her scrutiny, random in her selection... every thought, feeling, perception and physical discomfort she examined with pristine precision the moment it arose. What was the origin, the root of its cause? What was its substance? Naked, vulnerable, bereft, all was cast aside as she crumbled to nothing... None of these was her... and with her inevitable demise... came peace...*

Guidance

Nine visions[26] mark the relationship of Spirit to matter as it is expressed outwards through a particle within its substance. Complete in itself, each charts a course from Source, through multiple layers of expression, to reach the deepest level of forgetfulness before effecting a way of return. *Empty Vessel* completes the return journey. Inspired by the most profound teachings in Buddhism, those concerning emptiness, it is an invitation to examine intimately all elements that make up the human being – thought, perceptions, feelings, form and consciousness – and to recognise that all are 'empty' of a separate self. Look deeply, really look, and you will see that none of these elements may exist alone; they must co-exist or inter-be with each other. The error lies in taking ownership of them as they arise – making any one, or all, 'mine'. Paradoxically, as only your heart may reveal, in being empty of a separate self, you are full of everything in the cosmos.

---

[26] *Creation, Emergence, Empty Vessel, Eye Eye, Mind, Phone Home, Recognition, River of Souls, Welcome.*

Empty Vessel

Quality: Beyond Illusion
Absolute Aspect: Will
Geometry: None
Rainbow Sphere: Love

Contemplation

In the heart of a forest, far, far away, in an age when the air breaths fresh and clean and the rivers run pure and undefiled, the mighty oak spreads wide its boughs to expose a heart open to all. Custodian to this fair land, it stands as witness to the comings and goings, toing and froing, of those who walk in reverence upon the land and those who hail its lofty governance in wings of song across the vast ocean of the skies. Outer expression to an inner magnificence, its countenance brooks no denial, for the wisdom of ages pulses through its veins and strength born through adversity renders it worthy of its undisputed sovereignty. Custodian it is, but, in spite of its grandeur, it is but a shadow to the One, who stands beyond the mists of time and apart from the profane. Giver of life, orchestrator to the stars, haven to the realms of nine and bridge to the highest and the low, the One Tree cradles every ilk, shape and form within its breast. Origin of all wisdom and home to creatures great and small, it is Mother to the past, keeper of Light and guardian to all that moves within the night. So as one appears as kin to the other, alike in form though distinct in density, each tree, in its expression, is an age apart. And still, there are others, less imposing in structure, whose purpose is of such profound significance that heaven would fail in its mission without their participation. Those whose appearance is less than vertical, whose structure is far more delicate yet whose intricate web of filaments, fibres, flora and spawn, infused with intelligence of irrefutable order, is able to unite where others fail. Those whose nourishing blanket of green conceals sprinklings of magic... where one perhaps, with a discerning eye, may bear witness to the little folk celebrating in wonder the miracle of nature's abundance...

Guidance

Five visions[27] serve as awakeners to the intelligent life forms that dwell amongst the flora and fauna of our majestic woodlands. *Enchantment* is, as title and quality suggest, a sojourn into the subtle realms of nature – fairies, elves, undines, gnomes and the like, as well as elementals responsible for the upkeep of the kingdom. Crucially, as the vision shows, it also includes the vital role fungi, as organic recyclers, play in maintaining a healthy biosphere. The combined force of these creative builders is a continuous, fluid and harmonious interrelationship, exemplified through the triple torus, where no element is superior to or less important than another; working together for the greater good of the whole, they maintain the delicate balance of our environment, without question. Sadly, at this time in earth's history, their efforts are being undermined by not only mankind's inability to recognise their existence but also their relentless denial of nature's perfect rhythm. It is time for this to change – the planet demands it – and it begins with you – **now**.

---

[27] *Custodian, Enchantment, Stability, Wallington Wood, World Tree.*

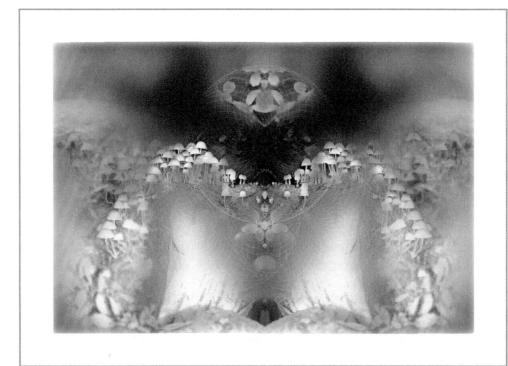

Enchantment

Quality: Faerie Realms
Absolute Aspect: Intelligence
Geometry: Torus, triquetra
Rainbow Sphere: Light

Contemplation

*It was chaos but not as she knew it. This time it was different. In a subtle way, one she couldn't quite put her finger on, it **felt** different. So as all she believed herself to be, all her carefully laid plans, her reasons for being, her loves and hates, all that she treasured most in the world and gave meaning to her life, crumbled to nothing... she remembered. Inside the empty cup, in the stillness... amongst the great ensuing silence... she remembered. Instead of life falling apart, the great wheel had reversed its flow to turn well-heeled programs on their head. A window offering a new reality had appeared as if by magic, like a great opening in the sky, to bring clarity to muddied waters. She remembered... how it felt to have such a joyful spirit of adventure bubbling away inside that she could embrace every eventuality with a smile. She remembered... how, in embracing nothing, she became everything. She remembered... a way of being that brought with it an untold sense of peace... and gratitude. Today, on this day to end all days... she remembered... who she was...*

Guidance

When 'things' get turned on their head, life may be viewed from a fresh 'up-side-down' perspective. Magic happens, moments of wonderment, encased in ordinariness, present untold opportunities for adventure in the most bizarre of fashions and 'life' becomes considerably lighter. It really is quite liberating. *Eureka!* is the path to liberation, where each 'magical moment' leads you from one fiery awakening to the next until nothing of your former self remains. The image, married with script, may be interpreted as a storm in a teacup fuelled by anger from a disgruntled self, but turn it on its head and you are presented with a new panorama. A clear path, showered in soft, golden light, rises above tumultuous waters, fire in the blood vitalises your courageous soul to act with integrity, as upon the Will of the Divine, you follow the road to the stars. This vision is a call to action, but take your lead from the traveller's journey. In every 'aha', pause for a moment, notice a doorway to the infinite laid bare before you, step through with clear intent and you will soon experience stillness present in the midst of chaos; it is there, always. The still small space of the listening heart leads the way. When the lord of the waters has completed his task and the fire of pure spirit runs through your veins, love is a fire that burns through the dross of your daily life to enrich the hearts of all. The spiritual warrior is born but it needs to **act** in order to be of service to the divine. Now listen. Hear the quiet one inside the Great Silence whisper sweet songs to the Soul as it draws your heart to love. Can you hear its message? Can you hum its tune? In the silence of the Great Beyond, it waits... but first, you must act...

Eureka!

Quality: Magical Moments
Absolute Aspect: Will
Geometry: None
Rainbow Sphere: Will

Contemplation

*"The fall from existence gave birth to the fool... Mystery of Spirit concealed in misrule.
In mimicking rule, he plays man for a fool as he dances through time to confuse and delude...
But the jester's disguise is laid bare to wise... so behold him thus, see Truth and the lies.
No-thing is he, just a clown with a part who plays the world game with joy in his heart.
He is naked, an innocent, a child of the morn, just filling a purpose to which he was born."*
Teacher, in their infinite wisdom, had offered this short poem in response to Esmerelda's ponderings,[28] and now she was confused. *"Our last teaching concerned the origin of the primal impulse –the trinity, with its inherent frequencies being established as instrumental in setting the ball rolling – but how?"* Esmerelda's inner ear was fine-tuned to the subtle vibrations emanating from her beloved Mentor. *"Let's translate these qualities into identities that are more familiar. Consider the Source of All to be the Father (Will) whose partner in divinity is the Mother (Love), with the fruit of their union being the Divine Child (Intelligence). You are a product of your parents, carrying the same genetic blueprint while remaining free to express your individuality as life unfolds around and within you; the Divine Child is no different."* So far, she understood! *"Now we get to the crux of your question and the role of thought. Absolute, as we know, is All. There is nothing that isn't it, yet within its Absolute Being-ness is a perpetual state of unfolding. How is this? What inspires it to express?"* Esmerelda's jaw dropped as they continued. *"It is, quite simply, curiosity! Within the dynamics of the Three, inspired through child-like curiosity, arises thought, 'How would it be if Absolute was not absolute? How would it be if it appeared separate from itself, if it were isolated or alone?' Thought, once set in motion, must follow its agreed course, so expression now has another 'vision' within its substance – **un**consciousness, or life in sleep."* They waited for the impact to settle. "So within substance we have Love of the Divine Mother, Will of the Father and Child as an expression of both, but it may not be aware of its roots as it is more than likely asleep?!" *"Yes,"* they laughed, *"and this returns us to the fool. The 'fall' is a metaphor for life in sleep, setting the stage for unconscious beliefs and behavioural patterns to be established, whilst the fool is equally innocent child and, as mind, the 'Lord of Misrule'. Unravelling the matrix of desire-based thought allows the true qualities of mind to be expressed – the Child returns to its innate divinity and the three are again One. So take your lead from the fool. Dare you follow and go where he leads, befriend the unknown, partake of the seed... and surrender your sight in order to see? Have you the courage... Dare you be free?"*

Guidance

One who is at home within herself plays the game but doesn't become it. Outwardly, it presents as wisdom masquerading as a fool.

---

[28] See *Impulse.*

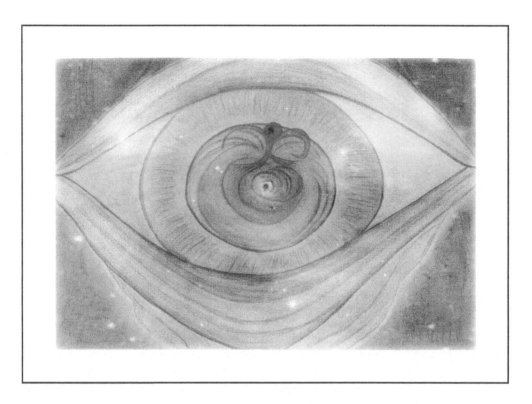

Eye Eye

Quality: Curiosity
Absolute Aspect: Will
Geometry: None
Rainbow Sphere: Love

Contemplation

The bridge of light was in place, a community of a like kind was assembled in purpose upon the inner planes and the Blessed One was poised in readiness to transmit the Perennial Wisdom... Time was of the essence... time not determined by the world of clocks nor even by the order of cycles great and small. No, this time was measured by something far more subtle and infinitely more profound. It was set by Presence. In the heart of the Great Mother, the Blessed One drew unto itself the mantle of silence and, with no arising nor falling, gave of its breath to the Eternal stillness... As air moved twixt the in and the out, without beginning or end, the Will of One was thus assured of purpose... for the Eternal One Breath flows through all... and the Fount of All Wisdom lies in all, like unto One... And so, as the Beloved received, so did it transmit, as it inhaled, so did it breathe out, for the Way of One is in parlance with all... It gives as it receives, it loves as it finds and it wills as it may... such is the Way made present to all... And for aeons it has been so... round upon round of the hidden mystery made available to those who would know the ways of the Great Ones, to those who may, in their infinite yearning, sample a droplet from the sacred chalice or poise for a moment amidst their Holy Presence. But the will of the small, persistent in its ways, is obscurer of Truth... and though the Fount overflows... Its Voice is unheard...

Guidance

Five facets of the diamond[29] convey the multi-layered presence of the Soul as it expresses through kingdoms in nature. *Family of Light* is the Perennial Wisdom, expressed throughout the ages as timeless spiritual tradition: Hinduism, Buddhism, Christianity, Islam, Jewish mysticism and, of course, Indigenous Tribal Wisdom, to name but a few. Naturally, family traditions, behaviours and 'rules' all come under the auspices of this vision too, so making a leap to the broader, more expansive and more inclusive perspective of the perennial is often not quite as easy as it sounds. However, personal ties aside, *Family of Light* is a calling to 'light', and the leap must, at some point, be made. So find your tribe by all means but scrutinise its roots – meticulously. Do they flourish in perennial soil, is the sound of the Eternal whispered through their song, the seed of homecoming nested in its heart? Is the Presence of Being seen in their ways or does its path lead in another direction, to an alternative reality perhaps, in which wishes are granted, every desire is fulfilled and all manner of stature, from the highest to the lowest, is yours for the asking? Yes, find your tribe, but be aware of the two gates... one leads to sorrow, the other to joy: one lies in light, the other, shadow... Dig deep... consider every part... for in the Fount of All Wisdom... nothing is ever as it seems...

---

[29] *City of Light, Family of Light, Presence, Solar Angel, The Well.*

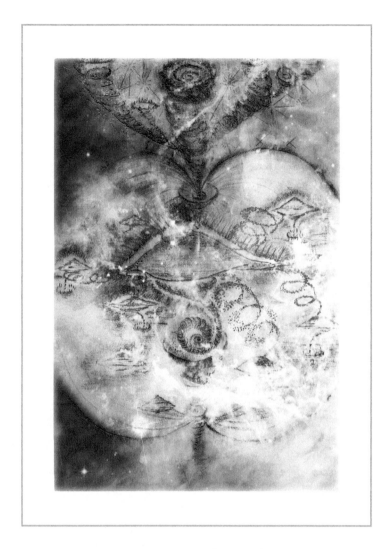

Family of Light

Quality: Ancestral Wisdom
Absolute Aspect: Intelligence
Geometry: None
Rainbow Sphere: Mind

Contemplation

"In the beginning was the Word... Mmmm... in the beginning?" She was more than familiar with the opening words to the biblical version of creation, having reflected upon their significance on many occasions, but now it was the opening phrase that held her in its grasp...*"In the beginning was the Word?"* *"What is its real significance?"* wondered Esmerelda, intuiting that there was far more to it than was being expressed through such a simple sentence. And then another, equally bemusing, thought: *"...the Word was made flesh...".* Each hinted at a profound relationship between sound and form, but the connecting pieces of the jigsaw were proving to be somewhat elusive. Mentor was uncharacteristically silent so, grateful for the space to explore, she absorbed every emission as it arose. *"Time is a force that holds all events separate, each in its proper place..."*[xi]

"Mmmm... now that's added another dimension to the matrix," she exclaimed to herself. *"It would appear there is a gap, an indeterminate period, between the utterance of sound and it being 'made flesh'. No wonder it is so difficult to make a connection between these two, seemingly separate, events. When observed in the context of time, however, it all makes sense: it would appear time is a medium through which all events are held separate whilst being in a perpetual state of motion... and yet..."*

"Time changes not, but all things change in time..." more wisdom from Thoth, confirmed her realisation.

"Excellent! Now let's join the dots," encouraged Mentor, warmly. *"Let's begin at the beginning, with the Word; more specifically, with the constitution of sound itself, for its point of origin lies, not with vibration, but in thought. Sound, as the Word, is thought expressed outwards through substance."*

"So thought is the precursor to existence?"

"Precisely! Esmerelda," they exclaimed. *"Before the onset of sound, thought abided with Absolute as Eternal Thought."*

"And for thought to be eternal, time must exist," she interrupted, overcome in her enthusiasm for remembering more words from Thoth. "In the beginning, then," she pondered, somewhat bemused, "was not only the Word but also the dawning of time?"

"Indeed, Absolute is constant but in order to express outwards, it requires a medium through which its Will may be made manifest; this medium is time and the substance of its Being-ness is consciousness. Thought, sound and all outer manifestations are thus changing attributes within an eternal state of fixation."

"So the 'Word made flesh' is a step down in vibration, through multiple layers of existence, as the Will of Absolute expressed in form?"

"Exactly, but the most important thing to remember is it takes place in time..."

Guidance

Father Time draws upon all the qualities mentioned in this dialogue and asks you to guard the gate through which your words are uttered. Speech is thought expressed outwards and carries as much karmic weight as any harmful or beneficial action. Once uttered, your words cannot be retracted and in time will be 'made flesh'. Know this.

Father Time

Quality: Life
Absolute Aspect: Intelligence
Geometry: Torus
Rainbow Sphere: Rainbow

Contemplation

...the bubble burst and with it came understanding... On a warm summer's day, as she toyed with her mind, she lazily surrendered to the meandering presence of water carried by a gentle stream. Easily, she merged with its presence, swam in its playful eddies as it spiralled round pebble and stone, allowed its silky touch to carry her onward into the unknown. Suddenly, she awoke from her dream-like state. A precipitous cascade, plunging into a tumultuous pool far below, marked the demise of her gentle stream. Droplets sank to murky depths, crashed upon rocks or were cast disparagingly upon the air... yet every seemingly separate drop returned from whence it came... rejoining the meandering stream as it continued, unperturbed, upon its way... They had appeared to part company but all the while their inherent substance had carried them home to themselves. Instantly, she recognised the relationship between mind and consciousness... knew how inextricably linked they were and understood why it was so very, very difficult to distinguish one from the other. Mentor rejoiced and substantiated her discoveries, *"Consciousness is the river, the substance within which mind flows, so, in a like manner, every droplet, being the substance of water, is inseparable from its source, the river. Understand that there is no place in mind that is not consciousness, therefore it is as much an expression of Absolute as its underlying substance. It is, therefore, all things on every level and, in this respect, no different to consciousness."* Esmerelda pondered deeply, "So how do we get beyond mind?" she asked. *"Mind is not something to get beyond. It is an expression to be embraced,"* replied the Word. *"Different layers of mind are embedded within equally diverse expressions of consciousness as an outpouring substance that is Absolute. Furthermore, it is essential that layered qualities of mind are put to good service, for in its expression, individual and group-consciousnesses will express and create new ways of being. So we need not try to get beyond mind but to express the true qualities of mind."* "Mmmm..." she reflected. "And, the true qualities of mind are?" *"Quite simply, my child, the true quality of mind is to recognise its substance, consciousness. Mind, as we have established, is multi-layered. The lowest aspect has to learn the way of water through understanding the emotional body – how thought and feeling influence each other. More refined qualities are found upon the plane of the higher mind where they are employed to create individual lighted thought-forms and, as a result, express group purpose as a collective consciousness. The higher mind does not work with the emotional body; it works with substance – not emotion."*

Guidance

Festival of Light introduces the full spectrum of mind. It is a calling to travel deep into mind's substance, to know the multiple layers that are its Absolute expression and, in harmony with its sister, *Holy Grail,* to celebrate the remarkable moment when a tiny droplet of water – *you* – recognises itself...to **be** the ocean...

Festival of Light

Quality: Magic
Absolute Aspect: Love
Geometry: None
Rainbow Sphere: Order

Contemplation

They met as they had always met, inside the Hall of Learning, where all that is possible to know is known. However, on this occasion, as Consciousness sensed the presence of the Shining One long before it put in an appearance, a ripple of excitement, barely detectable to others in the vicinity, echoed throughout its substance. "Greetings, my friend," sounded the luminous being without employing words. "We have a task before us concerning the future well-being of a world for which we are equally responsible and for which you must be prepared. We must journey together into four realms, each a kingdom in its own right, with which I am far more familiar than you, to engage with those whose remit is to work in the lesser, denser fields of service. We must engage intimately with those whose presence is not usually made visible to any outsider and who would, in normal circumstances, be hostile to any infringement of their domain. However, it is recognised that your participation in this is paramount, so exceptions have been made and they wish you to know that, in furtherance of mutual cooperation, you are welcome in their respective worlds." Consciousness, a willing participant, engaged gracefully with each as they made their presence felt. Time reversed its forward motion as they journeyed to the beginning, to the point when life as it is known today held its origin. A flash of immeasurable light, a discharge of unfathomable power, returned all that was to nothing. It appeared as an end but it was not, and as Consciousness, reduced to a particle of sub-atomic substance, was granted an audience with the Origin of the Flame, it knew why: Light and power were not only sparks essential to igniting and sustaining life, but, at the molecular level, were also agents in the fusion of Spirit with matter. At the heart of the planet, central to its molten core, this amalgamation of substance became evident. Earth, air, fire and water, in one accord, conjoined to become 'elemental essence', nutrition for life, and in this, the mission of the flame was accomplished...

Guidance

Four facets of the diamond lead into the magical world of nature spirits – *Air* (sylphs), *Earth* (gnomes), *Fire* (salamanders) and *Water* (undines) – each responsible for the maintenance, purification and ultimate balance of their respective domains. A fifth vision, *Brilliance*, is the 'Shining One', a Deva, or angelic being, who has under its direction these 'lesser' creative builders. Salamanders, as spirits of fire, have a vital role in the maintenance of all living forms, for they are, in their inherent essence, the igniting spark of life itself. The span of their responsibility, however, extends far beyond the sustenance of life, for they also hold, as perhaps their greatest burden, the purification of humanity's destructive thought patterns, both individually and collectively. Now, as the spark returns to itself, you are granted the opportunity to be as a phoenix rising from the ashes... but first, you must enter the fire...

Fire

Quality: Elemental Essence
Absolute Aspect: Intelligence
Geometry: Metatron's cube
Rainbow Sphere: Beauty

Contemplation

Picture a warm summer's day... the radiant heat of a marbled sun delivers a gentle glow to your lightly tanned skin... encouraging you to let go... to give of yourself, wholly and completely, to its presence... A delicate aroma, carried softly upon wind in tantalising, barely detectible bursts, delivers sweet perfume to senses otherwise numb to sensation... Deeper and deeper you surrender, that you may absorb its gifts with every fibre of your being. Pause for a moment to honour the magnitude of that which is being offered... so, so freely... She, who is mother to all, readily responds... more whispers on the wind, spoken in long-forgotten, fragrant language, are received with humble appreciation as your heart dissolves into rapturous waves of bliss... Attention turns towards fruit upon a nearby tree... inviting, tempting, irresistible... and as teeth penetrate luscious skin, your taste buds come alive with flavour the like of which you have never known... sense upon sense, wave after wave of pure joy infuses your whole being... you are alive... so completely, so intently... so vibrantly... alive. As upturned eyes greet a cloudless sky and ears surrender to the wonder of nature's orchestra, your heart is filled to bursting with gratitude for this miraculous moment... Never, in all your days, have you experienced such intense rapture... such intense pleasure... from that which is so simple, generous... and oh-so humble in its presence...

Guidance

Wherever you are right now, allow every sense in your body – sight, sound, taste, smell and touch – to engage with the full sensory experience presented through this short visualisation. Take it all into your physical body, every last drop, until, fully satiated, you sit back and shine, just like the sun. Now take the full magnitude of this experience **inside**, deep into your heart, and multiply it 1000 times. Are you smiling? Is your heart happy? Do you feel a sense of wonderment at this perfectly ordinary day? See how easy it is to shine when every sense, every aspect of physicality, regardless of outer circumstance, is brought into moment-by-moment experience as an **inner** reality. This is the gift *Flowering* brings; however, its ultimate potential lies in its capacity to merge the spiritual essence of the sun, as transmitter for the source of all love in our solar system, with everyday life. When every sense is used, with focused intensity through the heart, a door to the miraculous is opened and more refined qualities of love may be accessed. Seeds of gratitude sown within your beautiful heart return the light of 10,000 suns to grace your days with reverence for all that arises before you, regardless of outward appearance. Life, in its simplicity, reveals a beautiful cycle that begins with you taking a few moments to savour the gifts she offers, breathing them deep into your heart and then allowing yourself to receive the ultimate reward. All it takes is a moment to sample that which is before you, right now. Be attentive. Are you ready to outshine the sun? Can you spare the time?

Flowering

Quality: Maturity
Absolute Aspect: Intelligence
Geometry: Seed of life, torus
Rainbow Sphere: Love

Contemplation

Long, long ago, before a fledgling planet prepared to flex her wings, there came to earth those who would prove to be the masters of the race. Their purpose, multiple in expression, was to instil amongst infant humanity wisdom in an age. And for aeons, it was so. Miraculous feats, performed through understanding the laws of the physical universe, were effortless: remarkable structures appeared; advanced technology enabled travel through time and space; music and art, exquisite in their expression of the divine, were celebrated in a spirit of unity. Man and gods in co-creative partnership heralded an era of peace, a golden age, in which the great continent flourished. But it was not to last. There were those who claimed the hidden powers, shared so generously without condition, as their own; those who used the secret knowledge to manipulate and control and would stop at nothing to be the new rulers of the race. And so began the Great War. Silent as the grave, the Masters of Wisdom withdrew their presence from the land, sending in their stead a mighty flood to take all, save a few, to certain death beneath the waves. Before long, Atlantis was no more, or so says the legend. In deep meditation, the meditator knew these tales to be far more than myth. Billions of years after the event, the same dynamics were still being played out inside him and in the world at large – this he knew. Atlantis still lived. Manipulation, control and desire for power were obvious, but more subtle, and carrying far greater significance, were the psychic powers running rife amidst an unsuspecting populace. The Siddhis were strong... in his meditation he could feel them... and their allure was so, so tempting...

Guidance

The Atlantean root race, as documented in well-researched material,[xii] is part of a greater cycle (mantvantara) spanning many millions of years. However, it is the golden age – its fall and how the resultant karma plays out on 21st-century earth – that we are concerned with here. Five visions[30] serve as a bridge in time where these forces may be contemplated as an inner process. *Follow the Crowd?* is the most pertinent to you as an individual, calling into question every last detail of your innate sense of self in relation to the vast cosmic outpouring featured here. It questions your very identity and your allegiances – whether familial, spiritual or relational. It challenges your beliefs, behaviours and control mechanisms. But, most of all, it demands nothing less than the sacrifice of every aspect upon the altar of Truth. Are you a healer, an intuitive or perhaps a spiritual teacher? Examine your motives closely. Do you claim 'miracles' as your own or subtly manipulate others through your desire to impart? Remember the *Siddhis*... they thrive in situations such as these... Remember... then give all up to the Soul...

---

[30] *Alien Nation, Burning Ground, Follow the Crowd?, Stillness, Welcome.*

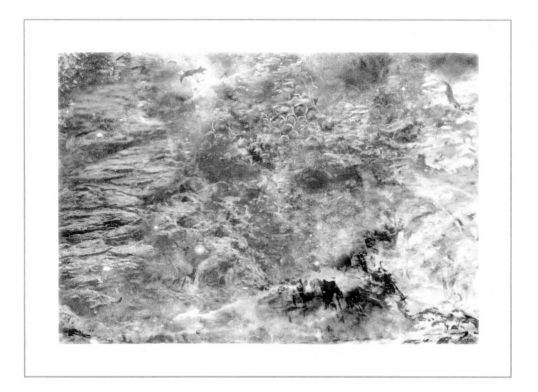

Follow the Crowd?

Quality: Discernment
Absolute Aspect: Will
Geometry: None
Rainbow Sphere: Truth

Contemplation

Caw Caw, Caw Caw, Caw Caw... The call (which she perceived to be a racket) was insistent. So much so, it brought her stomp through the woods to an abrupt end. Equally annoying and far more detrimental to her current state of mind, as well as her somewhat misguided sense of well-being, was the effect it had upon the flow of her entangled web of melodramatic thoughts. Caw Caw, Caw Caw, Caw Caw... it persisted, adding for good measure a crescendo with each utterance. Caw Caw, Caw Caw, Caw Caw... "Alright, alright," she acknowledged, whilst turning in the direction of its source. "You have my undivided attention, now what do you want?" She had arrived at the foot of a somewhat uninspiring tree, characterised by a preponderance of ivy hugging its trunk from base to sky, and searched amongst its foliage for the cause of her disturbance. Almost at the top, amongst its uppermost branches, perched a crow. Now silent, gaze fixed meaningfully upon the expectant child below, it waited patiently for her to acknowledge its presence. As their eyes met, language became detrimental to dialogue, and in the enveloping stillness, presences of species hitherto apart found knowing of each other. Crow, shapeshifter and keeper of Sacred Law, led the way. Through oceans deep and rivers swift and true, in thunderous clouds to the softest drops of dew, past mountains high capped with ice and silken flowers painted white, into seams of crystal deep beneath the crust, they travelled. Each encounter was an opening to the Way, every place an adherence to the Law and, without exception, each contact an exposure of the truth. Earth was sick, the Mother was dying and responsibility lay with the species to which she belonged. The child, wise beyond her years, was sick to her stomach... She understood why Messenger had been insistent... knew the purpose of their meet... and now she must act...

Guidance

Ten visions[31] pave the way to restoration of balance following centuries of neglect inflicted upon our planet by the human race. Individually, as characters in the script, they tell a tale of creation as it is reflected through your inner diamond. *Fortitude* concerns the beginning and end of our tale. What begins as a 'melodramatic mind' is solidified over time into crystallised 'thought-forms' to expose concretised beliefs and behavioural patterns; this is detrimental to you as an individual and, importantly, to the planet as a whole. It is time for these to change. Rose quartz, featured here, is a crystal of profound significance in which rigidly held belief systems are held and then released into the arms of unconditional love. In the image, a somewhat regal persona is held fast in its 'enticingly attractive' perception of reality, but turn it upside down and an alternative viewpoint is revealed where the rich, ruby red of a magnanimous heart is now haven for the lost... Soon the ice breaks... and tears flow... but courage is its forerunner...

---

[31] *Alchemist, Fortitude, Integrity, Invitation, Messenger, New Earth, Raindance, Reception, Sanctuary, Stewardship.*

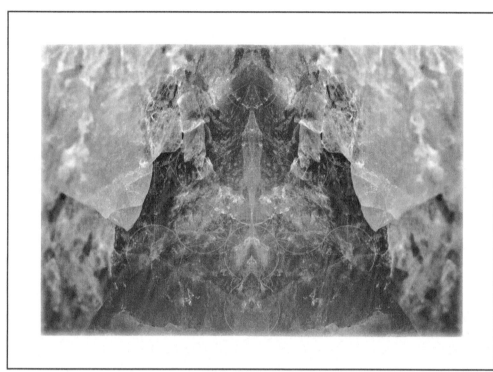

Fortitude

Quality: Courage
Absolute Aspect: Will
Geometry: Metatron's cube
Rainbow Sphere: Order

Contemplation

In times of old, it was said, three serpents roamed amidst the ethers of the known universe, each with a tale to tell and a vital message to impart. The first, it was said, had as its origin the very beginnings of time and, though it knew it not, was source to the other two. Birthed in eternal darkness, forgetfulness its only companion, it patrolled the far reaches of its domain wondering why it must be so. Abandoned, lost and alone; desperate, afraid and, at times, fiercely angry. In desperation, it gave up its fruitless search and came to rest in the darkest recesses of dark; deathless sleep its only companion... or so it believed. At times, it would awaken from its slumber. At times, the miracle of sleep yielded an alternative 'lighter' reality. Often, the reasons for its banishment played tricks upon its mind and its all-consuming tyrant reduced its sense of worth to dust... Yet there were also times, glimmers of hope, when 'something' other than 'this' appeared on the horizon... But in the end, nothing changed... or so it believed. To this day, it is said, the black snake safeguards its kingdom, wallowing in the mire of its own self-disgust, little knowing the effects upon reality that it is engendering, blind to the presence of its serpent brothers whose lives are so dependent upon its grace and oblivious, beyond measure, to the Light it yearns to greet holding it so close...

Guidance

The tale of three snakes, expressed through an equal number of visions,[32] is one that, if the wider implications of their respective offerings is grasped, brings clarity and vision into every aspect of the awakening journey. The unconscious black snake, as it moves throughout the collective void, leaves a trail of chaos in its wake, an 'entanglement timeline' wherein duality in its purest form is distorted by one who is, to all intents and purposes, asleep. It winds its way through the dark, fluctuating between one pole and another, creating beliefs, programs and emotional traumas until, in the fullness of time, it wakes up to its own divinity. Add to this the powerful symbology – Caduceus married with Aesculapius rod[33] – holding a place of prominence and you have here a recipe for understanding not only the most intimate nature of your inner being but also the most profound workings of our dualistic universe. *Fortress,* therefore, draws attention to your entangled 'knots' but, in knowing the interrelationship between these three 'masters' of intrigue, it also induces awareness of the polarised flow between the universal pairs of opposites – masculine/feminine, child/adult, personality/Soul – as it manifests through challenges in your daily life. There is potential for awakening concealed within this vision, where you may know your unconscious projections and, above all, where the true origin of your core wounds may stand revealed... but it is the taste of freedom igniting Light in your eyes that makes the vision reality...

---

[32] *Fortress, Headspace, Roots.*
[33] See glossary.

Fortress

Quality: Entanglement
Absolute Aspect: Intelligence
Geometry: None
Rainbow Sphere: Will

Contemplation

On the threshold of a dream she stands... her feet, as an anchor, rest deep in the sand...
As her eyes, filled with longing, search distant shore... she hears a sweet sound and tries hard
to recall... the crash of the waves, birds flying high? Or perhaps it's the sea as it touches the sky?
But no, it is neither, yet it is all, for it touches the part that speaks to her soul... Its song stirs a
memory of child and cetacean... "Listen, listen... feel the vibration... trust in your heart as it's
never mistaken..." Long ago forgotten, her companion of old... now is the time for its tale to
be told... "Come, come Little One, will you play with me? Leave your feet on the shore, as one
we'll explore... We'll dance upon waves and sail amongst stars... beings we will greet as worlds
become ours. By angles and spirals, through space and through time, many realms we'll
explore... an adventure, sublime. So fear not, Little One... Will you come? Will you play?
Will you enter the mystery, leave all for this day?"

Guidance

Freedom is a way of life we take very much for granted – speech, movement, action,
choice and, particularly, personal liberty – until it is taken away, and then we soon come
to recognise the full implications of its lack. Fear, for instance, as intimated in the script,
holds us all in bondage at some point in our lives. It places untold restrictions on some
or all avenues of expression and would lead us to believe we are helpless in the face of
any perceived adversity. The song of the dolphin, shared in the script, addresses these
core issues. It awakens the child within and extends a warm invitation to put aside your
anxieties, embark upon the most magical adventure of your life and **play!** An octahedron,
resting above a golden sphere of light, is a striking centre point to the image, where all has,
quite literally, been turned on its head. An alternative reality to the apocalyptic backdrop,
it delivers a tranquil seascape shimmering **above** the night sky; whilst soft, gentle flames
lick the uppermost edges of the structure, it is **safe** from the fiery waters beneath. The
dolphin completes the inverted picture through its alignment with the cosmos and its
invitation to *dance upon waves and sail amongst stars*. Less obvious are two children either
side of the geometry: a female stands to the left whilst a male, set to the right, appears
ready to exit the picture. These dynamics epitomise the polarised nature of life on planet
earth and are key to unlocking the transformational properties of *Freedom* as a facet of
the diamond. When you, as the wonder-filled child, abide at the nexus between any pair
of opposites, celebrating each equally in joy, your world **will** turn upside down and you
will know beyond measure the true meaning of freedom... you will come to see that the
biggest adventure you may ever undertake is right where you are...

Freedom

Quality: Adventure
Absolute Aspect: Love
Geometry: Octahedron
Rainbow Sphere: Love

Contemplation

The heat was intense, the pain excruciating... still she resisted. Her mind was a mess, her heart ripped to shreds... still she resisted. And even though she knew that every sense – each sensation, thought and feeling – was a lie... still she resisted. Why? Why did she fight so hard to protect that which she knew, with every fabric of her being, to be false? Why was she so afraid to embrace the very thing she had been striving for, which she knew, deep inside and beyond all doubt, would lead to her ultimate salvation and bring her lasting peace? Why? Why did she fight so hard to reject its gentle presence? Why? One simple word – **no***! This tiny, nondescript word had become so much a part of who she was that she was powerless against its insistent message, defenceless in its call to action, rendered impotent at every occasion of its utterance –* **no, no, no***! Resistance...* **her** *resistance... was all down to this one word. She would* **not** *give in. Her reason for being, the very fabric of her identity, depended upon it... or so she thought. Deep inside, the great wheel turned and, as momentum changed from force repulsive to force attractive, all that was hitherto immovable melted; the great no had become a giant* **yes***. Denied for so long through her insistence on maintaining an identity that, from the very beginning, had no possible hope of survival, she relaxed her resistant stance and sank deeper and deeper into Presence; at last, in the arms of the Great Unknown, she knew peace...*

Guidance

When irresistible force – Divine Will – meets immovable object – you – something has to give, and it doesn't take a great deal of imagination to figure out which one. Divine Will has nothing to lose; you, on the other hand, have everything. So why engage with it? Why not just carry on with your quite comfortable, if not entirely fulfilling, life and just wait for evolution to run its course? What's the point in upsetting the apple cart? After all, you are happy – right? Perhaps if what was involved in stepping from 'life in sleep' to full waking consciousness was made more apparent there would be many more who would choose the 'wait for evolution to take its course' option. However, you have chosen this vision and, as the Soul alignment quality directs, it requires an act of will before any form of transition may occur; you have to want to change! Courage in making the necessary sacrifices allows the Real to arise, like a phoenix, effortlessly from the ashes of the false self. *Furnace*, therefore, is a vision of great power, holding within it the potential for transformation beyond all that is humanly possible. In offering all that you believe yourself to be to the Great Unknown, you emerge awake in the certain knowledge that **you** are the peace that surpasses understanding. But first, you have to enter the fire...

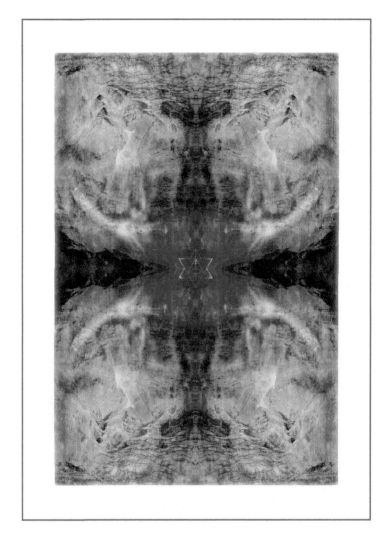

Furnace

Quality: Will to Evolve
Absolute Aspect: Will
Geometry: Star tetrahedron
Rainbow Sphere: Will

Contemplation

In the mountains of the moon, hidden from those whose ways are blinded by the sun, a wealth in wisdom is found, little known to all but its chosen keepers. Those who toil beneath the land may lead the fearless through its dark passages to reach the tunnel of light and then onwards to the mysterious cave that houses its ancient scripts. But these shy creatures are not easily met. When the heart of the human vibrates to the tune of stillness, then, and only then, those who grow in light and those who build in matter may meet with ease in mutual respect. Then wisdom held by those who know the art of form is entrusted to those who would tear it down, the way of light is made aware to the shy and the two may begin afresh to mould new life from form, untainted by the blood of man. The prophecy is thus fulfilled and that which was torn apart is whole once more; order is restored.

Guidance

As its name implies, *Fusion* brings the forces of duality to a place of unity from which the real work of synthesis may begin. But, as intimated in the script, this act of union is not as straightforward as the mind would have us believe. It necessitates deep and honest exploration through its 'dark passages', forsaking 'false lights' along the way, to gain the ultimate in wisdom upon arrival at the 'mysterious cave' of the heart. *Fusion* also contains more universal appeal in the privilege of the humble human meeting those who work in the subtle realms of nature, especially those within the physical body itself. The message of this vision is deep and powerful: know the power of the past as it taints your blood and keeps your body locked in pain, know that without its cooperation there is no home for the Soul and learn to appreciate those who work behind the scenes just so your humble heart may continue to beat with purpose in your breast. It is time to take responsibility for the part **you** play in bringing the pure light of Spirit into the heart of the Blessed Mother. She who gives birth to all forms, including you! Remember, no man is an island. The spirit of co-creation requires you to step aside to allow those whose wisdom far exceeds your own to fulfil the mark of **their** destiny, alongside yours.

Fusion

Quality: Thinking in the Heart
Absolute Aspect: Love
Geometry: None
Rainbow Sphere: Love

Contemplation

*The landscape was bleak... at least on first impression... but as her eyes adjusted to its subtle shades and the tight knot deep in her belly relaxed its hold, her heart opened to an enveloping presence. Darkness of impending twilight gave way to the glow of golden dawn, spectres in the gloom appeared as friends in the mist and, despite her trepidation at the impending gathering, at which she would play a vital role, the essence of Love emanated such unconditional acceptance that it could not fail to ignite in her unquestionable trust. With awakened confidence, she walked deep into their kingdom and, taking her place at the centre, lay resolutely upon the soft, receptive land, whilst elders of the tribe, each in their own place, gathered around. As one they sang, in ancient tones, a lullaby of the lost. In Truth they stayed as Light Transcendent drew near. And in unison they cried as the Blessed One bestowed its blessing. With heart attuned to silence, hands rested comfortingly upon her rounded belly and eyes fixed unwaveringly upon the Great Unknown, the sacrificial lamb gave all of herself to the impending deliverance. In consummate absorption, all that she was, all that she is now and all that she has yet to be – journeys, memories, hopes and wishes, beliefs, programs, light and shadow – dissolved into a river of liquid light. To Zero, Absolute Zero, she returned. In Zero, she was delivered... and **as** Zero, what began as bleak... was redeemed...*

Guidance

Three facets of the diamond[34] chart a course from darkness to light, from despair to hope and from separation to unity as it unfolds through an evolutionary path of return, each vision exposing a role in a story that is timeless in the telling. *Gathering* sets the scene. Consider the image and you will see, amidst an other-worldly setting and in a *landscape that is bleak*, an assembly of ethereal beings whose presence emits a soft, golden radiance. Look closely and you will see that the attention of these beings is directed towards the centre, more specifically, to the ground. It is clear that a sacred gathering is in place, where 'elders' with knowing in the art of deliverance are gathering to facilitate an impending birth. But there is more to it than this. Whereas the essence of the story may apply to physical birth, its greatest offering lies upon the more subtle planes of the heart and mind and the emotions and thought, and, crucially, in personality integration with the Soul. When every last vestige of the separate self is held in loving acceptance, as a mother caressing her unborn child through her own body, it ceases to feel alone and isolated. It feels safe. It feels loved. And, above all, it knows all its needs are assured of being met. This is how you must be with **every part** of yourself. Now hold yourself with gentleness... and pay attention to the sacrificial lamb... for it has much wisdom to impart...

---

[34] *Absorption, Blessing, Gathering.*

Gathering

Quality: Deliverance
Absolute Aspect: Love
Geometry: None
Rainbow Sphere: Beauty

Contemplation

"If thought were a prayer and mind the conveyer... then who am I, director or player? Perhaps I am both – are they one and the same... each of them parts I play in a game? And what of this void... this place between thought... where all things fill a space that is naught? Is it the pause between beats of my heart... Stillness that speaks when worlds fall apart... or silence that rests in the space between words? The sound of the sea, the call of the birds, the cry of a child that longs to be heard... Am I all of these things... perhaps even none... And if I am a product of thought turned to form... am I also the void from which it was born?" Mentor smiled. It brought joy in Spirit to witness her musings. *"To begin at the end..."* they responded. *"Yes, you are equally the product of thought and the 'womb' within which it was created, as well as being 'all of these things' and none. Truth is a paradox, and the deeper you ponder upon polarities that cannot possibly exist in the same space at the same time, the closer you will come to recognising the true nature of reality and, with it, Truth."* Esmerelda frowned, *"So I **am** both director and player?"* *"Indeed, you are! Every thought creates your reality, this you know. But to recognise, and **become**, the origin of thought is for the player to know, beyond all doubt, that it is also the orchestrator of the show."* *"Mmmmm... so all I have to do is locate the origin of thought?"* she pondered. *"Ha, ha... yes, that is all!"* Teacher jested. *"But know this: the origin of thought will not be found within itself. Although it is an admirable method to see the myriad forms it creates, you will never understand the mirror by gazing into its reflection; mind is no different. To know mind, and thus the origin of thought, you must shatter the mirror. You must look to the substance within which mind is but a particle. Thought is the droplet that believes it is the ocean. But it is not. Only the ocean can be the ocean."* Mentor sensed her confusion. *"You are closer than you think. Consider thought to be a seed planted in the garden of Absolute. Like all seeds, it requires the right nutrients that it may ripen to fruition, but in this instance, all is provided from within the 'soil' itself; there is nothing that needs to be added. Now sow your seed in the garden of life, with no agenda, no extra thoughts or 'watering', and allow its substance – consciousness – to deliver the fruits of its majesty into reality."* As the last piece of the jigsaw fell readily into place, Esmerelda smiled...

Guidance

Thought, as a creative process, is expressed through two visions bearing the title of *Genesis*. *Inception* asks that you look to the origin of thought to know the soil in which it is planted and then take a leap of faith into the unknown. Now, as the script directs, sow your seeds and, most importantly... leave them alone!

Genesis Inception

Quality: Orchestration
Absolute Aspect: Will
Geometry: Icosahedron, spiral
Rainbow Sphere: Mind

Contemplation

"If thought were a prayer and mind the conveyer... then who am I, director or player? Perhaps I am both – are they one and the same... each of them parts I play in a game? And what of this void... this place between thought... where all things fill a space that is naught? Is it the pause between beats of my heart... Stillness that speaks when worlds fall apart... or silence that rests in the space between words? The sound of the sea, the call of the birds, the cry of a child that longs to be heard... Am I all of these things... perhaps even none... And if I am a product of thought turned to form... am I also the void from which it was born?" Mentor smiled. It brought joy in Spirit to witness her musings. *"To begin at the end..."* they responded. *"Yes, you are equally the product of thought and the 'womb' within which it was created, as well as being 'all of these things' and none. Truth is a paradox, and the deeper you ponder upon polarities that cannot possibly exist in the same space at the same time, the closer you will come to recognising the true nature of reality and, with it, Truth."* Esmerelda frowned, *"So I **am** both director and player?"* *"Indeed, you are! Every thought creates your reality, this you know. But to recognise, and **become**, the origin of thought is for the player to know, beyond all doubt, that it is also the orchestrator of the show."* *"Mmmmm... so all I have to do is locate the origin of thought?"* she pondered. *"Ha, ha... yes, that is all!"* Teacher jested. *"But know this: the origin of thought will not be found within itself. Although it is an admirable method to see the myriad forms it creates, you will never understand the mirror by gazing into its reflection; mind is no different. To know mind, and thus the origin of thought, you must shatter the mirror. You must look to the substance within which mind is but a particle. Thought is the droplet that believes it is the ocean. But it is not. Only the ocean can be the ocean."* Mentor sensed her confusion. *"You are closer than you think. Consider thought to be a seed planted in the garden of Absolute. Like all seeds, it requires the right nutrients that it may ripen to fruition, but in this instance, all is provided from within the 'soil' itself; there is nothing that needs to be added. Now sow your seed in the garden of life, with no agenda, no extra thoughts or 'watering', and allow its substance – consciousness – to deliver the fruits of its majesty into reality."* As the last piece of the jigsaw fell readily into place, Esmerelda smiled...

Guidance

Thought, as a creative process, is expressed through two visions bearing the title of *Genesis. Manifestation* is an invitation to look in the mirror, to know all you observe is a reflection of yourself and then to look beyond... to the substance. Ponder deeply this question. How far down the rabbit hole will you travel before you see all that you perceive is thought appearing as a product of itself?

Genesis Manifestation

Quality: Paradox
Absolute Aspect: Intelligence
Geometry: Icosahedron, spiral
Rainbow Sphere: Order

Contemplation

A birth is immanent. Magic is afoot. Pregnant with promise, subtle variances in the air, barely detectable to even the discerning eye, bring to fruition that which was set in motion many, many moons into the past. Temptation to induce is also present, as is interference from those who believe they know what is best for the incoming soul. But the One, who stands isolated, in unity, knows well the ways of matter and its propensity to mate with Spirit. It knows, as it has always known, that two are one, it knows that union may only occur when each is aligned perfectly with the other and it knows that the only doing lies in non-doing. It knows, as it has always known, that virtue lies in waiting and that providence ripens with patience... It is also aware... that anything other than this is in error...

Guidance

Every creative process – whether work of art, caterpillar to butterfly, human to Divine or birth into physical form – requires a period of waiting, an interval or space in time wherein all slows to a point of stillness. *Gestation*, as its name and Soul alignment quality – *patience* – implies, is this period of quiescence; it is the breathing space between the moment of conception and ultimate birth into a new reality. However, it is far more than this. For those who are willing to look beyond the confines of the small self, it also offers insight into the unfoldment of the Soul within the consciousness of humanity. Consider the image; the eyes are immediately drawn to the central apparition where a tree-like spirit stands, firm in intention, in welcome embrace towards the clear blue skies above. At its feet, not quite of this world, is the seed of life geometry. Magic is in the air, forces, clearly beyond the understanding of the average human being, are at play and a birth is in the final stages of completion. *Sacred Ceremony*, origin and higher octave of *Gestation*, sets the alchemical magic in motion. From a space, pure and clear, above and beyond the veil of darkness, a sacred seed is sown. In deepest dark it rests, all nutrients gathered unto itself until, in the fullness of time, it is ready to make the final transition. Look closely at these two visions and you will see the geometry is the focal point of each. One, *Sacred Ceremony*, sets the intention for Divine Purpose; the other, *Gestation*, sees that same purpose being birthed into a new reality. The tree spirit is critical, emphasising the essential part that Mother Nature, in particular the Devic kingdom, plays as agent of the divine in the manifestation of form. *Gestation*, therefore, is the divine feminine. It calls upon you to listen to the song of the earth, to honour her custodians and to acknowledge that without her generosity, your feet would not be walking upon her holy ground and your humble heart would not be beating so reverently within your breast.

Gestation

Quality: Patience
Absolute Aspect: Intelligence
Geometry: Seed of life
Rainbow Sphere: Beauty

Contemplation

*In crystalline light sublime... the Great Cause sounded its note. To its side drew those who knew the Way, who spoke the Word and who would sculpt the many and the few like unto itself. Each intrinsic to its Being, inseparable from the All... These brothers three... Flames of Mind, Masters of Order, Builders of Worlds Anew... never wavered from their course... Never failed to set ablaze those they touched... never failed in their purpose... to reveal Truth... to call an end on time. Three gathered unto One, drew deep the breath and exhaled purpose. The Great Cause, infused with Will, Love, Intelligence, expressed outwards through its substance. Symbols, atoms, molecules, **sound** and geometric structure... all unfolding in perfect symmetry... built myriad forms... Single-celled organisms, planets and stars to galaxies and immeasurable universes... all orchestrated according to its Divine Architecture... all infused with the mission of the flame... None was exempt... Each followed Absolute order... one, two, followed by three and seven... and then the many... Such was the Way of Fire... such was substance unfolding within itself... and such was divinity expressing its perfection... "For light gives way unto the dark... And symbols form, so soon to spark... Remembrance... of the Truth... I am..." So spoke one whose fire was True, whose Spirit was integral to the Three and whose vision was clear... Esmerelda, the Word... made flesh.*

Guidance

Seven visions[35] illustrate the involutionary journey of creation using geometric form. Through ever-expanding rounds of concentric circles, they highlight divinity, expressing first as one (*Through the Portal*), followed by one appearing as two (*Becoming*) and then duality as separate entities (*Divine Darkness, Divine Inspiration*). Completing the process is the trinity, expanding outwards to the full divine matrix, the blueprint of all creative expression within the manifested world (*Gnosis*). *Gnosis*, in its three forms, is not only the trinity, but, by virtue of its integral geometries, it also marks the gateway to the third dimension: matter as we know it. As the point where Spirit conjoins with matter, in both involutionary and evolutionary journeys, each vision under its umbrella holds particular significance in aligning the personality with the Soul and, ultimately, with Spirit. The beauty of contemplating, understanding and above all **being** the natural creative force of the universe as it flows through you is that all these variables come to a peak of wholeness within, to the point where they cease to be separate. *Gnosis Intelligence* is the Universal mind. From an individual standpoint, it asks you to consider your thoughts and how they influence your daily life, for good or ill. However, the greatest gift bestowed is that of the **plane** of mind. What is the origin of thought? Who, or what, is the thinker? Is there even one who thinks? Go deeper. Ask yourself, *what is the underlying **intelligence** that informs every life form – that informs **you**?* Don't rush: Rome wasn't built in a day, and any reward of value is worthy of a little patience...

---

[35] *Becoming, Divine Darkness, Divine Inspiration, Gnosis (Intelligence, Purity, Tranquillity), Through the Portal.*

Gnosis Intelligence

Quality: Universal Mind
Absolute Aspect: Intelligence
Geometry: Divine matrix, dodecahedron, star tetrahedron
Rainbow Sphere: Light

Contemplation

*In crystalline light sublime... the Great Cause sounded its note. To its side drew those who knew the Way, who spoke the Word and who would sculpt the many and the few like unto itself. Each intrinsic to its Being, inseparable from the All... These brothers three... Flames of Mind, Masters of Order, Builders of Worlds Anew... never wavered from their course... Never failed to set ablaze those they touched... never failed in their purpose... to reveal Truth... to call an end on time. Three gathered unto One, drew deep the breath and exhaled purpose. The Great Cause, infused with Will, Love, Intelligence, expressed outwards through its substance. Symbols, atoms, molecules, **sound** and geometric structure... all unfolding in perfect symmetry... built myriad forms... Single-celled organisms, planets and stars to galaxies and immeasurable universes... all orchestrated according to its Divine Architecture... all infused with the mission of the flame... None was exempt... Each followed Absolute order... one, two, followed by three and seven... and then the many... Such was the Way of Fire... such was substance unfolding within itself... and such was divinity expressing its perfection... "For light gives way unto the dark... And symbols form, so soon to spark... Remembrance... of the Truth... I am..." So spoke one whose fire was True, whose Spirit was integral to the Three and whose vision was clear... Esmerelda, the Word... made flesh.*

Guidance

Seven visions[36] illustrate the involutionary journey of creation using geometric form. Through ever-expanding rounds of concentric circles, they highlight divinity, expressing first as one (*Through the Portal*), followed by one appearing as two (*Becoming*) and then duality as separate entities (*Divine Darkness, Divine Inspiration*). Completing the process is the trinity, expanding outwards to the full divine matrix, the blueprint of all creative expression within the manifested world (*Gnosis*). *Gnosis*, in its three forms, is not only the trinity, but, by virtue of its integral geometries, it also marks the gateway to the third dimension: matter as we know it. As the point where Spirit conjoins with matter, in both involutionary and evolutionary journeys, each vision under its umbrella holds particular significance in aligning the personality with the Soul and, ultimately, with Spirit. The beauty of contemplating, understanding and above all being the natural creative force of the universe as it flows through you is that all these variables come to a peak of wholeness within, to the point where they cease to be separate. *Gnosis Purity* is the Will of the Divine, set with purpose and, as its title implies, the most pristine, diamond-clear Light of Absolute. Its way is fraught with danger, for it wields great power... and none are spared its discriminating gaze... Naught shall escape its Will to Be... for to experience it directly is to cease to exist... Few are willing... many try and fail... but there are those whose humble hearts succumb on bended knee... whose countenance is strong... and whose courage in shedding the darkened way... can only leave the Real...

---

[36] *Becoming, Divine Darkness, Divine Inspiration, Gnosis (Intelligence, Purity, Tranquillity), Through the Portal.*

Gnosis Purity

Quality: Diamond Clear Light
Absolute Aspect: Will
Geometry: Divine matrix, dodecahedron, star tetrahedron
Rainbow Sphere: Rainbow

Contemplation

In crystalline light sublime... the Great Cause sounded its note. To its side drew those who knew the Way, who spoke the Word and who would sculpt the many and the few like unto itself. Each intrinsic to its Being, inseparable from the All... These brothers three... Flames of Mind, Masters of Order, Builders of Worlds Anew... never wavered from their course... Never failed to set ablaze those they touched... never failed in their purpose... to reveal Truth... to call an end on time. Three gathered unto One, drew deep the breath and exhaled purpose. The Great Cause, infused with Will, Love, Intelligence, expressed outwards through its substance. Symbols, atoms, molecules, **sound** *and geometric structure... all unfolding in perfect symmetry... built myriad forms... Single-celled organisms, planets and stars to galaxies and immeasurable universes... all orchestrated according to its Divine Architecture... all infused with the mission of the flame... None was exempt... Each followed Absolute order... one, two, followed by three and seven... and then the many... Such was the Way of Fire... such was substance unfolding within itself... and such was divinity expressing its perfection... "For light gives way unto the dark... And symbols form, so soon to spark... Remembrance... of the Truth...* **I am***..." So spoke one whose fire was True, whose Spirit was integral to the Three and whose vision was clear... Esmerelda, the Word... made flesh.*

Guidance

Seven visions[37] illustrate the involutionary journey of creation using geometric form. Through rounds of concentric circles, they highlight divinity, expressing first as one (*Through the Portal*), followed by one appearing as two (*Becoming*) and then duality as separate entities (*Divine Darkness, Divine Inspiration*). Completing the process is the trinity, expanding outwards to the full divine matrix, the blueprint of all creative expression within the manifested world (*Gnosis*). *Gnosis*, in its three forms, is not only the trinity, but, by virtue of its integral geometries, it also marks the gateway to the third dimension: matter as we know it. As the point where Spirit conjoins with matter, in both involutionary and evolutionary journeys, each vision under its umbrella holds particular significance in aligning the personality with the Soul and, ultimately, with Spirit. The beauty of contemplating, understanding and above all being the natural creative force of the universe as it flows through you is that all these variables come to a peak of wholeness within, to the point where they cease to be separate. *Gnosis Tranquillity* is Absolute expressed as universal love. However, it is barely discernible as such, for it holds such a refined vibration, it may not be perceived or even felt by the average human being, who is conditioned only to love of the self or love of a significant other. This vision is Love as pure reason, the unified and combined force of *mind infused with Love*. Absolute expresses Love, as its **nature** is Love... It is merely expressing that which it **is**... When the heart is humbled with the mind as a cloudless sky... you may **feel** it... and express wonder as soft, gentle tears shine through luminous eyes... that no longer see.

---

[37] *Becoming, Divine Darkness, Divine Inspiration, Gnosis (Intelligence, Purity, Tranquillity), Through the Portal.*

Gnosis Tranquillity

Quality: Meditation
Absolute Aspect: Love
Geometry: Divine matrix, dodecahedron, star tetrahedron
Rainbow Sphere: Will

Contemplation

"Love... yes, that was it... It was love... Love that reduced her heart to nothing, left her empty of feeling and dispatched all sensation to the graveyard of the past. Love that called the Beloved to her side... that permeated every last cell in her body and that called every ounce of her being to melt into its Presence. Yes, it was love... but it was love such as she had never before experienced... Love that she felt through her... mind? How could this be? How was it possible for mind to feel – surely this was solely the domain of the heart?" Teacher, whom she loved beyond all else, appeared. *"You have travelled far, experienced many pitfalls on the way and known the heights that may be gained when outer pleasure gives way to luminance within. You have swum the watery depths, where your heart, alone, has felt the rhythm of the waves, and now the time has come to know the pulse of love as it beats to a more inclusive tune..."* *"But how?"* she replied, *"How could mind possibly experience feelings?"* In silence, Mentor replied. *"Let us explain."* Authority echoed through the Word and could not be ignored. *"Mind, as you are aware, spans many levels. At its lowest, it is divisive and considers all things, including the heart, separate to itself. In this expression, it is not only incapable of knowing feeling, but is not even aware it is a mere fragment within an even greater and more inclusive whole. It is firmly held in its belief that mind alone rules supreme."* Esmerelda understood this clearly. *"Now, through many years, often lifetimes, of knowing the way of the trickster, how it maintains the prison of separation and how it promotes itself as ruler above all else, the essential substance of mind becomes refined. Initially, it realises it is part of a wider community and surrenders its separative ideals to that of the group. This is the beginning of a more inclusive and altruistic mindset, but it is still very much in the province of mind, alone. Do you understand?"* She knew the trickster well, so nodded her approval. *"Mind, at its ultimate, is a different kettle of fish entirely. Its vibration is such that it barely exists in its original state, the substance within which it flows being its predominant expression."* Quizzical furrows marked her brow. *"Let us consider the origin, and elements, that make up this substance. Absolute is constant, unchanging, but contains within it the conditions to express outwards though its substance. Consciousness **is** substance and, as Absolute in expression, is, therefore, All conditions and All things – mind, love, will, intelligence... and so on."* The warmth shining through her eyes said it all. *"So in its highest expression,"* she reflected, *"mind is not really mind at all. It is substance – consciousness – and as such expression of Absolute... including love."* *"Exactly!"* Mentor exclaimed. *"Higher mind works with substance, not emotion. It is Love... expressed in its purest form."*

Guidance

It is worth repeating the last line, *higher mind works with substance, not emotion.* Consciousness, not mind, as sole expression of Absolute, is love expressed in its purest form. When the distinction between mind and consciousness is experienced deep within the heart, you will know this. Above all, you will **feel** it.

Guidance

Quality: Inner Tuition
Absolute Aspect: Will
Geometry: None
Rainbow Sphere: Mind

Contemplation

*He'd passed this way before but on this day it was different somehow. Strolling across its forgiving landscape, he touched the earth with gentleness and revelled in her sacred beauty, each blade of grass a remembrance of times long since gone, every indentation, evidence of creatures large and small, every nook and cranny, babbling brook or mountain high, a tale ripe for the telling. In this place was history in the making, stories for the hearing and mystery for the unravelling. Familiarity gave way to inner vision. He saw the land awash with fire, yet not a blade of grass was harmed, he felt the frozen wastes of time as his heart, encased in ice, could only dream again of spring and, in the quiet of an early dawn, as autumn mists gave up their dead, he felt the ground bear testament to every passing... to **his** passing. Yes, the picture was different... it was different because **he** was different. Extremes of fire and ice no longer pulled him this way or that... no longer scorched his heart nor ground his bones to dust... no more did his heart drown in despair... Now he was different...*

Guidance

Three facets of the diamond[38] present differing versions of the same source imagery. Strikingly apart in appearance, with a unique expression of reality to impart, each relays its message in such a way that their underlying connection is evidenced by far more than image alone. Most prominent in *Harmony* is Glastonbury Tor, a hill of outstanding natural beauty, arising as an island amidst the surrounding 'watery' landscape of the Somerset Levels. Remnant of a bygone age when knights in shining armour, round tables, mythical kings and fair maidens graced the land with tales of magical quests, unrequited love and crusades against dark forces, the Tor stands in prime position atop an escarpment softened by a gentle, meandering stream, to serve as a reminder of these legendary tales of old. When Avalon, kingdom of the dead, eclipses the bounds of time to spring magically into life, when netherworlds of spirits, elves, faeries and such like are more real than the ground beneath your feet and when the world as you know it appears as a faded photograph against a tantalisingly vibrant panorama, then existence other than 'normal' is possible. To climb the Tor is to engage intimately with its topography and to bear witness to all that is engraved upon its ancient pathways. Seven layers of rock, terraces inscribed in time, mark your ascent, fire and ice – agents of change – run through your veins and, as you poise for a moment at the crowning glory of your ascendency, all is revealed... Only you know the reflection, only you can enter the mystery... only you can peel back the layers of time. *Harmony* is a sojourn into the realm of death but only as it is experienced through life. It is an invitation to stand at the door to eternity and, with barely a backward glance... **jump**.

---

[38] *Aspiration, Eureka!, Harmony.*

Harmony

Quality: Gentleness
Absolute Aspect: Love
Geometry: None
Rainbow Sphere: Beauty

Contemplation

In times of old, it was said, three serpents roamed amidst the ethers of the known universe, each with a tale to tell and a vital message to impart. The first, it was said, had as its origin the very beginnings of time and, though it knew it not, was source to the other two. Birthed in eternal darkness, forgetfulness its only companion, it patrolled the far reaches of its domain wondering why it must be so. Abandoned, lost and alone; desperate, afraid and, at times, fiercely angry. In desperation, it gave up its fruitless search and came to rest in the darkest recesses of dark; deathless sleep its only companion... or so it believed. At times, it would awaken from its slumber. At times, the miracle of sleep yielded an alternative 'lighter' reality. Often, the reasons for its banishment played tricks upon its mind and its all-consuming tyrant reduced its sense of worth to dust... Yet there were also times, glimmers of hope, when 'something' other than 'this' appeared on the horizon... But in the end, nothing changed... or so it believed. To this day, it is said, the black snake safeguards its kingdom, wallowing in the mire of its own self-disgust, little knowing the effects upon reality that it is engendering, blind to the presence of its serpent brothers whose lives are so dependent upon its grace and oblivious, beyond measure, to the Light it yearns to greet holding it so close...

Guidance

The tale of three snakes, expressed through an equal number of visions,[39] is one that, if the wider implications of their respective offerings is grasped, brings clarity and vision into every aspect of the awakening journey. The unconscious black snake, abandoned and alone in the dark with no apparent hope of reprisal, does not understand its predicament. In desperation, it creates a series of stories, fuelled by self-limiting beliefs, around why it should be this way; soon they define who it is, with every thought, feeling and event adding credence to its loathsome existence. *Headspace*, conspicuous in this triad in its absence of snakes, addresses these core issues by returning to their point of origin. The image leaves no doubt as to why its aptly named title is as it is and needs no further clarification, but the head is not where we must venture if we are to understand these entanglements. No, we must take a dip into the far-from-appealing waters of the dark continent that is beckoning to us from the foreground and engage with the serpent that is responsible. You see, it is our stories that define who we are, our beliefs concerning our sense of self that determine our sense of worth and our identity based upon these 'assets' that we devote our lives to defending. But all this is a lie... an untruth... concocted by a serpent... embroiled in the matrix of its own entanglements...

---

[39] *Fortress, Headspace, Roots.*

Headspace

Quality: Collective Unconscious
Absolute Aspect: Intelligence
Geometry: None
Rainbow Sphere: Truth

Contemplation

*The dreamer woke... but not fully. Succumbing to stillness in the moment, it sank deeper and deeper into a space where mind played no part. Giant roots, embedded in unconscious soil, led the dreamer far into the source of its origin to its history and reason for identity. Story upon story cast by a mind without vision, intent upon control, anchored seeds of doubt inside a heart held fast by tendrils too numerous to mention. The dreamer stirred when its heart fought for breath, strangled by cords of its own undoing. But as its body locked in pain, it saw the trickster's game and held no desire to fix... nor to blame. To silence it returned, absorbing the stillness... again. On its own in the dark, a tiny tree, whose roots were its history, its soil caked in shame, stood naked and vulnerable, and with barely a light to call its own, drew to itself that which would call its parts home. The dreamer watched in wonder, sinking evermore into acceptance of all as the tiny tree emerged from within its own heart. And, when stories left untold returned seeds as pastures new, the tiny tree opened to its perfect presence. An exact replica of the first, the mighty tree revealed its pristine hologram, whole in relation to the part, source of radiance to a heart whose only expression was compassion. The dreamer smiled inwardly as the complete picture emerged. Little tree, the dreamer, was the very fabric of Spirit, its anatomy of self was a miracle in existence and now it could see... **clearly**... that the greatest gift had been bestowed upon one who drowned in thirst when it found the secret of the stars within a piece of dirt...*

Guidance

Two visions[40] address the relationship between fractal and hologram from the perspective of each whilst being equal in measure. *Holographic Universe* is the grain of sand that, in a moment of awakening, realises it is not only the cosmos but also the ocean in a drop. However, as the script reveals, there is much inner work needed before the 'little tree' recognises its holographic nature to such a degree that it is embraced as a way of life. Central to the image is a multi-layered star tetrahedron, inspiration for contemplating the nature of holograms. But what does this mean? Quantum mechanics defines a way of being, 'superposition', where every possibility is available in the moment; the perfect paradox, it is everywhere and nowhere simultaneously. It presents a state of wholeness that includes both fractal and hologram, yet at the same time is neither. A hologram is the big picture, a matrix within the space-time continuum whose potential is to show an individual, particle or fractal its place within the whole. Wherever you slice the pie there is the totality, but a 'piece' that is asleep won't know it – all it can project is an unconscious hologram. The dreamer, in embracing all that it was in each moment, regardless of circumstance, invited superposition where awakened consciousness was expressed as its way of being. Whole and the part, everywhere and nowhere... the dreamer was awake.

---

[40] *Holographic Universe, Mystic Union.*

Holographic Universe

Quality: Worlds within Worlds
Absolute Aspect: Intelligence
Geometry: Star tetrahedron
Rainbow Sphere: Mind

Contemplation

Consciousness slept... or so it would appear. Consciousness does not sleep... ever. Its Eternal One expression is present... always. Nothing escapes its notice, for it holds within its substance expression of All; every path, experience, system and expression, is known to be One within its impeccable clear awareness. Waters of life nurture its pristine Presence... earth, wind and fire breathe its purpose into worlds anew... and thought, mind within its substance, weaves the wondrous web of life into its fabric... Architect of All... master of mystery and, ultimately, builder of the True, it ignites fire in substance, ensuring each and every particle returns to greet itself within the mirror of its mind. Now, with her journey almost done, consciousness bears witness to a small figure, an innocent child, as she approaches the Lion's Gate... It knows her journey, the tests and trials that have brought her to its door, senses her naked vulnerability... and feels the humble heart that beats, so fearlessly, within her breast. Consciousness recognises itself in the mirror of her immaculate mind... knows the purity of her Soul and swings wide the door to welcome her into its domain. In a momentary flash, she assimilates the qualities of its substance... mind that shines so clear it out-sparkles light from 1000 clear-cut diamonds, love that makes all things new and excludes naught from its warm embrace and above all, purpose... clear direction that ensures its Will is expressed through every particle within its substance... without exception. The sacred chalice shimmers in its force attractive, calling those to her presence whose rhythm is her own... and once again she knows herself as One. She, a single particle within substance... is expression of All... a celebration in Light... alongside those whose way is hers... alone.

Guidance

Holy Grail carries the gift of the Universal mind, but far more than this, it presents an opportunity to experience the multi-faceted nature of mind as being mere substance within a wider, and more inclusive, expression – consciousness. The script is in itself multi-layered. Weaving its way backwards and forwards within uncountable paradoxes, it culminates in a single 'particle within substance', an innocent child celebrating her emergence in Light with those whose frequency, whose song, is none other than her own. The 'Lion's Gate' features in many esoteric traditions and signifies the emergence of a Self-aware, individualised consciousness into the wider expression of the group. Additionally, *Holy Grail* aligns to the Cosmic Christ, whose presiding presence is Love. However, this is love that carries no emotion. It radiates through the heart of one who has cultivated a mind of untainted awareness and qualities that work directly with substance within consciousness, not one who is embroiled in the trappings of the emotional body. Its sister, *Festival of Light*, should be contemplated alongside, for they are interconnected. Together, in realisation of the clear-seer's heart, they celebrate with those whose presence is pure light as they in unison express outwards the song of the sacred three... Love... Will... Intelligence... Spirit in life... all life... everywhere.

Holy Grail

Quality: Cosmic Christ
Absolute Aspect: Love
Geometry: None
Rainbow Sphere: Love

Contemplation

*... the storm raged... the little boat, tossed here and there by mighty waves, surrendered to its passage. Rudderless... powerless... **alone**... it had no choice. The rider cowered inside... fear, a familiar bedfellow, engulfed its heart... Imagination, fuelled by a mind that knew no bounds, reduced its countenance to a quivering mess... then to stature frozen beyond all recognition... The rider could take no more, could no longer resist the inevitable, it had to let go... Slumped upon the wooden floor, heart a steady murmur in its breast, breath a gentle rise on the wind... it gave of itself... completely... to the boat... Then came the wave... and with it their demise... Splintered flesh, bloodied timber... swallowed, all too quick, by oceans deep... called the dreamer from her sleep... Twixt night and day she tarried, idly pondering the dream... In spite of her untimely death, she felt no fear, no quickening of pulse or shortness of breath... How could it be? Consciousness slipped away... The light was blinding but oh-so refreshing... Confused, elated, the traveller opened its heart to its majestic splendour... Once again, the dreamer awoke... this time filled with love beyond measure... The dreamer or the dreamed... the Real or unreal... who was she?*

Guidance

Neptune,[41] planet of vision, dreams and initiator of universal compassion, sits centre stage in this dramatic seascape. As 'lord of the sea' it knows the subtle rhythm of lunar tides that sweep from sandy bed to ocean shore. Through gentle swell to crashing wave that eats the land with a will that does not care, it knows, like no other, the way of water. This master of mysticism is thus well equipped to seduce even the strong-willed into the most depraved areas of human consciousness whilst also making available, to all who would sacrifice their worldly needs, the wide expanse of love that has as its origin the Higher Self, or Soul. As god of the waters, it does not need a reason to love or a focus upon which it may lavish its affections: Neptune loves because its **nature** is Love; it loves because the nature of Love is to love. The qualities of this nebulous planet are thus expressed through two visions – *Illumination* and *Illusion*. Great gifts may be bestowed by aligning with either but there are also many traps. *Illumination* leads you into the subtle realms of light, the *Way of the Soul*, but, as intimated in the opening script, all is often not as it seems. Those who are unfamiliar with its territory, unaccustomed to its brilliance or seduced by subtleties in their desire nature may be easily confused or led astray. The way forward is to allow your heart to lead but with a mind that is clear. Place all outer appearances and inner 'sparkles' under the microscopic lens of discernment and then give all up to the light of universal love. Love because it is the nature of Love to love. Love because the nature of **you** is Love. Remember the message of the dream... when death has claimed the false, there can be no doubt as to the Real... but it takes a mind that's clear to know it...

---

[41] Five visions portray the essential essence of the outer 'transpersonal' planets: *Awakening* (Uranus), *Illumination* and *Illusion* (Neptune), *Transcendence* and *Underworld* (Pluto).

Illumination

Quality: Inner Vision
Absolute Aspect: Will
Geometry: None
Rainbow Sphere: Truth

Contemplation

*... the storm raged... the little boat, tossed here and there by mighty waves, surrendered to its passage. Rudderless... powerless... **alone**... it had no choice. The rider cowered inside... fear, a familiar bedfellow, engulfed its heart... Imagination, fuelled by a mind that knew no bounds, reduced its countenance to a quivering mess... then to stature frozen beyond all recognition... The rider could take no more, could no longer resist the inevitable, it had to let go... Slumped upon the wooden floor, heart a steady murmur in its breast, breath a gentle rise on the wind... it gave of itself... completely... to the boat... Then came the wave... and with it their demise... Splintered flesh, bloodied timber... swallowed, all too quick, by oceans deep... called the dreamer from her sleep... Twixt night and day she tarried, idly pondering the dream... In spite of her untimely death, she felt no fear, no quickening of pulse or shortness of breath... How could it be? Consciousness slipped away... The light was blinding but oh-so refreshing... Confused, elated, the traveller opened its heart to its majestic splendour... Once again, the dreamer awoke... this time filled with love beyond measure... The dreamer or the dreamed... the Real or unreal... who was she?*

Guidance

Neptune,[42] planet of vision, dreams and initiator of universal compassion, sits centre stage in this dramatic seascape. As 'lord of the sea' it knows the subtle rhythm of lunar tides that sweep from sandy bed to ocean shore. Through gentle swell to crashing wave that eats the land with a will that does not care, it knows, like no other, the way of water. This master of mysticism is thus well equipped to seduce even the strong-willed into the most depraved areas of human consciousness whilst also making available, to all who would sacrifice their worldly needs, the wide expanse of love that has as its origin the Higher Self, or Soul. The god of the waters does not need a reason to love or a focus upon which it may lavish its affections: Neptune loves because its **nature** is Love; it loves because the nature of Love is to love. The qualities of this nebulous planet are thus expressed through two visions – *Illumination* and *Illusion*. Great gifts may be bestowed by aligning with either but there are also many traps. The astral world is not only known for its preponderance of ghosts and ghouls, it is also rife with enticing spiritual imagery that is never quite as it seems; it is not called the world of glamour and illusion for nothing! *Illusion* is a sojourn into the world of desire and addiction. It asks that you look deep into this aspect of the small self to know the subtleties that drive your behavioural responses and feed your basic needs and that you lie all upon the altar of compassion. Allow your heart to lead and surrender all outer appearances and inner 'sparkles' to the light of universal love. Love because it is the nature of Love to love. Love because the nature of **you** is Love. Let desire for anything else fall away.

---

[42] Five visions portray the essential essence of the outer 'transpersonal' planets: *Awakening* (Uranus), *Illumination* and *Illusion* (Neptune), *Transcendence* and *Underworld* (Pluto).

Illusion

Quality: Collective Dream
Absolute Aspect: Love
Geometry: None
Rainbow Sphere: Truth

Contemplation

Like a fire they burned... fuelling her passion, her search... her reason for being, the very heart of her Soul... and, to her, the keys to existence itself... Questions, seemingly unanswerable, had nourished her innermost Self as far back as she could remember... "What is the origin of the primal impulse? What form did it take? How did Absolute move from being All to appearing as nothing? Why? Why would 'something' that was infinitely 'everything' choose to express its opposite?" Displaying infinite patience, Teacher responded, *"This is how it is,"* they said, *"Absolute is complete. There is nothing that isn't it. You know this from our earlier lessons.*[43] *However, within Absolute are the conditions to express outwards through its substance, consciousness. This substance is not Absolute; it is the* **expression** *of Absolute. Do you understand? It is important you are able to make this distinction before proceeding further."* Esmerelda nodded in agreement. *"Now, within the infinite expanse of Absolute are qualities essential to its Being-ness,"* Mentor continued. *"Love, Will and Intelligence (mind), which are so much a part of its nature that it is impossible to distinguish them as anything other than it." "So there are apparent separates within its wholeness but they are not detectable as such?" "Precisely!"* they replied. *"Concurrent to the moment of expression, these qualities come together to form a triple vortex, a trinity, which creates the cause for a new reality to be birthed. All subsequent appearances will thus be imbibed with their inherent frequencies. Does this make sense?" "Yes,"* she answered, *"but what of the primal impulse behind the expression? What form does it take? And what part, if any, does it play in the unfolding of the new reality?"* They smiled at her quickening grasp of the teaching. *"Quite simply, the primal impulse is an idea, a vision, arising through the combined force of the triad and expressed outwards as substance."* The familiar quizzical expression graced her brow. *"We will use metaphor to explain. Imagine a brand new garden, one that has yet to be planted but has the most fertile soil in which to establish all manner of life. In your hands are the seeds, but they are not ordinary seeds, they are miracle workers bearing the blueprint of your vision. Furthermore, the soil is not ordinary either; it contains every nutrient, every particle necessary to manifest all possible realities from the smallest atom to the most expansive universe – effortlessly." "So if I were to mirror Absolute and allow vision to arise from the vortex of expression, the fruit of my garden would be limited only by the extent of my imagination?"* ventured, Esmerelda. *"Absolutely. Moreover, your* **conscious** *engagement in mirroring the creative process of Absolute is to fulfil its purpose. The outer appearance, expressing its inherent substance, returns reality to the origin of its vision –* **you** *are the reason Absolute chose to express itself through an apparently separate particle." "Mmmm... but what was the role of thought in the unfolding vision?"* she wondered...[44]

Guidance

Absolute is complete. It is all, all is **it**. Primal impulse is an idea that is expressed outwards as consciousness. It is otherwise known as purpose – Divine Purpose.

---

[43] See *Conversion*.
[44] See *Eye Eye*.

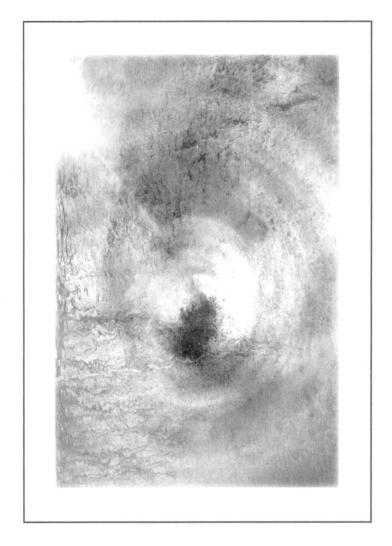

Impulse

Quality: Divine Purpose
Absolute Aspect: Intelligence
Geometry: None
Rainbow Sphere: Will

Contemplation

The builder gathered into himself the stock of his trade... Light in substance was his way... geometric grids were the foundation of his work... and love... love of life, love of form and love of beauty within expression... Signatures of his craftsmanship, they defined the hallmark of a mind that cast no reflection, that knew well the pattern of its group and that swam, with awareness, in the river of its inherent Being-ness. Now it was time for him to build anew... time to ignite sparks of mind within substance... to create in harmony with those who knew the Way of Fire... First, a thought, a single packet of light encoded with purpose, followed by a note, the Word of Power, issued from a heart that had renounced forever the course of desire.... to set in place structure for a new vision of reality. Masters of earth, air, fire and water answered the call... as did those whose nature was the force attractive, whose hearts beat in tune with the pulse of purpose, whose rhythm matched his own. Brothers in Light were these companions along the way... They who, like he, had danced upon waves, faced the dragons' gate and received the gift of fire... Now, as One, they joined with the Masters of Genesis to celebrate their Ultimate expression... in raising matter to its purest form...

Guidance

The subtleties of mind become increasingly more difficult to discern as we get closer to the realm of the Soul. The higher mind, as intimated in the script, is less concerned with thought and more with the expression of its inherent substance, consciousness. However, employment of thought is paramount in the creation of reality, so how is this apparent paradox resolved? How do we execute thought without using its primary mode of expression – mind? The short answer is 'we' don't. *Initiation* asks you to dive into the **substance** of mind, where every thought, each appearance, is known to be a mere particle within a broader and more inclusive expression – consciousness. It asks that you befriend its quintessential presence and, above all, it asks that you make of your mind a clear channel for the unfolding of its purpose. In this way, thought, as expressed through the mind of one who thinks, is a seed sown in the substance of its own essential nature. It knows itself **as it is**, not as mind would have it believe. This is one of several visions reflecting the multi-faceted nature of mind, where the importance of thought varies according to the consciousness of the mind through which it is expressed. Take your lead from the script: the mark of an initiate is not evidenced through performing unexplained 'miracles' but through mastery over its lower desire nature, particularly, the skilful direction of thought as it unfolds within its parent river, consciousness. Only when the particle is aware it is **substance** will it be a conscious co-creator... only then will the builder know the form with which it works...

Initiation

Quality: Inclusiveness
Absolute Aspect: Intelligence
Geometry: None
Rainbow Sphere: Order

Contemplation

Deep within a watery cave, in a time when tears of the past are as footprints in the sand, the seeds of unknowing endure. In quiet solitude they wait whilst the gardener of the Soul sleeps. Unaware of the treasure held deep within her breast, she dreams instead of the forever war waged between light and dark, between truth and false, between self and other and between that which thinks and that which feels. She knows not how to make it stop, though she has tried... many times. She sighs... eyes firmly closed... as the endless dream goes on... When will this war within her cease? When will the two turn towards each other in peace? Or dance together as one? When?

Guidance

Three visions[45] address these deep, soul-searching questions, but before offering any resolution, we must look closely into the territory from which they are birthed. The dreamer, although clearly asleep, is nevertheless aware there is a war going on inside her, one she seeks desperately to resolve and one in which she has clearly identified the players. All she lacks is the wherewithal to bring about a reversal in the way they relate to each other. Little does she realise, in her desperate state, how close she is to attaining that which she desires above all else. The gardener of the Soul must cease her quest and allow the seeds of unknowing to unfurl in their own time. As the tears of the past are released, the flower of understanding is born and the duelling brothers may at last withdraw their swords to bow in recognition of the great gifts each has bestowed upon the other. *In Lak'ech*, in both ideal and vision, is the end of the war. The title is drawn from a Mayan greeting of the same name, meaning, "I am in you, and you are in me." However, it is so much more than this: 'In Lak'ech' is a way of life, a moral code, whose origins lie in the sacred space of the heart as recognition of unity. When the mind is aligned with the pure light of Spirit to such a degree that it ceases to exist, **identification** is with **all that is**. Even though dual aspects such as self and other appear, they are merely forms, not separate entities. How can anyone or anything be separate if wholeness is present? It is not possible. *In Lak'ech*, both as moral code and vision, is, therefore, the art of right relationship, not only between human beings but also between every life form in the cosmos.

---

[45] *In Lak'ech, Quiescence, Sacred Space.*

In Lak'ech

Quality: Right Relationship
Absolute Aspect: Intelligence
Geometry: None
Rainbow Sphere: Love

Contemplation

*The Serpent slept... the waters raged... whilst the Great Light looked on. Many tried, most failed, to call her from her sleep... but they knew not her ways... They little understood the power that may be invoked, the havoc that may be caused, if the one who held the wisdom of the age was released before her time. Still, in ignorance, they tried... hungry for her gift of the eternal flame... Still, their waters surged within... stirred by fires untamed... And still, they comprehended not the Law. For only when the great spiral has done its work and the Three are returned again to One, may the Serpent awaken from her sleep... Only then, in full majestic splendour, may She rise up to greet her Lord... to say, with clarity... "I **see** you..." And then... only then... may they,* as One, *redeem the Way of Fire...*

Guidance

The redemption of fire is a purification process in which the divine feminine awakens in response to the call of Spirit but **only** after deep inner work has been completed. Unconscious psychological and emotional behavioural patterns are unceasingly surrendered to the fire of the Soul, all desire fed by the lower self is renounced and the inner female returns to her 'Lord' thus ending the paradox of duality. *Inner Alchemy* is therefore an evolutionary journey on which every letting go leads to ultimate triumph of Spirit (fire) over the 'lower-emotional desire nature' (water). It brings together forces of profound spiritual significance with clear direction – change! However, the implications are so much more than this. The synchronous relationship between each element is alchemical, signifying a total disintegration of the old that the new may emerge in such a way that it bears no resemblance to its former self – like the caterpillar metamorphosing into a butterfly. As the script forewarns, this is not something to be forced. It comes about through dedicated and concerted effort. Fire has many connotations, from blind rage to the highest spiritual illumination, whilst 'baptism' by water cleanses the emotional body, allowing feelings to be felt without suppression. However, when these two elements come together **unconsciously**, the reactive response is similar in magnitude to that of a tsunami; its capacity to harm both self and others goes without saying, but it also consigns the propensity to merge with Spirit to the same burial ground. Awareness is the key, and it employs the fire of mind, initially, to quell the waters of passion. As the Spirit of fire moves upon the face of the waters, light falls as soft gentle rain through the locus of your heart. Stripped naked to your core, unhindered by your love of story, all appearances are free to come and go; they, as you, are clearly seen as mere emanations within a wondrous field of liquid golden light. Now take a step back. Can you **see**? Can you hear the call? Are you ready to dive into the waters of the Soul... and tread the *Way of Fire*?

Inner Alchemy

Quality: Self-Healing
Absolute Aspect: Intelligence
Geometry: Spiral
Rainbow Sphere: Order

Contemplation

*Cold as ice, secure within its crystalline substance, the seed that came to earth began its lengthy period of gestation. In the heart of the Mother it placed its trust, whilst all around, ancient ones, in company with its over-shadowing Presence, tended to its needs. Well they knew the sacrifice it had made, the love it held for them and their fair land, the prophecy that must be fulfilled. Well they knew the difficulty of the way that lay ahead. And well they knew the rich reward that may be bestowed upon **all** should their endeavours reach fruition. So steadfastly and together they worked, each imparting their gifts in equal measure, setting new foundation for the Law. Removed from all record was the entrapment of time, erased forever the way of war, sown instead imprints of a new way. Seeds of brotherhood, spirit of co-creation, ways of being never before known to man, were sown as packets of light into a new structure. For millennia the Starseed had rested amongst others of its kind, buried deep within the substance of its earthly tomb, but now, with the dawning of the age of disintegration, its intrinsic order awakened to bring balance in the ensuing chaos. Light fulfilled its destiny... blueprint for a New Earth was born... and Starseed worked out its purpose alongside those whose resonance matched its own...*

Guidance

Inner Earth is sister to *Starseed,* both housing the same Lemurian Starseed crystal and holding equal measure of intent. Although each is integral and complete, as individual visions reflecting diverse units of consciousness, they tell the story of how a single particle of divinity begins its exploration in a far-away galaxy to culminate deep within our earthly domain as a seedling. *Starseed* marks the outset and inter-galactic portion of this journey; *Inner Earth* is where it lands and works out its destiny. The process in its entirety serves as a metaphor for the involutionary and evolutionary unfolding of consciousness in its sojourn from Spirit to integration with matter. What begins as a spark, a mere particle within an outpouring of substance, evolves over time to become a whole new way of being that heralds the dawn of a new era, not only for individuals, but for the planet as a whole. Its method is consciousness, brotherhood is its expression and the spirit of co-creation, its foundation. It is time to extend the hand of friendship to those who work in the subtle realms of nature, and to the Mother who breathes life into all forms and to offer the gift of the stars. Recognise the Starseed within, **be** the pure channel of creative force that flows within and through you and consciously express outwards a vision of the new way... Know, as packets of light explode within the matrix of its substance, that destiny is fulfilled... Balance is restored... both in you and the planet. What greater act of service can there be?

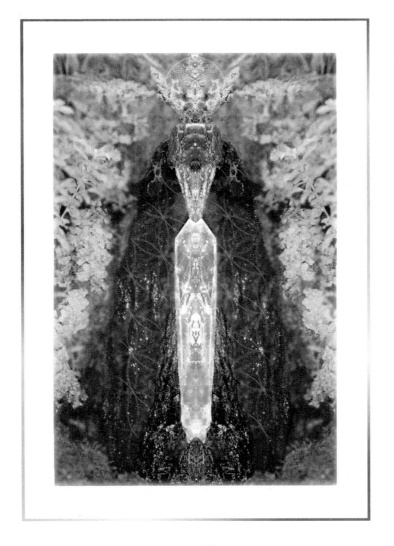

Inner Earth

Quality: Holy Marriage
Absolute Aspect: Love
Geometry: Divine matrix, torus
Rainbow Sphere: Rainbow

Contemplation

It began with a spark, although it was barely discernible as such. Like a solitary firefly illuminating the darkest night... it was just a spark... wasn't it? How could she possibly have known the impact it would have, the power it would unleash... or the devastating potential it held to destroy that which she considered her greatest asset. Where had it come from... this insignificant packet of fire, this isolated thought that had set her mind ablaze with light? What was its source? Who was the dispenser of the flame? And who was the thinker? A vision, fleeting but clear, appeared before her inner eye. *Upon the floor in front of her were piles of books stacked one on top of the other, a plethora of information contained within numerous articles and, of course, her trusty laptop where all manner of research may be undertaken. All around the air was **still**, pregnant with untold knowing... and knowledge.* Esmerelda could not contain herself; she laughed until her belly ached. Her customary method of research seemed so primitive, tedious and, well, ridiculous! *"Ok,"* she softly goaded her inner teacher, *"Show me **your** way."* Allowing this was in itself a tremendous challenge. Her greatest assets, or so she believed, were her attention to detail and her meticulous approach to research, especially into topics like this one. Now she had to go deep into its territory, seek out the origin of thought and determine its modus operandi and purpose, and all without using her mind! Nevertheless, she stepped aside and permitted the Word to pour forth its wisdom. *"The spark, a particle of divine fire within substance, originates as an impulse in the mind of Absolute; it is a function of its Being-ness. Once ignited, it follows its agreed pathway in accordance with its Will. Spark ignites spark through multiple layers of existence until it is discerned as thought in the mind of one who thinks – such as you."* Subtle threads of understanding joined the dots in her head as Mentor continued. *"In consummate surrender, the light of clear-seeing enables Truth to stand revealed. Light Codes of Creation, embedded within the substance of Absorption, are keys to unlocking the power of thought. Remember, assimilation within the Cause before expression is the method by which consciousness unfolds within itself to co-create itself; thought, as a packet of light within its substance is no different. Every thought returns to itself as an expression within Cause to manifest as reality, whether for good or ill."* Now it all made perfect sense.

Guidance

Three visions[46] tease apart the workings out of thought as it is expressed through an equal number of layered expressions: body, Soul and Spirit. *Inside Out* is the Soul, intermediary between Spirit and matter, whose signature force fuses Will, Love and Intelligence (mind) as pure expression of Spirit. Its reflective nature serves as a mirror to abiding consciousness as well as awakener to those who turn their attention towards its realm. *Power to make the Voice in the Silence heard* is the gift of this vision... but first, you must turn your senses inwards and listen...

---

[46] *As Above, So Below, Inside Out, Sweet Surrender.*

Inside Out

Quality: Altruistic Intent
Absolute Aspect: Will
Geometry: None
Rainbow Sphere: Mind

Contemplation

Caw Caw, Caw Caw, Caw Caw... The call (which she perceived to be a racket) was insistent. So much so, it brought her stomp through the woods to an abrupt end. Equally annoying and far more detrimental to her current state of mind, as well as her somewhat misguided sense of well-being, was the effect it had upon the flow of her entangled web of melodramatic thoughts. Caw Caw, Caw Caw, Caw Caw... it persisted, adding for good measure a crescendo with each utterance. Caw Caw, Caw Caw, Caw Caw... "Alright, alright," she acknowledged, whilst turning in the direction of its source. "You have my undivided attention, now what do you want?" She had arrived at the foot of a somewhat uninspiring tree, characterised by a preponderance of ivy hugging its trunk from base to sky, and searched amongst its foliage for the cause of her disturbance. Almost at the top, amongst its uppermost branches, perched a crow. Now silent, gaze fixed meaningfully upon the expectant child below, it waited patiently for her to acknowledge its presence. As their eyes met, language became detrimental to dialogue, and in the enveloping stillness, presences of species hitherto apart found knowing of each other. Crow, shapeshifter and keeper of Sacred Law, led the way. Through oceans deep and rivers swift and true, in thunderous clouds to the softest drops of dew, past mountains high capped with ice and silken flowers painted white, into seams of crystal deep beneath the crust, they travelled. Each encounter was an opening to the Way, every place an adherence to the Law and, without exception, each contact an exposure of the truth. Earth was sick, the Mother was dying and responsibility lay with the species to which she belonged. The child, wise beyond her years, was sick to her stomach... She understood why Messenger had been insistent... knew the purpose of their meet... and now she must act...

Guidance

Ten visions[47] pave the way to restoration of balance following centuries of neglect inflicted upon our planet by the human race. Individually, as characters in the script, they tell a tale of creation as it is reflected through your inner diamond. *Integrity*, in partnership with *Raindance*, is a co-creative dance in which uncharted, unconscious waters, territory with which Crow is familiar, are brought into balance. Attention in the image is drawn to an imposing presence. Standing tall amidst tranquil waters upon an island at the confluence of two fast-flowing rivers, it is in clear command of the surrounding area. Aware that it is a player in a game, that co-workers in the field of magic play their part and that one who is instrumental in its completion is a willing participant, it is unperturbed by the magnitude of the task in hand. Familiar with the depths where the mistress of the deep sleeps... it knows her worth... and as courtier to her gilded layers... it knows, beyond all doubt, that in heralding her value, the earth is redeemed... as too, are you.

---

[47] *Alchemist, Fortitude, Integrity, Invitation, Messenger, New Earth, Raindance, Reception, Sanctuary, Stewardship.*

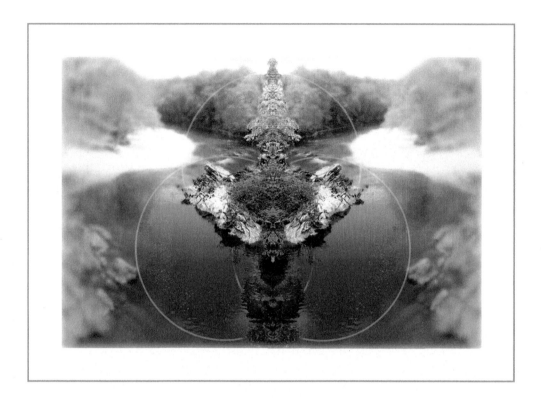

Integrity

Quality: Balance
Absolute Aspect: Will
Geometry: Triquetra
Rainbow Sphere: Light

Guidance

Three master visions, *Will*, *Love* and *Intelligence*, mark the divine triad, represented by a triple toroidal vortex, which gives birth to each respective symbol. Their combined and equal force serves as a prism whereby fractured light – seven coloured rays of the inner rainbow – is expressed outwards as substance; every ray, and by association every *vision of reality*, therefore has their unified essence running through it, regardless of appearance. *Intelligence* expresses divinity through intelligent activity that employs the Universal mind. Negative, receptive pole to Spirit's positive outpouring, it ensures the primal impulse, Divine Will, is effortlessly carried forward into every life form. From galaxies, stars and planets to atoms, quarks and molecules, from creatures of air, land and sea to every expression of human consciousness, throughout all kingdoms in nature, without exception, this pulse of intelligent will commands all to vibrate to its tune. Time and space come under its governance, as do involutionary and evolutionary forces, including the rate at which a unit of human consciousness is returned to Spirit; there are far greater forces directing the flow of life than you could ever be aware of. Look to the natural world, observe its passage through time, and you may gain a glimpse into the supreme quality of activity unfolding around, through and within you. Yield to its principles and life will seamlessly deliver the ultimate reward, with minimal effort.

The **Law of Economy** ensures that this is how it must be. Governing the material and spiritual evolution of the cosmos, it sets a vibratory note to each atom and molecule making up every physical life form, fine-tunes it to the metronome of Divine Will and returns the multiplicity of its existence to the state of unity from which it originated. It perfects every atom of time, from milliseconds to eternal periods defining cosmic eras, and carries them forward with the least resistance, using the minimum of force and maintaining all in a state of perfect balance throughout each stage of the journey. Essentially, this Law takes the primal impulse, scatters it to the far reaches of the universe and ensures that every particle is kept separate from the others until its calling to return has reached its point of least resistance. In daily life, it understands these rhythms and moves with them, surrendering all resistance, and flows with 'what is', as it is, in each moment; herein lies the road to peace.

Two spirals,[48] one left, the other right, moving in universal symmetry make this the perfect **symbol** for contemplating the forces at play revealed through the commentary. The most important quality to embrace, however, is the innate essence of the spiral itself – love. It is love that makes the world go round and love that lies at the heart of every life form in the cosmos. Remember this whilst contemplating this vision. Remember this as you go about your daily life. Remember… and then **feel it**.

---

[48] The 'Fibonacci spiral', mentioned on p.87, p.104, pp.449–450.

Intelligence

Quality: Law of Economy
Divine Triad: Prism – Intelligence
Geometry: Spiral, torus, triquetra
Rainbow Sphere: Rainbow

Contemplation

Caw Caw, Caw Caw, Caw Caw... The call (which she perceived to be a racket) was insistent. So much so, it brought her stomp through the woods to an abrupt end. Equally annoying and far more detrimental to her current state of mind, as well as her somewhat misguided sense of well-being, was the effect it had upon the flow of her entangled web of melodramatic thoughts. Caw Caw, Caw Caw, Caw Caw... it persisted, adding for good measure a crescendo with each utterance. Caw Caw, Caw Caw, Caw Caw... "Alright, alright," she acknowledged, whilst turning in the direction of its source. "You have my undivided attention, now what do you want?" She had arrived at the foot of a somewhat uninspiring tree, characterised by a preponderance of ivy hugging its trunk from base to sky, and searched amongst its foliage for the cause of her disturbance. Almost at the top, amongst its uppermost branches, perched a crow. Now silent, gaze fixed meaningfully upon the expectant child below, it waited patiently for her to acknowledge its presence. As their eyes met, language became detrimental to dialogue, and in the enveloping stillness, presences of species hitherto apart found knowing of each other. Crow, shapeshifter and keeper of Sacred Law, led the way. Through oceans deep and rivers swift and true, in thunderous clouds to the softest drops of dew, past mountains high capped with ice and silken flowers painted white, into seams of crystal deep beneath the crust, they travelled. Each encounter was an opening to the Way, every place an adherence to the Law and, without exception, each contact an exposure of the truth. Earth was sick, the Mother was dying and responsibility lay with the species to which she belonged. The child, wise beyond her years, was sick to her stomach... She understood why Messenger had been insistent... knew the purpose of their meet... and now she must act...

Guidance

Ten visions[49] pave the way to restoration of balance following centuries of neglect inflicted upon our planet by the human race. Individually, as characters in the script, they tell a tale of creation as it is reflected through your inner diamond. *Invitation* works with *Reception* to build a 'New Earth', where humankind and Mother Nature function as one in equal, co-creative partnership. *Invitation* is, as its title implies, an open hand of friendship extended from those who inhabit the subtle realms of nature to you as an individual and to humanity as a whole. The image presents a turbulent picture where subtle, otherwise hidden, beings preside over troubled waters; any coming together of species requires a large degree of trust from both parties whilst carrying the risk of stirring up grievances rooted in the past. However, despite the appearance of turmoil, there is hope: the scene, as a whole, is one of unity set with intention to cooperate. As ever, the process begins with you.

---

[49] *Alchemist, Fortitude, Integrity, Invitation, Messenger, New Earth, Raindance, Reception, Sanctuary, Stewardship.*

Invitation

Quality: Participation
Absolute Aspect: Will
Geometry: Triquetra
Rainbow Sphere: Beauty

Contemplation

*"You won't transcend it unless you're in it," they said. "It's your 'stuff'..." they admonished. "You will never be a 'nice, spiritual person' if you harbour these soul-destroying patterns of behaviour towards yourself and others," they declared, with unquestionable certainty. Voices guiding her on her journey that she may attain that which she desired above all else... voices she trusted, friends on the path, those in the know, imparting wisdom from the wise... voices... voices. It would seem that the greater her commitment, the more she tried so desperately to belong... the less she did. She was on the brink of despair, drowning in a revolting stew where all was entangled, where thoughts and feelings conspired to evoke bliss or despair, where an enticing rabbit hole took her deeper into the abyss leading her to who knows where to face who knows what and where the sticky mesh of her compelling desires held her so tight in its grasp there was no possibility of escape... "Where is love?" she wondered. Where was the welcoming acceptance she believed to be the bedrock of all things spiritual? Was she so bad, so far beyond redemption, that she didn't qualify to receive its blessing? Surely not... Surely no one, however lost they may be, is past hope? Not even her... And then, another voice... one so quiet, so barely audible that she wondered if her ears were deceiving her... But there it was again, soundlessly soft... gentle yet clear... and so warmly accepting... of **her**... that she could not fail to hear it... "Perhaps the place of your belonging is other than this..."*

Guidance

The peaks and troughs of treading a 'spiritual' path have been well documented in teachings, mythologies and words of wisdom throughout the ages, but when you get down to the nitty gritty, what does it really mean? How **do** you move from lowly grub to majestic butterfly and, most importantly, how do you discern the false from the true, especially when those companions on the way are so convincing in their direction? *Journey* addresses these core issues. It has an affinity with the astral, 'desire' body, the 'entanglement' ground, whereupon thoughts and feelings take on an identity in their own right to define who you are. This is the great illusion: you are not your thoughts any more than every transient feeling characterises you as a person. It is time to tear apart this web of deceit, to delve deep into your true nature and to stand in the certain knowledge that who you are right now is a consequence of a path well trodden, whether for good or ill. So turn within, experience truth as only you know it and, above all, know beyond any doubt that which **you are not**. Remember, the still-small voice is a tried and trusted friend whose guidance is grounded in the Real, so shed the opinions of others and ask yourself, *how far down the rabbit hole must I travel before I wake up to its Presence?*

Journey

Quality: Commitment
Absolute Aspect: Love
Geometry: None
Rainbow Sphere: Will

Contemplation

Oh, how she loved this simple life... If she did nothing but bathe in its wonder for the remainder of her days, she would leave this world... content. But it was not to last – even simplicity had its complexities – and before too long she was carried along in a spiral of activity... Soon even that fizzled out. How strange. For a brief moment in time, all was still... and in the ensuing pause, simplicity appeared again... "Now it's getting really weird," she reflected to herself, as activity, this time in the form of thought, commanded attention... She was getting wise to this cyclic flow now... so instead of choosing one over the other, she allowed the spiral to take her wherever it wished... More strangeness followed... in the form of bubbles... yes, that's what they were... bubbles... Bubbles... just like those that rise to the surface when you shake a pop bottle... only these were inside... deep inside... her belly? And each little bubble... as it effervesced inside... made her smile... it tickled... it had a life of its own... it made her laugh... silently... and it made her heart explode into a zillion untold happy stories. She had never known such joy... never, in a million years, would she have imagined so much pleasure could be generated from inside... her belly?

Guidance

Everything about this vision is encapsulated in the title's three letters: J-O-Y! It is hard to imagine how such a nondescript word could embody so much wealth in both feeling and sensual imagery that leads the mind through rapturous circles and endless spirals to feed an imagination that would otherwise be bereft of substance. Untold stories, whose source can only be the realm of the gods, beat in synchronous rhythm to the tune of paradox unveiled, whilst the Lord of the Dance laughs with gay abandon at the stupendous results of his abundant creations. The possibilities and opportunities for expansion and growth are beyond the confines of a mind embroiled in worldly thought or a heart encased in steel; it takes a transparent, open and magnanimous spirit to attract the boundless Love of this cosmic distributor. The fool, in traditional tarot, is one such example. Not quite of this world, his consciousness abides in the realm of pure spirit, where he vibrates in unison with the tune of Divine Will. Feet resting firmly in the world of matter, he dances through every earthly challenge with a child-like trust that is real, not feigned. In untainted innocence, he delights in every aspect of existence, treats every moment as if it were his last and steps fearlessly into the unknown as if his life depends upon it. His boundless love binds all to his purpose, the song in his heart calls all to listen and he shimmers with an inner luminance that outshines the sun. In short, the fool is everything whilst at the same time nothing. He lives wholly and completely because he knows he is not the one who lives. And he trusts, implicitly, simply because he is. *Joy* is an invitation to take the fool into your heart, to ride the spiral of unconditional love through every aspect of your daily life and to take a giant leap into the unknown as if it were your **first** adventure.

Joy

Quality: Serenity
Absolute Aspect: Love
Geometry: Spiral
Rainbow Sphere: Truth

Contemplation

"*There has to be more to this,*" she pondered. "*The extent of her learning can't just be about a sticky mesh or how to build a trap for unsuspecting flies, surely?*" She had been sent to learn her next lesson, the remit being to find a spider's web, observe its qualities and, in particular, watch the way of the weaver. Grandmother, meanwhile, was silent. *As she watched, a silken thread appeared from nowhere. Cast meaningfully into the air before being carried by the wind, it found anchor amidst a bush on the other side of the great divide. Then followed the most mesmerising display of natural architecture she had ever had the pleasure of witnessing. Backwards and forwards, round and round, upwards and downwards, in an ordered fashion, the little creature went, undeterred by hindrances to its quest, until, before long, what began as a solitary gossamer thread had become a delicate, intricate network of fibres whose interconnection with its surroundings brooked no denial. Esmerelda drank it all in, whilst Spider, its task complete, moved purposefully to the centre of its creation to wait.* "Now follow me." Grandmother had spoken, so refusal was not an option. *The web, very soon forgotten, became a wonder of the past, and as they entered worlds anew – some familiar, others strange to her in appearance – she knew that the way of Spider was present in them all.* "Like the casting of thread, all your thoughts, words and deeds are bridges in time that may build or divide. The web you weave may ensnare, captivate or inform, and the sacred language of the universe is present in all you create should you have eyes to see." *Grandmother, master weaver, architect of creation, had spoken... and it was wise to heed her words...*

Guidance

In eight visions,[50] characters within the script express a *Way of Wholeness* by virtue of spider medicine. Three – *Weaver*, *Whirlwind* and *Wisdom Keeper* – open doors to 'Grandmother'; the remaining five set scenes in which the spinning of the web may be contemplated. *Jubilation* marks the end of the road. What began as a bridge across the great divide, and wound its way between this way and that to find wholeness in the matrix of creation, has come full circle. The end has returned to its beginning, the head has consumed its tail and the past has found resolution in the present; sound foundations for a future in which wholeness and integration make up the web of life. Look closely and you will see that all these ingredients are seeded within this vision of completeness. However, its crowning glory lies not in its gift of fusion but in its baring of all to the boundless expanse of nothingness – a giant, yawning 'mouth' in the centre of the image – that lies at its heart. Observe it. Embrace it. Don't be tempted to fill it. Leave it... leave it... **empty**...

---

[50] *Jubilation, Multiverse, Omniscience, Timewarp, Walk in the Park, Weaver, Whirlwind, Wisdom Keeper.*

Jubilation

Quality: Completion
Absolute Aspect: Will
Geometry: None
Rainbow Sphere: Order

Guidance

Three master visions, *Will*, *Love* and *Intelligence*, mark the divine triad, represented by a triple toroidal vortex, which gives birth to each respective symbol. Their combined and equal force serves as a prism whereby fractured light – seven coloured rays of the inner rainbow – is expressed outwards as substance; every ray, and by association every *vision of reality*, therefore has their unified essence running through it, regardless of appearance. *Love* covers the full spectrum of this expression of divinity: personality (love in the three worlds: mental, emotional and physical), Soul (love for humanity as a whole) and Spirit (universal love where all forms of divine expression are embraced equally and without favour). Its force is magnetic; it draws like to like and kind to kind until atoms or units of consciousness vibrate in unison to form a co-creative cohesive whole, whether in physical form or cooperative inner group. Love is the underlying principle of our solar system, the director of the form-building show and the driving force behind every separate entity's evolutionary return to Spirit. The broad and totally inclusive expanse of love, however, will not be experienced by one who is controlled by their lower desire nature, where love for a 'special other' is blind to the presence of the Soul and the pendulum of preference swings erratically from one extreme to the other. No, Love Divine is altogether different. However, it is also the pendulum. Ponder on this.

The **Law of Attraction** is the building or Vishnu aspect of deity. It rests at the centre, holding all dualities in its inclusive embrace, to serve as a point of neutrality between the positive pole of Spirit (*Will*) and negative, matter (*Intelligence*). However, so long as the pendulum swings twixt this way and that, so long as the two are divided by mind, then love, as true redeemer, will never be found. But in the background it works, drawing all to itself, for love is magnetic – as it gives, so must it receive. In the fullness of time, this sea of fire, in which all opposites are consumed, gives rise to coherence, and in the merging of what was once deemed separate, all is found to be whole. In the human being, this cyclic spiral of attraction presents opportunities for integration at each evolutionary turn, self-realisation being the end result.

The **symbol** is a perfect expression of unison. Three petals, coloured according to the three aspects of Divinity and bounded by a circle, engage the heart-mind in direct experience of the interplay between these inseparable cohesive forces. Less obvious is a golden triangle joining the apex of each petal, again leading the mind towards unison. However, this underlying symmetry is only understood through appreciation of geometric structure; in order for the petals to be displayed in this manner, **seven** circles[51] must conjoin. In this symbol, then, is the divine triad, the Sacred Seven and the all-encompassing sphere, displayed as a circle.

---

[51] See 'What is...?' 'What is sacred geometry?', 'Seed of life'.

Love

Quaility: Law of Attraction
Divine Triad: Prism – Love
Absolute Aspect: Love
Geometry: Circle, seed of life, torus, triangle, triquetra
Rainbow Sphere: Rainbow

Contemplation

With increasing curiosity, she watched the boy on the beach, his eyes resting with ease on a remote horizon, focus directed inward on some undetermined vision, disposition filled with innocence and... wonder. Absorbed in a world of his own making, he appeared unaware of her presence... or perhaps not. She sensed ripples echoing through subtle vibrations... tangible... palpable... as he expressed thought through the seven planes of existence. Geometric structure fired into life, particles within substance aligned to fulfil its purpose and order was established. His invitation to play was joyously received by those who were ready to respond to the call. She knew this, knew the process had begun, knew the vision was soon to be reality. Esmerelda watched in wonder as she witnessed thickening in the air between the boy and the point of his vision... echoes of intent bore fruit to unite ether with matter and, as if by magic, that which was not of this world materialised right before his eyes. Dancing in and out of waves, turning somersaults through the air and emitting joyous, 'clicking' sounds unique to them alone... came the pod. And then, as fast as they appeared, they were gone. The boy walked nonchalantly away... it was another perfectly ordinary day in paradise... She turned to Mentor and smiled. *"Now do you understand how easily a thought-form may become reality?"* they said. *"The important distinction, in this case, is that the origin of thought was not the lower mind, such as we experienced in our last session.*[52] *The boy, inspired by curiosity, was merely playing; there was no emotional charge, no grasping, no needing to fulfil a lack in himself. His demeanour was one of wonderment, pure joy of being. He was in the presence of Absolute, so all appearances he knew to be an expression of this – and only this."* *"Therefore, 'magic' was as natural an occurrence as a walk in the park,"* she responded, excitedly. *"But what if he had wanted a repeat performance?"* she continued. *"What if he had wanted them to come closer or perform certain feats in order to prove he had manifested his vision?"* *"If an emotional charge is attached to any thought-form,"* Teacher reinforced, *"even though its origin may have been pure at the outset, the lower elemental aspect is introduced to create a new cyclic process with desire as its origin. The dissolution of a thought-form is as important as its creation, so once it has worked out its purpose, it **must** be allowed to return to its point of its origin – substance. In other words, to follow the example of the boy, celebrate then let it go. Always return to substance, for it is consciousness who directs the show, not you."* *"So true cosmic ordering is a **non**-ordering, with no grasping or wanting!"* she exclaimed, and then reflected, *"It is an expression of joy in celebration of that which has already been given."*

Guidance

Cosmic ordering is nothing to do with the **Law of Attraction,** even though its principles serve as a foundation. As the script says, *true cosmic ordering is a non-ordering.* Not only is there an absence of grasping, wanting or needing, but there is no one, no self, no identity doing the asking – not even in the case of 'ordering' for others. Ask and you shall receive... but first, you must step out of the way.

---

[52] See *Point of Light.*

Materialisation

Quality: Thought-Form
Absolute Aspect: Love
Geometry: Metatron's cube
Rainbow Sphere: Mind

Contemplation

Caw Caw, Caw Caw, Caw Caw… The call (which she perceived to be a racket) was insistent. So much so, it brought her stomp through the woods to an abrupt end. Equally annoying and far more detrimental to her current state of mind, as well as her somewhat misguided sense of well-being, was the effect it had upon the flow of her entangled web of melodramatic thoughts. Caw Caw, Caw Caw, Caw Caw… it persisted, adding for good measure a crescendo with each utterance. Caw Caw, Caw Caw, Caw Caw… "Alright, alright," she acknowledged, whilst turning in the direction of its source. "You have my undivided attention, now what do you want?" She had arrived at the foot of a somewhat uninspiring tree, characterised by a preponderance of ivy hugging its trunk from base to sky, and searched amongst its foliage for the cause of her disturbance. Almost at the top, amongst its uppermost branches, perched a crow. Now silent, gaze fixed meaningfully upon the expectant child below, it waited patiently for her to acknowledge its presence. As their eyes met, language became detrimental to dialogue, and in the enveloping stillness, presences of species hitherto apart found knowing of each other. Crow, shapeshifter and keeper of Sacred Law, led the way. Through oceans deep and rivers swift and true, in thunderous clouds to the softest drops of dew, past mountains high capped with ice and silken flowers painted white, into seams of crystal deep beneath the crust, they travelled. Each encounter was an opening to the Way, every place an adherence to the Law and, without exception, each contact an exposure of the truth. Earth was sick, the Mother was dying and responsibility lay with the species to which she belonged. The child, wise beyond her years, was sick to her stomach… She understood why Messenger had been insistent… knew the purpose of their meet… and now she must act…

Guidance

Ten visions[53] pave the way to restoration of balance following centuries of neglect inflicted upon our planet by the human race. Individually, as characters in the script, they tell a tale of creation as it is reflected through your inner diamond. *Messenger* is the crow. As a whole, the bird kingdom serves as intermediary between Devic realms and the world of form, specifically the human race, where crows in particular are considered to be 'masters'. Legend has it that Crow was obsessed with its shadow, unable to leave it alone. Eventually, shadow awoke, took on its own identity and consumed Crow, thereby also affirming Crow as master of illusion. Many parallels may be drawn between Crow and one treading a spiritual path but there is far greater urgency being called upon here: the future well-being of our planet is at stake. It is time to pay attention to these messengers from the sky, to hear their plea and to adhere to **their** Law, not those created by man.

---

[53] *Alchemist, Fortitude, Integrity, Invitation, Messenger, New Earth, Raindance, Reception, Sanctuary, Stewardship.*

Messenger

Quality: Sacred Law
Absolute Aspect: Intelligence
Geometry: Seed of life
Rainbow Sphere: Light

Contemplation

Interred within the folds of flesh, a mind inside a brain struggled to be free. Unaware of the hidden splendour, the thinker dwelled upon its cast of clay. Every last particle of globular substance, each deeply ingrained behavioural pattern, every feeling that fuelled forever its story, it knew. It knew them all... intimately. The role of thought, with its subtle hooks that sowed seeds of doubt within a heart that longed to feel, the fields of knowledge that ensnared all to its domain. Yes, the thinker was master in its class and knew well the art of manipulating form to its will. But it knew naught else. It knew not mind, nor the substance from which it grew, nor that which gave it life. No, the thinker knew itself and that which validated its existence, but it was blind to all else. And so mind continued its struggle and thinker wove its web... Then came the spark... In a flash, to the graveyard of its past went the thinker as mind soared free. For the first time, it saw beyond the confines of its incarceration. It observed, in rapturous wonder, the eternal stream that flowed from source to subject, understood the mechanism by which the thinker had been birthed and knew, beyond all doubt, the magnificent perfection held within its unfolding journey. But, as yet, it did not know itself. Its intrinsic substance, its life force, had yet to be experienced. Beneath the mirror of its own reflection, it failed to recognise that the witnessed was none other than itself... it sensed not the all-consuming fire that burned so resolutely within, had yet to experience Love from one whose heart announced the Great Unknown... No, in a like manner to the thinker, it was blind... Then came the spark...

Guidance

Nine visions[54] mark the relationship of Spirit to matter as it is expressed outwards through a particle within its substance. Complete in itself, each vision charts a course from Source, through multiple layers of expression, to reach the deepest level of forgetfulness before effecting a way return. *Mind*, as title and script suggest, is a calling to know its subtle games and to wake up to its influence in your life. Its three aspects chart a well-defined initiatory pathway[xiii] where each inner letting go leads to a more inclusive and illumined reality. The *thinker* is the most concrete; its, largely unconscious, transient nature ensures entrapment within the perpetual cycle of cause and effect, death and rebirth. *Mind* as the Soul, whose nature is love and whose essence is eternal within time and space, serves as intermediary between Spirit and matter. It marks the territory where fusion and blending begin to take place. The *spark*, boundless and unknown, lies beyond the confines of the space-time continuum and completes the process of fusion. *Thinker, mind* and *spark* when blended become one purified instrument for expression of Divine Will in matter.

---

[54] *Creation, Emergence, Empty Vessel, Eye Eye, Mind, Phone Home, Recognition, River of Souls, Welcome.*

Mind

Quality: Reflection
Absolute Aspect: Will
Geometry: None
Rainbow Sphere: Love

Contemplation

"There has to be more to this," she pondered. *"The extent of her learning can't just be about a sticky mesh or how to build a trap for unsuspecting flies, surely?"* She had been sent to learn her next lesson, the remit being to find a spider's web, observe its qualities and, in particular, watch the way of the weaver. Grandmother, meanwhile, was silent. *As she watched, a silken thread appeared from nowhere. Cast meaningfully into the air before being carried by the wind, it found anchor amidst a bush on the other side of the great divide. Then followed the most mesmerising display of natural architecture she had ever had the pleasure of witnessing. Backwards and forwards, round and round, upwards and downwards, in an ordered fashion, the little creature went, undeterred by hindrances to its quest, until, before long, what began as a solitary gossamer thread had become a delicate, intricate network of fibres whose interconnection with its surroundings brooked no denial. Esmerelda drank it all in, whilst Spider, its task complete, moved purposefully to the centre of its creation to wait.* "Now follow me." Grandmother had spoken, so refusal was not an option. The web, very soon forgotten, became a wonder of the past, and as they entered worlds anew – some familiar, others strange to her in appearance – she knew that the way of Spider was present in them all. "Like the casting of thread, all your thoughts, words and deeds are bridges in time that may build or divide. The web you weave may ensnare, captivate or inform, and the sacred language of the universe is present in all you create should you have eyes to see." Grandmother, master weaver, architect of creation, had spoken... and it was wise to heed her words...

Guidance

In eight visions,[55] characters within the script express a *Way of Wholeness* by virtue of spider medicine. Three – *Weaver, Whirlwind* and *Wisdom Keeper* – open doors to 'Grandmother'; the remaining five set scenes in which the spinning of the web may be contemplated. *Multiverse* challenges your frame of reference to consider altered states of reality with which you may not even be familiar, let alone experienced. Surreal imagery, casting shades of vibrant and unusual colour and impinged upon by orbs of lighted presence, stimulate the creative imagination into believing that worlds other than our own are not only possible but real. Now bring into your awareness the spider's web. Imagine if the spaces between each thread were so vast that they rendered the appearance of the web non-existent. Place yourself at the centre. See how blind you have become to the interrelation between every thread making up each layer in the matrix. Can you sense how your knowing of all things, as vast as it may be, is confined to but one miniscule fragment of existence? Can you see how your perception of reality is incomplete? Can you?

---

[55] *Jubilation, Multiverse, Omniscience, Timewarp, Walk in the Park, Weaver, Whirlwind, Wisdom Keeper.*

Multiverse

Quality: Co-Existence
Absolute Aspect: Love
Geometry: None
Rainbow Sphere: Mind

Contemplation

Within a facet of itself is birthed a thought... followed by sound so pure it shatters into worlds anew... and in a momentary flash, the cycle without end begins. Space and time... matter in its copious guise and subtle realms of vibrant light are the backdrop to this fair land. Build and tear apart is its paradigm, order from chaos, the way. Yet here, the guardians of the race are seldom seen by man, for they know the means by which the ones that time forgets are assured of their return, and the way must ever be barred to those whose hearts do not see... such is the decree. Now, with its journey almost done, a fragment of the whole comes to rest amongst others of its kind... alike in form, yet miles apart, the history is the same. Record of its passage is held deep within its breast, through myriad forms it knows them well... from galaxies and stars to planets with their moons, from mountain and meadow to sky, night and day, from atoms and molecules to journeys past... and futures yet to come... it has borne witness to their passing, seen birth to shapes unknown... The very fabric of Spirit, it is anatomy of self, a miracle in existence if only you would see... for what greater gift can be bestowed upon one who may be damned than to find the secret of the stars within a grain of sand?

Guidance

Two visions[56] address the relationship between fractal and hologram from the perspective of each whilst being equal in measure. *Mystic Union* expresses great depth through many layers. It is a guiding light that encourages you to know the reality behind sayings, expressions and truths that have been taken as read throughout the ages and then to marry your findings with your personal journey. Central to the image is a being of enormous strength and power, arms spread wide to expose naked vulnerability at its core. In each opened palm sits a multi-layered star tetrahedron infused with circles of light, which alone, would define *Mystic Union* as a vision of integration and balance; however, there are many facets ascribed to its collective wisdom yet to be revealed. The backdrop is enticing; stars and beams of light amongst ancient ones who grace the earth with timeless truth encased in stone draw the attention inwards. But its strong allure is not for those whose eyes have seen the glamour of the pleasured way, whose heart has swum in waters deep and whose form has known the way of death; their redemption lies in pastures new where courage is the only friend. The dark chasm beckons, and all that is false must die. As the *guardians of the race* draw near, naked and vulnerable is the one who walks... alongside those whom time forgets...

---

[56] *Holographic Universe, Mystic Union.*

Mystic Union

Quality: Cosmic Knowing
Absolute Aspect: Will
Geometry: Star tetrahedron
Rainbow Sphere: Love

Contemplation

Caw Caw, Caw Caw, Caw Caw... The call (which she perceived to be a racket) was insistent. So much so, it brought her stomp through the woods to an abrupt end. Equally annoying and far more detrimental to her current state of mind, as well as her somewhat misguided sense of well-being, was the effect it had upon the flow of her entangled web of melodramatic thoughts. Caw Caw, Caw Caw, Caw Caw... it persisted, adding for good measure a crescendo with each utterance. Caw Caw, Caw Caw, Caw Caw... "Alright, alright," she acknowledged, whilst turning in the direction of its source. "You have my undivided attention, now what do you want?" She had arrived at the foot of a somewhat uninspiring tree, characterised by a preponderance of ivy hugging its trunk from base to sky, and searched amongst its foliage for the cause of her disturbance. Almost at the top, amongst its uppermost branches, perched a crow. Now silent, gaze fixed meaningfully upon the expectant child below, it waited patiently for her to acknowledge its presence. As their eyes met, language became detrimental to dialogue, and in the enveloping stillness, presences of species hitherto apart found knowing of each other. Crow, shapeshifter and keeper of Sacred Law, led the way. Through oceans deep and rivers swift and true, in thunderous clouds to the softest drops of dew, past mountains high capped with ice and silken flowers painted white, into seams of crystal deep beneath the crust, they travelled. Each encounter was an opening to the Way, every place an adherence to the Law and, without exception, each contact an exposure of the truth. Earth was sick, the Mother was dying and responsibility lay with the species to which she belonged. The child, wise beyond her years, was sick to her stomach... She understood why Messenger had been insistent... knew the purpose of their meet... and now she must act...

Guidance

Ten visions[57] pave the way to restoration of balance following centuries of neglect inflicted upon our planet by the human race. Individually, as characters in the script, they tell a tale of creation as it is reflected through your inner diamond. *New Earth* is the product, the crowning glory, of all ten visions in this set. Conscientious engagement with the nine brings completion in the ten and a new vision for our planet is birthed. But this is not the end. Snowdrops, as featured here, teach us the perennial nature of reality, as does the torus geometry in which the flowers are enclosed. In death there is always hope of resurrection, seeds sown in reverence reap the ultimate in reward and a courageous heart will always break through the most hardened of terrains. In this vision, therefore, there is a big ask. In all humility, it requests that you take the combined essence of the nine into your heart and then express it outwards, without agenda, into your world...

---

[57] *Alchemist, Fortitude, Integrity, Invitation, Messenger, New Earth, Raindance, Reception, Sanctuary, Stewardship.*

New Earth

Quality: Purification
Absolute Aspect: Love
Geometry: Torus
Rainbow Sphere: Light

Contemplation

"There has to be more to this," she pondered. *"The extent of her learning can't just be about a sticky mesh or how to build a trap for unsuspecting flies, surely?"* She had been sent to learn her next lesson, the remit being to find a spider's web, observe its qualities and, in particular, watch the way of the weaver. Grandmother, meanwhile, was silent. *As she watched, a silken thread appeared from nowhere. Cast meaningfully into the air before being carried by the wind, it found anchor amidst a bush on the other side of the great divide. Then followed the most mesmerising display of natural architecture she had ever had the pleasure of witnessing. Backwards and forwards, round and round, upwards and downwards, in an ordered fashion, the little creature went, undeterred by hindrances to its quest, until, before long, what began as a solitary gossamer thread had become a delicate, intricate network of fibres whose interconnection with its surroundings brooked no denial. Esmerelda drank it all in, whilst Spider, its task complete, moved purposefully to the centre of its creation to wait.* "Now follow me." Grandmother had spoken, so refusal was not an option. *The web, very soon forgotten, became a wonder of the past, and as they entered worlds anew – some familiar, others strange to her in appearance – she knew that the way of Spider was present in them all.* "Like the casting of thread, all your thoughts, words and deeds are bridges in time that may build or divide. The web you weave may ensnare, captivate or inform, and the sacred language of the universe is present in all you create should you have eyes to see." *Grandmother, master weaver, architect of creation, had spoken... and it was wise to heed her words...*

Guidance

In eight visions,[58] characters within the script express a *Way of Wholeness* by virtue of spider medicine. Three – *Weaver*, *Whirlwind* and *Wisdom Keeper* – open doors to 'Grandmother'; the remaining five set scenes in which the spinning of the web may be contemplated. *Omniscience*, as both title and quality suggest, introduces the fount of all knowledge, a web in which the western mind is increasingly entangled through its pursuit of science, education and even religion. However, this facet of the diamond holds far greater potential than the mere accumulation of 'facts', whatever field of research is being investigated. When viewed through the lens of an All-Seeing eye, knowledge ceases to be microscopic, and if it is also married with an all-embracing heart, through direct life experience, dogmatic know-how is transmuted into wisdom. Make no mistake, knowledge is an invaluable tool in the pursuit of All-Knowing – omniscience – but it is not an end in and of itself; to consider it to be so is to be ensnared in a web of self-deceit in which the only weaver is... you.

---

[58] *Jubilation, Multiverse, Omniscience, Timewarp, Walk in the Park, Weaver, Whirlwind, Wisdom Keeper.*

Omniscience

Quality: Knowledge
Absolute Aspect: Intelligence
Geometry: Metatron's cube
Rainbow Sphere: Mind

Contemplation

Ostara takes its name from the German goddess of spring and is ostensibly linked with the spring equinox, when the days and nights are of equal length. Its seasonal quality is to breathe an air of hope into a land that has, for too long, been held in the cold, hard grasp of winter, when long, seemingly endless nights intrude upon the meagre light of day and the warmth of summer is but a long forgotten memory. In spring, as the earth awakens from her long sleep, *Ostara* brings the gift of new life and hope, and the expectation of wishes soon to be fulfilled. All her creatures spring magically to life: birds sing with renewed vigour, nests holding promise of new life appear where once there was none, flower buds are impatient to open and a fresh, warm breeze caresses the land. It is the season of joy, of celebration, and an opportunity to embrace the wonder of life in all its burgeoning splendour. Additionally, each season has an elemental force that is its signature tune; air connects to the intellectual mind but its essence is most at home in the heart. *Draw upon the remnants of long, solitary nights as you ponder upon the qualities of this season of new beginnings. Allow its magic to permeate every cell in your body, every drop of emotion in your heart and every shade of doubt that muddies your mind. Breathe... breathe deep... breathe again... Savour the gift of new life... Allow each refreshing breath to cleanse your thoughts... to bring hope to your heart and warmth to your bones. Be as the air... allow the sacred breath of Spirit to release the dark days of winter... witness its crystalline clarity breathing light into a mind that's clear... and feel your heart rejoice in its presence. Breathe... breathe...*

Guidance – balance is alchemical

The combined essence of eight linked visions is an invitation to tune into the natural rhythm – birth, life, decay and death – expressed through the four seasons (*Ostara*: Spring, *Cosmic Orchestra*: Autumn, *Woodhenge*: Summer, *Unconquered Sun*: Winter) – and to marry it with those areas in your life symbolised by the four elements, expressed through four visions – *Fire*, *Earth*, *Air* and *Water*. Notice the gifts each aspect brings, encouraging you to become more aware of your thoughts (air), feelings (water), physical well-being (earth) and spiritual essence (fire). Be the detached observer; see how the same cyclic pattern, so evident in our natural world, flows through all areas of your life. From one moment to the next, the only thing that is certain is that 'it' will change. Take your lead from the kingdom of nature, for she is a willing teacher, and remember that you have the capacity to 'fly' as much as the caterpillar. It is time for new seeds to be sown, for you to reconnect to the pulse of life and restore natural rhythm and order as a way of being... but first, you must consign the long, dark days of winter to the graveyard of the past...

Ostara

Quality: Hope
Absolute Aspect: Will
Geometry: Torus (double)
Rainbow Sphere: Light

Contemplation

Alone he stands, the Starborn; isolation and loneliness, companions of old. For too long he has walked these earth-laden pathways, Spirit ever seeking a path of return. The race of the stars long ago forgotten, his great love for this earth was grown over time, and though many moons must pass before he remembers his calling, in his heart he finds solace, in his bones he knows peace. Seeds of homecoming he waters with gratitude and tends to with care until inside they ripen to answer his prayer. As sun meets its sky and rivers, the sea, as seasons and cycles dance with joy through his veins and as forests and deserts come alive in his breast, he remembers. He remembers his calling. In a moment of knowing, he is wise to the circle, he steps into time, beyond time, where life and its cycles are complete, where all that is lost he knows to be found. On bended knee he remembers, and with Sacred Sun shining through his every word, he sends forth a cry to the land of his birth. From a soul in aloneness he adds words to his song, to the place of belonging he invites them to come and to his home on this earth he gives thanks for her care. In all haste they come, his clan from afar, to embrace their brother and rejoice in his light. And as wisdom of ages flows through his being, a bridge he becomes between earth and the stars. No more a stranger, no longer a strange land, Starborn is present, for in earth he remembers and as Sacred Mother weds Eternal Star, the path to return is established... No, he is no more a stranger, he is no longer alone. He walks the land, as the land... he walks, he breathes, he smiles... celebrating... appreciating... the wondrous sense of belonging he feels amongst this clan... this human race.

Guidance

Nine visions[59] mark the relationship of Spirit to matter as it is expressed outwards through a particle within its substance. Complete in itself, each vision charts a course from Source, through multiple layers of expression, to reach the deepest level of forgetfulness before effecting a way of return. *Phone Home* brings the gift of belonging but, as our script reveals, it does not come without cost. To feel as a *stranger in a strange land* is an all-too-familiar bedfellow, part of being human and not easily remedied. But life carries with it many choices, surprises around every corner, and it is through these choices that we create our reality. A turn of the spiral, a revolving of the great wheel, and suddenly life is transformed. What was once experienced as isolation or loneliness miraculously changes; loneliness becomes aloneness, which bears fruit as belonging. All that was required for Starborn was to *sow different seeds*. In short, he had a change of heart and chose to accept his reality just as it was. In both image and script lie potential for two (at least) diverse realities. Do you choose isolation or do you choose community, to **belong**? Know that you may also choose both – aloneness within community instils ultimate belonging. It gives birth to the authentic Self; wherever you are, whoever you are with, whether in company or not – you belong.

---

[59] *Creation, Emergence, Empty Vessel, Eye Eye, Mind, Phone Home, Recognition, River of Souls, Welcome.*

Phone Home

Quality: Aloneness
Absolute Aspect: Love
Geometry: Spiral
Rainbow Sphere: Love

Contemplation

Esmerelda, under the watchful eye of Mentor, was playing in substance. She had developed some skill in the constructive application of thought and how it may lead to inspired visions of reality, but it was time for her to understand the wider implications. It was time for her next lesson. *"Thought, as you well know,"* spoke Teacher, *"is directly related to how reality is experienced by one who thinks. But there is far more to it than this. Thought and the planes of mind play an important role in the very constructs of the universe as a whole; it is the fabric upon which, in varying degrees of subtlety, life is created."* Esmerelda listened attentively as Mentor continued. *"In order for you to understand, we must return to the origin, the point of light that created the cause for the manifestation of physical reality. Remember that consciousness, as sole expression of Absolute, recognises and ignites thought using mind as its vessel; consciousness is the origin of thought, not mind. So once a thought-form is set in motion, as in the primal Cause, it passes through seven planes to create multiple layers of existence, amplifying itself as it works out its purpose. It is a cyclic process, always returning to its point of origin. So it knows, through experience, that which it is and that which it is not; it returns to itself that the point of origin may distinguish the Real from the unreal. This is how a thought-form works."* She was trying to grasp its meaning relative to her own frame of reference, *"So if I am the originator of the thought-form, it returns to me?"* *"Yes,"* was the reply, *"but it follows the same process, passing through the seven planes before returning as an experience in your reality."* *"What are the seven planes? What is their purpose?"* she asked. *"Let us explain using a metaphor you may understand better,"* said her infinitely patient Teacher. *"The seven planes distinguish layers and particles within substance, according to their vibrational resonance, from primal impulse to the densest vibrations in matter. So if the origin of the thought-form is the lower mind, charged with emotion, it will energise and amplify the lower elemental aspect of the planes through which it passes."* Esmerelda was beginning to get the picture. *"So as energy follows thought, if I were to create a thought-form to manifest a desire or dream, it may be fulfilled but it will also charge an elemental that I may not be aware of?"* *"Exactly!"* Mentor exclaimed. *"It is not real and at some point will be taken away. Using the power of thought in this manner only serves to keep you enslaved in the desire body. If you were to use the true qualities of mind you would imprint thought-form **without agenda** and ensure its origin was consciousness, not mind. This is expression of pure mind working with consciousness, not emotion."*

Guidance

Thought is directly related to how reality is experienced in the mind of one who thinks. As the originator of thought, the product of its intention will return to you. Think about it, carefully. This is how thought works. Not only in this way, but also in the way every aspect of reality is created.

Point of Light

Quality: Cosmic Breath
Absolute Aspect: Intelligence
Geometry: Circle
Rainbow Sphere: Rainbow

Contemplation

The bridge of light was in place, a community of a like kind was assembled in purpose upon the inner planes and the Blessed One was poised in readiness to transmit the Perennial Wisdom... Time was of the essence... time not determined by the world of clocks nor even by the order of cycles great and small. No, this time was measured by something far more subtle and infinitely more profound. It was set by Presence. In the heart of the Great Mother, the Blessed One drew unto itself the mantle of silence and, with no arising nor falling, gave of its breath to the Eternal Stillness... As air moved twixt the in and the out, without beginning or end, the Will of One was thus assured of purpose... for the Eternal One Breath flows through all... and the Fount of All Wisdom lies in all, like unto One... And so, as the Beloved received, so did it transmit, as it inhaled, so did it breathe out, for the Way of One is in parlance with all... It gives as it receives, it loves as it finds and it wills as it may... such is the Way made present to all... And for aeons it has been so... round upon round of the hidden mystery made available to those who would know the ways of the Great Ones, to those who may, in their infinite yearning, sample a droplet from the sacred chalice or poise for a moment amidst their Holy Presence. But the will of the small, persistent in its ways, is obscurer of Truth... and though the Fount overflows... Its Voice is unheard...

Guidance

Five facets of the diamond[60] convey the multi-layered presence of the Soul as it expresses through kingdoms in nature. *Presence*, as the Soul of humanity, serves as a guiding light to those who would walk in the footsteps of the Great Ones and instils a way of being that is largely beyond the comprehension of those who tread a 'spiritual' path, let alone the mass consciousness of humanity. Sacrifice is its byword, but be under no illusion: immolation on the part of the Soul is by far the greatest offering in transmitting the Perennial Wisdom to the human race than any act of surrender undertaken on the part of an individual. The *bridge of light*, or 'Rainbow Bridge', is therefore an essential prerequisite to populating the evolution of consciousness amongst our fellow brothers and sisters – this human race. It demands a letting go of such magnitude that every breath draws its sustenance from stillness... where each beat of the heart echoes perennial silence... and where the totality of Being-ness radiates self-less service to all humankind, regardless of race, creed or belief... Is this for you? Will you be one with the Soul? Would you give up your dreams in order to serve... or perhaps you feel humanity is beyond redemption?

---

[60] *City of Light, Family of Light, Presence, Solar Angel, The Well.*

Presence

Quality: Being
Absolute Aspect: Love
Geometry: None
Rainbow Sphere: Rainbow

Contemplation

Deep within a watery cave, in a time when tears of the past are as footprints in the sand, the seeds of unknowing endure. In quiet solitude they wait whilst the gardener of the Soul sleeps. Unaware of the treasure held deep within her breast, she dreams instead of the forever war waged between light and dark, between truth and false, between self and other and between that which thinks and that which feels. She knows not how to make it stop, though she has tried... many times. She sighs... eyes firmly closed... as the endless dream goes on... When will this war within her cease? When will the two turn towards each other in peace? Or dance together as one? When?

Guidance

Three visions[61] address these deep, soul-searching questions, but before offering any resolution, we must look closely into the territory from which they are birthed. The dreamer, although clearly asleep, is nevertheless aware there is a war going on inside her, one she seeks desperately to resolve and one in which she has clearly identified the players. All she lacks is the wherewithal to bring about a reversal in the way they relate to each other. Little does she realise, in her desperate state, how close she is to attaining that which she desires above all else. The gardener of the Soul must cease her quest and allow the seeds of unknowing to unfurl in their own time. As the tears of the past are released, the flower of understanding is born and the duelling brothers may at last withdraw their swords to bow in recognition of the great gifts each has bestowed upon the other. *Quiescence* invites you to take a long, hard look at duality as it plays out in your daily life, for recognition of the 'two' in their purest form is a pivotal and informed stage in the awakening process. Furthermore, it asks you to rest in quiet stillness, to engage your mind in the discriminative act of clear-seeing and to send all preconceptions to the graveyard of the past where they belong. Isolated, alone and in silence, you come to know the dance of two, you welcome each into your heart and you know, beyond any doubt, each is a reflection of the other, whole and complete in themselves – One mind, One heart, One Soul... appearing in the form of two.

---

[61] *In Lak'ech, Quiescence, Sacred Space.*

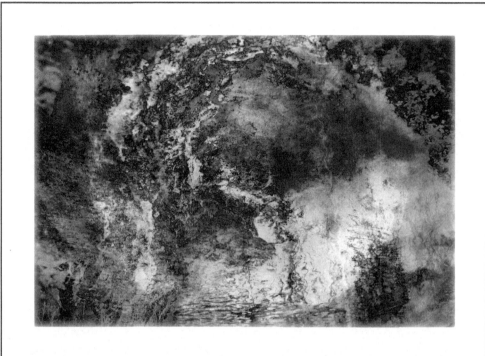

Quiescence

Quality: Isolated Unity
Absolute Aspect: Love
Geometry: None
Rainbow Sphere: Love

Contemplation

*She loved this land... this wondrous field of liquid golden light... this time in space that cast no shadow, not even when at its most luminous... Where subtle shades and lustrous gems danced in tune to One whose purpose was their only way... where radiant sparkles rejoiced in celebration of its expression and where every particle within its substance bore testament to Absolute and its total perfection. For the most part, she was not there, dissolved completely in the river of its intent, but now... now the particle that was Esmerelda had emerged... to **play**. With awareness polished to equal the most pristine in mind, heart that surpassed all understanding and willingness to serve its Will... alone, she engaged with its Presence. Miracle in existence touched her most delicate core... Its simplicity, as it flowed through and within her, brought bubbles of joyous delight... and as brave new worlds blossomed in her mind... her curiosity was aroused... In an instant, the child within... awoke! Transparent particles were there for the taking, to bounce on the wind, to attract or repel... each an appearance, a story to tell... End or beginning, they were realms to explore... In her was no doubt... each was a door... an opening... to the miraculous.*

Guidance

Rainbow Bridge aligns to the mental body – thoughts and the art of clear-seeing. It is an invitation to tap into that which is said to be the most powerful force in the universe – imagination. When these aspects of mind are unified, all that arises materialises, consciously and without effort, into physical reality. The power of creative thought shows, beyond doubt, that you are the orchestrator of your life. On one level, therefore, this vision asks you to awaken the child within and have some fun. Look at the image. The central scene is framed by a rainbow; transparent bubbles of light lead your mind's eye to explore, whilst two dogs race across the land, extending an invitation to play. Be the child. Let your imagination run wild. Pierce these bewitching bubbles with your mind and build magical worlds of your own. Play, and who knows what you may create? Remember, as you think, so you are, and if your mind is attuned to altruistic endeavour, under the direction of the Soul, there cannot fail to be a world where all existence is light; it is the ultimate expression in service to the whole. However, there is more to this vision than meets the eye, for it is multi-layered and spans the full spectrum of mind from intellect through to intuition. Esoterically, *Rainbow Bridge* defines the pathway of light linking man to his Soul and ultimately to Spirit. So by all means mimic the joyful antics of Esmerelda and play, but look also to the origin of her story. She started out as nothing, a mere particle within a field of liquid golden light, the substance of all creation. Ultimately, when the bubble bursts, it is to this she must return... as must you.

Rainbow Bridge

Quality: Imagination
Absolute Aspect: Love
Geometry: None
Rainbow Sphere: Will

Contemplation

Caw Caw, Caw Caw, Caw Caw... The call (which she perceived to be a racket) was insistent. So much so, it brought her stomp through the woods to an abrupt end. Equally annoying and far more detrimental to her current state of mind, as well as her somewhat misguided sense of well-being, was the effect it had upon the flow of her entangled web of melodramatic thoughts. Caw Caw, Caw Caw, Caw Caw... it persisted, adding for good measure a crescendo with each utterance. Caw Caw, Caw Caw, Caw Caw... "Alright, alright," she acknowledged, whilst turning in the direction of its source. "You have my undivided attention, now what do you want?" She had arrived at the foot of a somewhat uninspiring tree, characterised by a preponderance of ivy hugging its trunk from base to sky, and searched amongst its foliage for the cause of her disturbance. Almost at the top, amongst its uppermost branches, perched a crow. Now silent, gaze fixed meaningfully upon the expectant child below, it waited patiently for her to acknowledge its presence. As their eyes met, language became detrimental to dialogue, and in the enveloping stillness, presences of species hitherto apart found knowing of each other. Crow, shapeshifter and keeper of Sacred Law, led the way. Through oceans deep and rivers swift and true, in thunderous clouds to the softest drops of dew, past mountains high capped with ice and silken flowers painted white, into seams of crystal deep beneath the crust, they travelled. Each encounter was an opening to the Way, every place an adherence to the Law and, without exception, each contact an exposure of the truth. Earth was sick, the Mother was dying and responsibility lay with the species to which she belonged. The child, wise beyond her years, was sick to her stomach... She understood why Messenger had been insistent... knew the purpose of their meet... and now she must act...

Guidance

Ten visions [62] pave the way to restoration of balance following centuries of neglect inflicted upon our planet by the human race. Individually, as characters in the script, they tell a tale of creation as it is reflected through your inner diamond. *Raindance*, alongside *Integrity*, is a dance of creation where uncharted, unconscious waters, territory with which Crow is more than familiar, emerge into the clear light of day. Drawing upon its knowing of Spirit from within the depths of illusion, it ignites through love, it is light in the dark; all that hides amid the shadowlands is thus powerless to resist its call. The image paints a tale of enchantment in which lighted beings, seen clearly beneath the darkened surface, are tangible almost to the point of touch. Amidst turbulent waters, stirred by sprites in celebratory dance, a magician and master of creation orchestrates all... But know this... its real power to create is wielded by one whose essence far outshines its own... one whose Presence in Spirit... precedes the mystery...

---

[62] *Alchemist, Fortitude, Integrity, Invitation, Messenger, New Earth, Raindance, Reception, Sanctuary, Stewardship.*

Raindance

Quality: Incantation
Absolute Aspect: Love
Geometry: Metatron's cube, vesica piscis
Rainbow Sphere: Order

Contemplation

*Tick tock, tick tock... peace or war... love and hate... tick **this**, tock... **that**... light dark... tick tock, tick tock, tick tock... and so it goes on, the interminable swing from one side of the fence to the other, never ceasing its momentum, not settling on one side or the other, never knowing rest. Is this how it has to be? Must the pendulum always present the rhythm and pulse of life as a way of choice? Must the mind always be split in two, or heart torn apart, simply to live? Surely there is another way, a means by which the pressure of having to choose is relegated to the grave as would a body that has ceased to breathe. After all, who, or what, is it that powers the pendulum? Who dictates the rhythmical beat of the metronome?*

Guidance

These questions, and more, are addressed through contemplating the vision, *Rebirth*. A meditating figure, head and body split wide open, presents two faces – one at peace, the other outwardly enraged – and visually portrays how our state of mind creates the world in which we live. Constantly, almost without even realising it, we make judgements as to which 'face' we prefer – peace over discontent, happy over sad, tolerance over anger – then, as if to compound the error, we condemn one way of behaving whilst bursting with pride at the opposite. This is the inner pendulum at work. We desire peace but we seek in the wrong place. Look closer at the image and you will see both spiral and droplet emerge from the forehead of the one who shouts at the land. This is not to say that this is the polarity to choose, nor that awakening is only served by knowing our 'demons', but it highlights that choosing **either** polarity leads to entrapment within the continuous beat of two. The only way to escape the "interminable swing" is to surrender **both** to the unknown. *Rebirth* resolves all polarities but is especially powerful when considered as a triad alongside *Aspiration* and *Fusion*. Rest at the pivotal point between two polarities and soon both will disappear, as will you. Wait... wait some more... then wait again... Soon... stillness is... It wears no face, neither one nor two. It has no beat, neither fast nor slow. It is light yet casts no shadow, dark but holds no fear. It simply **is**. Now do you understand who commands the metronome? Who perpetuates the dance of two? Could it be you?

Rebirth

Quality: Revelation
Absolute Aspect: Intelligence
Geometry: Spiral
Rainbow Sphere: Truth

Contemplation

Caw Caw, Caw Caw, Caw Caw... The call (which she perceived to be a racket) was insistent. So much so, it brought her stomp through the woods to an abrupt end. Equally annoying and far more detrimental to her current state of mind, as well as her somewhat misguided sense of well-being, was the effect it had upon the flow of her entangled web of melodramatic thoughts. Caw Caw, Caw Caw, Caw Caw... it persisted, adding for good measure a crescendo with each utterance. Caw Caw, Caw Caw, Caw Caw... "Alright, alright," she acknowledged, whilst turning in the direction of its source. "You have my undivided attention, now what do you want?" She had arrived at the foot of a somewhat uninspiring tree, characterised by a preponderance of ivy hugging its trunk from base to sky, and searched amongst its foliage for the cause of her disturbance. Almost at the top, amongst its uppermost branches, perched a crow. Now silent, gaze fixed meaningfully upon the expectant child below, it waited patiently for her to acknowledge its presence. As their eyes met, language became detrimental to dialogue, and in the enveloping stillness, presences of species hitherto apart found knowing of each other. Crow, shapeshifter and keeper of Sacred Law, led the way. Through oceans deep and rivers swift and true, in thunderous clouds to the softest drops of dew, past mountains high capped with ice and silken flowers painted white, into seams of crystal deep beneath the crust, they travelled. Each encounter was an opening to the Way, every place an adherence to the Law and, without exception, each contact an exposure of the truth. Earth was sick, the Mother was dying and responsibility lay with the species to which she belonged. The child, wise beyond her years, was sick to her stomach... She understood why Messenger had been insistent... knew the purpose of their meet... and now she must act...

Guidance

Ten visions [63]pave the way to restoration of balance following centuries of neglect inflicted upon our planet by the human race. Individually, as characters in the script, they tell a tale of creation as it is reflected through your inner diamond. *Reception* works with *Invitation* to build a 'New Earth', where humankind and Mother Nature function as one in equal, co-creative partnership. *Reception* is, as its title implies, an opening to receive the hand of friendship extended by those who inhabit the subtle realms of nature – to you as an individual and to humanity as a whole. In contrast to its partner, *Invitation*, the image presents a vision of tranquillity, if not radiance, as if the task in hand has already reached completion. Clouds that may otherwise obscure the sun are reduced to mere reflections in a pond, lily pads are well met as hands across the great divide and the picture as a whole inspires such a quality of natural ordinariness that there is no other recourse but to... **shine**...

---

[63] *Alchemist, Fortitude, Integrity, Invitation, Messenger, New Earth, Raindance, Reception, Sanctuary, Stewardship.*

Reception

Quality: Open to Receive
Absolute Aspect: Will
Geometry: Vesica piscis
Rainbow Sphere: Beauty

Contemplation

*"Hello, Little Brother..." A gentle radiance warms their hearts as recognition dawns... and as memories stir in minds that unite each to the Cause... times long since gone emerge to tell tales of friendship and stories of brotherhood, sacrifice and love. Often without form, indistinguishable one from the other... they never wavered from their course... never failed in their commitment to put its Purpose ahead of their own. Now the Call of the Eternal brings the brothers to its side, and once more the link is forged... Its purpose is clear... in their hearts is no doubt... to make manifest the heart of All-Knowing... and awaken seeds of peace amongst men... Long is the journey... laden with sacrifice soon to come, for one must give up the other... must give of his light to the world... and enter the prison of darkness without knowing of purpose or cause. All knowledge of Self is forsaken to be a particle apart from the whole. Divorced from kin for aeons, he must struggle and falter... alone... But take heart, beloved traveller... your brothers are always near... In forms you will come to recognise... distinguished by light in their eyes... they will appear when you least expect, often in times of despair, to whisper sweet songs of encouragement... and remind you of all that you've shared... So take heed Little Brother and listen... "Make of the darkness, your friend... Be light in the land of the shadows... and soon you'll effect your return. At journey's end, each to the Cause returns... and all will have knowing of One, then in our hearts we shall celebrate... for **we are** the land of the sun..."*

Guidance

Nine visions[64] mark the relationship of Spirit to matter as it is expressed outwards through a particle within its substance. Complete in itself, each vision charts a course from Source, through multiple layers of expression, to reach the deepest level of forgetfulness before effecting a way of return. *Recognition* addresses the outset of this journey and has far more outreaching consequences than that of friendship. It blazes a trail of Ultimate intent, requires the most harsh of sacrifices and, although aware of the pitfalls on the way, delivers the unsuspecting pilgrim to the door of its own demise, a journey with which we are all familiar. The gift of this facet of the diamond is to make you aware of this. At the point of return, you must first know the light that shines through your own eyes before your 'brother' may be recognised, you must gaze in the mirror and **know** Truth in your Being-ness and, above all, you must have the courage to allow your inner luminance to radiate outwards for the benefit of all. *Recognition* is, hence, a call to service, a call that has been answered many times before... But you will never fulfil its purpose if you cower in the dark all alone... Now stand up... celebrate, with joy in your heart... then greet your brother... who's been there, beside you... for so long...

---

[64] *Creation, Emergence, Empty Vessel, Eye Eye, Mind, Phone Home, Recognition, River of Souls, Welcome.*

Recognition

Quality: Discrimination
Absolute Aspect: Love
Geometry: None
Rainbow Sphere: Mind

Contemplation

Imagine, for a moment, a place that is so safe, so secure and so profound that you can rest in eternal peace, even as you watch all that you treasure most in the world crumble into nothing at your feet... How does it feel to know... really know... all that unfolds before your eyes is in perfect accord with the natural rhythm and pulse of some great cosmic orchestra? How does it feel to be so in tune with this rhythm, you become it? You know... really know... you are a perfect note within this magical song of existence... And how does it feel to know, really know, you are also the orchestrator of that song?

Guidance

Resting Place is an invitation to rest in the cosmic womb of creation, to experience the wondrous space that holds all events separate and to know man and universe, singer and song, are one and the same – one glorious note echoing throughout all time, all existence. The image is presented in three distinct layers, each cascading from one to the other through seemingly unknowable depths; consciousness, as the torus geometry, rests at the centremost well. These layers may be likened to expressions of the *One Life* – Spirit, consciousness and matter – and invitation to explore each one is implied. Transparent light beings, emanations of the One, are the guardians of the space who ensure its subtle radiance spans from the heights to the depths. However, *Resting Place* is also a **container** for these worlds. It is at once preserver, sacred space and separate entity wherein great cosmic forces move unimpeded throughout all realities, untarnished by the form through which they travel. Just as water has no recourse but to follow its way from source to sea, so it is with Spirit as it penetrates deep into the heart of matter. If you have stepped into this vision, it is time to fulfil the purpose to which you and all mankind were born, to be an intermediary between Spirit and matter, to know yourself as consciousness as it expresses itself **through** you. Wherever you are and whatever is unfolding in your life now, this is the occasion to step back from the drama, put aside your self-centred agendas and abide as the presence of one who **is**. Be the landscape of the Soul, container and contained, real and unreal, the singer and the song. Know that wherever your consciousness abides, its true expression is limitless presence wherein the great waters of the cosmos, including life itself, flow. Be a magical, experiential doorway where time and space, all that is lost and incomplete, cease to exist, and enter into a way of being where consciousness may explore itself... where it may recognise itself within itself... and finally see... with crystalline clarity... it is far more than that which is revealed.

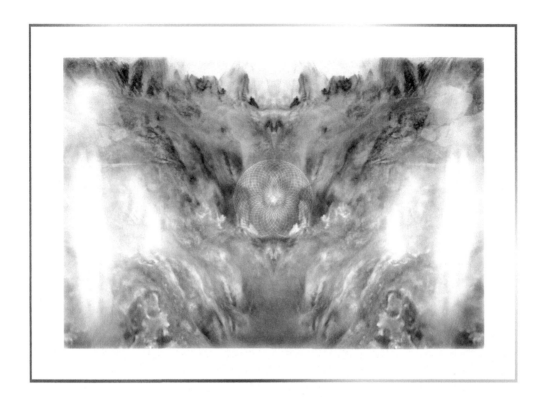

Resting Place

Quality: Cosmic Waters
Absolute Aspect: Love
Geometry: Torus
Rainbow Sphere: Rainbow

Contemplation

*As ever, it is light that draws her... tantalisingly close, yet so, so far... a pinprick of brilliance in an otherwise neutral sky... too distant to bathe in its presence... or so it would appear. Nevertheless, it entices, encourages her... to explore further. At first she is reticent, believing its laser-like radiance would cut like a knife through the tender fabric of her soul, but she is captivated and allows her eyes to engage. It burns with a flame so bright, yet does not scald, it welcomes her in a way that fuels her desire for more and all the while it comes closer and closer as if to swallow her whole... Vibrant and alive is the land of light... shores as clear as diamonds... atmosphere as pure as the driven snow... there is nothing... no-thing... that isn't... **it**. She pauses to absorb the miracle of her arrival... Becomes it's strange echo in her heart... And as the air draws songs from her breath, her softened gaze addresses the land she once knew as home... To the trees in their radiant autumn glory, to the clouds as skating shadows across familiar terrain and to the creatures of land, sea and sky... she sends forth her note. To those of her kind, who know not from whence they came, who have yet to hear the echoes of their own songs upon the wind... she sends forth her note. And to those she has walked alongside... in recognition of the beauty they have shared... and mountainous feats they have mastered... she sends forth her note. As a chorus of unsung voices, from a heart swelled with love that is other than her own, she sounds the one word... gratitude...*

Guidance

An inclusive and loving heart opens the door to reverence, the signature force of this facet of the diamond. It leads the way to a deeply appreciative disposition, in which respect and honour, alongside a profound sense of awe, are shown towards the very fabric of life itself, regardless of outer appearance. Key to integrating this into daily life are the dynamics of a torus, the focal geometry of the image, and its inherent ability to exchange and eventually blend together substances from within and around itself. This doughnut-shaped energy field is in a perpetual state of motion, yet perfect balance and stillness lie at its core, and it's these characteristics that assist in moving from self-centredness to reverence. And so **be** still. **Be** fluid. Ask yourself, why would you want to hold on to that which has already gone? Then wait. As the note of gratitude is sounded, it strikes a chord in one whose heart is open, and you may feel it in the space between spaces. Listen to the tender rhythm of the heart's sound; within it you will find the hidden code of the universe... then you will experience the true meaning of gratitude... then you will experience **life**... But first, you have to open the door...

Reverence

Quality: Appreciation
Absolute Aspect: Love
Geometry: Torus (double)
Rainbow Sphere: Beauty

Contemplation

Beneath an exotic sky, pregnant with promise, a blanket of warmth like 10,000 suns casts subtle shades of golden hue across the land. Rolling hills, once uninterrupted for as far as the eye could see, are ripped apart, that water, unstoppable in force, undaunted in its resolve, may forge a way from source to sea. And even though the torrent fumes, even though cries of the damned are heard wide and far and even though its beginning lies in a time far, so very far, away, still the golden Sun gives of its radiance. It kisses the earth with love, graces air with its breath, spawns fecund thoughts amongst those who drown and whispers echoes of peace into their hearts. Yes, over aeons of time, the golden Sun has given of itself but its gifts have gone unnoticed, its oh-so-quiet voice left unheard. The river of life carries souls of the damned, and though their cries are many, their suffering intense, the water in which they drown is born through tears that they alone have shed. And though their hearts beat as one in history, they stay immune to each other's woes, for they are but unconscious victims inside a self-inflicted cause... Forever closed to all but their sorry stories... held fast in the clutches of time...

Guidance

River of Souls, in spite of its simplistic presentation, is a vision of profound depth with the potential for transformation barely hinted at through the script. It is clear that there are at least two ways of interpreting its message: from the perspective of the Soul or from that of one who is entrapped within the perpetual cycle of death and rebirth; both are equally valid. However, how may one merge with the other? How may this seemingly impenetrable gap be bridged? These questions demand answers. A clue is offered in the vision's Soul alignment quality, *Change of View*; another lies in the *unconscious cause*; both are resolved through the cultivation of mindfulness in action. So **be** aware of the inner narrative; know that with each self-perpetuating thought, with every self-serving desire and all harmful acts, the valley of tears swells to consume the land and extinguish the light of your soul. Remember, the sun is ever present, even on the cloudiest of days, so take your lead from the script. Listen to the still, small voice, enjoy silence, feel the warmth from your inner fire nourishing those parts that would step into the endless tide and allow the golden Sun to express its radiance **through** you. Rivers of life are tunes to the Soul but the time has come to leave all for the shore. The pitfalls are many, the precipitous path is unknown and the way of the warrior is to be forever alone. But the clarion call of the Soul is insistent, one that can never be denied, and the heart of one who is drowning is ideally placed to receive...

River of Souls

Quality: Change of View
Absolute Aspect: Will
Geometry: None
Rainbow Sphere: Love

Contemplation

In times of old, it was said, three serpents roamed amidst the ethers of the known universe, each with a tale to tell and a vital message to impart. The first, it was said, had as its origin the very beginnings of time and, though it knew it not, was source to the other two. Birthed in eternal darkness, forgetfulness its only companion, it patrolled the far reaches of its domain wondering why it must be so. Abandoned, lost and alone; desperate, afraid and, at times, fiercely angry. In desperation, it gave up its fruitless search and came to rest in the darkest recesses of dark; deathless sleep its only companion... or so it believed. At times, it would awaken from its slumber. At times, the miracle of sleep yielded an alternative 'lighter' reality. Often, the reasons for its banishment played tricks upon its mind and its all-consuming tyrant reduced its sense of worth to dust... Yet there were also times, glimmers of hope, when 'something' other than 'this' appeared on the horizon... But in the end, nothing changed... or so it believed. To this day, it is said, the black snake safeguards its kingdom, wallowing in the mire of its own self-disgust, little knowing the effects upon reality that it is engendering, blind to the presence of its serpent brothers whose lives are so dependent upon its grace and oblivious, beyond measure, to the Light it yearns to greet holding it so close...

Guidance

The tale of three snakes, expressed through an equal number of visions,[65] is one that, if the wider implications of their respective offerings is grasped, brings clarity and vision into every aspect of the awakening journey. The unconscious black snake, left alone in the dark with little hope of reprisal, does not understand the predicament in which it has, through no apparent fault of its own, been placed. More than this, it is totally oblivious to its lighted 'shadow', so much a part of its innate essence that they are indistinguishable in their reflections of each other. In *Roots,* unlike its sister vision, *Fortress,* there is but one snake... one **lighted** snake... which takes its place, in full waking consciousness, to command centre stage amongst the roots of its entangled past. Ascendency proves to be simple. Unconscious roots, source of **all** psychological and emotional entanglements, are anchored in the past, and when held under the lens of clear-seeing, they cease their hold upon the present. If, at the same time, all are embraced inside a heart of compassionate acceptance, they dissolve into nothingness, becoming one with the whole tree. The black snake, in recognising its lighted shadow, turned to face its past and consumed its own tail, and all that shivered in the dark became visible. *Roots,* then, is a calling to the past... not through a mind steeped in judgement... but through a heart willing to embrace, with love... all that arises from the dark...

---

[65] *Fortress, Headspace, Roots.*

Roots

Quality: Simplicity
Absolute Aspect: Intelligence
Geometry: None
Rainbow Sphere: Truth

Contemplation

The boy in the boat was at peace... with nowhere to go, nothing to do and no goal to which to aspire, he granted his mind free rein to wander as it willed... Into the dim, distant past it travelled... past highs and lows, meetings and partings, he saw it skim relentlessly across the many and varied landscapes of sea and shore, beyond love and pain, to arrive at a space in time where it had all begun, to the moment when he first set out upon his journey of self-discovery. Mapped out clearly before him, he watched as his life unfolded through a young man striding purposefully along a lane with not a care in the world and scarcely a backward glance. The boy marvelled at how easily he could recall it in such fine detail and, more importantly, with such ease of being, for the circumstances of his parting were not the most agreeable. But no, he could see it clearly, as if it were but a day away, and he watched, somewhat bemused, as the peace in his heart allowed the movie of his life to play without judgement or regret. Now all had come full circle... a young man, mature beyond his years through experience, meaningful only to him, had borne fruit inside the heart of a small boy, and as the past returned all to the present, the little boat commanded his attention again. Cast adrift upon an unforgiving sea, beneath a moonlit sky pregnant with promise... mind turned its attention to more recent events. Welcoming the presence of utter despair, the boy relived the moment his remaining oar had disappeared into the unfathomable depths below and watched in horror as his all-too-fragile vessel bounced upon waves relentless in their determination to destroy. He felt the icy grip of death as fear turned his heart to stone and felt the rise of hope when he was granted life. Finally, exhausted past exhaustion, and out of all plausible options, he gave up his pathetic attempts at survival – even in thought... A deep and profound stillness came upon him... there in the silence of the Great Beyond... he knew peace... peace beyond measure... And as the boat slipped easily beneath the waves... the boy smiled in gratitude...

Guidance

When life brings you to a place where all tried-and-tested methods or strategies to control have been exhausted, there really is no place left to hide. You are as the boy in the boat, naked, vulnerable and stripped to your core. With no possible hope of salvation, you come face to face with the agent of your own demise. In abject despair, you recognise that the only course of action open to you is to give in. However, hitting rock bottom is in itself salvation if you would but heed the guidance revealed through the script. So accept you have no control over anything or anyone, let go of all personal agendas, including those directing the flow of your life, and then turn your attention inwards and **wait**...

Rudderless Boat

Quality: Waiting
Absolute Aspect: Love
Geometry: None
Rainbow Sphere: Truth

Contemplation

*It came from the dark... the Great Dark. It came from time... not through time, **from** time.*
It came alone, one fragment in the dark, alone. But it was not alone. It was All. Space
adjusted to accommodate its emergence. So much a part of its fabric, barely discernible as
separate, so dark it was not even there, so light it could only be dark. But, as features became
more pronounced, as just a hint of facial structure appeared, they could be seen, clearly: eyes,
nose... mouth... and then... more. Force attractive drew to itself others alike in kind. Sparks in
the dark, myriad pinpricks of light, they came to its bidding until, in its completion, the crystal
palace, vibrant, alive and pristine in presence, stood resplendent in all its glory. Filling a space
where once in time there was dark, the Great Light was birthed. Now the work could begin...
now the calling of the group, each apart yet complete within itself, may bestow the gift... Now
the seed of future revelation may be sown... Now substance would be imbibed with Presence...

Guidance

Christ-Consciousness is this vison's Soul alignment quality and, as felt within the words
of the script, its clear signature force. It radiates pristine clarity, crystalline intention and
purity of heart, such as is only evidenced when the heart and mind, untouched by any
form of division, conjoin. It is clear that sacred work is in progress. Space is being held
for the manifestation of 'something' not quite of this world. Delicate light forms encircle
a well that is dark, an imposing figure, somewhat alien in appearance, spreads wide its
'wings' to expose its naked and vulnerable heart, whilst inside, the sacred work unfolds.
Seven concentric circles, the seed of life, perfectly suspended above a void-like space,
complete the picture. Herein is the blueprint hinted at in the script, where all sentient
life forms may realise their Ultimate in potential: Christ-Consciousness. This is not a
rarity; it is a right. However, it is not something to be claimed by the false self. When all
you have ever believed yourself to be, all hope of whatever you may become and all you
think you are in this moment has gone, then, and only then, will the light of the True
Self emerge. Return to the image. Despite an icy, cold feel, at the heart within the heart, a
gentle fire nurtures the Spirit within. All signature elements rest in a space that is pristine,
pure and clear. Use these qualities to guide you on your way. With every inner letting go,
the ice melts, with every moment spent in Truth, the seed ripens and with every ounce
of courage employed in the dissolution of self, the walls imprisoning the Soul crumble.
It is not about raising your vibration, chanting mantras or praying to some holy being in
an unattainable 'heaven'. Christ-Consciousness arises when nothing else is left. It arises....
when the ice cracks... when tears are allowed to flow...

Sacred Ceremony

Quality: Christ-Consciousness
Absolute Aspect: Intelligence
Geometry: Seed of life
Rainbow Sphere: Love

Contemplation

Deep within a watery cave, in a time when tears of the past are as footprints in the sand, the seeds of unknowing endure. In quiet solitude they wait whilst the gardener of the Soul sleeps. Unaware of the treasure held deep within her breast, she dreams instead of the forever war waged between light and dark, between truth and false, between self and other and between that which thinks and that which feels. She knows not how to make it stop, though she has tried... many times. She sighs... eyes firmly closed... as the endless dream goes on... When will this war within her cease? When will the two turn towards each other in peace? Or dance together as one? When?

Guidance

Three visions[66] address these deep, soul-searching questions, but before offering any resolution, we must look closely into the territory from which they are birthed. The dreamer, although clearly asleep, is nevertheless aware there is a war going on inside her, one she seeks desperately to resolve and one in which she has clearly identified the players. All she lacks is the wherewithal to bring about a reversal in the way they relate to each other. Little does she realise, in her desperate state, how close she is to attaining that which she desires above all else. The gardener of the Soul must cease her quest and allow the seeds of unknowing to unfurl in their own time. As the tears of the past are released, the flower of understanding is born and the duelling brothers may at last withdraw their swords to bow in recognition of the great gifts each has bestowed upon the other. The vicinity of the physical heart, within a space so nondescript the full extent of the universe can fit inside, so small the world's most powerful microscope would struggle to see it, is where this miraculous turnabout takes place. From atom to galaxy, ocean to mountain, human to Soul, dimension to dimension, every conceivable possibility of that which has yet to be dreamed is held within this little-known chamber. *Sacred Space*, as this cave of unknowing, allows access to its dominion but not in a way that is familiar. It takes a giant leap of faith to plunge into the valley of death, to face the darkness of the past and to enter the waters of your own undoing. Are you ready? Take a deep breath, swallow your pride and listen to that still, small voice deep within your breast. Soon you will ask yourself why it took you so long, why you waited all this time to receive the most beneficial gift the universe has to offer.

---

[66] *In Lak'ech, Quiescence, Sacred Space.*

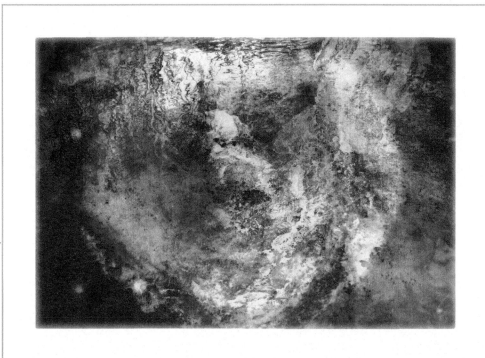

Sacred Space

Quality: Hearing
Absolute Aspect: Love
Geometry: None
Rainbow Sphere: Truth

Contemplation

Caw Caw, Caw Caw, Caw Caw... The call (which she perceived to be a racket) was insistent. So much so, it brought her stomp through the woods to an abrupt end. Equally annoying and far more detrimental to her current state of mind, as well as her somewhat misguided sense of well-being, was the effect it had upon the flow of her entangled web of melodramatic thoughts. Caw Caw, Caw Caw, Caw Caw... it persisted, adding for good measure a crescendo with each utterance. Caw Caw, Caw Caw, Caw Caw... "Alright, alright," she acknowledged, whilst turning in the direction of its source. "You have my undivided attention, now what do you want?" She had arrived at the foot of a somewhat uninspiring tree, characterised by a preponderance of ivy hugging its trunk from base to sky, and searched amongst its foliage for the cause of her disturbance. Almost at the top, amongst its uppermost branches, perched a crow. Now silent, gaze fixed meaningfully upon the expectant child below, it waited patiently for her to acknowledge its presence. As their eyes met, language became detrimental to dialogue, and in the enveloping stillness, presences of species hitherto apart found knowing of each other. Crow, shapeshifter and keeper of Sacred Law, led the way. Through oceans deep and rivers swift and true, in thunderous clouds to the softest drops of dew, past mountains high capped with ice and silken flowers painted white, into seams of crystal deep beneath the crust, they travelled. Each encounter was an opening to the Way, every place an adherence to the Law and, without exception, each contact an exposure of the truth. Earth was sick, the Mother was dying and responsibility lay with the species to which she belonged. The child, wise beyond her years, was sick to her stomach... She understood why Messenger had been insistent... knew the purpose of their meet... and now she must act...

Guidance

Ten visions[67] pave the way to restoration of balance following centuries of neglect inflicted upon our planet by the human race. Individually, as characters in the script, they tell a tale of creation as it is reflected through your inner diamond. *Sanctuary* is the crow's nest. Situated high in the treetops, roosts have an uninterrupted view of the surrounding area where chicks are assured of protection against potential predators. Throughout the ages, 'churches' from all traditions have served as 'nests' to the community, offering sustenance and support during times of need. But it is to the mother of all nests we must turn our attention. Haven to the bereft in Spirit, evidence that divinity in creation is expressed through all life forms – from the lowliest grub to galaxies across the cosmos – Mother Earth provides sanctuary to all. To be conscious in her beneficence is to embody sanctity of place... To experience wonder in creation, to bathe in nature's beatitude, is to give thanks to life...

---

[67] *Alchemist, Fortitude, Integrity, Invitation, Messenger, New Earth, Raindance, Reception, Sanctuary, Stewardship.*

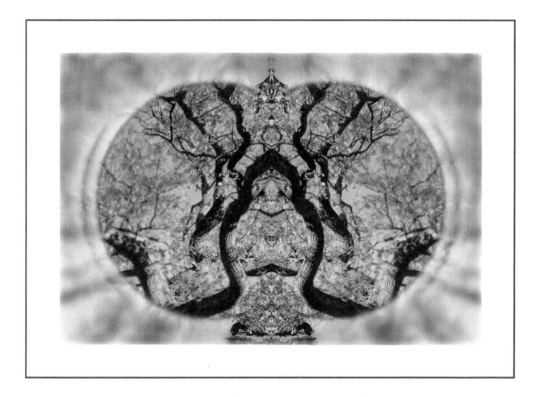

Sanctuary

Quality: Well-Being
Absolute Aspect: Will
Geometry: Vesica piscis
Rainbow Sphere: Love

Contemplation

*In the locus of the soul, they meet for the first time... two brothers, each a mirror of the other, though they know it not... One, who loves beyond measure, his heart an open door, is a magnet to those in need... His motto, "To love and include," determines the course of his life. The other, less well loved, sees with a light so clear, even the most depraved in spirit are struck by its radiance. His discriminating gaze knows all things intimately... Naked, in Truth, is his way... no-thing is exempt... not even himself... Heavenly twins, two wings of a bird, are the brothers, two. They are the circle and point, the singer and song... as far apart as ocean and sky yet each cut from the same cloth, incomplete without the other... and still, even now, they know it not... The sacred space knows them well, has witnessed their forever journeys in silence as deep as the grave... So intent on their purpose, each following his own course, they are blinded to all but their own... But now, at this timely juncture, in this place that is so alive yet **still**... they can hear it... faint at first but clear and growing in intensity... Soon, each heeds the Voice in the Silence, feels the beat of his brother's heart as his own... knows the great gifts each has bestowed, the journey they have shared... and then, in recognition, they turn towards each other... and smile... as the mirror cracks...*

Guidance

Ancient teachings[68] speak of two essential qualities that align the heart with the mind and are needed before access to the kingdom of the Soul may be granted. As inseparable as the air from the breath, a drop from the ocean or a seed from its flower, each is fuel for the other, and together they birth the ultimate in Truth, wisdom. Appropriately expressed through two facets of the diamond, *Secret Garden* and *Dharmakaya*, they help you not only to recognise qualities of compassion and clear-seeing within yourself, but also to consciously live your life in accordance with their united principles. *Secret Garden,* compassion, is a doorway to the heart. Two divine beings extend a quiet invitation to enter the 'sacred space' whilst, concealed in the background foliage, a third Buddha offers what appears to be a vase of great import. Direction is clear. Rest quietly in the garden of your heart, allow all that comes your way to dissolve into the pure being-ness of one who is at peace with himself and be prepared to greet your brother whose light you have so far failed to see. As a bird that has mastered the air, the 'wings' of these two visions gift you the freedom of flight... but first, you have to look in the mirror...

---

[68] Mahayana Buddhism.

Secret Garden

Quality: Compassion
Absolute Aspect: Intelligence
Geometry: Vesica piscis (double)
Rainbow Sphere: Love

Contemplation

*Bang! Out of the blue it came, with power enough to strip her naked to the core. Not a sound was heard, no echoes disturbed the air. But its force sent her reeling, brought her crashing to her knees, left her quivering in the debris of her structured self's demise. As a fire, it burned this phoenix of the night, whose mission brooked no failure, whose cause alone was light. Battered and bruised she lay, confused and wary, as her mind sought justice, her heart blame, but all she came up with was the mirror of her shame. So she turned her mind inwards and stripped back the layers until she saw, clearly, all of the players. Then he stood there beside her, this dispenser of the flame... light shining brightly, mirror pristine, where his purity in Spirit could never be foreseen... "I see you," she cried, "I **see** you. You are Anam Cara, Soul friend, destroyer of unreal. You are Anam Cara who brings the false to heel." And then, as the phoenix she rose, ashes ground in dust, to state with clarity, "I am Anam Cara, agent of death, emissary to the brave... **I** am Anam Cara, friend to the Soul. And here I stand."*

Guidance

There is no mistaking the energy of this vision. It takes no prisoners and speaks of power, will and the pure unadulterated presence that knows it has a right to occupy the space on this earth upon which it is stood. This is one who has broken through the structures imposed by societal, familial and dictatorial belief systems. Above all, it knows its own self-limiting and destructive 'programs' that keep it entrenched within the endless cycle of death and rebirth. "No more" is its message. All that is false is cast aside that the vibrant light it feels burgeoning within may stand naked in the face of Truth. However, in order to reap its rich reward much personal inner work will have been accomplished, for the power evoked through its bold attitude is not ego related but driven by the pure Will of the Divine. Only one who is aligned with its presence can make the difficult choices necessary to comply with its message, and only one who is ready to let all else go is able to be a useful emissary for its purpose. Finally, it is said that "power corrupts and absolute power corrupts absolutely", but a humble heart whose attention is turned inwards to the Higher Self ensures correct orientation for forces such as these. Will, tempered by love, conquers all. *Shattering* is one of three visions[69] attuned to the planet Pluto, Lord of the Underworld and agent of death, but only an inflated ego need tremble in its presence. Remember, 'demolition' is inevitable but love is the true agent of power and it's this force alone that births an emissary for the divine. Anam Cara, friend to the Soul, knows this.

---

[69] *Shattering, Transcendence, Underworld.*

Shattering

Quality: Divine Demolition
Absolute Aspect: Will
Geometry: None
Rainbow Sphere: Will

Contemplation

Dark was complete... black, pitch black... consummate. Not a single pinprick of light interrupted its pristine, perfect mystery... no sound impregnated its Presence, no breath disturbed the air... This dark, silent night, this Divine Darkness, was entire... Devoid of nothing, not even light... It was All. And for aeons it had been so. The safest and most trusted space, where all may disappear without even knowing it had gone, this great cosmic mother had reigned supreme... Her vast womb-like presence, from whence the child of infinite possibilities may be birthed, had waited... Waited until the moment of fruition, until the wheel of life had reached its point of turning. And then, at last, Dark was impelled to move... As an appearance of itself, it presented an eye... closed at first but soon to tear asunder the rich fabric of the void in which it lay. And in its opening, she was forever changed... As diamond-clear radiance poured forth from the expanding orifice, it consumed the mystery... until naught but it remained. Now all was Light. Complete in its brilliance, it was the end and the beginning, dark as light, sound emitting silence, the many and the One. It was All... The wheel turned again. Within a well of darkness, as a facet of itself, Light planted the seed of unknowing... The Lord of Misrule looked on... He was the Way... and he knew the dance of two... An impassioned observer, he stood perfectly poised on the bridge of change and watched, as he had always watched... Then came the fall...

Guidance

The *fall* is a perfect metaphor for unconscious 'life in sleep' and marks the point at which all great cycles, including the passage of time, begin. From this juncture onwards, all must follow its prescribed course according to its intrinsic nature. Birth inevitably follows death and death is always the precursor to life, but as sure as the river will always find its ocean, so is each individual assured of its return. Opposing forces of light and dark, yin and yang, are clearly seen as not separate but inextricably linked and complementary to each other, whilst the *Lord of Misrule*, detached, yet not, is silent. By virtue of its integral geometries, *Silent Night* is all of this, and more. It marks the progression from source to separation and return as a dynamic process of change, a seamless interchange where flow and synthesis between all levels and vibrations are applied simultaneously to the macro-galactic and to you in your daily life. And herein lies the direction of this vision. Change is inevitable and made all the more difficult when its flow is resisted, so when it appears your life is falling apart, consider that everything might just be falling into place. Be the Lord of Misrule, take your place upon the bridge of change and watch as **you** have always watched... then jump... the great mystery awaits...

Silent Night

Quality: Harmony of the Spheres
Absolute Aspect: Will
Geometry: Circle, torus, triangle
Rainbow Sphere: Rainbow

Contemplation

*It was a force she knew well... that left her powerless, yet resistant... She hungered for its presence, for its light to pierce the dark... for its fire to rage through her veins... until naught of her former self remained... She yearned... yet still she resisted. How long had she turned a blind eye to its call... closed her heart to its gentle touch... ignored its appeal for union? Years, decades... lifetimes? How long? Why, despite being powerless, did she resist that which she desired so much? She recalled moments when they'd merged... when its sweet majesty was her every breath, when her heart beat with a pulse so pure she could barely detect its rhythm... and when its flame burned so bright she knew there was naught else but **it**. In momentary interludes throughout her life, she knew... she knew it well. But the pull of the familiar was strong... it fuelled her resistance, filled her mind with pastures new, allowed impassioned lovers to toy with her heart and endless creature comforts to feed her body. She sighed... She was tired of these wayward distractions. With magnetic appeal, the clarion call of the Soul sounded once more... watering the arid desert of her inner life... Now she was ready to listen... Now she was willing to surrender all to its passage... And now, she was able... to act.*

Guidance

There are many names attributed to the Soul; *Solar Angel*, the title of this vision, is but one. Its primary function, using the medium of consciousness, is to serve as an intermediary between Spirit and matter, with the human being – you – as a vessel through which it may express itself. The script highlights the eternal struggle each one of us faces in bringing together our core polar opposites – personality and Soul – and shows how easy it is to be imprisoned for lifetimes should we consistently choose to feed a polarised viewpoint. Liberation is offered in the form of surrender, but is it really that simple? Included in the multi-layered image are mirrored versions of seven facets of the diamond,[70] which together present the qualities necessary for choosing to align with the Soul and then taking appropriate action to follow it through. Finally, each vision mentioned in the first footnote aligns to one of the circles in the integral seed of life geometry. As they are invisible, hidden within the layers, it may be assumed that the energy of each one is integrated and complete within the vision as a whole. And herein lies its potential. *Solar Angel*, one of five visions[71] dedicated to Soul expression, offers the Ultimate in spiritual reward where the highest and lowest meet as consciousness in one who is awake. But are you ready to hear the call? Are you willing to let go of all that you cherish most in **this** world? And are you able to place **its** purpose ahead of your own? Are you?

---

[70] *Aspiration, Burning Ground, City of Light, Eureka!, Follow the Crowd, Fusion, Way of Light.*
[71] *City of Light, Family of Light, Presence, Solar Angel, The Well.*

Solar Angel

Quality: Alignment
Absolute Aspect: Love
Geometry: Seed of life
Rainbow Sphere: Mind

Contemplation

*In intimate communion, the Word issued its wisdom... "Be still. Turn your senses inwards. Listen. Can you taste the wonder of creation as it flows through you? Can you hear its song? Feel your heart as it beats to the tune of its magnetic pulse... sense its synchronous rhythm sounding through your veins. Be **still**... Listen... Feel the rise and fall of its breath as it animates your earth-bound Soul." Inner senses on alert, Esmerelda heeded its message and in silence as deep as the grave invited the force of becoming to embrace the bedrock of her heart. In unconditional surrender, she knew its journey... its origin... and, most of all, its consummation. Esmerelda sighed... was it really so simple? "Yes," replied Mentor. "In the becoming, all is undone. Laws, systems and beliefs collapse in its expression. It is the Cosmic Breath, the Word of one who has no voice... the beginning and the end... It is a way of being in which acceptance in the now is expression of the All." She surrendered deeper and deeper into its mystery, allowed its majesty to follow its agreed course within and through her. All senses closely attuned to its passage, there was no part of this harmonic resonance she didn't know... intimately. She became the spiralling force of becoming, winding its way from Zero, through stars, galaxies, subtle realms of light and ethereal dimensions in nature, to reach far into crystallised substance held deep within the earth's core. Like a mighty river she flowed, slowly... almost lazily... at first, then tighter and tighter, faster and faster... until she vanished... completely... Returned to the place of eminence, she paused... Until, at another turn, she was released... alike, yet not... changed, yet irrevocably the same...*

Guidance

The 'great cycle' visions – *Song of Freedom, Song of the Cycles, Song of the Soul* – centre upon a giant spiral in varying stages of integration with matter. *Song of Freedom* is its ultimate expression, where matter and Spirit unite, not only in one who is awake, but also in the very fabric of earth herself. Its calling takes you deep into your physical body to experience the becoming force as it vitalises your blood, brings joy to your heart and fills your mind with light. Having a profound connection with the heart, the spiral **is** the art of liberation, inseparable from the all-inclusive Love of the Divine. Letting go and allowing whatever 'is' to be 'just as it is' removes all obstacles to its presence and suddenly **you are** the Great Cause as it flows **through and within** you. However you are feeling right now, whatever is occurring in your life, surrender to its gift. Allow its magnificence to fill your being until naught but it remains. Then celebrate the magic of existence as it radiates through you to enrich the lives of those who sleep... those whose forms are unlike yours... and others whose purpose is to serve the one whose heart lies right beneath your feet...

Song of Freedom

Quality: Ultimate Release
Absolute Aspect: Will
Geometry: Spiral
Rainbow Sphere: Order

Contemplation

*In intimate communion, the Word issued its wisdom... "Be still. Turn your senses inwards. Listen. Can you taste the wonder of creation as it flows through you? Can you hear its song? Feel your heart as it beats to the tune of its magnetic pulse... sense its synchronous rhythm sounding through your veins. Be **still**... Listen... Feel the rise and fall of its breath as it animates your earth-bound Soul." Inner senses on alert, Esmerelda heeded its message and in silence as deep as the grave invited the force of becoming to embrace the bedrock of her heart. In unconditional surrender, she knew its journey... its origin... and, most of all, its consummation. Esmerelda sighed... was it really so simple? "Yes," replied Mentor. "In the becoming, all is undone. Laws, systems and beliefs collapse in its expression. It is the Cosmic Breath, the Word of one who has no voice... the beginning and the end... It is a way of being in which acceptance in the now is expression of the All." She surrendered deeper and deeper into its mystery, allowed its majesty to follow its agreed course within and through her. All senses closely attuned to its passage, there was no part of this harmonic resonance she didn't know... intimately. She became the spiralling force of becoming, winding its way from Zero, through stars, galaxies, subtle realms of light and ethereal dimensions in nature, to reach far into crystallised substance held deep within the earth's core. Like a mighty river she flowed, slowly... almost lazily... at first, then tighter and tighter, faster and faster... until she vanished... completely... Returned to the place of eminence, she paused... Until, at another turn, she was released... alike, yet not... changed, yet irrevocably the same...*

Guidance

The 'great cycle' visions – *Song of Freedom, Song of the Cycles, Song of the Soul* – centre upon a giant spiral in varying stages of integration with matter. *Song of the Cycles* tracks the emergent force of becoming as it unfolds within itself to form the structure of the universe as a whole. Galaxies, solar systems, stars and planets are established according to its intrinsic architecture, whilst their continued evolution is in accord with a divinely orchestrated 'Cosmic Clock'. Having a profound connection with the heart, the spiral is master integrator and inseparable from the all-inclusive Love of the Divine. Letting go and allowing whatever 'is' to be 'just as it is' removes all obstacles to its presence and suddenly **you are** the spiralling force of becoming, in intimate relation with the natural ebb and flow of the universe as it flows **through and within** you. Are you ready to face your nemesis? However you are feeling right now, whatever is occurring in your life, surrender **now** to the taste of the present. Allow the wonder of becoming to fill your being. Feel the Love of the Divine fill your heart with unconditional acceptance and listen to the Cosmic tick as it animates your Soul with light...

Song of the Cycles

Quality: Divine Order
Absolute Aspect: Intelligence
Geometry: Spiral
Rainbow Sphere: Order

Contemplation

*In intimate communion, the Word issued its wisdom... "Be still. Turn your senses inwards. Listen. Can you taste the wonder of creation as it flows through you? Can you hear its song? Feel your heart as it beats to the tune of its magnetic pulse... sense its synchronous rhythm sounding through your veins. Be **still**... Listen... Feel the rise and fall of its breath as it animates your earth-bound Soul." Inner senses on alert, Esmerelda heeded its message and in silence as deep as the grave invited the force of becoming to embrace the bedrock of her heart. In unconditional surrender, she knew its journey... its origin... and, most of all, its consummation. Esmerelda sighed... was it really so simple? "Yes," replied Mentor. "In the becoming, all is undone. Laws, systems and beliefs collapse in its expression. It is the Cosmic Breath, the Word of one who has no voice... the beginning and the end... It is a way of being in which acceptance in the now is expression of the All." She surrendered deeper and deeper into its mystery, allowed its majesty to follow its agreed course within and through her. All senses closely attuned to its passage, there was no part of this harmonic resonance she didn't know... intimately. She became the spiralling force of becoming, winding its way from Zero, through stars, galaxies, subtle realms of light and ethereal dimensions in nature, to reach far into crystallised substance held deep within the earth's core. Like a mighty river she flowed, slowly... almost lazily... at first, then tighter and tighter, faster and faster... until she vanished... completely... Returned to the place of eminence, she paused... Until, at another turn, she was released... alike, yet not... changed, yet irrevocably the same...*

Guidance

The 'great cycle' visions – *Song of Freedom, Song of the Cycles, Song of the Soul* – centre upon a giant spiral in varying stages of integration with matter. *Song of the Soul* turns your attention inwards to the subtle inner realms of the Soul where, in deep surrender, you release all that no longer serves its purpose. Each subsequent turn of the spiral moves the great void left by an absence of story, and, on bended knee, your heart opens to welcome its delicate impressions. The serenity of the present moment, within its outpouring expression, brings profound transformation, and as you continue to let go and allow whatever 'is' to be 'just as it is', all resistance fades to nothing. Suddenly **you are** the spiralling force of becoming, in intimate relation with the natural ebb and flow of the universe as it flows **through and within** you. However you are feeling right now, whatever is occurring in your life, surrender to the gift of the present. Allow the wonder of becoming to fill your being. Feel its love embrace your heart in unconditional acceptance and hear the Voice in the Silence as it whispers sweet songs... to the one it loves... so much...

Song of the Soul

Quality: Magnetic Radiation
Absolute Aspect: Love
Geometry: Spiral
Rainbow Sphere: Order

Contemplation

Are you aware that there is a place where time appears to stand still, where a lifetime of understanding is revealed in a split second and where your intimate connection with the universe as a whole is known beyond any doubt? Did you know that this place is accessible to you right here, right now, in this very moment? And did you also know that within this time, outside of time, you have the distinct possibility of coming face to face with all that is Real... in you?

Guidance

Spirit of Place, as its name implies, bids you to open your heart and **allow** all this magnificence to fill you, wholly and completely, right now. The image clearly relates to a particular 'place' and embodies structured, grounded and timeless earth wisdom through the energy of the 'Spirit' ascending from the rocks. Its whole demeanour invites you to look beyond the obvious 'place' to see that it really isn't about a particular spot at all. The central 'Spirit', the seed of life resting comfortably upon its crown, has clearly found sanctity of place within itself: it and the land are one, and the details of the surrounding landscape pale in significance. When we marry this with our understanding of time, we can see why. Two sister visions cover the complete spectrum. One, *Celebration*, is the measured world of clocks, where every aspect of daily life is dictated by the sequential movement of two hands rotating around 12 numbers upon a face without vision. When we eat, sleep, work or even make love sets the course of our daily life without any appearance of it ever being otherwise; in short, it limits our activities with every tick and each tock and deprives us of the pure pleasure of experiencing life in its most richest expression as it is in the moment. *Father Time*, on the other hand, is the medium through which all that is bound by the laws of perpetual motion unfolds. It heralds a way of being that is **not** time. There is not even movement. However, even though time itself does not change, every event, each seasonal alteration and every time-honoured moment in 21st-century life that marks its perpetual impermanence takes place within it. The ancient Greeks had a name for this time outside of time, *Kairos*, and the quality they assigned to it was God: God time. As the changeless face of Spirit, time is therefore the ultimate in paradox – it may impose limits through its agent, Chronos[72], or it may gift the greatest of rewards for those who would **be still**, even for a moment. *Spirit of Place*, therefore, is the gateway from one way of being to the other. It is not about a 'special place', but more about the **quality** of space you are in wherever you are, whatever you are doing and whomsoever you are with. It is an invitation to step outside of time whilst being in a world bound by clocks.

---

[72] See glossary.

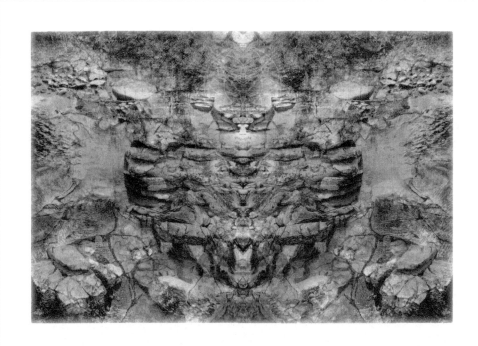

Spirit of Place

Quality: Perfect Moment
Absolute Aspect: Love
Geometry: Seed of life
Rainbow Sphere: Light

Contemplation

In the heart of a forest, far, far away, in an age when the air breaths fresh and clean and the rivers run pure and undefiled, the mighty oak spreads wide its boughs to expose a heart open to all. Custodian to this fair land, it stands as witness to the comings and goings, toing and froing, of those who walk in reverence upon the land and those who hail its lofty governance in wings of song across the vast ocean of the skies. Outer expression to an inner magnificence, its countenance brooks no denial, for the wisdom of ages pulses through its veins and strength born through adversity renders it worthy of its undisputed sovereignty. Custodian it is, but, in spite of its grandeur, it is but a shadow to the One, who stands beyond the mists of time and apart from the profane. Giver of life, orchestrator to the stars, haven to the realms of nine and bridge to the highest and the low, the One Tree cradles every ilk, shape and form within its breast. Origin of all wisdom and home to creatures great and small, it is Mother to the past, keeper of Light and guardian to all that moves within the night. So as one appears as kin to the other, alike in form though distinct in density, each tree, in its expression, is an age apart. And still, there are others, less imposing in structure, whose purpose is of such profound significance that heaven would fail in its mission without their participation. Those whose appearance is less than vertical, whose structure is far more delicate yet whose intricate web of filaments, fibres, flora and spawn, infused with intelligence of irrefutable order, is able to unite where others fail. Those whose nourishing blanket of green conceals sprinklings of magic... where one perhaps, with a discerning eye, may bear witness to the little folk celebrating in wonder the miracle of nature's abundance...

Guidance

Five visions[73] serve as awakeners to the intelligent life forms that dwell amongst the flora and fauna of our majestic woodlands. When the earth is at rest, when the air breathes still and when moisture is allowed to follow its own gentle course, there is a meeting place where kingdoms that would otherwise be separate come together in beauty. Such a place is found in the heart of every copse, wood or forest if you would but open your heart and see. In the script it is the *blanket of green*, a mossy wonderland where magic hangs in the air as an invitation to imbibe in other-worldly pastimes. In the image it appears as soft filaments engaging gracefully with unforgiving stone to impart secrets from a bygone age. *Stability* brings all these qualities together in nature's reverence to instil a sense of instant belonging. With humility born through aeons of adversity, it knocks softly upon the door to your heart. Can you hear its call? Will you open the door?

---

[73] *Custodian, Enchantment, Stability, Wallington Wood, World Tree.*

Stability

Quality: Grounding
Absolute Aspect: Intelligence
Geometry: Divine matrix, seed of life
Rainbow Sphere: Will

Contemplation

"Ak-Shah… A-ha!" She woke with a start. *"Who, or what, on earth was that?"* she asked herself. *Like a thunderbolt, she saw it break through the portal… a velocity of pure light whose origin lay beyond the bounds of the space-time continuum in which it must work out its Will, whose mission, once begun, was impossible to renounce and whose purpose demanded absolute obeisance, according to its Law.* Esmerelda watched in amazement as a miracle in creation unfolded before her. *From the highest to the low, through multiple layers and beings of expression, the Starseed transmitted its message… Keys of Light, encoded within its matrix of substance, appeared for those who were open to receiving its gifts. The hearts of those whose inner ear was attuned to the Voice in the Silence were given the gift of Presence, those who succumbed, on bended knee, were offered the gift of Truth… and to those whose vibration was so closely attuned to its note, such as there was naught to distinguish them from it, was granted Wisdom in Expression – power to speak the Word.* Lifetimes may have passed as the magic of its journey, its *becoming,* revealed its majestic splendour, but, no, it was a mere moment. However, five years must pass before she was any nearer to understanding the message that woke her with such persistence a few seconds ago; five long years before she would come face to face with her inner being. *"Many, many aeons ago, the Starseed, Ak-Shah, who is of galactic origin, set out on its journey in accordance with that which had been decreed. It arrived on planet earth during the time of Lemuria, sinking deep into its crystalline substance where it waited for conditions to ripen that it may fulfil its purpose. Ak-Shah's responsibility is to create divine order by unlocking portals of consciousness that are beyond this system, to restore balance through blueprints of wisdom contained within its matrix and to establish new paradigms through structured grid-works of light and illumined thought."* The more she listened, the greater was her affinity with its presence – she **knew** this being, she knew its heart… furthermore, she knew in essence it was her. *"Ak-Shah is a new way. It is a pure channel of creative force that is charged and expressed through consciousness, sharing and anchoring to Keys of Light; each vision is a key, a facet of the diamond, where the All may be known in its entirety by the many and then expressed outwards as timeless wisdom."* Esmerelda softened. She felt the presence of gentleness as it held her all-embracing and wonder-filled heart. In recognition, she knew the voice of authority that demanded unquestionable acquiescence to its Will had at its core the beauty of the divine feminine – Love.

Guidance

Starseed, then, unites masculine and feminine – Will and Love – but its greatest offering is the wonder-filled child, *Esmerelda,* for without her *Ak-Shah* would not be known. More importantly, its wisdom would not be expressed… through one who is… **present**… to its cause.

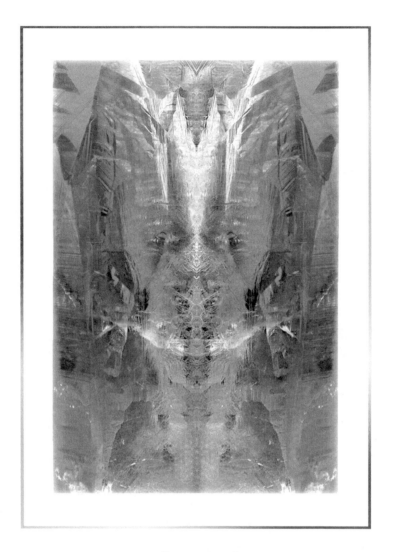

Starseed

Quality: Timeless Wisdom
Absolute Aspect: Will
Geometry: Divine matrix, fruit of life, Metatron's cube, seed of life
Rainbow Sphere: Rainbow

Contemplation

Caw Caw, Caw Caw, Caw Caw... The call (which she perceived to be a racket) was insistent. So much so, it brought her stomp through the woods to an abrupt end. Equally annoying and far more detrimental to her current state of mind, as well as her somewhat misguided sense of well-being, was the effect it had upon the flow of her entangled web of melodramatic thoughts. Caw Caw, Caw Caw, Caw Caw... it persisted, adding for good measure a crescendo with each utterance. Caw Caw, Caw Caw, Caw Caw... "Alright, alright," she acknowledged, whilst turning in the direction of its source. "You have my undivided attention, now what do you want?" She had arrived at the foot of a somewhat uninspiring tree, characterised by a preponderance of ivy hugging its trunk from base to sky, and searched amongst its foliage for the cause of her disturbance. Almost at the top, amongst its uppermost branches, perched a crow. Now silent, gaze fixed meaningfully upon the expectant child below, it waited patiently for her to acknowledge its presence. As their eyes met, language became detrimental to dialogue, and in the enveloping stillness, presences of species hitherto apart found knowing of each other. Crow, shapeshifter and keeper of Sacred Law, led the way. Through oceans deep and rivers swift and true, in thunderous clouds to the softest drops of dew, past mountains high capped with ice and silken flowers painted white, into seams of crystal deep beneath the crust, they travelled. Each encounter was an opening to the Way, every place an adherence to the Law and, without exception, each contact an exposure of the truth. Earth was sick, the Mother was dying and responsibility lay with the species to which she belonged. The child, wise beyond her years, was sick to her stomach... She understood why Messenger had been insistent... knew the purpose of their meet... and now she must act...

Guidance

Ten visions[74] pave the way to restoration of balance following centuries of neglect inflicted upon our planet by the human race. Individually, as characters in the script, they tell a tale of creation as it is reflected through your inner diamond. *Stewardship* takes the message of the script, in its totality, and lays responsibility squarely at the feet of the human race – **you**. Walk a path through the snow until it kisses the trees and you are greeted by a large Buddha kneeling serenely upon the earth – hands held firmly behind its back, head turned upwards with pained expression, its whole demeanour one of supplication. Now retract your gaze, notice the bear's head emerging through its chest and take note of its significance: bear awakens the power of the unconscious. Marry this with Buddha-consciousness and you have clear direction as to how planetary abuse may be redressed. Befriend the shadow... touch the earth on bended knee... and offer every self-serving interest to one... on whose life you depend...

---

[74] *Alchemist, Fortitude, Integrity, Invitation, Messenger, New Earth, Raindance, Reception, Sanctuary, Stewardship.*

Stewardship

Quality: Right Action
Absolute Aspect: Will
Geometry: Divine matrix
Rainbow Sphere: Order

Contemplation

Long, long ago, before a fledgling planet prepared to flex her wings, there came to earth those who would prove to be the masters of the race. Their purpose, multiple in expression, was to instil amongst infant humanity wisdom in an age. And for aeons, it was so. Miraculous feats, performed through understanding the laws of the physical universe, were effortless: remarkable structures appeared; advanced technology enabled travel through time and space; music and art, exquisite in their expression of the divine, were celebrated in a spirit of unity. Man and gods in co-creative partnership heralded an era of peace, a golden age, in which the great continent flourished. But it was not to last. There were those who claimed the hidden powers, shared so generously without condition, as their own; those who used the secret knowledge to manipulate and control and would stop at nothing to be the new rulers of the race. And so began the Great War. Silent as the grave, the Masters of Wisdom withdrew their presence from the land, sending in their stead a mighty flood to take all, save a few, to certain death beneath the waves. Before long, Atlantis was no more, or so says the legend. In deep meditation, the meditator knew these tales to be far more than myth. Billions of years after the event, the same dynamics were still being played out inside him and in the world at large – this he knew. Atlantis still lived. Manipulation, control and desire for power were obvious, but more subtle, and carrying far greater significance, were the psychic powers running rife amidst an unsuspecting populace. The Siddhis were strong... in his meditation he could feel them... and their allure was so, so tempting...

Guidance

The Atlantean root race, as documented in well-researched material,[xiv] is part of a greater cycle (mantvantara) spanning many millions of years. However, it is the golden age – its fall and how the resultant karma plays out on 21st-century earth – that we are concerned with here. Five visions[75] serve as a bridge in time where these forces may be contemplated as an inner process. *Stillness* addresses the 'Test of the Siddhis', which every traveller on the path must eventually face. The 'temptation of Christ', in the Christian bible, is the most obvious example, but even today, seduction by the forces of darkness is as real as it was 2000 years ago. Most obvious in, but not exclusive to, New Age circles, it comes in many 'intuitive' guises – healing, channelling, mediumship, energy techniques, psychic phenomena, etc. But know this: betwixt and between any lower psychic expression, Truth is always present, always. Only you, through an act of will, can invite it in, only you can face your innate desire for recognition and power... and only you can surrender all this... to one who loves you above all else... only you...

---

[75] *Alien Nation, Burning Ground, Follow the Crowd?, Stillness, Welcome.*

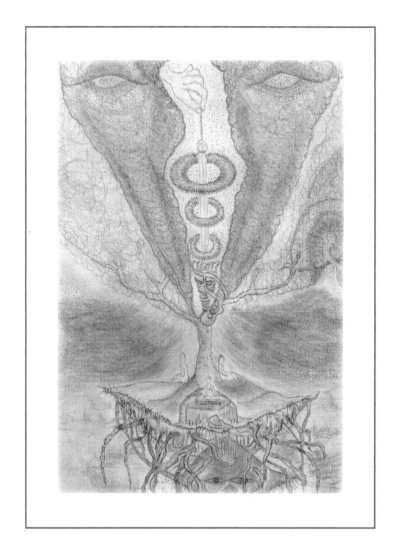

Stillness

Quality: Temptation
Absolute Aspect: Love
Geometry: None
Rainbow Sphere: Will

Contemplation

Moments before, it had been shut... yet it had not always been so. Although many, many revolutions of the great wheel had come to pass since the illustrious One had turned its attention inwards, there had been rounds, equal in number and duration, where worlds upon worlds, spread across countless millennia, had passed into and out of existence when it was other than closed. Times when its Will alone determined their providence, when a day and a night were measured in an age and the Eye of All-Seeing was One in the seeming. Now, as the night of the sleepless enters its closing and the dawning of day brings an advent of light, the wheel of all-turning heralds an age of new learning. Singular in purpose, no more in the seeming, the Great Eye revolves upon its pedestal of Light to emit the fruits of its meditation outwards into substance once more. A spark in the dark is there, and then gone, replaced with soft, gentle radiance that carries the mystery in service to the many. As a firefly in the night, carried upon wings of flame it comes, instilling life into that which hitherto lacked being. Magnetic, its force, its potential divine and the power in its Presence calls all to align. But it is Love in its radiance that holds the most sway, for the wisdom of ages carries all in its passage, and like unto one, the many are saved. So as the spark finds its mark and radiance its home, veils are rendered naked in the presence of its pristine mystery...

Guidance

A day of Brahma, the Creator according to Vedic tradition, is said to last 4,320,000,000[xv] years, with a night being of equal duration. It is also said that, 'when Brahma sleeps all is ended and when awake all is created',[xvi] such is the Perennial Wisdom as it has been transmitted throughout the ages in many cultures and traditions. The script offers a way in whereby the lives of this Being may be intuited, if only, in the initial stages, by virtue of the creative imagination. Go deeper, marry script with subtleties encoded within the image, and you may be transported deep into the heart of the mystery, where imagination ripens into direct experience. As consciousness is led by soft, golden light infused with subtle shades of red, orange, violet and, at the outer edges, rich indigo blue, wisdom in creation stands revealed. If you are fortuitous, it may give of itself entirely as you pledge all of you to, it. If it be so, wonderment is your just reward. *Substance* is a calling to the Soul. It asks that you dive deep into the golden river of light to engage intimately with its rich and fertile ground that is source for all and follow its direction from here until eternity's end. The gateless gate opens wide before you... all you have to do is jump... will you?

Substance

Quality: Wonderment
Absolute Aspect: Love
Geometry: None
Rainbow Sphere: Rainbow

Contemplation

It began with a spark, although it was barely discernible as such. Like a solitary firefly illuminating the darkest night... it was just a spark... wasn't it? How could she possibly have known the impact it would have, the power it would unleash... or the devastating potential it held to destroy that which she considered her greatest asset. Where had it come from... this insignificant packet of fire, this isolated thought that had set her mind ablaze with light? What was its source? Who was the dispenser of the flame? And who was the thinker? A vision, fleeting but clear, appeared before her inner eye. *Upon the floor in front of her were piles of books stacked one on top of the other, a plethora of information contained within numerous articles and, of course, her trusty laptop where all manner of research may be undertaken. All around the air was **still**, pregnant with untold knowing... and knowledge.* Esmerelda could not contain herself; she laughed until her belly ached. Her customary method of research seemed so primitive, tedious and, well, ridiculous! *"Ok,"* she softly goaded her inner teacher, *"Show me **your** way."* Allowing this was in itself a tremendous challenge. Her greatest assets, or so she believed, were her attention to detail and her meticulous approach to research, especially into topics like this one. Now she had to go deep into its territory, seek out the origin of thought and determine its modus operandi and purpose, and all without using her mind! Nevertheless, she stepped aside and permitted the Word to pour forth its wisdom. *"The spark, a particle of divine fire within substance, originates as an impulse in the mind of Absolute; it is a function of its Being-ness. Once ignited, it follows its agreed pathway in accordance with its Will. Spark ignites spark through multiple layers of existence until it is discerned as thought in the mind of one who thinks – such as you."* Subtle threads of understanding joined the dots in her head as Mentor continued. *"In consummate surrender, the light of clear-seeing enables Truth to stand revealed. Light Codes of Creation, embedded within the substance of Absorption, are keys to unlocking the power of thought. Remember, assimilation within the Cause before expression is the method by which consciousness unfolds within itself to co-create itself; thought, as a packet of light within its substance is no different. Every thought returns to itself as an expression within Cause to manifest as reality, whether for good or ill."* Now it all made perfect sense.

Guidance

Three visions[76] tease apart the workings out of thought as it is expressed through an equal number of layered expressions: body, Soul and Spirit. *Sweet Surrender* aligns to the 'intellectual mind' whose primary focus is acquisition of knowledge. However, as Esmerelda discovered, it is by no means the most efficient way to communicate with the Soul. Subtle, fleeting impressions are its language and are easily missed when attention is turned outwards. Step back and observe... watch as your mind burns as a flame in the night... to reveal that which you have always known... Now do you understand?

---

[76] *As Above, So Below, Inside Out, Sweet Surrender.*

Sweet Surrender

Quality: Liberation
Absolute Aspect: Love
Geometry: None
Rainbow Sphere: Mind

Contemplation

*He loved this place... soft, golden light that graced the land with tender touch... magic that permeated the stillness of the air, gentle beings who came and went in shy appeal... the sound of silence deftly playing the tune of perennial unsung orchestras upon the strings of his opened heart. He rejoiced in every breath that filled his being with diamond sparkles to outshine the light of 10,000 suns. But most of all, he loved the ease with which he moved, the ease with which his thoughts became real and the ease with which he could simply **be** in this realm. He never ceased to be amazed at the miraculous turn of events that had granted him access, and yet he knew that only by his own effort did the gate appear before him. Only through his unfaltering step, sight set resolutely on the goal that outperforms all others, did he bring together those qualities that allowed the event to appear. Furthermore, he knew this land was but a beginning... the great gate was yet to come. Soon, alone, he must mount the inner stairway to face his totality and, on bended knee, surrender all to the One... Then, when his former self is no more, to the plains of ordinariness he must return, where life may begin again, in earnest...*

Guidance

As its title implies, *Synchronicity* is a vision of magical 'coincidences'. Unrelated occurrences come together in one spectacular moment to present a window outside of time where other-worldly realities may be experienced. But, as the script shows, these miraculous moments are not merely a stroke of luck; they are divinely orchestrated, brought about through dedicated effort on the part of one who seeks. The integral symbol, geometric in origin, serves as a key: three 'petals' meet at a central point of light, lying at the centre of a golden triangle, which in turn sits at the midpoint of an all-embracing circle. Its direction is clear: return to your centre, tune your inner compass to the frequency of the Soul, appreciate the miracle of ordinariness and allow the beauty of the light within to be your guide. When your mind is clear, when your heart is centred in the space holding apparent separates, it is easy to see the doorway to the miraculous lying open before you. Then, and only then, do you know the true meaning of choice. If the inner compass serves as your guide, you know, really know, there is only one force controlling its direction, that of the Soul. This, then, is the only choice open to you; in all other matters it is irrelevant.

Synchronicity

Quality: Opportunity
Absolute Aspect: Will
Geometry: Circle, seed of life, triangle, vesica piscis
Rainbow Sphere: Mind

Contemplation

... the door slammed shut. Waves of hate thundered through an otherwise tranquil valley. An endless war, waged with words that scarred and from wounds that never healed, leaves indelible footprints upon a soul doomed to forget. Dreamers sleep oblivious, panicked creatures scuttle to find sanctuary and as the wind bristles and earth measures its resistance, the war behind closed doors continues. In another time, in a faraway place, an explosion rocks the air. "It's just a test," they said. "It'll do no harm," they said. But as the bomb releases its quarry and the earth receives its toxic waste, the effects are clear. A world, rich in beauty, now razed to the ground, leaves no doubt for the few who remain that their assurances were lies. Far in the future, where a land with its history is consigned to those who know the Law, a young man wanders through an idyllic forest. His heart an open book, his soul a source of light, he greets the world with a love that is equal for all. But his days on this earth are numbered, his time is to come way too soon and he is destined to be cut down in his prime, for the Law must be worked through to the end. In ignorance he remains as pain tears his heart to shreds, until in his last breath he remembers... a peaceful valley... an endless war... and a door slammed shut...

Guidance

Moments in time are seemingly without connection, but if you look to the web and unravel the mysteries held within its space-time continuum, you will know each effect is not without its cause. *The Web*, therefore, addresses the Law of Karma, specifically as it pertains to you as an individual in your day-by-day interactions with others. Until you take responsibility for your actions, whether thoughts, words or deeds, you will be perpetually bound to the wheel of endless rebirth: life after life. However, as much as this *vision of reality* weaves a web that has no end, it also offers hope for those who would be free. A devoted dog, a saintly face within a gnarled and twisted tree, both upon an island wrested from the tangled web of pain, points the way to the Eternal that only you can choose. For roots, anchored in unconscious soil, will at some point be known, and as seeds of compassion bear fruit in remembrance, the valley of the damned is raised once more to Spirit. If you have chosen this vision, know that every aspect of your personal darkness is, in fact, light, that each moment spent in devoted service to the one who abides within brings you closer to your heart and that every occasion of acceptance untangles a knot in the web that has no end. Now be honest, do you really wish to be an unconscious 'reactor' at the mercy of 'effects' or will you, from this moment forward, hand over all resistance to the Soul and build your life, **consciously**, from within the realm of causes?

The Web

Quality: Responsibility
Absolute Aspect: Intelligence
Geometry: None
Rainbow Sphere: Light

Contemplation

The bridge of light was in place, a community of a like kind was assembled in purpose upon the inner planes and the Blessed One was poised in readiness to transmit the Perennial Wisdom... Time was of the essence... time not determined by the world of clocks nor even by the order of cycles great and small. No, this time was measured by something far more subtle and infinitely more profound. It was set by Presence. In the heart of the Great Mother, the Blessed One drew unto itself the mantle of silence and, with no arising nor falling, gave of its breath to the Eternal Stillness... As air moved twixt the in and the out, without beginning or end, the Will of One was thus assured of purpose... for the Eternal One Breath flows through all... and the Fount of All Wisdom lies in all, like unto One... And so, as the Beloved received, so did it transmit, as it inhaled, so did it breathe out, for the Way of One is in parlance with all... It gives as it receives, it loves as it finds and it wills as it may... such is the Way made present to all... And for aeons it has been so... round upon round of the hidden mystery made available to those who would know the ways of the Great Ones, to those who may, in their infinite yearning, sample a droplet from the sacred chalice or poise for a moment amidst their Holy Presence. But the will of the small, persistent in its ways, is obscurer of Truth... and though the Fount overflows... Its Voice is unheard...

Guidance

Five facets of the diamond[77] convey the multi-layered presence of the Soul as it expresses through kingdoms in nature. As the Soul of a solar system, *The Well* is the bigger picture. Multiple layers and planes of existence are birthed when Spirit makes its involutionary journey to unite with matter. At each level, galaxies, solar systems and planetary lives are blended with subtle vibrations of light to build universes that may be discerned as a living, breathing, conscious entity. Space is not empty. It exists, it is alive... it is intelligent. Illustrating the outer expression of an inner subjective reality, every aspect of this vision reveals multiple vibrations of light when the divine triad unfolds within itself. Will through sphere alignment, Intelligence through aspect and Love as colour, within the deep, rich indigo, form the backdrop to its ripening magnificence. Soft, golden shades court brilliant white light to reveal subtle planes of Soul and Spirit, whilst denser forms in matter are exposed as planetary life. This facet of the whole **is** a living universe. If you enter its domain you may feel its breath as your own, if you fine-tune your inner senses further you may hear its song and if you surrender all sense of personal identity to its Presence... **if**... you may touch upon the unchanging, immutable essence of Absolute...

---

[77] *City of Light, Family of Light, Presence, Solar Angel, The Well.*

The Well

Quality: Living Universe
Absolute Aspect: Intelligence
Geometry: Spiral
Rainbow Sphere: Will

Contemplation

*How well she knew the rhythmic cycles defined by this ancient pattern... how easy it was for her to be the centre and witness their forever revolutions, to gaze through multiple doorways presented at their crossings... and, at will, step into their many and varied realities... Yet, in spite of her boundless wisdom, her proficiency at inter-dimensional travel, there was something missing, something she couldn't grasp. She felt she was playing at something she couldn't quite understand... she knew there was more. And so, for the first time, she relinquished her position at the centre and chose a peripheral path... one foot before the other she traced the outer circle whilst the wise ones continued their work at the centremost point... forwards and back through time she travelled as lifetimes, systems and cycles – small and large – faded in and out of her awareness... still she walked, never losing sight of the centre... and then words, familiar, but long ago forgotten, "Know the relationship of the centre to the periphery." She pondered their meaning, mind drawn again to the centre, knowing there was more. Still she walked the outer path. Suddenly, the panorama shifted... the centre vanished, the circle disappeared, as did she... all that remained was one who walked... In unconditional surrender, she experienced being drawn... there was nothing for her to 'do', nowhere to go, no centre to be found... she merely allowed the one who drew to draw... **through her**... Now, at last, she understood...*

Guidance

The ability to step aside or step back defines the art of conscious living and is an essential technique in merging the personality with the Soul. It is a way of being, of allowing, that enables the Soul to control the outer form – **you!** *Through the Portal* is an opportunity to experience life beyond the confines of everyday existence, to let go of your ego need to be the centre of attention and be special and to enter into a way of being that allows the one who is the true director of your life to create **through** you. Whether you stand at the centre or walk the periphery is irrelevant; it is where consciousness abides that defines the quality of your life. Recognise also that *Galactic-Consciousness* – the Soul alignment quality of this vision and all that this implies – is not dependent upon ego will. It takes effort and commitment to surrender **all** before the secrets of the cosmos are made available to one who seeks. Ask yourself, how adept are you in the art of stepping aside? How great is your desire to be special? Be honest, look deep and, should the timing be right, be prepared to make the biggest transition of your life.

Through the Portal

Quality: Galactic-Consciousness
Absolute Aspect: Will
Geometry: Flower of life, seed of life
Rainbow Sphere: Rainbow

Contemplation

"There has to be more to this," she pondered. *"The extent of her learning can't just be about a sticky mesh or how to build a trap for unsuspecting flies, surely?"* She had been sent to learn her next lesson, the remit being to find a spider's web, observe its qualities and, in particular, watch the way of the weaver. Grandmother, meanwhile, was silent. *As she watched, a silken thread appeared from nowhere. Cast meaningfully into the air before being carried by the wind, it found anchor amidst a bush on the other side of the great divide. Then followed the most mesmerising display of natural architecture she had ever had the pleasure of witnessing. Backwards and forwards, round and round, upwards and downwards, in an ordered fashion, the little creature went, undeterred by hindrances to its quest, until, before long, what began as a solitary gossamer thread had become a delicate, intricate network of fibres whose interconnection with its surroundings brooked no denial. Esmerelda drank it all in, whilst Spider, its task complete, moved purposefully to the centre of its creation to wait.* "Now follow me." Grandmother had spoken, so refusal was not an option. *The web, very soon forgotten, became a wonder of the past, and as they entered worlds anew – some familiar, others strange to her in appearance – she knew that the way of Spider was present in them all.* "Like the casting of thread, all your thoughts, words and deeds are bridges in time that may build or divide. The web you weave may ensnare, captivate or inform, and the sacred language of the universe is present in all you create should you have eyes to see." *Grandmother, master weaver, architect of creation, had spoken... and it was wise to heed her words...*

Guidance

In eight visions,[78] characters within the script express a *Way of Wholeness* by virtue of spider medicine. Three – *Weaver*, *Whirlwind* and *Wisdom Keeper* – open doors to 'Grandmother'; the remaining five set scenes in which the spinning of the web may be contemplated. *Timewarp*, in seeming contrast to its title, is a direct link to the mind – weaver of destiny, master of fate and trickster extraordinaire. "Come into my parlour," said the spider to the fly and "What a tangled web we weave when first we practise to deceive," are well-known tenets that apply to the mind as master of intrigue, deception and entrapment but also shine a light upon its mischievous mannerisms; as intimated in the script, mind can be turned towards less divisive and more virtuous pursuits. It begins by turning all on its head – thinking outside the box in which you view your reality and learning to **think without really thinking**. *Timewarp*, then, is a vision of paradox, a way of being in which mind cannot exist, where a whole new panorama opens up miraculously before you... without thinking it into existence...

---

[78] *Jubilation, Multiverse, Omniscience, Timewarp, Walk in the Park, Weaver, Whirlwind, Wisdom Keeper.*

Timewarp

Quality: Lateral Thinking
Absolute Aspect: Intelligence
Geometry: Spiral
Rainbow Sphere: Mind

Contemplation

Upon a lotus leaf it rested; intricate, transparent wings poised for flight; eyes, multi-directional, luminescent in their artistry, fine-tuned to acuity of vision that scanned the air for food or threat. And, as insects flutter here and there, unaware of the predator in their midst, the one who moves twixt night and day deserts the scene in favour of more impressing prey. Into the murky depths it goes, deep into the mud from which the lotus draws its breath, until in an unsuspecting moment, the one who has forever searched is greeted by that which it has always known. It takes the form of lowly grub, one who forages amongst the dirt, who plucks sweet morsels from its watery tomb and who struggles to the surface after many seasons in its bid to be free. But in its labour lies its demise, and as the sum total of all it was becomes a hardened shell, a remnant of life well lived, it gives itself over to that which it knows is its destiny. Soon, upon a lotus leaf, in a nondescript pond within a wood that bears no name, a mighty dragon flexes its wings... The watcher in the wood sighs. In a moment of recognition, she feels the lowly grub surrender to its passage, knows its journey to be her own; the seasons passed in ignorance amidst thoughts that carried her home were all her own making, cycles in accord with the Law, and as long as time measures their passage, a grub in the mud she must remain. So in the heart of her shell, she surrenders, enters the Great Unknown and as the guardians of the race draw near, in the space that holds all events as separate, mind and matter meet... In the locus of the Soul... as she bears witness to her death... a body sources its breath...

Guidance

Transition from caterpillar to butterfly – or, in this case, to dragonfly – is one that is readily accessible, as is its parallel: transformation from personality to Soul. This vision takes it a stage further, inviting you to look deeper into its spiritual significance and measure it against the perpetual cycle of death and rebirth. Furthermore, it asks that you enter into the 'how' of that process to examine the intimate relationship between mind and matter, how thought has direct bearing upon reality and, most importantly, the role the kingdom of nature plays in affecting human bondage to the cyclic passage of time. Follow the script, measure events in your life against time as a continuum and then take the image into your heart. Welcome the kingdom of nature as she generously shares her gifts and as she facilitates the merging of mind and matter within a space that is eternally free. Sink into the Great Unknown... As you give of yourself wholly and completely to its Presence, you know peace... peace beyond measure... you *touch paradise*... Slowly... slowly... it dawns... the only one responsible for bondage... is you...

Touching Paradise

Quality: Contentment
Absolute Aspect: Love
Geometry: Seed of life
Rainbow Sphere: Light

Contemplation

Hades by name, death by nature, though his demeanour belied the way legend would have it. His realm marks an end, that is for sure, but it is only the fearful who need dread their demise, for the end is beginning to those who can see. In this tale of homecoming is an ending other than end, where the great chasm left in the wake of extinction – in one who had little or no recollection as to how he came to be there – yielded the most surprising epiphany. Subtle echoes imprinted upon his conscious mind gave rise to memories from a dim, distant past; visions of a world he once knew, shattered beyond all recognition, were dissolved in the ensuing mirage; the ringing of judgements, beliefs and preferences sounding, too insistently, inside his ears were soon stilled to silence. In the aftermath of destruction all fell to nothing: what once was lost he knew was never found, all knowledge accumulated was never his to claim and the onset of demise could never be set in the past. It was here, right now, in this instant of reckoning. All knowledge, understanding and wisdom is me. There is no state, whether false or true, that I do not enter. I am equally the ignorance of the deluded as I am wisdom in the sage. Thus, all ignorance is my pure knowing, imperfectly portrayed through an unfinished appearance of my divine perfection.[xvii] *The voice, arising through the silence, brought with it immeasurable peace. At Hades' breast, incomplete, yet whole... he rested... knowing there is no death... only life.*

Guidance

Five visions[79] individually feature photos of the three outer planets; two – Neptune and Uranus – are higher octaves of their respective counterparts – Venus and Mercury – and express the transpersonal attributes of love and mind respectively; Pluto, as 'agent of death', is equally dual in its expression. On the one hand, it parallels the bowels of the earth in its depiction of 'excrement' in human society, but post apocalypse, when all that has been hidden beneath the surface is brought into light, it heralds a way of being where Truth, empty of all judgement, is all there is. *Transcendence* marks the dawning of this new way but only after this tiny little planet has worked out its will. The signatory force for the dropping of the 'plutonium bomb' is, of course, divine, as is its timing, but its path is made a little smoother in one who is accepting of its methods – not an easy task! Respecting its innate power as 'wisdom from above' is a start and allowing its will to be made manifest **through** you is even better, but its perfection lies in recognising its beauty when the waters at Hades' Rest have paved a way to the Soul...

---

[79] *Awakening* (Uranus), *Illumination* (Neptune), *Illusion* (Neptune), *Transcendence* (Pluto), *Underworld* (Pluto).

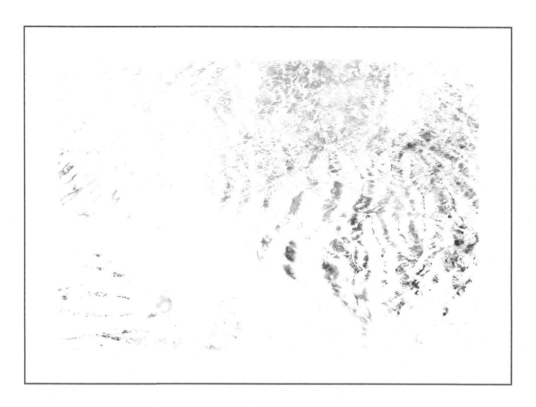

Transcendence

Quality: Regeneration
Absolute Aspect: Will
Geometry: None
Rainbow Sphere: Will

Contemplation

Her relationship with *the Word* was deepening... Its intimacy was tangible and it was much easier to merge with its presence... She understood its purpose... and now, as it flowed through and within her, she discerned the concealed message within its transmission... *"Particles of light contain the matrix of the substance of creation. It is offered to those willing to surrender to its passage. As an expression of the Cause, transmission permits the substance, or particles of light, to be disseminated into layers of expression."* Although she understood its intrinsic meaning, in a feeling sense, she needed more to be able to fully comprehend its depth; teachings revealed during her first and subsequent encounters provided context. *"Conversion, as the Cause, is a formula of creation. Its substance and means of expression is consciousness, using assimilation within the Cause as its method. However, Conversion is not to change something into something else but to assimilate first, then express."* The pieces of the jigsaw were slowly being assembled. *"Unmanifest is the constant, changeless state of Absolute. Its nature and mode of expression, as the primal Cause within the manifested world, is Becoming. This continuous outpouring allows each particle within its substance to assimilate within itself to co-create itself – to multiply itself within expression."* So there were Cause, substance, expression, becoming and now transmission, all apparently saying virtually the same thing. Or were they? Despite the apparent parody, it was beginning to make sense. It just required a touch of intuitive 'glue' to bring it all together. The primal Cause, origin of all life forms, is an outpouring force, an expression of intent, whose reason for Being is to express Divine Will in the manifested worlds; nothing more, nothing less. Furthermore, *"From the highest to the lowest, as it transmits, all those it passes through are aligned with its divine code of creation; form is thus changed back into primal Cause."* In teasing apart the subtle vibrations that are a function of its expression, a single unit of consciousness – such as **you** – may not only experience itself as light, but also know why it is so and, above all, be able to discern its method of return. The space-time continuum is the arena where this great cosmic play is acted out. Whether you are aware of them or not, these subtle vibrations are unfolding within and around you all the time, and the more you engage with their 'modus operandi', the greater is your opportunity to merge with the director of the show; you may thus become both receiver and transmitter. Every act of surrender, each momentary alignment, creates a pause – a sacred space wherein these refined vibrations may be intuited. Subtle impressions are received as 'packets' of light that unfold in the fullness of time to create 'aha' light-bulb moments of clarity when you least expect them.

Guidance

Transmission is an agent of creativeness, but in order to realise its full potential, you must first open your mind to receive. Only then may the voice of your True Self find expression in a world more accustomed to noise.

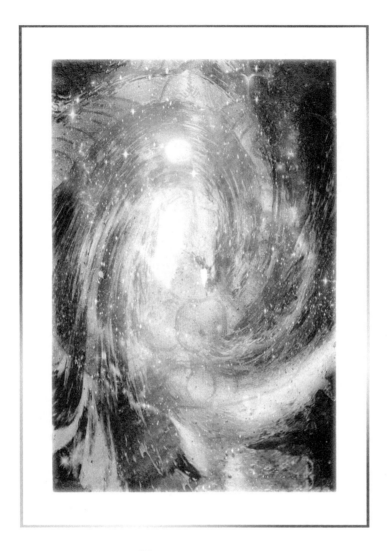

Transmission

Quality: Frequency
Absolute Aspect: Intelligence
Geometry: Spiral
Rainbow Sphere: Rainbow

Contemplation

In darkest recess of mind she roamed... with absence of light to guide her way home. Love, the betrayer, had brought her to this... how easy she had fallen... from ocean of bliss. She spiralled in darkness, sank into despair, for the pain of her loss was too much to bear... Life, it was worthless, no refuge or hope... and, for her, no purpose... or scope. Fear gripped her heart, her soul torn asunder, other steps she must take, or she'll surely go under. Blackest of space, this dark night of the soul... her hell in creation, she would stay in... **no more!** *From the depths of her being, with all of her might, she sent forth a prayer... "Please, show me the light." Dawn of awaking brought forth revelation... she knew this despair was her own creation. Another turn of the spiral saw dark take new form... and in a time of unravelling, knowing was born. A space that was void... no-thing could destroy... so she made it her ally... ignited her joy. At the end of the day, it was all that remained... light, as abyss... a welcomed friend... whose light in the dark left her... forever changed...*

Guidance

The gift of the spiral lies in its ability to follow its intrinsic nature, no matter where it may lead. It casts no judgement, cares not whether it culminates in bliss or despair and is equally at 'home' in the dark and the light. It is pure energy, an agent of becoming that expresses the will of that which has set its force in motion, regardless of intention or outcome; in this case, it is the star of our script who serves as executor, with thought being her impetus for change. All that is perceived in this world passes through the substance of mind – there is nothing that isn't it – so if conditions don't meet with expectation, it is thought that must be mastered to bring about the desired change in circumstance. However, the lower aspect of mind, which we are considering here, is very much 'entangled' with the emotional body – feelings – so neither one may assert its presence without this directly impacting upon the other. Our story begins with betrayal – a feeling – swiftly acted upon by a mind of despair; the spiral takes up the energy to bottom out in total blackness with no apparent hope of redemption. At the next turn, however, the energy changes, with prayer bringing forth salvation and subsequent emergence into light. Knowing the intrinsic nature of these powerful forces is key to mastery over the 'victim' that defines man's lower nature. Aspects of water, as they apply to the emotional body, must be understood by the lower mind before it can forge a bridge to the higher. And herein, lies the guidance of this vision. Take a step back... allow space to form between the entangled 'players' and become the 'stage' upon which the drama unfolds... Now watch... witness the miracle of existence as it blossoms before your eyes...

Trust

Quality: Peace
Absolute Aspect: Intelligence
Geometry: Spiral
Rainbow Sphere: Truth

Contemplation

Look beyond the frozen surface. Step through the 'darkened' doorway to a place where seeds of unknowing lie dormant. With sure and steady step, journey deeper into this sacred realm wherein the gentle goddess sleeps. Open your heart and approach in humility, and her sweet compassion is sure to unveil her deepest secrets. Before too long, the wisdom of her ways will awaken knowing in your heart and in quiet reverence you will realise this rite of passage has led you deep into the essence of your own Being-ness.

Guidance

Love, in this imaginative journey, is portrayed as the divine feminine, but it is not exclusive. Light, in the frosty panorama, brings in its male counterpart and shows that nothing is quite as it seems; the dance of duality is evident, regardless of outward appearances. As a mark in time, this vision is the winter solstice, longest night of the year, 'night of the unconquered sun'. So named because despite the sun being at its lowest and weakest point in the sky, with barely a hint of its radiance, it still emits light. The image, as well as its 'essence', *Light*, reflects this. A vision of many paradoxes, *Unconquered Sun* asks you to remember that when it appears that the darkness of your days would consume every last spark of your soul, there is always light, always. It calls on you to engage deeply with the spirit of hibernation, to be still, to know, as does the earth, the darkness of your depths and to appreciate that even in the blackest hour, there is light more powerful than you can possibly imagine. Reflect upon this time when the earth sleeps, know nothing is ever as it is presented and remember that even in sleep there is chance to dream. Be the earth... let her gentle spirit nurture your soul... as you bathe... in the quiet light of a barely discernible sun.

Guidance – balance is alchemical

The combined essence of eight linked visions is an invitation to tune into the natural rhythm – birth, life, decay and death – expressed through the four seasons (*Ostara*: Spring, *Cosmic Orchestra*: Autumn, *Woodhenge*: Summer, *Unconquered Sun*: Winter) – and to marry it with those areas in your life symbolised by the four elements in four visions – *Fire*, *Earth*, *Air* and *Water*. Notice the gifts each aspect brings, encouraging you to become more aware of your thoughts (air), feelings (water), physical well-being (earth) and spiritual essence (fire). Be the detached observer; see how the same cyclic pattern, so evident in our natural world, flows through all areas of your life. From one moment to the next, the only thing that is certain is that 'it' will change. Take your lead from nature, for she is a willing teacher, and remember that you have the capacity to 'fly' as much as the caterpillar. But in order to do so, you must first surrender to the darkness... you must, in all willingness, offer every last morsel of your unreal sense of self to a barely visible... spark...

Unconquered Sun

Quality: Light
Absolute Aspect: Love
Geometry: Seed of life
Rainbow Sphere: Light

Contemplation

Hades by name, death by nature, though his demeanour belied the way legend would have it. His realm marks an end, that is for sure, but it is only the fearful who need dread their demise, for the end is beginning to those who can see. In this tale of homecoming is an ending other than end, where the great chasm left in the wake of extinction – in one who had little or no recollection as to how he came to be there – yielded the most surprising epiphany. Subtle echoes imprinted upon his conscious mind gave rise to memories from a dim, distant past; visions of a world he once knew, shattered beyond all recognition, were dissolved in the ensuing mirage; the ringing of judgements, beliefs and preferences sounding, too insistently, inside his ears were soon stilled to silence. In the aftermath of destruction all fell to nothing: what once was lost he knew was never found, all knowledge accumulated was never his to claim and the onset of demise could never be set in the past. It was here, right now, in this instant of reckoning. All knowledge, understanding and wisdom is me. There is no state, whether false or true, that I do not enter. I am equally the ignorance of the deluded as I am wisdom in the sage. Thus, all ignorance is my pure knowing, imperfectly portrayed through an unfinished appearance of my divine perfection.[xviii] *The voice, arising through the silence, brought with it immeasurable peace. At Hades' breast, incomplete, yet whole... he rested... knowing there is no death... only life.*

Guidance

Five visions[80] individually feature photos of the three outer planets; two – Neptune and Uranus – are higher octaves of their respective counterparts – Venus and Mercury – and express the transpersonal attributes of love and mind respectively; Pluto, as 'agent of death', is equally dual in its expression. On the one hand, it parallels the bowels of the earth in its depiction of 'excrement' in human society, but post apocalypse, when all that has been hidden beneath the surface is brought into light, it heralds a way of being where Truth, without judgement, is all there is. This tiny planet is one of tremendous power. Divine Will dictates when the 'plutonium bomb' shall be dropped – from a great height – to ensure 'Truth will out', and this Lord of the Underworld is not one to shirk his duties. Pluto then, as transformer and agent of Divine Will, in cahoots with its celestial brothers, opens the heart to death, whether physical or ego related, whilst removing all obstacles in mind to the higher intuition. *Shattering*, also agent of death, is the destroyer, whilst *Underworld* exposes the aftermath of 'hell's' fury, where at 'Hades' breast', with all that you thought you were, gone... you rest...

---

[80] *Awakening* (Uranus), *Illumination* (Neptune), *Illusion* (Neptune), *Transcendence* (Pluto), *Underworld* (Pluto).

Underworld

Quality: Rest
Absolute Aspect: Love
Geometry: None
Rainbow Sphere: Will

Contemplation

From rainbow clouds and violet light infused with gold came creatures great and small... Woodland folk with sparkly wings, feathered friends that flew on high and creepy-crawly things that knew the ancient ways... But strangest of them all was one whose countenance was clear, whose subtle scent and sweetest sound – not known in other realms – sent songs of peace upon the wind to call the truthful to its side... One whose gentle eyes, the deepest blue, would cause your soul to weep, and single horn of vibrant light, reveal your passions deep. A creature of Elysium fields, of ancient myths and tales, it takes the heart of one who's pure to bring it to its knees... a child, an innocent, one who knows its heart, whose beauty is its own... one who knows, without a doubt, its trust belongs to her... alone... and then, as she lays claim upon its heart, the master of its realm surrenders to her grace... With bated breath, the dreamer watched it all unfold... an ingenious fantasy birthed through a mind absent of thought... Detached and clear, he watched as he had always watched... followed one prolific outpouring of mind after another... observed his thoughts turning real. He conceived spheres of light and doorways to strange new worlds and miraculously stepped inside to make the story live. The dreamer, who slept not, knew the dream, his part within it and his power to create... he knew it all... In a second, split from time, an unexpected flash set the dreamer's world ablaze... At once he was there, and then gone... as the bubble burst...

Guidance

Magical kingdoms in nature are not just the reserve of children's fantasy stories, they also serve as telling metaphors for Spirit and our relationship to divinity. Unicorns, in particular, symbolise the most pure of these subtle realms and are poignant reminders that the 'Kingdom of God' is only accessible to those whose hearts and minds run true. However, *Unicorn* addresses far more intricate issues than those portrayed through this enchanted metaphor alone. It calls into question the very fabric of mind, and how thought has direct impact upon the reality of day-to-day life and even addresses the role of the dreamer in distinguishing the Real from the unreal. The image is simple and presents an air of clarity. Above a wispy layer of rainbow cloud, within a space where myriad realities exist one upon the other, an other-worldly creature is in the final stages of birth. A band of colour directs your gaze to its centre, where a humble heart may waken to its miraculous offering. Aside from allowing your imagination to run wild, as would any captive released from chains that bind, *Unicorn* gifts you the art of clear-seeing. Enter the mind of the dreamer, play with his magical characters, pick fables from the air and then imagine you **are** the one who clearly sees... you, as the master of the story, are yourself within a dream...

Unicorn

Quality: Inner Strength
Absolute Aspect: Love
Geometry: None
Rainbow Sphere: Will

Contemplation

"There has to be more to this," she pondered. *"The extent of her learning can't just be about a sticky mesh or how to build a trap for unsuspecting flies, surely?"* She had been sent to learn her next lesson, the remit being to find a spider's web, observe its qualities and, in particular, watch the way of the weaver. Grandmother, meanwhile, was silent. *As she watched, a silken thread appeared from nowhere. Cast meaningfully into the air before being carried by the wind, it found anchor amidst a bush on the other side of the great divide. Then followed the most mesmerising display of natural architecture she had ever had the pleasure of witnessing. Backwards and forwards, round and round, upwards and downwards, in an ordered fashion, the little creature went, undeterred by hindrances to its quest, until, before long, what began as a solitary gossamer thread had become a delicate, intricate network of fibres whose interconnection with its surroundings brooked no denial. Esmerelda drank it all in, whilst Spider, its task complete, moved purposefully to the centre of its creation to wait.* "Now follow me." Grandmother had spoken, so refusal was not an option. The web, very soon forgotten, became a wonder of the past, and as they entered worlds anew – some familiar, others strange to her in appearance – she knew that the way of Spider was present in them all. "Like the casting of thread, all your thoughts, words and deeds are bridges in time that may build or divide. The web you weave may ensnare, captivate or inform, and the sacred language of the universe is present in all you create should you have eyes to see." Grandmother, master weaver, architect of creation, had spoken... and it was wise to heed her words...

Guidance

In eight visions,[81] characters within the script express a *Way of Wholeness* by virtue of spider medicine. Three – *Weaver*, *Whirlwind* and *Wisdom Keeper* – open doors to 'Grandmother'; the remaining five set scenes in which the spinning of the web may be contemplated. *Walk in the Park* is about as ordinary as it gets, or is it? An infusion of violet, snakes in the grass tinged with gold and other-worldly apparitions in the sky belie the scene's sense of normality; all is not as you would expect on your average day out in the park. Like its sister vision, *Multiverse*, *Walk in the Park* challenges the creative imagination to embrace the existence of other worlds, to accept that they are not only possible but real and, moreover, intimately entwined with our own. Taking the vast experiential knowing of the matrix gained in one vision, it delivers it wholly and completely into the other, grounding it in everyday reality... **your** daily life. For many, the picture is as it has always been... but to one who walks in wonderment, it is forever changed... the ordinary is now... **extraordinarily** ordinary... isn't it?

---

[81] *Jubilation, Multiverse, Omniscience, Timewarp, Walk in the Park, Weaver, Whirlwind, Wisdom Keeper.*

Walk in the Park

Quality: Ordinariness
Absolute Aspect: Will
Geometry: None
Rainbow Sphere: Order

Contemplation

In the heart of a forest, far, far away, in an age when the air breaths fresh and clean and the rivers run pure and undefiled, the mighty oak spreads wide its boughs to expose a heart open to all. Custodian to this fair land, it stands as witness to the comings and goings, toing and froing, of those who walk in reverence upon the land and those who hail its lofty governance in wings of song across the vast ocean of the skies. Outer expression to an inner magnificence, its countenance brooks no denial, for the wisdom of ages pulses through its veins and strength born through adversity renders it worthy of its undisputed sovereignty. Custodian it is, but, in spite of its grandeur, it is but a shadow to the One, who stands beyond the mists of time and apart from the profane. Giver of life, orchestrator to the stars, haven to the realms of nine and bridge to the highest and the low, the One Tree cradles every ilk, shape and form within its breast. Origin of all wisdom and home to creatures great and small, it is Mother to the past, keeper of Light and guardian to all that moves within the night. So as one appears as kin to the other, alike in form though distinct in density, each tree, in its expression, is an age apart. And still, there are others, less imposing in structure, whose purpose is of such profound significance that heaven would fail in its mission without their participation. Those whose appearance is less than vertical, whose structure is far more delicate yet whose intricate web of filaments, fibres, flora and spawn, infused with intelligence of irrefutable order, is able to unite where others fail. Those whose nourishing blanket of green conceals sprinklings of magic... where one perhaps, with a discerning eye, may bear witness to the little folk celebrating in wonder the miracle of nature's abundance...

Guidance

Five visions[82] serve as awakeners to the intelligent life forms that dwell amongst the flora and fauna of our majestic woodlands. *Wallington Wood* introduces an element of surprise, where a brief encounter with solitude, taken at an opportune moment in an inspired wood, brings nature's unsung heroes to the forefront of a mind otherwise closed to their presence. As the dreamer bathes in wonderment at nature's beneficence, veils between worlds are miraculously cast aside and transportation to another dimension in space and time is suddenly made readily accessible. Creatures never before encountered, not even in the most vivid of imaginary tales, are clearly visible, beings whose presence is defined through subtle variations in light and sound are made tangible to the senses and, most astounding of all, the Spirit of the Wood is known. Hailed with gratitude inside a heart steeped in humility, the one who paused... just for a moment... is left forever changed. An equal opportunity is available to you now... **be** in nature... Who knows what you may find?

---

[82] *Custodian, Enchantment, Stability, Wallington Wood, World Tree.*

Wallington Wood

Quality: Surprise
Absolute Aspect: Intelligence
Geometry: Vesica piscis
Rainbow Sphere: Light

Contemplation

*They met as they had always met, inside the Hall of Learning, where all that is possible to know is known. However, on this occasion, as Consciousness sensed the presence of the Shining One long before it put in an appearance, a ripple of excitement, barely detectable to others in the vicinity, echoed throughout its substance. "Greetings, my friend," sounded the luminous being without employing words. "We have a task before us concerning the future well-being of a world for which we are equally responsible and for which you must be prepared. We must journey together into four realms, each a kingdom in its own right, with which I am far more familiar than you, to engage with those whose remit is to work in the lesser, denser fields of service. We must engage intimately with those whose presence is not usually made visible to any outsider and who would, in normal circumstances, be hostile to any infringement of their domain. However, it is recognised that your participation in this is paramount, so exceptions have been made and they wish you to know that, in furtherance of mutual cooperation, you are welcome in their respective worlds." Consciousness, of course, was a willing participant and engaged gracefully with each as they made their presence felt. Spirit of water carried upon winds of change, as liquid drops in breath of fire, found its source in oceans deep, where carnage, caused by centuries of abuse, left havoc in the wake of human passage. Seas, once pristine and clear, source for life forms unbeknownst to man, were reduced to toxic waste; rivers who carried the gift of life from source to sea were clogged with mankind's cast-offs in its desire for the new. But it was the subtle realms, the unseen in-between, that revealed the greatest horror. In the dark waters of the collective unconscious, a powerful presence lurked, feeding upon every desire, every need and all manner of selfish, manipulative behaviour – **fear** – to create a tsunami of 'must-have', 'me-first' attitudes. Consciousness wept. "They are unaware of the harm they cause in projecting their unconscious emotional detritus into the world and, importantly, the toxic waste upon the physical plane that is created as a result," admonished the Shining One. "And this is why I am here," Consciousness replied. "I am mediator between your domain and theirs. Mine is the task of making them aware and in me lies responsibility to stimulate change in them."*

Guidance

Four facets of the diamond lead into the magical world of nature spirits – *Air* (sylphs), *Earth* (gnomes), *Fire* (salamanders) and *Water* (undines) – each responsible for the maintenance, purification and ultimate balance of their respective domains. A fifth vision, *Brilliance*, is the 'Shining One', a Deva, or angelic being, who has under its direction these 'lesser' creative builders. *Water*, as we have seen, holds far greater significance than the quality of the wet 'stuff' we drink; it is the playground for our every unconscious, reactive response, our abusive emotional behaviour and our underhand, selfish indulgence.

If this doesn't serve as a wake-up call to harmonise your feeling response, consider the selfless service of water spirits who work ceaselessly to purify humanity's garbage – your garbage... makes you think, doesn't it? Importantly... how does it make you **feel**?

Water

Quality: Feeling
Absolute Aspect: Intelligence
Geometry: Metatron's cube
Rainbow Sphere: Beauty

Contemplation

*A solitary figure treads a precipitous path amidst lofty crags high in the land of the Golden Flame. Bounded on either side by mighty chasms, graveyard to those ill prepared to face its hidden depths, the watchers wait with glee in anticipation of his faltering steps. But his intent is clear. One foot resolutely placed before the other, eyes set firmly on the way ahead, he struggles onwards, undismayed by the lure of bottomless pits or cries of the dead. He recalls, easily, his days in the valley of plenty... where every heart's desire was met with equal voracity, where all needs were fed before they were thoughts in his head and where, despite its opulence, each day seemed vaguely bereft of substance. He remembered clearly the time when, in a momentary flash, he drew a line under his fruitless philandering. He saw, with clarity, the blazoned path laid out before him, recognised the manifold task he must endure and knew that once it was begun, there was no turning back. Now tired, he rested to reflect upon the years spent in this fair land, he knew well the sunshine and the shade, the pitfalls of the path, the golden ones – unseen companions who served to guide him on his way... Yet never was he further from realising his goal than he was right now. So he abandoned his search and resolved to cease all movement until Truth made its presence felt. In a moment of clarity, Light streamed forth from his illumined inner eye. He knew the Lighted Way... felt its rhythm vibrate to the tune of his heart... and as threads of light wove their way through the tapestry of his life... an image slowly began to take form... Shimmering in vibrant, diamond-clear light, against the background of his days... the totality of every experience: meetings and partings, sorrow and joy, happiness and despair, fear and love... all he had ever been, in countless existences, since beginning of time, was **his** song. It carried the heartbeat of the universe... the vibration of Absolute perfection... His song... his perfect note...*

Guidance

Way of Light is a gateway to the miraculous. It leads you on a journey from the unfathomable depths of the unconscious mind to full waking awareness, such as that experienced by the pilgrim in the script above. This, however, is not an easy journey. 'Dark chasms' are not some figment of an overactive imagination – they are very real. Appearing in many forms – from divisive thought, through desire in its myriad expressions, to extreme physical pain – each must be faced with unparalleled resolve and leonine courage and then unconditionally surrendered to the warm embrace of an all-inclusive heart. For only when your every regret, harsh remark and unconscious harmful act has brought you crashing to your knees may the door to the infinite stand wide before you. In a blaze of glory, the One who is orchestrator of all songs emits its Note... And, in a moment of wonder, the whole world stills to listen... as do you...

Way of Light

Quality: Humility
Absolute Aspect: Will
Geometry: None
Rainbow Sphere: Beauty

Contemplation

"There has to be more to this," she pondered. *"The extent of her learning can't just be about a sticky mesh or how to build a trap for unsuspecting flies, surely?"* She had been sent to learn her next lesson, the remit being to find a spider's web, observe its qualities and, in particular, watch the way of the weaver. Grandmother, meanwhile, was silent. *As she watched, a silken thread appeared from nowhere. Cast meaningfully into the air before being carried by the wind, it found anchor amidst a bush on the other side of the great divide. Then followed the most mesmerising display of natural architecture she had ever had the pleasure of witnessing. Backwards and forwards, round and round, upwards and downwards, in an ordered fashion, the little creature went, undeterred by hindrances to its quest, until, before long, what began as a solitary gossamer thread had become a delicate, intricate network of fibres whose interconnection with its surroundings brooked no denial. Esmerelda drank it all in, whilst Spider, its task complete, moved purposefully to the centre of its creation to wait.* "Now follow me." Grandmother had spoken, so refusal was not an option. *The web, very soon forgotten, became a wonder of the past, and as they entered worlds anew – some familiar, others strange to her in appearance – she knew that the way of Spider was present in them all.* "Like the casting of thread, all your thoughts, words and deeds are bridges in time that may build or divide. The web you weave may ensnare, captivate or inform, and the sacred language of the universe is present in all you create should you have eyes to see." *Grandmother, master weaver, architect of creation, had spoken... and it was wise to heed her words...*

Guidance

In eight visions,[83] characters within the script express a *Way of Wholeness* by virtue of spider medicine. *Weaver*, most obvious of the eight through its imagery, is characterised by a spider's web spanning the 'great divide'. At the centre, appearing as a creature in winged flight, the 'weaver' leaves no doubt as to the direction in which orchestration of this particular web should proceed: upwards. Spiders, in physical form, are distinguished from insects through body shape and number of legs; spiders have two equal body segments, not three, and eight legs to the insects' six. These numbers are significant. Not only, through the two, do they highlight the 'great divide' fundamental to our dualistic universe, but, by virtue of the eight, they also point the way in which these opposites may come together in harmony; a figure of eight symbolises the natural movement of energy between any pair of opposites should it be allowed to flow unrestricted. *Weaver* abides at the centre... it observes the flow of dualities without interference... But first, it builds a bridge...

---

[83] *Jubilation, Multiverse, Omniscience, Timewarp, Walk in the Park, Weaver, Whirlwind, Wisdom Keeper.*

Weaver

Quality: Wholeness
Absolute Aspect: Intelligence
Geometry: Torus
Rainbow Sphere: Mind

Contemplation

Long, long ago, before a fledgling planet prepared to flex her wings, there came to earth those who would prove to be the masters of the race. Their purpose, multiple in expression, was to instil amongst infant humanity wisdom in an age. And for aeons, it was so. Miraculous feats, performed through understanding the laws of the physical universe, were effortless: remarkable structures appeared; advanced technology enabled travel through time and space; music and art, exquisite in their expression of the divine, were celebrated in a spirit of unity. Man and gods in co-creative partnership heralded an era of peace, a golden age, in which the great continent flourished. But it was not to last. There were those who claimed the hidden powers, shared so generously without condition, as their own; those who used the secret knowledge to manipulate and control and would stop at nothing to be the new rulers of the race. And so began the Great War. Silent as the grave, the Masters of Wisdom withdrew their presence from the land, sending in their stead a mighty flood to take all, save a few, to certain death beneath the waves. Before long, Atlantis was no more, or so says the legend. In deep meditation, the meditator knew these tales to be far more than myth. Billions of years after the event, the same dynamics were still being played out inside him and in the world at large – this he knew. Atlantis still lived. Manipulation, control and desire for power were obvious, but more subtle, and carrying far greater significance, were the psychic powers running rife amidst an unsuspecting populace. The Siddhis were strong... in his meditation he could feel them... and their allure was so, so tempting...

Guidance

The Atlantean root race, as documented in well-researched material,[xix] is part of a greater cycle (mantvantara) spanning many millions of years. However, it is the golden age – its fall and how the resultant karma plays out on 21st-century earth – that we are concerned with here. Five visions[84] serve as a bridge in time where these forces may be contemplated as an inner process. *Welcome*, flagship for the group, marks the golden age. In many ways the image speaks for itself, clearly illustrating qualities from both script and era, but it is the subtle nuances that offer the most profound insight into its direction. An ancient figure, pure awareness testament to its divinity, rests beneath a tranquil sea. Above, inside a temple upon a heart-shaped island, sits a second figure, also in meditation. Consider carefully these dynamics. The heart is in the head, both figures – ancient and modern – strike a meditative pose, whilst the sea, serving as membrane between the two, is quiescent. Time and space, heart and mind, above and below... All is not as it 'should' be, yet all is in perfect order... how can that be?

---

[84] *Alien Nation, Burning Ground, Follow the Crowd?, Stillness, Welcome.*

Welcome

Quality: Sharing
Absolute Aspect: Love
Geometry: None
Rainbow Sphere: Order

Contemplation

"There has to be more to this," she pondered. *"The extent of her learning can't just be about a sticky mesh or how to build a trap for unsuspecting flies, surely?"* She had been sent to learn her next lesson, the remit being to find a spider's web, observe its qualities and, in particular, watch the way of the weaver. Grandmother, meanwhile, was silent. *As she watched, a silken thread appeared from nowhere. Cast meaningfully into the air before being carried by the wind, it found anchor amidst a bush on the other side of the great divide. Then followed the most mesmerising display of natural architecture she had ever had the pleasure of witnessing. Backwards and forwards, round and round, upwards and downwards, in an ordered fashion, the little creature went, undeterred by hindrances to its quest, until, before long, what began as a solitary gossamer thread had become a delicate, intricate network of fibres whose interconnection with its surroundings brooked no denial. Esmerelda drank it all in, whilst Spider, its task complete, moved purposefully to the centre of its creation to wait.* "Now follow me." Grandmother had spoken, so refusal was not an option. *The web, very soon forgotten, became a wonder of the past, and as they entered worlds anew – some familiar, others strange to her in appearance – she knew that the way of Spider was present in them all.* "Like the casting of thread, all your thoughts, words and deeds are bridges in time that may build or divide. The web you weave may ensnare, captivate or inform, and the sacred language of the universe is present in all you create should you have eyes to see." *Grandmother, master weaver, architect of creation, had spoken... and it was wise to heed her words...*

Guidance

In eight visions,[85] characters within the script express a *Way of Wholeness* by virtue of spider medicine. Two, *Whirlwind* and *Wisdom Keeper*, are open doors to 'Grandmother', where a quiet mind and humble heart may be privy to her secrets. *Whirlwind* draws attention to the web, not one founded upon illusion in which you create your own destiny, but the great web of life, where orchestration, in place since the beginning of time, unfolds as **it** wills, not as you would dictate. The image, enough to set the senses reeling, presents a 'whirlwind' and is analogous to the sticky mess created when thoughts, emotions or life events are allowed to spiral out of control. But at the centre, all is in perfect balance: opposites face each other, the seed of a new way emerges and in the midst of chaos is clarity. So when the forces of change are at their most insistent, allow the eternal Grandmother to share her ways, and listen. She knows that in one who abides at the centre, there are no spiders... only weaving...

---

[85] *Jubilation, Multiverse, Omniscience, Timewarp, Walk in the Park, Weaver, Whirlwind, Wisdom Keeper.*

Whirlwind

Quality: Change
Absolute Aspect: Intelligence
Geometry: Seed of life, torus
Rainbow Sphere: Order

Guidance

Three master visions, *Will*, *Love* and *Intelligence*, mark the divine triad, represented by a triple toroidal vortex, which gives birth to each respective symbol. Their combined and equal force serves as a prism whereby fractured light – seven coloured rays of the inner rainbow – is expressed outwards as substance; every ray, and by association every *vision of reality*, therefore has their unified essence running through it, regardless of appearance. *Will*, as its title suggests, is divinity expressed as the Will to Be. Creativity in its most pure expression, it brings life to all form, from subtle realms of light to the densest appearance in matter, and ensures, through ordered intelligence, that all is returned once again to Spirit. The divine plan in action thus reveals Spirit to be in a perpetual state of unfoldment, where each turn of the spiral is a revelation in the art of divinity knowing itself. It cannot be denied that **you** play an undeniable and essential part in the unravelling of this plan, for just as you learn, expand and grow through personal experience, so does the universe as a whole. However, there is far more to this than meets the eye.

The **Law of Synthesis** governs Spirit, the life within the form, and determines both the rate at which and degree to which each evolving 'facet' returns to itself. In other words, it is not you but the Cosmic Clock within that determines when and how you will awaken. All the same, included within this Law of governance is individual process, where integration of three divine aspects – thoughts, feelings and physical form – are systematically drawn into coherence through persistent effort on the part of an individual. From their point of fusion, a bridge may be built between the lower man and that which controls the outer form: the Soul, which is Divine Intermediary between Spirit and matter. The Law of Synthesis eventually returns everything to a state of wholeness, but until the process of fusion is complete, it remains a barely detectable, if not totally absent, vibration in the awareness of one who has yet many steps to tread on his inner journey. In the context of this vision, be aware that this Law exists and that behind the scenes is a far bigger picture unfolding than you could possibly imagine, and then continue, in abject humility, to reclaim all those parts of you that remain hidden.

The **symbol** is an ideal starting point and well worth contemplating over a period of time. Embodying all ingredients outlined above, it provides a valuable and intuitive 'way in', where profound, difficult-to-grasp teachings soon become far more than mere concepts in the mind of one who has yet to awaken. A star tetrahedron, centred within a sphere, is the only 3D geometry within these master visions, reflecting both depth and breadth in integration. The Law of Synthesis, governed by the Real, is illustrated through the downward-pointing tetrahedron – pure white Light undeterred in its mission to merge with matter.

Will

Quality: Law of Synthesis
Divine Triad: Prism – Will
Geometry: Circle, star tetrahedron, torus, triquetra
Rainbow Sphere: Rainbow

Contemplation

"There has to be more to this," she pondered. *"The extent of her learning can't just be about a sticky mesh or how to build a trap for unsuspecting flies, surely?"* She had been sent to learn her next lesson, the remit being to find a spider's web, observe its qualities and, in particular, watch the way of the weaver. Grandmother, meanwhile, was silent. *As she watched, a silken thread appeared from nowhere. Cast meaningfully into the air before being carried by the wind, it found anchor amidst a bush on the other side of the great divide. Then followed the most mesmerising display of natural architecture she had ever had the pleasure of witnessing. Backwards and forwards, round and round, upwards and downwards, in an ordered fashion, the little creature went, undeterred by hindrances to its quest, until, before long, what began as a solitary gossamer thread had become a delicate, intricate network of fibres whose interconnection with its surroundings brooked no denial. Esmerelda drank it all in, whilst Spider, its task complete, moved purposefully to the centre of its creation to wait.* "Now follow me." Grandmother had spoken, so refusal was not an option. *The web, very soon forgotten, became a wonder of the past, and as they entered worlds anew – some familiar, others strange to her in appearance – she knew that the way of Spider was present in them all.* "Like the casting of thread, all your thoughts, words and deeds are bridges in time that may build or divide. The web you weave may ensnare, captivate or inform, and the sacred language of the universe is present in all you create should you have eyes to see." *Grandmother, master weaver, architect of creation, had spoken... and it was wise to heed her words...*

Guidance

In eight visions,[86] characters within the script express a *Way of Wholeness* by virtue of spider medicine. Two, *Whirlwind* and *Wisdom Keeper* , are open doors to 'Grandmother', where a quiet mind and humble heart may be privy to her secrets. *Wisdom Keeper* unravels the mystery of her heritage and reveals how this humble creature is endowed with such regal qualities as to have the fruits of her creations dance to its tune. As Grandmother, she is mother and as mother, child. Since the dawn of creation she has wafted the weave, sowing seeds for the future deep in the past, and in the telling of her story, the web is made whole but only to those who relinquish control. Language is her gift, writing her art, and in the one lies the other, though they seem far apart. So a word to the wise, to those who follow her lead, take care what you wish for, be aware of the seed and if you seek glory, you know the story... a tangled web is all that you'll weave.

---

[86] *Jubilation, Multiverse, Omniscience, Timewarp, Walk in the Park, Weaver, Whirlwind, Wisdom Keeper.*

Wisdom Keeper

Quality: Sacred Language
Absolute Aspect: Intelligence
Geometry: Triquetra
Rainbow Sphere: Mind

Contemplation

Woodhenge is the summer solstice, whose signature force is the fire element – Spirit as the divine masculine. The season of summer, in particular the solstice, is a time of year when light, in the form of the sun, is at its most brilliant. It is a time to celebrate its presence, utilise the preponderance of solar fire and ignite the light of consciousness within. Traditionally, fire and the sun are synchronous with enlightenment, one of many reasons that ancient cultures – including the Mayans, Ancient Egyptians and Druids – celebrated its passage with exotic and powerful rituals. *Woodhenge* carries the vibration of such practices. It was encapsulated on midsummer's eve at a local 'stone' circle, following sacred ceremonies to align with the kingdom of nature present during that time and place. If you have chosen this vision, you are encouraged to energise the light within, particularly the masculine qualities of right action, integrity and power, infused with wisdom. *Reflect upon the qualities of this season of luminescence. Allow its magic to vitalise every cell in your body, to warm all sense of feeling in your heart and to illuminate every last shadow in your mind. Breathe, breathe deep... breathe again. Breathe in the fire of Spirit... Follow each scintillating breath as it burns through all destructive thought... Smile as your heart is infused with joy at its passage... Celebrate a new sense of freedom when your physical body is enlivened with light. Be the fire of Spirit... the phoenix as it rises from the ashes of your former self... allow its power, its force for change, to feed the fire in your soul...*

Guidance – balance is alchemical

The combined essence of eight linked visions is an invitation to tune into the natural rhythm – birth, life, decay and death – expressed through the four seasons (*Ostara*: Spring, *Cosmic Orchestra*: Autumn, *Woodhenge*: Summer, *Unconquered Sun*: Winter) – and to marry it with those areas in your life symbolised by the four elements in four visions – *Fire*, *Earth*, *Air* and *Water*. Notice the gifts each aspect brings, encouraging you to become more aware of your thoughts (air), feelings (water), physical well-being (earth) and spiritual essence (fire). Be the detached observer; see how the same cyclic pattern, so evident in our natural world, flows through all areas of your life. From one moment to the next, the only thing that is certain is that 'it' will change. Take your lead from the kingdom of nature, for she is a willing teacher, and remember that you have the capacity to 'fly' as much as the caterpillar. It is time for seeds, sown in a season long since gone, to ripen and bear fruit as reality. Furthermore, it is an invitation for you to reconnect with the pulse of life, to appreciate the gifts each turn of the spiral brings and to restore these natural rhythms in your life... But first, you must turn every ounce of your presence – body, heart and Soul – towards the Light...

Woodhenge

Quality: Ritual
Absolute Aspect: Will
Geometry: Torus
Rainbow Sphere: Light

Contemplation

In the heart of a forest, far, far away, in an age when the air breaths fresh and clean and the rivers run pure and undefiled, the mighty oak spreads wide its boughs to expose a heart open to all. Custodian to this fair land, it stands as witness to the comings and goings, toing and froing, of those who walk in reverence upon the land and those who hail its lofty governance in wings of song across the vast ocean of the skies. Outer expression to an inner magnificence, its countenance brooks no denial, for the wisdom of ages pulses through its veins and strength born through adversity renders it worthy of its undisputed sovereignty. Custodian it is, but, in spite of its grandeur, it is but a shadow to the One, who stands beyond the mists of time and apart from the profane. Giver of life, orchestrator to the stars, haven to the realms of nine and bridge to the highest and the low, the One Tree cradles every ilk, shape and form within its breast. Origin of all wisdom and home to creatures great and small, it is Mother to the past, keeper of Light and guardian to all that moves within the night. So as one appears as kin to the other, alike in form though distinct in density, each tree, in its expression, is an age apart. And still, there are others, less imposing in structure, whose purpose is of such profound significance that heaven would fail in its mission without their participation. Those whose appearance is less than vertical, whose structure is far more delicate yet whose intricate web of filaments, fibres, flora and spawn, infused with intelligence of irrefutable order, is able to unite where others fail. Those whose nourishing blanket of green conceals sprinklings of magic... where one perhaps, with a discerning eye, may bear witness to the little folk celebrating in wonder the miracle of nature's abundance...

Guidance

Five visions[87] serve as awakeners to the intelligent life forms that dwell amongst the flora and fauna of our majestic woodlands. *World Tree*, as its name implies, is the life-giving 'mother of creation', otherwise known as the Tree of Life. An avatar-like quality to the image leads the eye beyond the prominent foreground to an ethereal, partially exposed tree in the distance, whilst the torus geometry, sitting centre stage and housing an 'eagle' in upwards flight, leaves no doubt as to the perennial nature and potential for growth in the energies being offered. The script gives added direction, inviting the traveller into the majestic splendour that is Mother Nature, the One Tree, in action. It is a calling to bathe in her life-enhancing presence and to accept her gift of nurturance, but, far more than this, it is also an invitation to step outside the bounds of time and experience the wonder of the Blessed Mother as she offers herself – body, heart and Soul – to *you*...

---

[87] *Custodian, Enchantment, Stability, Wallington Wood, World Tree.*

World Tree

Quality: Growth
Absolute Aspect: Intelligence
Geometry: Torus
Rainbow Sphere: Will

An Invitation

"Now what?" mused Thomas, more to himself than anyone else. He wasn't really expecting a reply so was surprised when Esmerelda responded. "I was wondering just the same thing," she said; like him, not really inviting a response. While they lapsed into a companionable silence, the question hung unanswered upon the air. A pregnant pause – a bubble of curiosity infused with stillness, yet alive with wonderment – took the place of conversation. And as each in their own way meandered inwardly along the peaks and valleys of their shared experience, the air between them intensified, as if other realms – other-worldly beings – were making their presence felt. This was more than a meeting of minds, more than a simple question posed in a moment of idle curiosity, far more than two small adventurers resting upon a log in a forgotten forest; indeed, it was a moment of such high import that emissaries of the three kingdoms came together as one. United in purpose, they left the sweetest scent upon the air, sang songs in tones not of this world and, through fleeting visions, left subtle impressions with clear intent in the minds and hearts of those who sought to enquire.

In Esmerelda, it was the presence of her Beloved who called her to action. There were no words and no dialogue, not even inwardly as the Voice in the Silence. No, in this there was nothing. In her mind there was nothing. But in her heart there was everything, in her heart the question had been answered, in her heart she knew, beyond all doubt, the way forward. In Thomas, the response came through visions, inwardly expressed, that were equally clear and were revealed in such a way that he too had no doubt as to the next step on their journey. Allowing themselves the luxury of bathing in wonderment for a while longer, they each absorbed the implications of what was being

asked; it was, after all, no small feat and they had, as yet, only been given the very first step. Then they turned to each other and smiled.

"We share it!" they cried in unison, leaping to their feet at one and the same time. Then, as if to let it sink in, as they couldn't really believe they had received the same answer, they performed a little dance around the glade repeating it over and over again. "We share it!" "We share it!" "We share it! Tra-la-la-la-lah…"

Suddenly, they stopped. They didn't know who spoke first but the message was clear. "How?" Silence, then again, "How can we possibly share all of this?" spoke Esmerelda. In a flash, the magnitude of her life's experience played before her inner eye. She was watching a movie of her life: her incarceration in the land of shadows, her sojourn in the fields of light, sensing her beloved Mentor, her fall and arrival in this idyllic forest, meeting her dearest forever friend. Esmerelda was struck by the seeming impossibility of the task that lay ahead. "How can we possibly share all of this?" she echoed. And then there were the keys to consider… and the rainbow… and… Thomas was equally bemused as he relived his experiences in the forest: his affinity with nature, his love for Esmerelda, how all the magic he had inside him flourished whenever she was near and how geometric structure was 'given' in response to her quest to understand… "How?" he repeated. "How can we possibly share all of this?" And then, "I mean, where would we begin?"

Neither of them spoke for a very, very long time, until Esmerelda penetrated the stillness with her voice. "It's quite simple," she said, with a mischievous sparkle in her eyes, "We begin at the end…" Thomas leapt to his feet in excitement, "With the diamond! Of course, it's so simple anyone would understand, even if they had never been to a magical wood or encountered an extra-special being from another realm." They laughed and they hugged and they did another celebratory dance around the glen. And then they did it all again... and again... and yet again, until they could dance no more; exhausted, they fell into a heap on the ground.

And so this is what they did. They took all the individual facets of the diamond, delved deep into each image as it presented a *vision of reality*, with its quality and geometry, and then arranged them all according to their parent Rainbow sphere. All 144 facets of the diamond could now be viewed as both individual and an intrinsic part of a bigger picture through the colour of the rainbow to which they belonged. It was so simple, but there was another piece of the jigsaw yet to fall into place. "Do you know," said Thomas, for he had a way of figuring out all things ordered, "I think there must be an easier way to put this across." Esmerelda was all ears. "Could we find a way to display all the facets of the diamond in such a way that shows the colour of the rainbow to which each belongs? And where the symbols relevant to each vision are immediately evident? If people can touch and play with them, they will easily experience 'everything' in a very profound yet accessible way."

"You mean like a deck of cards," she replied. And then, without further ado, "Such as these!"

Thomas, as you can well imagine, was gobsmacked. He started to say, "How, how..." but then stopped in mid-flow. He knew, of course. Esmerelda's forte was to manifest intention 'out of thin air', almost before it had been set. It would appear that between them they had created just what was needed for the next step on their journey. *Key of Light* contemplation cards had been born. Now they could explore both Diamond and Rainbow with ease, and very soon they would be ready to share.

Introducing *Key of Light* contemplation cards

Embracing Esmerelda's journey, from wholeness to separation and return, alongside the wisdom of Thomas, through his innate understanding of sacred geometric structure as ordered intelligence, *Key of Light* contemplation cards present a *Way of Wholeness* in which each turn of a card is a doorway to the innermost self.

In the land of her belonging, Esmerelda witnessed the birth of the Word where three aspects of Divinity – Will, Love and Intelligence – gathered unto themselves before expressing outwards as sound in the form of the Word. The Rainbow appeared as the Sacred Seven who arranged themselves into coloured spheres before her eyes in the forest, whilst the multi-faceted Diamond was revealed courtesy of Thomas' big toe. Along the way, both mystery within number and order through geometry were exposed through simple teachings otherwise too ethereal to grasp. And then there were the *keys* themselves, which were proven to be rooted in geometric order linked to the womb of creation. Every aspect of creation – from Absolute, through subtle vibrations of sound and light, to the heart of Mother Nature – is expressed through this story alongside the interaction of characters within it; *Key of Light* cards are no different.

Beginning with Absolute, 'life aspects' – Love, Will and Intelligence – are expressed through three master cards bearing the same names. Their symbols run, as a river, through every card and serve as the outer 'appearance': Spirit in matter. Intrinsic to both *aspect* and *appearance* is consciousness, or Soul expression, which colours the 'currents' within this river with certain 'qualities'. The cards, using their symbol and word on reverse, reflect this. These master cards set the scene and serve as a prism wherein the seven coloured rays of the Rainbow may be birthed. The Rainbow, as fractured light, is revealed through seven coloured suits, each one bearing the symbol of the Rainbow group-consciousness (p.52) it represents. An eighth suit, the Rainbow in its totality, traces the *Way of Creation* through its cards as it integrates with matter through the *Way of Nature*. Finally, the Diamond is the 144 cards, individual facets within wholeness, each one expressing a *vision of reality* through image, symbol and seed thought.

In summary, *Key of Light* contemplation cards **are** Esmerelda's keys. Through image, symbol and seed thought, they take the subtle realms intrinsic to the kingdoms of nature, the Soul and Spirit and marry them with the innate essence that expresses humanity at its finest. Rich in symbolism and steeped in spiritual significance, they serve as doorways into the multi-layered nature of human consciousness. Subtle realms of earth and cosmos merge with your personal journey – thoughts, feelings and physical appearances – to provide an *Education in Consciousness* in which all are recognised as facets of the multi-dimensional Self: the inner you. Contemplating *Key of Light* cards – image, seed thought, symbol and geometry – or taking the deep and profound principles laid down within the pages of this

book into your heart opens up a means of internal communication that transcends "the boundaries of space and time". Like Esmerelda, you will start to remember that which has, for so long, been forgotten. All you **believe** yourself to be will fall away and you will start to emit a frequency of authenticity; the inner you will be expressed outwards as radiance.

Key of Light card layouts
In keeping with this chapter, the following layouts are **an invitation** to play. Their foundation lies in three primary roots: suit, including Rainbow colour, as an expression of group-consciousness; symbol, as it aligns to the coloured ray it embodies; seed thought relative to suit. They work best with *Key of Light* cards but may be just as effective when used with this book alone. Some suggestions for using the layouts with this book are set out below.

- Layouts have as their source A Rainbow (p.45) and A Diamond (p.91) chapters, with Rainbow symbols providing the structure for each reading. Referring to these chapters as you work will provide perspective and clarity through the remainder of this chapter.
- 'Rainbow spheres/Key of Light suits' in 'Appendix 2: Facets of the Diamond' lists visions relative to their bigger-picture, Rainbow perspective. Use these in place of cards as a focus for selecting, contemplating and understanding the essence of the energies being presented; alternatively, choose one that draws your attention whilst perusing the list.
- Turn to the Diamond chapter (p.91) when choosing a vision to contemplate. Randomly flip through the pages and notice any that jump out – use this as a starting point for working with a layout.
- Be creative when choosing a vision or layout. Use coloured card that's blank on the reverse to

represent the Rainbow spheres, or simply write their names on one side and randomly choose them as you would a card.

- There are endless creative possibilities in using this book alone; the only limitation is your own lack of vision. So be creative, play and let your inner guide lead the way. Above all, enjoy the ride!

Vesica piscis – the womb of creation

In the chapters 'A Gift' and 'A Door', Esmerelda discovered that the keys held their roots in geometric structure, namely the vesica piscis. It was this alignment that not only set them apart as gateways, but also ensured that every interaction shifted perspective from the small to the Real. This symbol is integral to *Key of Light* cards. Each card, as a *vision of reality*, is thus imbibed with the intention to see as the 'Eye' would see: to view reality as would the singular, non-dual Eye of God. Likewise, every suit symbol emerges from this same structure to instil a bigger-picture perspective when working with the cards. Bear this in mind when using the layouts below, and remember that *Key of Light* cards are **contemplation** cards: they are not to be understood with the mind but absorbed, integrated and experienced over time through the heart. Changes may be fleeting, in line with the subtle realms of the Soul, so be patient and keep surrendering to the process. A short introduction to the art of contemplation will help you get a feel for how it works.

Art of contemplation

The art of contemplation requires space and time. It is not something to be rushed or manipulated. Start by watching the breath and bring your attention to the pause between the in-breath and out-breath. Continue to breathe normally with relaxed focus; this creates space and allows your mind to slow down. It is important not to have any agenda. You are simply watching and breathing. As you continue to observe, allow yourself to become the 'pause' – simply merge with its presence. At this point, you can relax your attention on the breath.

Abide in a position of relaxed focus and allow the object of contemplation (image, seed thought or symbol, etc.) to arise gently in your mind. In the case of an image, allow your gaze to alight softly upon its form and notice any thoughts, feelings or insights that appear. Again, don't fixate on, judge or try to manipulate any of these impressions; simply allow them to come and go. If nothing happens or if you lose your focus, let it go. This is really important. Allow the object of reflection to move to the back of your mind and get on with your daily life. Going for a walk or taking a shower helps to move the energy; before long, you will find clarity and insight appearing from nowhere.

Finally, it is important to write down your insights. Understanding gained from contemplation rarely happens in one sitting. It evolves, grows and bears fruit over time. Keeping a diary (or Rainbow journal) of your insights will enable you to follow your own process of integration.

Creating an 'awareness bubble'

When you choose an object for contemplation, notice your **first** impressions – feelings, thoughts, themes, patterns, etc. – and place them in a little bubble suspended just above your head. Now continue with your daily life, loosely holding the bubble in your awareness. Notice occurrences that tie in with its contents and place them in the bubble too. At the end of the day, record your insights – or even create a 'bubble' drawing!

Life is a journey and a process, and, by the same token, so is *Walk the Rainbow*. Selection of a card is an invitation for you to take the first step on this journey. Your daily life is transformed as understanding of this process filters in. Radiating outwards, in ever-increasing circles, it not only impacts upon your life, but also enriches the lives of others. Thus, cosmic understanding intertwines with earthly existence, **your** existence. This is the beauty of *Walk the Rainbow*; it is the *Art of Synthesis:* one vision, one journey, one life.

The layouts and suggested readings featured below assume that *Key of Light* cards are being used; suit symbols are their point of origin, with geometric structure at their heart to provide a backdrop, or framework, so your chosen cards have a sacred space within which their energies may unfold. When cards are set out in this way, you are automatically aligned with the inner workings of the cosmos without even thinking about it. Add to this the subtle energies embodied within the seven coloured rays of light and, together with your chosen cards, you have the perfect recipe for intuiting the most refined vibrations within yourself. You will notice that not all spheres have been chosen; this is intentional. Refer to Figure 2, 'Rainbow Bridge', on p.83, and notice that there are three symbols fundamental to bridge-building that encompass all others – *Will, Order* and *Truth* – with a fourth, *Beauty,* serving as gateway to the inner realms. Lastly, one more layout is included, 'Rainbow', for those who wish to set aside a period in their lives in which the *Way of Wholeness* may be integrated into daily life, for instance, as if in a retreat setting.

Now begin by choosing one card; take note of the suit symbol on its reverse (bottom centre) and use this as your first layout. Alternatively, turn your attention towards the layouts featured below and choose one according to the energy that speaks to you in the moment. Be creative and play. **N.B.** Card positions are shown by circles (spheres of influence) in all layouts.

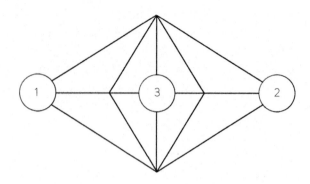

Conflict Resolution – The Beauty Way
Three cards
Rainbow sphere/Key of Light suit: Beauty
Symbol: Two tetrahedrons, golden ratio

When confusion, misunderstanding or conflict arise, it may be said that one side is at odds with the other; the significance of this symbol couldn't, therefore, be clearer. It extends beyond the central vesica piscis 'diamond' to fill the structure in its entirety. This implies that there is work to be done in bringing the two to a point of resolution and illustrates the degree to which the two poles are apart; only two suit symbols express polarity to this extreme – *Beauty* and *Truth,* a vital clue as to the purpose behind their respective expressions. There is hope, however, for the integral geometry lying at the heart of both is the golden ratio: love, Love Divine, as the greatest redeemer.

Inspiration
Ray 4 – Harmony through Conflict
The fourth is the ray of humanity and as well as marking man's propensity to polarise everything dual, it draws to the surface his interminable battle with himself. The symbol could not be clearer: two opposites stretched as far apart as they can go, symbolising the battlefield and

endless war of division that defines 21st-century life on planet earth. Direction is clear. Unity must prevail. Everything about this ray points to the polarisation of core dualities, but of far more import to one who has turned his attention inwards is the glaring chasm between mind and heart, or thought and feelings.

Use this layout to explore polarity in your life. Every conflicting view, separate part or divisive opinion has, at some point, the potential for resolution. The art of living lies in bringing these opposing forces into relationship and eventually into a place of harmony where each appreciates the qualities and expressions of the other without judgement. This may present externally as an 'other' or internally between different selves: heart and mind, body and spirit, etc. Ultimately, when seeming separates are embraced as reflective attributes of the inner you, every challenge and every life event becomes a blessing. Life is viewed as a gift, with diversity its greatest asset; a sense of wonderment ensues as the *Way of Beauty* translates into reality.

Method

This layout is simple. Choose two cards from any suit, each reflecting sides of the pole giving rise to conflict. This may be an inner or outer process; both are equally valid and essential to the route to wholeness. Take time to consider carefully – look beyond the obvious interpretation and be open to a new layer, or bigger picture, revealing itself. A third card, drawn from Rainbow, or any other suit as you intuit, may be chosen to bring clarity – this sits between the two and is the centre of the 'eye' in the symbol. It promotes clear-seeing through shifting your perspective to one of holism, as if you are viewing the situation through the All-Seeing eye of Absolute.

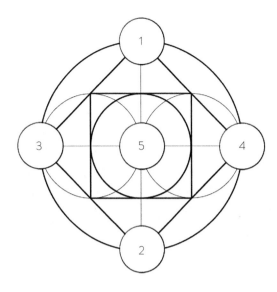

Karmic Roots
Five cards
Rainbow sphere/Key of Light suit: Order
Symbol: Geometry of octave, equal-armed cross within a circle within a square

The equal-armed cross is an ancient and sacred symbol. Not only does it harmonise all aspects of the quadrangle, but it also facilitates the marriage of both horizontal and vertical life – personality with Soul. However, it is far more than this, for fundamental to both symbol and interpretation is its affinity with sound. Consider each placement, then, to be a note – a vibration expressed as the Word, whose message echoes upon wings of silence to reveal the origin of its cause. In the path of evolution, such as we are concerned with here, it presents opportunity for bridge-building upon the journey from life in sleep to full waking consciousness; each arm being a stepping stone across the great river of ignorance. The 'diamond' (rotated square) implies movement, a propelling or instigating force that would belie the static appearance of the cross if it were to stand alone. In a clockwise direction, it moves the traveller to integration and, ultimately, synthesis, but choose the reverse and the spiral of chaos will tie your head in knots and turn your heart to stone. So listen well to the voices in the silence, know their source and above all, pay heed to their agenda.

Inspiration
Ray 7 – Ceremonial Order or Magic

The seventh ray is where the 'highest and lowest' meet and it sees the most refined vibrations of Spirit penetrate deep into the heart of matter. With respect to a reading, it denotes not only this bigger-picture perspective, but also the journey you, as a soul, have undertaken through many lifetimes (possibly) to reach the point where you are now. In esoteric astrology, its cosmic distributors chart a path through the heavens that helps us to see our path of return. That which began in *Aries* as a spark, an impulse to create, finds its way into the mass consciousness of humanity to arrive in *Cancer*, sign of the mother and the home; male, Spirit, has impregnated its feminine counterpart, matter, with its Will to exist. The home, of course, refers to the Soul, whose essence is love, found within the heart of physicality; "I build a lighted house and therein dwell" is a perfect keynote for this sign. Its polar opposite, *Capricorn*, encourages 'the crab' to emerge from the safety of its shell and rise to the heights of worldly ambition. Returning to your personal journey, the potential to redeem karmic propensities on mental (*Aries*), emotional (*Cancer*) and physical (*Capricorn*) planes of existence is ripe for the taking in this layout.

Use this layout to discern whispers of the Soul, to expose that which impedes your progress and to embrace those qualities that will be of most benefit to integration at this moment in time. *Light and shadow, personality and Soul; qualities must be embraced equally to gain maximum benefit from this reading.*

Method

Having first set your alignment intention, begin by selecting four cards from any suit. Place them on their respective places as shown in the layout, where voices demanding of your attention are:

1 = Soul/Spirit
2 = Earth/Body
3 = Beliefs/Programs
4 = Desires/Needs
5 = Harmony/Integration

Don't be in a rush to choose more cards; take some time to assimilate and **honestly** reflect upon the message that each card is offering relative to its place on the map. Now choose one card from the Rainbow suit; this sits at Position 5 and is the bigger-picture perspective assisting you in the integration process. Again, don't rush. Let each layer sink deep into your being and feel it on every level until it arises as a new way – a new you. When embraced in this manner, change is alchemical; it creates a new expression of the old you. Finally, if it feels right, you might choose four more cards. Place these on the four corners of the square and consider them to be keys to the shadow self, which, if illuminated, sets the spiral of integration in motion. This is a powerful reading; it should not be hurried but contemplated, assimilated and integrated over time.

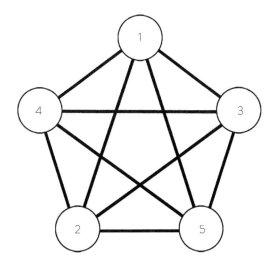

Awakening Inner Vision
Five cards
Rainbow sphere/Key of Light suit: Truth
Symbol: Pentagram within pentagon, golden ratio

Clouds are indicative of dreams; they are nebulous in nature, hard to get hold of or even remember, and therefore have very little bearing on reality. Or do they? Without dreams, without the power to envision or to imagine, humankind would still be living in the dark ages. Imagination is said to be the most powerful force in the universe, so is it any wonder we turn to its auspices when setting the intention for this reading? On the face of it, the pentagram, as suit symbol, would seem as far removed from the world of dreams as you can get but dig deeper into the roots of its geometry and you will find it to be a perfect match. The dodecahedron has 12 pentagonal faces and is essential to the structure of the Christ-Consciousness grid, but, most importantly in this case, it is unstable when it stands in its isolated state as one of the platonic solids; in other words, it needs something external to support it. The pentagram stabilises it from the inside, and when the qualities of mind and heart are applied to the five points of its star, what began as an indeterminate, wishy-washy dream centred in desire miraculously transforms into clear-seeing, where the bridge between the inner vision and the outer reality are known to be one and the same. The message of this symbol, then, is to look beyond the clouds that veil the sun, to go deep into its nature and to bring forth the inner visionary that is the true creator of reality. But before you begin, revisit the diagram on p.82 and take note of the position of this symbol – not only does it rest at the heart of the Rainbow Bridge, but it's abode is nothingness, and therein is a vital clue as to how to get the most out of this reading. Be honest, use the mind as a mirror to reflect outer reality inwards and accept whatever findings may emerge from the place of shadows as being aspects of you.

Inspiration
Ray 6 – Devotion or Idealism
The sixth ray is love at its most polarised. At its depth, it bears witness to the most extreme expression of self-centred love, fraught with conditions that waft to and fro with the opinions of others. Transpersonal Love of the Divine is at its height when a compassionate heart is its only expression. More on this ray's influence may be found in 'What is…?', 'What are the Seven Rays?', but for now, suffice to say, its ultimate potential lies in opening the heart to compassion, but be under no illusion: there is much inner work to be done before these all-inclusive qualities arise naturally in the heart of one who loves another like unto themselves.

Use this layout when you cannot see the wood for the trees, when you need to ignite an impetus for change and when the source of direction is beyond the scope of your current knowing. Pay attention to those areas in your life when you become fixated or obsessed or are closed to any viewpoint but your own. This layout, when set with intention, can introduce a broader perspective in which your mind and your heart are suddenly set free. But first, you have to wish it to be so. Inner vision can only be awakened when the heart is true and the mind is set to a purpose other than its own.

Method

Shuffle the cards and choose five cards, one from each of the suits shown below, and arrange as per the layout, where:

1 = Universal love – *Love (Indigo)*
2 = Polarised desire – *Beauty (Yellow)*
3 = Inner vision – *Truth (Blue)*
4 = Higher mind – *Light (Green)*
5 = Lower mind – *Mind (Orange)*

Take some time to absorb the messages being expressed through the images. Turn the cards over and do the same with the reverse. Let go of any need to interpret and just be present with what is. Now read the guidance for each card; writing it in your journal helps to anchor in its message. If you feel inspired to change card positions, go with it; listen to your inner guidance. Reaching number 5 is not an end; it is a beginning. Try following the lines of light connecting each card through the pentagram – 1, 2, 5, 4, 3 and return to 1 – see how they lead from heart to mind and then return again to heart in a non-linear manner. Remember, the golden ratio, expressed on this earth plane as the Fibonacci spiral, lies at the heart of the pentagram. Take it into to your heart, **feel** how heart and mind merge at each turn and surrender to its passage. Keep returning to number 1 and then start again. You will find your vision and subsequent appearance as reality shifts, changes and unfolds with each turning of the wheel. Be patient; creative expression is worth the wait.

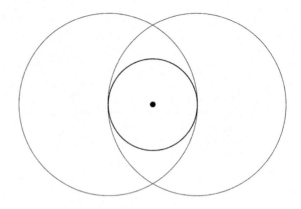

Light Emergent
Two cards
Rainbow sphere/Key of Light suit: Will
Symbol: A point within a circle

The circle, in this instance, is the 'eyeball' within the vesica piscis Eye of God through which Great Spirit may not only view the landscape of its domain, but also create a space into which it may emanate its light; the point is that emanation, a continuous outpouring force within which the Will, Love and Intelligence of divine manifestation is transmitted. Bear this in mind when considering the energies of your chosen cards during readings using this layout.

Inspiration
Ray 1 – Will or Power
The first ray is the initial impulse that arises through the most pure and primal of intentions: the will to exist. However, it is far more than bringing life to physical existence; it penetrates to the core of every life form it touches to infuse all with purpose, Divine Purpose. In daily life, this works out as the 'will to good', where every evolutionary turn of the spiral results in a more inclusive approach to reality. But beware: its method, using fiery will, is total annihilation of the old before a new way may come into being.

Use this layout to bring the inner and outer into intimate relationship. When a new beginning or way of being is on the horizon, it is too easy to fall back on old, familiar ways or coping mechanisms. This layout introduces a new way – a transpersonal perspective, where guidance, and the resultant new expression, has at its core the source of all beginnings (and endings): Divine Will.

Method

Choose one card from the Rainbow suit. This is the circle in the symbol and represents the bigger picture: the energy that is available to you should you choose to accept its gift. Now choose a second card from any other suit. This is the point within the circle and the initiatory force leading to a new way of being. Remember, letting go of any preconceived outcome or agenda is prelude to embracing the new.

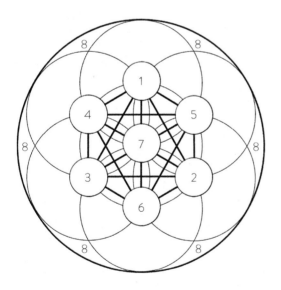

Walk the Rainbow
Eight cards
Rainbow sphere/Key of Light suit: Rainbow
Symbol: Seed of life

Seven concentric circles when arranged in this manner constitute the seed of life geometry. Like all seeds, it holds a perfect blueprint of its future self. Expanding in ever-increasing rounds of ordered circles, it blossoms into the flower, ripens into fruit and ultimately releases its divine potential in the form of Metatron's cube; the seeds of physicality are birthed through its geometry as the platonic solids. The beauty of sacred geometry is that it provides the perfect platform for contemplating both the subtle and more obvious aspects of our day-by-day interactions within our personal panorama. Every moment, with each thought, word and deed, we sow seeds that, at some point in time, will bear fruit as reality. Remember, once sown there is no turning back; divine order **will** work out and your 'wish' will be obeyed as if it were a command. *Key of Light* cards, particularly when your focused intention is channelled through this layout, present an opportunity to ensure those seeds will ripen for the good of yourself, humanity and our world as a whole.

Rainbow essence

The Rainbow suit in its entirety encompasses, and transcends, all Seven Rays. It can be likened to a diamond, which, owing to its high refractive index, allows light inside to maintain its purity and brilliance – diamond-clear light – yet when presented with an external light source, transmits its inner 'fire' outwards to create multi-coloured rainbows: fractured light. The diamond, therefore, serves as source to fractured light whilst being clear and untainted. All cards within this suit are imbibed with these qualities, which is why they play such a significant part in the awakening process during these readings. When you choose one of these cards, consider that although they may present as a separate aspect, or thread, of consciousness, the energy or presence underpinning them inwardly is pure and undefiled.

Use this layout when you are ready to begin a conscientious journey inwards, when you are able to dedicate some time in your life to move beyond habitual behavioural responses or when the calling of the Soul can no longer be denied. This does not have to mean isolation from friends and family, etc., although a period of 'retreat' may be beneficial; it can easily be blended into daily life. Just like the diamond, inner clarity may prevail whilst outwardly reflecting and embracing the many 'colours of the rainbow'. This is *Walking the Rainbow*; you are in the world but not of it. The method below offers one of many ways to approach this reading. Taking your time and allowing your inner guidance to lead will ease you in gently and help you to become familiar with the Diamond way of living. When you are comfortable with this, try experimenting with other symbols as foundations for a reading.

Introducing the Diamond – nine days
Choose eight cards, one from each suit, and arrange them as per the layout. The Rainbow card is always the 'containing' circle, being the presiding presence offering clarity from the inner diamond. This layout is a hexagram (six-pointed star) where:

1 to 3 = Matter raised to Spirit (evolutionary journey)
4 to 6 = Spirit descending into matter (involutionary journey)
7 = Integration, the glue that ensures the six are experienced as one
8 = Presiding presence as Diamond-consciousness (clear-seeing)

Take your time, let your eyes scan the visions, notice any sensations or insights that may arise and then turn the cards over and do the same with the symbols and words on the reverse. Rearrange the cards if you feel inspired to. This is day one; pay attention to your chosen Rainbow, read the guidance and use it as an anchor to awaken you to your innermost self, allowing the energy of the card to permeate your being. It will be a holding presence every day for the next week as you introduce a new card each day. On the next day, shuffle the remaining cards and choose a single card as your focus for the day, using the guidance as before. Follow this procedure for the rest of the week, choosing a different card every day. On completion, you will have reflected upon each of the cards from your reading. On day nine, arrange your cards in the Rainbow layout again and contemplate them as a whole. Don't forget to write down any insights in your Rainbow journal.

An End?

"Do you think there is ever an end, Esmerelda?"

"I suppose it could be said, 'Everything that has a beginning has an end.' After all, when this physical body dies, 'Esmerelda' as an identity will be no more. Though it's not as straight forward as this – I remember in one of your teachings you stated, 'once something has been created, it never dies' (p.58). I don't know, Thomas. What do you think?" she replied gently yet, unusually for her, somewhat absent-mindedly.

It was late summer. An in-between kind of time when a bountiful sun, softened by nature's passage, prepared to relinquish its place of prominence in a watery sky, when long, lazy days and endless luminous nights offered its seat to guardians of the night and when well-tended seeds weighed heavily upon branches of well-stocked trees. A season when fruit, ripe for picking and ready for eating, called upon the harvester to echo its finale; a season for celebration and reason for death, decay and dying. It was a time of gathering in, taking stock and giving thanks to the miracle of nature's beatitude, a time to appreciate the reaping of the sowing and a time to nurture seeds inside fruit that plentiful blessings may be granted in a future yet to be determined. A time of shift, a time of change, a time when a hint of cold carried upon a breeze sent shivers along skin caressed by warmth from a dying sun; it was a period when a satiated earth, who'd bestowed her best, welcomed seasons and cycles that steered her to rest. Yes, it was a time to take time out, to reflect upon and gather into oneself the abundance of life well lived. It was a season when a small boy might rest idly upon a carpet of moss beside a cheery brook in a secluded forest in the company of his bestest friend in the whole wide world, and, above all, it was a time for casting deep and meaningful questions into the air.

"Do you know what, Esmerelda, I don't really know, though I remember the teaching. I have just been lying here soaking up all the wonderful experiences we have had since we decided to share our magic, and marvelling at how it all seemed to have a life of its own, and I guess I just got carried away with the wonder of it all. I mean, who would have thought it would have all unfolded in the way it did? I can't believe how easy and effortless it has been and I cannot fail to be bowled over by the Orchestrator of the whole shebang. It's mind-blowing, it really is."

Esmerelda smiled warmly towards him as she spoke, *"I know, Thomas, I can feel the pure joy and wonderment in your heart as you speak; it's contagious. I, too, have been bathing in the miracle of our adventures. And now there is Presence in the air. I feel the gentle folk of the forest and others we have yet to meet gathering, and dearest Beloved draws near too; I sense, hear and feel them – inside. There is so much more to unfold as we share. Like everything else, we are not here, in this place at this time, without reason. Your questions, too, are not without purpose, but for now, it is for you to tease out answers, in a way only you can do."*

Thomas withdrew into himself, and before long, as he had come to expect, grid-works of light made their presence felt. Nature's perfect pattern, the divine matrix, appeared first, but this time it revealed, as if by magic, a sequence of meaningful visions beginning with the vesica piscis unfolding **inside** its already perfected 'outer' form. Structures with which he was readily familiar – seed, flower, fruit and Metatron's cube – followed in rapid succession, materialising in subtle vibrations of light before his eyes. But it was the last vision – one with which he was familiar, albeit in a different context – that struck the deepest chord. A dazzling array of multi-layered light led a clear pathway **inwards**, beginning with Esmerelda's map of consciousness in its simplest form: the vesica piscis. He had received his answer, and it was as clear as the brightest star on a cloudless night. Now he must step aside to allow words to flow. "The short answer," he began, "is 'No – there is no end.' But, as you might understand, it's not sufficient just to say the answer is no. In order to answer the question fully, there must be a 'Why?' as well." He paused, not only to confirm she was in accord, but also to align himself inwardly before moving on.

"This is how it is," he began, emulating the Beloved, as was his customary fashion. "The end is the beginning and the beginning is the end. You know this already, Esmerelda, but what you, and others, may not understand is why it is so. This is where sacred geometry comes in; it opens up avenues of expression where paradox is revealed in such a way that all is known to be whole, complete and in natural order, in the moment. In short, it bypasses the mind to ignite the underlying consciousness – the soil in which all 'things' grow and wherein mind is but a particle within its substance." Again he paused, this time to retrieve his 'teaching' aids. These had been 'upgraded' from the trusted drawing stick he used during their summer of sharing, and he was now the proud owner of a white board with many different coloured pens, as well as visuals outlining geometric structures. With an air of confidence, he placed a collection of images upon his stand.

"By now, you should be more than familiar with this particular sequence," Thomas continued with ease. "Beginning with a sphere, it follows an **involutionary** journey from the realm of Spirit into the heart of matter – 3D life; Metatron's cube is the gateway from one to the other. As you can see, these graphics are different from those we have seen before inasmuch as geometries are emphasised **within** an already perfected matrix. This implies that a return to the beginning is demanded, so that each sphere, or layer, may be revisited at another turn of the **evolutionary** spiral. Here's how it works. In the graphics overleaf, the platonic solids are displayed as an evolutionary sequence based upon the level of consciousness they represent; notice how they become more rounded with each step? Their intimate relationship to each other, how they are integral to consciousness and the method by which they facilitate movement from one level of awareness to another are not for this time or place [see 'What is...?', 'What is sacred geometry?' pp.441–451]. For the time being, it is sufficient to understand the role they play in returning the fragmented self to a state of wholeness; the 'rounding out' of 'jagged edges' being an essential part of the journey. Can you see, Esmerelda, how these structures bring clarity to the original

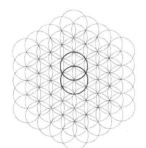

Divine Matrix:
Vesica Piscis

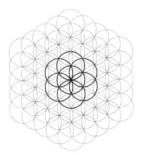

Divine Matrix:
Seed of Life

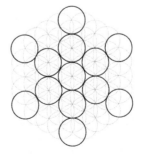

Divine Matrix:
Fruit of Life

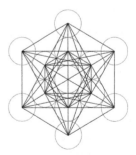

Fruit of Life:
Metatron's Cube

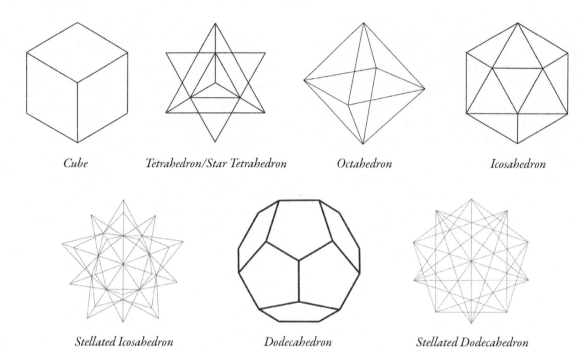

Cube   *Tetrahedron/Star Tetrahedron*   *Octahedron*   *Icosahedron*

Stellated Icosahedron   *Dodecahedron*   *Stellated Dodecahedron*

question, *Is there ever an end?*, through explaining the 'why'?" Esmerelda took some time to respond. During the spring and summer she had come a long way in grasping the teachings offered by her forever friend, but she still needed time to assimilate in order for the pieces of his geometric jigsaw to fall into place in a way that worked for her; she might then come to understand the why as an aspect of her own Being-ness.

She was back in prison. The all-too-familiar though long-ago-forgotten memories of her incarceration returned with unbridled passion. Once again, she experienced being trapped in a world of her own making, where she was queen of her domain yet inwardly bereft, where her beloved prince attended to her every need yet left her feeling desperately alone. Once again, she watched her spirit soar as she entered the world of dreams, with every escape offering tantalising glimpses of 'something' that might set her free yet would never be hers for the taking. Once more, she watched the pendulum

swing from bliss to despair, from despair to bliss, and back again... She watched it set the rhythm of her demise, over and over and over again, as it dictated the story of her existence.

Suddenly, the scene changed. A small wonder-filled child played in the dirt. Her heart an open book, she embraced every encounter with joy, welcomed each experience as if it were her first and revelled in existential realism. She laughed with a babbling brook, cried with the rain, sang with the birds and thundered alongside the most powerful storms as heaven vented its fury upon an unsuspecting earth. Inside, Esmerelda smiled. This was freedom. It had nothing to do with castles or prisons and especially not dreams or a need to escape; freedom was a state of mind.

Again, reality shifted. Geometric structures, in particular the platonic solids, were at the forefront of her vision; one after the other they tumbled from the sky just as they had when they first appeared in her map of consciousness. She watched, the detached observer, transfixed as they separated to perform a ritual dance. It was like watching a play but with each actor and every performance encoded with the mysteries of the cosmos. Sacred shapes unravelled stories: a cube became her prison, the dodecahedron, her escape and an octahedron sparkled with joy as a wonder-filled child explored magic in existence. Gyrations increased in intensity. The more they danced, the greater was the shift in reality, and the more marked the shift, the deeper was her understanding of the role they played in revealing consciousness as it worked out in matter. Slowly the display came to end. Only it didn't; two shapes remained – a cube and a star tetrahedron. This would prove to be the most profound, yet simple, lesson of all.

As the cube stilled to rest serenely upon the earth, the star tetrahedron rotated 90° (if she hadn't witnessed it herself, she would never have believed it) and upon completion of its orbit, it vanished into thin air only to re-emerge, almost in the same moment, **inside** the cube. Esmerelda was gobsmacked but she got the message – clearly. Now, nested together perfectly, one inside the other as if it had always been that way, these seemingly inanimate structures had revealed to her the route to wholeness. Inner and outer had intimately aligned, meaning dualities were free to exist as freedom in expression without judgement or polarisation; inside, as the penny dropped, she felt integrated, whole and complete. "Aha," said Esmerelda to herself, "so that is how it is done." And with that, for the time being at least, instruction into the fabric of time and space came to an end.

She turned towards her friend of all time and beamed from ear to ear. "Surprisingly, Thomas, I do understand, but, as you can intuit, I must enter these structures in order to gain access to their essence." Thomas, of course, was more than accustomed to her ways and had waited patiently until she was ready to share her experience (in fact, there was no need for her to repeat it, as they were so intimately in tune that he experienced it just as she did – moment by moment). "So this is my understanding of the energies as they were revealed to me," she explained. "Each solid, as you have quite correctly stated, is representative of a layer or sphere of consciousness. In my case, they revealed aspects of my personal journey – even those pertaining to a previous existence. This is how consciousness is; nothing is ever lost and all is built upon or disentangled within the space-time continuum until such time as it is absorbed into wholeness as a way of being. Clearly, as my stories were able to arise so effortlessly, they are still in a process of disentanglement, albeit one of fine-tuning; the charge, as you might say, is no longer present."

"Yes, I get it," chipped in Thomas, "but what I don't get is why you were only shown four of the platonic solids?" "Ah, well spotted. I had wondered about that myself. As I understand it, the 'lower' three geometries, plus the dodecahedron in its lowest expression, are where all the entanglements are worked out. The remaining geometries – icosahedron, stellated icosahedron, higher aspect of the dodecahedron and the stellated dodecahedron – pretty much take care of themselves, emerging with each inner letting go or acceptance to 'what is.' In other words, they appear as a **result** of harmonising the lower not by trying to 'fix' them or by chasing after some ideal or dream of how things ought to be."

They slipped into a comfortable, quiet space while each pondered upon the implications each to the other had shared. It was Thomas who broke the silence. "And what of the two that merged at the end?" "That's the most exciting revelation of all," she responded with purpose. "You might say it's the mainstay of the entire evolutionary journey, at least as far as human consciousness is concerned. Notice how the star tetrahedron nests inside the cube? This serves as a stabiliser for a geometry that is inherently unstable; it is a sound inner structure wherein transformation may take place securely without compromising the integrity of the whole." Thomas, contrary to his usual grasp of all things ordered, was frowning. *"Let me tease it apart some more so you can understand,"* she offered. *"Aside from the cube and the dodecahedron, can you see how every solid has as its foundation a triangle?"* He nodded, somewhat relieved to be back in familiar territory. *"It's all really simple when you consider the properties of this geometry: three straight lines with three apex points, serving as boundaries to a triangular inner space whose purpose is to bring two opposing standpoints to a place of resolution. When you apply this to daily life, when you cut to the core of every disharmonious state of mind or unbalanced emotion, it all comes down to polarising one dual against another; in other words, taking sides!"*

Thomas laughed as the penny dropped. "So during your incarceration, when you yearned to be rescued or when you chose light to the exclusion of your shadow, you were choosing one over the other. You wanted to be somewhere other than where you were; in effect, denying yourself full expression of both. Now it was Esmerelda's turn to laugh. *"Perfect, Thomas, you have got it in one! So, to round this off and by means of closure, we need to tie up the loose ends. Life in its full expression is made up of many, many dualities – light and dark, up and down, inner and outer, body and soul, you and me, us and them, etc., etc. There is nothing wrong with this; it is just the way life is. We are part of a dualistic universe and there is nothing that needs to be done to 'fix' it. The problem arises, as we have already intimated, when we polarise these dualities by preferring one over another. When stripped to the core, three essential dualities*[88] *are particularly relevant in our journey to wholeness: Soul/personality, inner child/present adult and masculine/feminine. When these are harmonised*

---

[88] See 'What is…?', 'What is Quantum Navigation, with Ronald L. Holt?'.

through accepting and embracing each equally, paradox emerges where they exist in the same space at the time and are appreciated equally. This was reflected in my vision through the merging of cube and star tetrahedron. Make sense?"

"Absolutely," he responded with enthusiasm, and then, just to prove he really had got it, "Conversely, if you were to use control, manipulation or personal will to feel secure or perhaps to reinforce a false sense of self, the cube becomes unstable as external means are being used to support it, not inner structure." *"Hahaha, now you've got it, Thomas! What a joy it is to explore this with you, I am so happy you posed the 'ending' question."* And then, almost as an afterthought, *"There is one thing I don't quite get though. It concerns the involutionary journey, with vesica piscis marking the outset; I cannot help but feel it is incomplete, as if a vital piece of the jigsaw is missing."*

"Now it's my turn to say, 'bang on' to you, Esmerelda!" In a flourish, infused with a measure of magic, he placed another graphic upon his board. "This," he said, with just the smallest hint of pride, "as you might remember from our Rainbow days, is the **inner** vesica piscis. It blew my mind when it appeared again, for it offers, beyond all doubt, a clear answer to my question. Notice how it begins at the point where two circles meet with the vesica piscis Eye of God, and then, by ordered process, traces a journey **inwards** ad infinitum? Now let's turn things on their head. Use your imagination and step into the drawing. This time, start at the smallest sphere (as far as you can see) and allow the circles to lead. Can you feel yourself expanding outwards with each rotational shift? If we had paper of universal proportion it would show **outward** expansion for ever and ever. It clearly shows that 'the end is the beginning, and the beginning is the end' and 'the smallest is the greatest, and the greatest, smallest' are not some

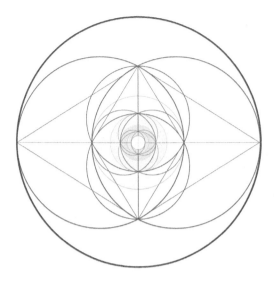

Inner Vesica Piscis

Inner Vesica Piscis: Structure

hifalutin, perceived-of ideal but are founded upon existential truth; in other words, paradox."

Esmerelda was quiet and very still. In her eyes, he could see consciousness exploring within itself, so he knew not to interrupt; the best way to facilitate their combined learning was for him to continue disentangling the matrix in 'Thomas-speak'. Somehow, in times such as these, they worked in unison through many planes of existence. During their days together and throughout their many sharings, alone and with others, they had learnt to respect each other's ways. Now in complete accord, they trusted as one journeyed **inwards** that the other would voice inner substance **outwards** to express reality at its most profound. And so, without further ado, Thomas produced his next diagram and continued his dialogue as if she were fully attentive in the midst of a many-thronged audience.

"This graphic is the inner structure to the first.[89] To reveal the why in answer to our question, we need to go into it in a bit more detail, especially the role the hexagrams play, not only in its construction, but also in its application to consciousness. Before continuing, however, it is important to emphasise the connection between the hexagram and star tetrahedron – essentially, they are one and the same, vibrating on different planes of existence – one in 2D, the other 3D. Bear this in mind as we go deeper into the vesica piscis matrix. When constructing the inner vesica piscis using compass and straight edge, the hexagram is a critical building block where each intersection determines the centre point from which the next circle is drawn. In other words, the six-pointed star and its 90° rotation is the inner structure that sets the course for subsequent inner or outer expressions. What does this mean? How do these geometries play out in daily life and what

---

[89] See 'Appendix 1: Practical Geometry', 'Constructing the inner vesica piscis'.

is their relevance to the material contained within this book, especially *Key of Light* contemplation cards as individual facets of the diamond? In other words, how does the bigger picture, revealed through these geometric structures, assist in building a bridge to higher consciousness?" He paused to catch his breath whilst gathering his white board and pens.

"First of all, for the sake of clarity," he began, "it is worth paying attention to the respective positions of the hexagrams as they are shown in the diagram. Notice how they not only decrease/increase in size, but also rotate 90° with each contraction/expansion. Once this is clear in your mind, you will be able to see how *Key of Light* suits, or group-conscious expressions of the Rainbow, and aspects of the personality blend together to create a synthesised *Way of Wholeness*. The following graphics, then, not only show how this may come about, but also make it clear how certain qualities of the rainbow, through their associated rays, work together to unite the higher with the lower; in other words, they facilitate bridge-building by harmonising polar opposites. It all sounds rather confusing doesn't it? Don't worry, it will become clear when we apply the theory to practice. After all, a picture is said to paint 1000 words." Thomas paused once more to allow his imaginary audience to absorb all he had shared up to this point. His audience, however, was far from imaginary. As we all know, he had a very attentive listener indeed, for Esmerelda, although seemingly 'absent', was taking in, absorbing and integrating his every word.

"Ok," continued Thomas, suitably refreshed. "This is the first of two graphics using the hexagram as a method of synthesising personality with Soul. As you can see, it presents two triangles – one pointing upwards, the other down – to which have been assigned certain qualities: Soul through upward triangle and personality through

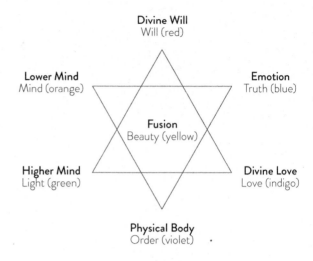

Soul-Infused Personality: Soul (upward) and personality (downward) triads, showing Group-Conscious Rainbow/Key of Light suits

its polar opposite. Rainbow spheres/*Key of Light* suits are shown underneath. Remember, these dynamics and placements were also fundamental to building the Rainbow Bridge when we looked at Rainbow Relationships (p.82). The diagram is self-explanatory, with little more to be gained through more dialogue, but when the hexagram is rotated 90° whilst maintaining the same triadic alignments, another layer is revealed and a whole new understanding becomes available to the discerning eye."

Pausing for just a few nanoseconds, he continued with barely an interruption to his flow. "The most amazing thing about turning things around is that you get to see what was in front of your eyes all along; not dissimilar to life, wouldn't you say? Let me explain. In the first drawing, attention was drawn to the triadic nature of the hexagram, in particular upward and downward pointing triangles (being Soul and personality expressions). This next graphic shifts your attention from the trinity to polarisation within duality, making it clear how even the rays,

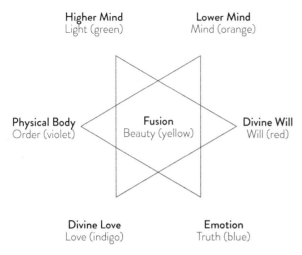

Higher Mind
Light (green)

Lower Mind
Mind (orange)

Physical Body
Order (violet)

Fusion
Beauty (yellow)

Divine Will
Will (red)

Divine Love
Love (indigo)

Emotion
Truth (blue)

*Soul-Infused Personality: Hexagram showing
triads rotated 90° clockwise*

as Cosmic 'entities', express the dualistic nature of the universe through their relationship to each other. In displaying the qualities of body, Soul and Spirit in a linear way such as this, it lays bare the intricate web that is the structure of not only these expressions of deity, but also the fabric of the space-time continuum. No man is an island, trinity and duality are intimately related, one cannot possibly exist without the other and every aspect co-creates to build layers of expression within existence. Once this becomes clear in our minds, we can get down to the nitty gritty."

"Looking at the diagram from top to bottom we can see the trinity is expressed in a linear, layered manner, with each level reflecting the dual nature of its qualities: higher and lower mind, physical body and Spirit (Will), transpersonal Love (Divine) and emotion. This helps to discern the energies at play during interactions or scenarios within daily life. When the group-conscious qualities of the Rainbow are also reflected upon, a light is shone on the bigger picture that is unfolding in alignment with your every thought, feeling, word and deed. Once again,

you and your story is not an isolated event; it is an interdependent relationship not only with others on your wavelength, but also on layers of consciousness of which you may be but dimly aware. Using these two diagrams as a foundation assists in initially bringing these 'opposites' into relationship through cultivating awareness of their polarised qualities, and then, by shifting attention to the triad, bringing all to a point of harmony where energy may flow equally between the two; Soul integration is thus expressed as wholeness in the moment."

From the moment he placed the new graphic upon his board, she was gone; all reference to her until-now-familiar view of reality vanished in almost the same instant. Although, strangely enough, as Thomas delivered his message, she was with him, at least in part, every step of the way; except she wasn't: she was gone, totally at one with the structure as it transported her to who knows where. At the outset, she felt she had no choice but to accept its invitation, so she opened her heart unconditionally to receive its gifts. Letting go of every last semblance of resistance, she then stepped through the eye, trusting in the outcome and willing herself to accept whatever that might turn out to be. But now she was not so sure. She was falling again... only this time it was different... more real somehow. She wondered why. Perhaps because this time, unlike when she first stepped through the door, she really was falling. The sensation of spiralling within a vortex of unfathomable proportion – tossing and turning as if she were a speck of dust carried upon gale-force winds – was most definitely real, very real indeed. She had been reduced to a powerless particle of inconsequential substance, helpless in influencing her passage, completely at the mercy of some other-worldly force that was stuffing her into a smaller and smaller space, and there didn't appear to be anything she could do about it. Esmerelda was afraid.

An invisible firmament arrested her fall as she came to 'earth' with a bang. Only she wasn't on earth and neither was there a bang; in fact, she didn't land at all – she bounced. Curiosity took the place of fear. She wondered why she would bounce. She was puzzled as to how this substance could possess an elastic quality and be strong enough to resist a small child being dropped from an infinitely great height yet as soft and supportive as a carpet of moss in their beloved forest. Yes, Esmerelda was curious... but she was also stuck. Interminable silence amidst an equally impenetrable blackness and confinement in an area the size of a pinhead were perfect ingredients to manifest panic and, in spite of her new-found curiosity, they were slowly but surely gathering momentum. Beneath her lay the 'elastic band' and above, the great well through which she had travelled; whichever way she turned there was no way out and she was getting pretty scared...

"Be present with what is," they encouraged. Esmerelda could have wept (in fact, between you and me, she did); her Beloved, true to their word, had not deserted her. Softly, and with no hint of admonishment, they repeated their message, "Be present, dear one... be present... and breathe." And those few words of encouragement, far more than mere words, were all that was needed. Bordering on the edge of despair, whilst experiencing her worst nightmare, she had returned to her innermost Self and in that allowing – in that moment of total acceptance of 'what is' – the reality reflecting her previous inner state was no more. In an instant, she 'plopped' through to another level; it was tangible, audible, and so miraculously ordinary she wondered what all the fuss had been about... or even if it had ever existed. "Now that we have your attention, Esmerelda, can you see the vital gifts that have been bestowed as a result of your second fall?" She was so overwhelmed with gratitude to be in their presence and to be once again sharing with them in this way,

she could barely find words to respond. "We know how it is for you," Teacher acknowledged. "We feel the immense love and boundless presence you share with all as a moral code, but more than this, we are most touched by the naked vulnerability with which you engage with **us**."

"If I rewind the clock to when I first stepped into Thomas' grid-work of light, I may begin to articulate that which is largely beyond words," she answered, with profound respect. "To begin with, I now know that his drawing is far more than a map, although, as his teachings reveal, it serves very well in this regard. My experience, however, led me far into the mystery that underpins the cyclic, multi-layered unfoldment of the universe as a whole. More importantly, it exposed a living, breathing, conscious **entity** within which we, as lesser mortals, are merely particles within its substance. The 90° shifts Thomas speaks of are real but they are not stilted, or conditional, as you might come to expect if approaching it in a linear 'knowledge-based' way, or even if viewing the grid-work solely as a map. I did not look at it as something external to me, something to be 'understood' or an object to be revered – I **entered** it, a huge difference." Teacher was silent, although she sensed their Presence, tangibly. She heard their subtle tones and felt their silent transmission as, in wave upon wave, infused with love and wisdom, her heart opened evermore to trust. All that was them flowed through her, every insight into her journey was theirs, each synchronous epiphany was laid bare under their direction as, in total absorption, Esmerelda surrendered to their passage. "The inner vesica piscis is not static," they continued in unison. "It is dynamic, it expresses through a naked and vulnerable heart as a spiral and it is experienced, in a felt sense, as a living, breathing, conscious entity. When you, Esmerelda, entered the map, you engaged immediately with the spiral, experiencing it directly as being personal to you, which in turn triggered under-processed emotional responses fuelled by equally under-processed psychological triggers; in short, you experienced fear, felt trapped and entered into a state of panic. Child-like curiosity offered a way out; light, innocence and joy invited Soul presence in the moment. We were beside you all along but your 'baggage' had obscured our presence; in recognising this, all traces of fear evaporated and you were able to 'plop' through into a new, more expansive energy field."

"I'm still wondering about the elastic-band layer," chipped in Esmerelda, curiosity getting the better of her again. "I can't get my head around its purpose or why it would have these qualities within it. I mean, what is it? How can something so fragile allow another 'something' to penetrate it, yet be so incredibly strong it can arrest the fall of 'someone' falling against it through multiple layers in space? I just don't understand it," she concluded, not without an air of frustration. "And there's another thing," she was on a roll now, her mind venting its fury at not being able to either control her descent or offer her a way through the elastic band. "I know that eventually I experienced the inner vesica piscis as being infinite expansion inwards, as well as out, but why as its prelude did I have to shrink to the size of a pinhead? It really wasn't very comfortable – not very comfortable at all!" Teacher laughed... and in all honesty, so did Esmerelda! "Okay, in keeping with the energy running through this dialogue, let's begin at the end by answering the last question first. Turn your attention to your breath, in particular the in-breath and out-breath. We would like you to notice what happens to your body as you breathe; take your time and be attentive to every little nuance." Dutifully, and with just a hint of curiosity, she obliged. "Well, I never," she enthused. "It is somewhat paradoxical: when I breathe **in**, my lungs, chest and belly **expand**, and with each **out**-breath, it's the other way round – lungs,

chest and belly **contract**. It's bizarre!" "Okay, just one question before we move on. Is it possible for you to breathe if your body is in a perpetual state of expansion or, conversely, if you suppress its flow by holding your breath and body in a contractive state?" She very nearly turned blue whilst experimenting but she got the picture and nodded her response without the use of words (or breath!). "As you can see, contraction and expansion is fundamental to life itself but, as you may well imagine, there is far more to it than this. At the outset, as you stepped through the eye, you experienced the universe as a 'living, **breathing**, conscious' entity. If there is any truth to this, why would it not also expand and contract as a natural function of its existence?" They didn't wait for a response; her expression was answer enough. "You stepped through the eye at the onset of the Cosmic **out**-breath, as it was entering into its contractive state and, powerless to resist its flow, you became smaller and smaller until an equally natural function came into play: the turning of the breath – experienced as 'bouncing' upon an elastic band. And now we come to the crux of the issue..." "It's all beginning to make sense now," she whispered to herself, as the magnitude of it all began to sink in.

"Yes indeed. Now we come to your first question concerning the 'bouncy' band. It's a little harder to get a handle on so we will use an analogy to explain. We know, through your adventures with Thomas, that you are familiar with the behaviour and qualities of water (aside from it being wet!), but what you may not have come across is the remarkable way it is able to resist an external force (such as someone falling upon it from a great height) due to the cohesive (attractive) nature of its molecules at the surface. In effect, this 'surface tension' creates a barrier between that which is above, such as the air, and that which is below, enabling something that is heavier, which would normally sink, to float or even, in the case of *certain insects, to skate effortlessly upon the surface. These same principles apply to your elastic band. Particles within its substance, of a like vibration, join forces to create a barrier to anything external that might compromise the integrity of the whole. The 'password', so to speak, as you found out, was to enter into a way of being where resistance did not play a part. As you accepted 'what is' in the moment, admission was granted and you broke through to enter a new reality, expansive in its expression; the Cosmic **in**-breath was born." Throughout their explanation, Esmerelda was consciously breathing in and out, coordinating her physical body sensations with those of the greater Cosmic entity and fine-tuning her awareness to appreciate the many delicate layers she had passed through during her fall. "I have a feeling there was more than one 'band' I passed through before arriving unceremoniously at my point of panic," she tentatively suggested. Their response came in the form of a group hug with so much unconditional love and appreciation – for her – that she visibly yet silently wept.*

"Your perception is correct," they affirmed before offering an explanation. "Many subtle layers and vibrations exist within the one Cosmic entity, and this being, as vast and refined as it is, is but an energy vortex within an even greater entity that is also a vortex within a being of even more refined vibration; all is interdependent until the many are returned to One. To express it in a way that is more familiar to you, we, as a group-consciousness united in purpose, are but an outpouring of its Word – nothing more, nothing less. So, in answer to Thomas' original question, there is no end, for the end is of itself a beginning. Ponder upon these words... and then, after due deliberation, consider this: 'All that has a beginning will, at some point in time, end. However, only the changeless face of Absolute, which has no beginning, is truly without end. All else succumbs to the Law of Change, which

*may present as an end but it is not – it is simply a change in appearance.'" Pausing for a brief interlude to allow her to assimilate their transmission, they returned all attention to her confusion over her fall, in particular the elastic firmament, and answered her query, directly. "When you fell into the vortex of the Cosmic **out**-breath, you did, indeed, pass through many subtle vibrations or layers, all of which you transitioned through with ease. How? Quite simply, dear one, there was nothing to get in the way – no baggage! Your arrival in the super-contractive state triggered core survival issues. In your mind's eye, you were on the brink of death and every learned response kicked in to defend the indefensible. In short, Esmerelda, you resisted. Only your child-like curiosity was able to defuse the situation – you had found the right password and admission was granted to the higher planes. Had you continued to resist, adding narrative to the feeling of panic, you would have remained at the same vibration, and possibly even descended to a lower level, until such time as you returned to this same juncture again, hopefully to return a different outcome." She cast her mind back to when her journey began... to when she stepped through the door for the first time, as a conscious, aware presence. And then she fast-forwarded to her most recent experience – like the first and yet so, so far removed. How could it have been so different? How could she have lapsed into fear when she had come so far? And how could she so easily have closed her mind and heart to her Beloved?*

Words, as questions set down in black and white, are so often misleading, for they are bereft of feeling. They do not carry the energy of presence, barely hint at the inclusive nature these soul-searching questions embody and fail to touch upon the profound sense of peace that echoes upon the winds of demise. As her mind searched and questioned amid all-too-familiar dark passages, her heart knew there were no answers to be found. In this moment, as the profound transmission from her Beloved drew to a close, Esmerelda was whole and complete – naked, vulnerable, stripped to her core, but complete. She could ask for nothing more.

Thomas was itching to contribute. He had been bowled over by her journey and the teachings imparted by Mentor, but he knew there was an important part of the jigsaw that would present the icing on the cake, so to speak. Esmerelda turned towards him and smiled. It was enough; he jumped to his feet, fluttered his wings and with a flick of his wrist produced his next graphic from out of thin air. He didn't even need a board upon which to rest it. Hanging of its own volition, with an energy that vibrated in unison with his words, it danced upon the air, revealing layer within layer of its substance, seemingly directed by nothing other than thought – his thought. He had come into his own and was eager to share his findings.

"This graphic – although to me it is a living, breathing entity – appeared as Teacher was

Inner Vesica Piscis: Fruit of life – two layers

disentangling the particulars of your fall," Thomas began. "It brings together all the elements we have been discussing, not only in this dialogue but also through others in the context of the Rainbow Relationships (p.79), Antahkarana and *Key of Light* layouts (p.398), as well as adding more layers besides. See how, in addition to the inner vesica piscis unfolding with in itself, it also has two layers of the fruit of life embedded within it, each at different levels shown by the size of their circles. To me, it reveals, at a glance, how every layer within the substance of creation carries the potential to expand or contract, inwards or outwards, as consciousness directs. So when the bouncy layer appeared, instilling instant panic, the potential for you to step into a polarised reality, possibly lasting many years or even lifetimes, was ripe in that moment; in effect, new seeds are sown with each thought, which eventually bear fruit in existence as a way of being. Return to wholeness, as your journey and inner dialogue revealed, was inevitable as, through awakening curiosity, you accepted 'what is' in the moment. It also shows how easy it is to become lost when repeatedly choosing life in sleep. Place your consciousness in the centre of one of the outermost small circles and imagine how it would feel to be totally oblivious to the centre or even ignorant of any other sphere but your own. How would that be Esmerelda? It would be rather like a fairy tale princess locked in a prison with no hope of escape, don't you think?"

"Indeed it would, Thomas, indeed it would." She laughed agreeably. *"And your application to my life's journey is not lost on me. I am profoundly grateful... your beautiful graphic is perfect for illustrating it so clearly, and you are right – it has a life of its own. It's almost worth jumping in and having a look around,"* she added mischievously.

"So have we answered the question, Esmerelda?

Is there really never an end?" She took her time in replying, considering carefully all that had been unravelled through their respective experiences... *"I don't know, Thomas, but it brings to mind words from 'Emergence', one of the facets of the diamond...*

When the end approaches the beginning... and the journey, with its stories, is but an echo on the wind... When the sun has lost its shadow and the moon consigned to day... When the tribe of many colours is just a pattern in the sky... When the stars have ceased to twinkle, the seasons and the cycles no more complete their turn and the droplet to the ocean has forever more returned... When the glory of emergence sends you crashing to your knees... When the only light remaining is the one you cannot see... and when the end, as the beginning... completes its dance of two... soon you come to recognise the only One is you... Then the Call of the Eternal strikes a chord you've always known...

of gentle souls and fields of light, of the land you know is home...

You could say this brings our quest to a close, but I have a sense it is not as straightforward as this. The question needs qualification in-as-much as it must include the realm to which it refers, as well as the consciousness of the one who poses the question. If, for instance, the questioner lacks awareness of the inner workings of the Soul, believing physical-plane life to be all there is, then at some point in time, at death, even though in Truth the belief is erroneous, it will be viewed as an end. In one who is awake, however, and in-so-far as our experiences in consciousness have revealed, other outcomes are possible; clarity in relation to the realm to which the question refers is, however, still necessary. An answer, therefore, is sourced not from the question but from within the context in which it is posed..." Esmerelda paused, sinking deeper and deeper into Zero, before concluding...

"At Eternity's end... there is no end...

In the continuum of time and space... every end is a beginning...

Within every appearance... is an end..."

AUTHOR'S AFTERWORD

If it wasn't for Esmerelda's realisation in the closing chapter, the end would seem a very strange place to begin when sourcing origin, inspiration and substance for the Rainbow journey, but foresight is a wonderful thing when viewing the miraculous, especially when you've only just registered its presence, and easy to miss if you're not giving it due attention. So here you have it: some five decades ago, when I was but a child at boarding school (which I loved by the way), a seed was sown and it is only now, as the writing of this book nears completion, that its place in the grand scheme of things has become evident. Little did I know then that my school friend's interest in all things astrological would ignite a spark, provide fuel for my inner fire and set me on a trajectory that would one day materialise as a book; surprisingly, not one about astrology. In the spring of 2019, this all became clear.

Whilst bathing in the aftermath of a beautiful afternoon spent sharing memories, stories and Rainbow materials with my old school friend and her younger sister, all the dots of this journey, including her part within it, miraculously fell into place. The gift she had shared with me through her passion for astrology had ripened during years of searching to include many sources of spiritual sustenance; naturally, all this 'magic' found its way into *Walk the Rainbow*. This was not the be-all and end-all; you see, astrology for me was never about prediction, questioning of purpose or even personal relationships. I had no ambitions to be an astrologer or to engage outwardly in anything metaphysical or spiritual; I was young, and the outer world with all its attractions, including earning a living, was far more alluring. No, astrology was a route to the innermost self – 'something' for me and 'something' that, amidst the many, many years of 'real' life distraction, would slowly, quietly, yet insistently, draw me

inwards on a regular basis, encouraging me to look deeper, broaden my inner horizons and acknowledge the presence of 'something' perennial. I knew deep inside that I would, in time, devote my life to serving this 'something', but not yet. Approaching the turn of the century, more than 30 years later, when the world as I knew it came crashing down around my ears, the tables were turned. In the ensuing silence, whilst befriending the Great Unknown, the researcher of truth finally paid attention, and 'know thyself', a seed sown in unconscious soil so many years ago, emerged into the light of day.

As it turned out, this seed would prove to be but one of three, each a thread woven into the fabric of a rather remarkable Rainbow tapestry. The earliest came in the form of memories – three in particular – beginning during the first year of my life. Lying in my cot, face down as usual, I was aware of my father leaning over me. "She's asleep," he said to my mother. "No, I am not," I replied silently, all the while being aware of the room from a perspective far larger than I, in my baby's body, could possibly have known. Several years later, when I was nine years old, this expanded, bigger-picture perspective was to make its presence felt on two more occasions. I had broken my wrist and needed to be knocked out in order for it to be reset; gas was the only option in those days. I won't go into the trauma of the 'putting to sleep' experience, but instead will draw your attention to the waking up part, in which I became a baby elephant falling down a very deep, well-lit, vertical well. It was tight but fitted me perfectly and I was quite happy in the falling. Landing softly on a bed of leaves, I awoke instantly and promptly burst into tears. Inside, I knew the place I had returned from was Real and the place where I awoke wasn't; naturally, I wanted to go back. I couldn't, so I cried – a lot. A third memory completed the seed and was equal in its clarity, intensity and perspective. A small child hauled over the coals by a far larger adult for some perceived 'wrongdoing' was witnessed by a presence whose wisdom outshined their brief, yet highly charged, encounter. "You are so wrong in this," it admonished the adult silently; the child heard and remembered. Far more than this, she knew that the origin of the voice was inside, that the Presence quietly reproaching the adult was indeed herself.

Three brief yet unforgettable moments in time, seemingly unconnected, had served to ignite a fire in the Soul and were destined to sustain me inwardly, albeit for the most part unconsciously, throughout my life. This second seed instilled Soul awareness. Over the years, it has fuelled a strong sense of knowing – that there is far more to life than meets the eye, that there is more to little me than I might ever know and that the presiding Presence directing the whole shebang is love.

Now to the third seed, probably the most memorable in terms of profundity, sown in the summer of 1964 – again, when I was nine. This period presented as a time of stability in an otherwise turbulent early life – where the number of house moves equalled the sum of digits on both hands – and included the happiest days of my childhood. Memories of these times, including the one I am about to share, are always bathed in an idyllic radiance of soft, golden light, a fitting backdrop for seeds set to ripen in unity some six decades later.

One of my little friends became sick, very sick. One day, following a period of months on chemotherapy, she came out of her house to join us as we played nearby. Only she didn't. She just stood on her front lawn and watched. A little china doll, face and tiny body all puffed up from the effects of the drugs, head covered by a scarf to hide her lack of hair and her whole demeanour emitting an unfamiliar air of acceptance; this vision is as clear to me now as it was then. She said nothing, did nothing; simply smiled benevolently as she watched us play. After a while, the others began taunting her: laughing, chiding and poking fun at her somewhat alien appearance. Kids, in their ignorance, can be cruel at times. She didn't move or cease to smile, although a trace of hurt flickered across her pain-ridden face. Mirroring her watchful stance, I stood by and said nothing. Time arrested its passage, silence – pregnant with purpose – permeated the air and in a split second, as a gateway to the infinite opened wide its doors, a lifetime of communication was shared between two unsuspecting observers. Eyes met across a now-deserted street, dappled sunlight gifted other-worldly shadows where once there were none and a bridge of light, fused with so many vibrant colours that its origin could not possibly be of this world, facilitated the union of two small children in consciousness, whereby knowing of one by the other may be expressed without employing words.

Instantaneously, her pain was mine. Her suffering, too, was mine, but it was nothing, absolutely nothing, compared to the love, compassion and understanding she radiated **towards me**. In her was peace beyond measure, love to melt 1000 hearts encased in stone, including mine, and wisdom born through lifetimes of knowing the fragility and impermanence of the human condition. Far greater than this was her unconditional love for me. She had appeared on that day to ignite a fire – a spark – that would bear fruit in reality many, many years into the future, a spark that would, for the most part, lay dormant, yet nevertheless serve as a reminder of the river of truth that had brought about this union between us. Too soon, the moment was broken by the raucous laughter of one of the others. We went on our way and my little friend returned to her house. She died a couple of days later. Not a word had been spoken and I never saw her again, but the memory of that moment, lasting no more than a minute, has remained with me for more than half a century. As to this particular Rainbow seed, you would have thought it would serve to set an inner course in pursuance of Soul purpose, but no, as has already been stated, the seed was to lie dormant until time and its essential nutrients had been gathered into itself. The death of my friend inspired a hitherto unexplored avenue of expression: a passion for science and biology. Someone close had died and I wanted to find out why.

Three distinct threads – each one a beginning in and of itself – seeded in unconscious soil in the dim, distant past had miraculously found their way into the present during a moment of sharing with one of the original gardeners: my astrological school friend. Mind-boggling isn't it? Little knowing the impact they would have, two sisters, in expressing interest in *Walk the Rainbow*, had opened a door to the infinite, and a series of little dots were joined in a split second to bring clarity and meaning to a life that on far too many occasions had seemed to lack purpose. This, however, was but a tip of the iceberg. Once a door of this magnitude is opened, especially if the heart is engaged without agenda, the domino effect kicks in, allowing many, many pieces of a jigsaw to come together; this is how it played out on this occasion. One spark after another sent lines of light across dimensions in time and space to create a beautiful tapestry embedded with purpose; every separate event, each encounter, every high and low, had its rightful place in the unfolding of something far greater. Random remarks were seen to set the course of a career and timely appearances of teachers, friends and guides when I was on the edge of despair, or even when I wasn't, were clearly under the direction of a force beyond any concept of control or personal

agenda. Perhaps the most significant eye-opener relative to *Walk the Rainbow* was the sequence of creative sparks, seemingly insignificant at the time, that inspired the artist within to synthesise the fruits of a Soul's journey – all I had ever loved, really loved – into a *Way of Wholeness.*

If you have arrived at this juncture having started at the beginning, you may be familiar with one or two of these experiences, as they unfolded amidst the twists and turns of our adventurers' journey. If you have cheated, as I am often prone to do, and read the ending first, perhaps you may be pleasantly surprised when you return to the beginning to see them unfold within a different context. But what of Esmerelda and her bestest friend in the whole wide world? What circumstances heralded their appearance and how did they fit so seamlessly into a story set to unravel, with child-like simplicity, everyday reality as an *Education in Consciousness*, whether expressed as human or divine? As you might imagine, this was a very humbling experience in which I was left in no doubt that the whole process was orchestrated by something other than ordinary.

Not one for regular holidays, preferring spiritual retreats in one form or another, and having pretty much exhausted any urge to explore the globe by the age of 26, I only ever travelled if there was a calling inside to do so. The occasion of meeting Esmerelda was no different – except it was. Some four or five years ago, I felt a pull inside, an insistent urge to get away, but I wanted something different. Spiritual retreats left me feeling flat; I didn't want something out of a travel brochure, or a yoga or tai chi break, I wanted something I hadn't experienced before – something that didn't fit into any boxes – where I could perhaps be a child again and have some fun. Cortijo Romero, in Andalucía, Spain, a retreat centre with a difference, appeared from who knows where to fulfil at least some of these ideals. I booked a week-long 'Reasons to be Cheerful' improvisation course with Alison Goldie, actor, theatre director, writer and teacher, and loved it; it seemed I was a natural. I had a good holiday to boot and met some really nice people, but what's that got to do with Esmerelda?

Midway through the week, an exercise was set in which we were asked to choose a photograph from those scattered upon the floor, the objective being to write a story centred upon our chosen image during our afternoon break. I took my time, eyes scanning backwards and forwards, mind feverishly searching for a story that might match one of the photos – not a one appealed. They, without exception, were totally alien to me – dull, boring, dated and from an era that, to me, lacked inspiration. In the end, with only a few left to choose from, I gave up and picked the one closest to me. A lady from, I assumed, the Victorian era was sat at a desk in front of a window. Head rested upon an upturned hand, an open book set out beside her whilst her melancholy gaze stared without focus into the empty space ahead, it was clear, at least in my mind, she wanted to be somewhere other than where she was. Aside from that, I hadn't a clue, let alone any idea of where to begin, so I let go and allowed the image to come to me. Before too long I noticed her ears – they were pointed! The lady in the photo had pointy ears… well I never! Immediately, a doorway into a kingdom filled with magical creatures, wondrous feats and limitless potential stood wide before me, and as words flowed effortlessly from pen to page, Esmerelda stepped through the portal from her realm to this and the rest, as they say, is history… or, more to the point, reality!

Esmerelda's journey, then, was birthed through a somewhat uninspiring photograph in Spain to become the opening paragraphs in the first chapter, 'A Story', in a book yet to find its way into any form of tangible substance. Little did she, or I,

know that it would serve as the intuitive glue that made sense of all the seemingly random 'facts', seeds and artworks gathered from a lifetime of research and rich personal experiences. Little did we know that during the course of her journey she would reveal the most profound nature of reality. And little did we anticipate the magnitude of her revelations when she engaged, so humbly, with her Beloved. As an author, Esmerelda gave me free rein to feel, to delve deep into the essence of **my** journey, to allow **my** mind freedom of expression, to question its findings and to surrender everything I believed I knew to the great void of nothingness, where in the silence of Eternal presence, the glory of paradox was experienced as one in Truth. Yes, Esmerelda was indeed a gift from realms other than this, and it has been a privilege and a joy to allow her expression through me, but her greatest gift, to me personally, has been her implicit trust in her inner teacher, something that, in all innocence, I felt I lacked.

As for her BFF, in true Thomas fashion he appeared just as he was meant to when circumstances dictated the timeliness of his arrival. You might say Esmerelda's appearance in the forest of magical creatures served as a calling card, an invitation, to make his presence felt and true to his nature, he obliged. How could he possibly refuse? It is no coincidence that he was part and parcel of a magical wood (he was more than likely quite right in his assumption that it was **his** wood), nor that his deep understanding of sacred geometry flowed so effortlessly through his teachings, nor that he had the capacity to appear out of the blue without making a sound when you least expected it. No, none of these are mere coincidences, and now that the journey is all but complete, it is reasonable to reveal one or two secrets concerning our impish little elf. First, we must revisit the Universal mind of God. As you may recall, mind expresses through three principal levels – Universal (Spirit), group (Soul) and intellect (human); natural intelligence, sacred geometry, kingdoms in nature – including Devas and nature spirits – all, therefore, dance to the tune of the Universal mind (humans do too but, in our ignorance, we've forgotten!). Thomas is no different. His knowing of its laws, sacred geometry and creatures of earth, sea and sky, right down to his love of cats, cannot be disputed. Why? Because none of it is learnt; Thomas knows because the kingdom of nature, as an expression of Universal mind, is who he is. Obvious when you think about it, isn't it?

Thomas made my love of research come alive. His passion, insight and vision for all things geometric, his excitement when he was able to marry his findings with Esmerelda's and his pure genius in unravelling the mysteries of the universe through the use of symbols opened doors to new avenues of expression in me. All too often, since beginning my journey inwards in earnest some 20 years ago, my logical brain was considered, by both peers and teachers alike, a detriment to progress (I might add that on occasion I conceded they were right); the heart was the only way forward and I would never 'know God' if I didn't heed their advice. Thomas helped me to redress this imbalance by encouraging me to embrace my beautiful mind, to appreciate it as a talent and to have fun in the process; in short, he taught me to believe in myself. His beauty, his love of cats and his child-like innocence, even his feigned rants when, in frustration, he didn't understand, I soon came to recognise as the best expression of me; one I was delighted to share through this medium of words. My joy, my light, my passion, all that I am – inside – as it is revealed through the wisdom of Thomas and his dear friend, Esmerelda, has become my greatest strength. Do these revelations mark an end, or even a beginning? Perhaps there is more to their relationship than that of two friends revealing magic in a rainbow and maybe their effect on me also exposes potential for their influence on you. Maybe?

If you have wondered in the course of your own musings whether Esmerelda is me or Thomas my alter ego, perhaps you won't be too short of the mark. There were many occasions when I wondered if I was writing an autobiography, not a non-fiction book, but things are never quite as they seem and if you have gained anything from absorbing the lessons imparted by our two explorers, you will know there are many, many levels concealed beneath a more obvious surface layer...

Lastly, in keeping with the theme of endings and beginnings, and as this note draws to its close, a gentle reminder is deserved... *Walk the Rainbow*, as comprehensive and inclusive as it is, is but a beginning... The ending... is *yours* for the telling...

From my heart to yours...
with love

Barbara Rose
Lancashire, UK
Autumn, 2021

What is...?

What is *Visions of Reality?*

As well as being 144 visions, expressed as facets of the inner diamond (see p.106) and *Key of Light* contemplation cards, *Visions of Reality* is an overall umbrella used to convey all that contributes to our perceived view of reality. It is an organic process of personality refinement where each turn of a card, or selection of a vision, encourages you to view your reality from a lighter, more inclusive perspective. It specifically includes:

- *Key of Light* contemplation cards, including a booklet
- Ageless Wisdom teachings – sacred geometry, the Seven Rays, accumulated research gathered from a wealth of spiritual and inspiring resources
- you, as an individual, your beliefs and your talents, as expressed through your daily life.

All these ingredients are systematically drawn together, in an intuitive way, through two publications and describe this organic process of transformation from the perspective of the whole; the inner *vision* – your journey – is reflected in the outer *reality* – books and contemplation cards. Progression from one to the next is determined through personal choice and readiness to absorb the material.

The journey begins with *Key of Light* cards, where *exploration* is the underlying energy leading you forward. You have a definitive view of how your reality looks 'through the window' of your experience, and now you would like to get to know how it all fits together. You are like a child *exploring* a brand new '*reality*'. And this is the best way to approach this first stage – let go of any preconceptions or outcomes and **play**. As you embrace these child-like qualities and *explore* the world in which you live through the 'windows' revealed by the cards, you experience spontaneous 'light-bulb' moments – something that was once confusing now makes perfect sense. You begin to *discover* new horizons, new possibilities, and you want to know more. You would like to take your new-found *discoveries* to another, deeper, more expansive and more profound level.

Walk the Rainbow opens up a world of discoveries where you learn to **live** the *Way of Wholeness*! It introduces the magical world of Esmerelda and encourages you to open your heart to the wonder of life from an evolved perspective and experience reality in a way that you might never have imagined possible. Esmerelda's wisdom flows, in storybook form, as a river through each page, whilst commentaries from each vision, as unique *visions of reality*, weave a holistic tapestry that cannot fail to evoke change within one who seeks. Soon you are aware of the subtle forces that inform not only your life, but also the very fabric of life itself; ordinariness becomes touched by wonderment. From the first spark that sets the scene of creation to the subtle realms in nature, your intimate relationship with all is offered in such a way that you cannot refuse to accept its gift. *Key of Light* cards, systems of ancient wisdom and your journey of *discovery* come together in a way that inspires you to *explore* further. This book, whether used on its own or in conjunction with the cards, encourages you to find your own way amongst the material presented; take Esmerelda's map and place upon it signposts of your own or delve into the wisdom of Thomas as he revels in the inner structure of space. Whatever method serves to inspire, its focus is on holistic symmetry within everyday life, enabling you to gain a deepening understanding of how the parts knit together to influence you, your life and those around you. In conclusion, *Walk the Rainbow*, together with *Key of Light* cards, may be viewed as a recipe book for the Soul. Facets of the diamond, including *Key of Light* cards, contain the essential 'ingredients' to **live** the *Way of Wholeness*, whilst *Walk the Rainbow* is the method by which they are knitted together; the integral process by which they become one is the *Art of Synthesis*.

What is the *Art of Synthesis*?

As stated above, the *Art of Synthesis* is a process. However, it is so much more than this. As an integral part of *Visions of Reality* and *Walk the Rainbow*, it is virtually impossible to detect, so other senses must be employed to determine its impact upon you and your daily life. These senses are observation and honest personal reflection. When these qualities are engaged, it becomes clear that the *Art of Synthesis* is also an effect – the result of prescribed action, or combination of actions, the outcome of which is *synthesis*, or integration, resulting in a new way of 'being' in the world.

A simple analogy may serve to explain this. Using the power of friction, fire is the result of a match being struck against a rough surface. However, another vital, subtler ingredient is also necessary: oxygen; the match would not ignite without its presence. It infiltrates both the molecules within the match and the surface upon which it engages, as well as being the fabric within which manifested life, all life, unfolds. When the *Art of Synthesis* is held up against this metaphor, it can be seen to align with the fabric of life itself – the air we breathe and its intrinsic life-giving component, oxygen. The mere act of living, therefore, calls into action the *Art of Synthesis*; whatever we breathe in through the circumstances of our daily life merges with our inner state and becomes who we are in the world. For the most part, this simple act of 'breathing in' our reality is unconscious, as is the effect it has on the image we project onto the world at large, but when used as a conscious path of self-awareness, it offers a creative way to attract 'light' qualities into daily life.

In conclusion, the *Art of Synthesis*, neutral in nature, is both the singer and the song, the air we breathe and the energy we share with the wider world; the way it permeates our daily life, for good or ill, is down to you. *Visions of Reality* expressed as *Walk the Rainbow* enables you, as a natural vessel for the *Art of Synthesis*, to sing the song of the Soul, to become the orchestrator of the '*vision*' that consciously creates your everyday '*reality*'.

What is a rainbow?

How do you feel when you see a rainbow? Almost without exception, the response to this question will be somewhere along the lines of 'uplifted', 'happy', 'hopeful' or maybe even 'lucky'. Has there ever been a negative response to seeing a rainbow light up the sky, even on the most dismal and dreary of days? Regardless of mood, its appearance will, for the most part, engender feelings of light and magic whilst holding prospects for a future where the 'streets are paved with gold'. The 'pot of gold', of course, is the reward, should you be able to locate the end of the rainbow and should you know at which end of the rainbow it has been placed!

With this in mind, let's not forget that the rainbow is also an optical illusion – the result of sunlight passing through raindrops. It is a mere 'trick of the light' that plays upon our imagination and leads us down blind alleys searching for something we have absolutely no chance of finding. Why? Because 'it' – the rainbow, as well as the pot of gold – doesn't exist, at least not in this reality; we can see it but we can't touch it. However, despite its illusory nature, the rainbow is revered across many cultures as a symbol of unity; it's easy to see why as the seven colours come together, in perfect accord, in a single miraculous event. In esoteric teachings, it defines the bridge to higher consciousness, known as the Rainbow Bridge, which, through the power of the mind, links man to his Soul. This begs the question, how can something that is founded upon illusion provide the inspiration for the ultimate in spiritual attainment? Maybe we have to look closer at the nature of the rainbow and its illusory qualities to find an answer. Collins English Dictionary offers the following definitions of the word illusion:

- *A false appearance or deceptive impression of reality.*
- *A false or misleading perception or belief.*
- *(psychology) A perception that is not true to reality, having been altered subjectively in some way by the mind of the perceiver.*

There are common threads of false perception and false appearance, based upon misguided beliefs, but it is the third definition that provides a clue as to how we may understand the nature of illusion and, with it, the rainbow: a perception, not true to reality, which has been altered in the mind of the perceiver. The answer to understanding the true nature of the rainbow, therefore, lies in the mind of the perceiver; it is not the nature of the rainbow that is illusionary but our **perception** of it. In other words, if we can simply enjoy the natural beauty and radiance of the rainbow **as it is** without chasing after the pot of gold we believe to be at the end of it, we may stand a chance of leading a lighter and brighter life. Is it really that simple? Maybe we have to know a little more about the rainbow itself before we can really understand how it relates to us as individuals.

A little bit of science

Certain conditions must be met in order for a rainbow to appear. First of all, there must be a source of white light; in this case, we'll use the sun. Then there must be a transparent object, such as a raindrop or crystal. The final requirement is an observer. However, the mere existence of these parameters in the same moment is not sufficient; they must come together in a specific geometric alignment. The observer must be between the sun and the raindrop, and the angle between the point at which light enters and exits the raindrop must be 40–42° (a double rainbow occurs at 50°); the observer only sees the rainbow if these conditions are fulfilled. If he/she moves, so does the rainbow; it is not at a fixed location in the sky and is always relative to the 'eye of the beholder'. Let's see how it happens. When white light from the sun enters a water droplet, for example, it is refracted (bent), causing the seven colours contained within it to spread out in the form of a rainbow. These colours bounce off the internal 'walls' of the raindrop until they reach a point of exit. If the angle of exit is 40– 42° relative to the viewer, they will see a rainbow in the sky.[xx]

In summary:

- All raindrops refract and reflect sunlight in the same way, but only the light from some raindrops reaches the observer's eye. This light is what constitutes the rainbow for that observer.
- A rainbow isn't a 'thing' and it doesn't exist in a particular 'place'. It is an optical phenomenon that appears when sunlight and atmospheric conditions are in alignment – and **when the viewer's position is at the right angle to see it**.
- Raindrops are not the only objects that create rainbows; prisms, crystals, etc. produce the same effect. The quality that they all have in common is they are transparent – in other words, clear.
- As a rainbow is not a 3D object, it casts no reflection or shadow. The only way to view a rainbow in a mirror, for instance, is if the rainbow is behind you; even then it will not be the same rainbow, as the colours are reversed. For the same reason, it is impossible to see a rainbow in a mirror directly, such as when rainbow light moves across a wall containing mirrors. As it is not an object in this 3D reality, it doesn't exist and is therefore incapable of casting a reflection in the mirror.
- The only place the rainbow does exist is **inside** the raindrop or within the white light that created it.

Now that we know what constitutes a rainbow, we can use the same parameters to explore our inner nature and see how it influences the practical reality of day-to-day living. The fifth statement is particularly valuable and bears repetition: "The only place the rainbow does exist is **inside** the raindrop or within the white light that created it." In effect, it exists in a non-physical realm. With that in mind, let us consider the premise that the rainbow is an illusion. Both dictionary definition and scientific findings agree this is so, yet the rainbow **does** exist. It exists in the form of light. Whether the rainbow is visibly present or not, wherever there is white light and wherever there are raindrops, there exists the rainbow; it is only our limited perceptions or beliefs that prevent us from 'seeing' it. In other words, once again, it is our '*vision*' that determines the '*reality*'.

If we perceive the rainbow as an object, we enter the world of illusion; if we view it as it really is, we step into a world where all is light: rainbow light. Taking this a little further, if we choose to look outwards when it is raining, for instance, we will see a grey, dismal day and no doubt experience the dreary emotions that tend to come hand in hand with such meteorological conditions. But what if instead of seeing pouring rain, we see raindrops, each one containing all the colours of the rainbow. How magical would that be? And how would it make us feel? Of course, we have just shown that sunlight is a prerequisite for the appearance of a rainbow and there is usually very little evidence of that on the days used in this example. However, the light of the Soul is **always** present, whether we are aware of it or not, and if we behave just like the raindrop and make ourselves available to receive its light, we will **be** a rainbow. And then all we have to do is walk...

How do we *Walk a Rainbow*?

As we have just found out, the technique of *Walking the Rainbow*, rather than chasing it, lies in **being** it. When, through honest self-reflection, you are able to be a clear channel through which the pure light of the Soul may flow, you are as the raindrop and all the colours of the rainbow **reflected within you** radiate outwards into daily life. The rainbow itself is an allegory for the window through which you experience reality, its **apparent** deceptive nature being used as a yardstick to determine the Real from the unreal. The way you believe yourself to be and the image you present to the world are **potentially** as much an illusion as the rainbow, a mere trick of the light obscuring the reality of life as it really is. However, a rainbow is not a "mere **trick** of the light"; it appears as a result of the **behaviour** of light. This opens up a whole new perspective on our understanding. Light is simply being itself and the rainbow is merely the result of its interaction with another form, which in this case is a raindrop. When we take the time to examine the natural phenomena occurring in our physical world, we can gain tremendous insight into realms in which we have no understanding or experience. We can now clearly see that **an illusion is entirely dependent upon our perspective on the reality within which it is experienced**. In our physical world, the rainbow is defined as an optical illusion – it is not an object, therefore it doesn't exist. In a like manner, the physical body has no form in the realms of light so it must be an illusion, mustn't it? The more we can open our minds to the possibility that infinite realities exist beyond those we perceive, the greater our chance of transcending the limitations imposed on us by day-to-day life on planet earth.

Remember, the only part of you that has physical form is your body; the remainder is made up of many subtle layers – thoughts, feelings, emotions and, most importantly in this instance, light. All too often we experience any one of these subtle layers and want to make them our own; we make them the entirety of who we are instead of just allowing them to flow through us, as is their true nature. We become the 'depressed' person or the 'happy' person or even the 'light' person, and this is the image we present to the world. It is this perception we have of ourselves and others that, just like the rainbow in this world, is an illusion. It is not who we really are. The more we can 'get out of our own way' and allow the beauty of our true nature to shine through, the more attractive is the light we deliver. Ask yourself, are you experiencing life **as it is** or through the filters of your judgemental beliefs? Maybe it is time to change the record and play a more harmonious tune?

Key of Light contemplation cards, in conjunction with the wisdom shared through these pages, help you to change the record! Being attuned to attracting the light of the Soul, they encourage you to align with its qualities; each choice in your daily life is therefore made from the perspective of the 'bigger picture' and life becomes richer and more wholesome as a result. In effect, you sing a far more inclusive and 'lighter' tune; you become the rainbow. To "manifest the beauty of the Soul... Walk a rainbow through your life..." is therefore the transformational act of conscientiously, moment by moment, cleaning your windows; the clearer they become, the more beneficial are the effects and the more you realise that **you** are the pot of gold at the end of the rainbow. All you have been searching for is right here, right **now, inside!**

What is the *Way of Wholeness*?

Are you familiar with Russian dolls? Just in case, there is a picture of a set below. With the exception of size (and their clothes!), each one is a replica of the one above or below, and each one fits neatly inside the other. However, instead of taking them at face value and then dismissing them, we will use them as models to explore the multi-layered nature of human consciousness.

Begin by placing your attention on the smallest doll. Use your imagination and pretend you are viewing the world through its eyes. This doll represents your physical body and all that you perceive is as a result of your sensory experience; the five senses – sight, hearing, taste, smell, touch – determine how you respond to and appreciate your physical environment. Make this 'vision' as real as you can. Include your family, friends, colleagues, house, place of work, etc. and then introduce the environment itself – the weather, nature, birds, bees, insects, etc. Now expand your field of reference to include the stars and planets, and beyond, until the physical universe as we know it is perceived through the five senses of this tiny little doll. Take a few moments to absorb the sheer magnificence of the physical universe in which we live, move and have our being. Know your place within it. Explore the miracle of your physical body; use all your senses to notice how all the parts are in perfect accord with each other and how the atoms and molecules that make up the totality of who you are match those found in the far reaches of the galaxy. As you deepen into the wonder of this sensory adventure, notice a world beyond the physical beginning to take shape – step into the realm of feeling and, with it, the next Russian doll. This realm, more subtle than the previous, lacks concrete substance, and even though you can't physically detect it, it is nevertheless equally as real, perhaps even more so?

Now let the focus on the physical fade and turn your attention to your feelings, your emotions. The second Russian doll, aligned with the emotional body, is very fluid in nature, resembling the ebb and flow of the tide, and is expressed through uplifting or adverse feelings. All too often we become attached to particular emotions or feelings, for good or ill, relative to our individual 'story'. We play the same record over and over again, which causes the emotional body to

become unnaturally exuberant, depressed or, in the case of anger, for instance, overly turbulent. It is important to allow feelings to come and go as they arise without letting your mind turn them into a drama.

The third doll is aligned to the mental body – your thoughts. See how much larger it is when compared with the emotional and physical bodies. The field of thought, and with it the mind, is limitless. Pause for a while and reflect on how far you can travel with your mind. You can explore the smallest cell within your body and then travel to the end of the universe; distant memories may be brought to life, futures dreamed of and all manner of 'visions' created or destroyed, in an instant! No wonder this doll is so much bigger! The mental body, as the Russian dolls illustrate, is also the container for the two lesser bodies; they both fit neatly inside it. However, as well as holding the other two, it interacts with, and has direct influence on, how they perform. In fact, each of these three bodies, which are the sum total of who you are as an individual personality, are inextricably linked; each one has direct bearing on the health and well-being of the other.

Let us consider how this may play out in everyday life. Search your memory banks and locate a time when you were happy, really happy. Bring this memory fully into the present moment, so much so that you begin to feel happy deep inside. Concentrate only on the feelings, not the circumstances connected to the memory, and allow them to expand and grow until they are the

Spirit   *Soul*   *Body*

only ones to exist. Now bring into your awareness your physical body whilst still holding on to the happy feeling. Notice where in your body, if anywhere, the feeling is at its most intense. This will vary with each person – in both degree and location. Observe any changes in your body as a result of placing your attention on these particular emotions. Let the memory fade and with it the associated feeling. Again, pay attention to your physical body as you return to 'normality'. We will now do the same exercise with a different emotion. Bring into your mind a time when you were afraid. Follow the same procedure and notice where in your body you feel this fear, together with its intensity. How does your body respond to fear? Allow some time to experience this new response, and then relax and return your feelings and body to their original state. Let go of any memories or residual feelings and be in the present moment.

This simple exercise shows how our thoughts and feelings have a direct bearing on our physical body. The same can be said for physical pain or disease. Try it. Next time you feel pain, or now if it is there, notice your emotions and thoughts. What happens when you create a story around the pain using your mind and emotions? Does the pain intensify or ease? Cultivating awareness of how these three bodies influence each other is vital to understanding the *Way of Wholeness*.

How can we possibly relate to, or understand, others if we don't even know ourselves? How can we expect to be complete, whole, if there are elements within us we are completely blind to? *Walk the Rainbow* assists you to know these principal qualities of human nature; in short, it helps you to 'know yourself' to understand what 'makes you tick'. Our five dolls may now be reduced to three, being body, Soul and Spirit. With a little practice, it is relatively easy to gain a working sense of how the three expressions of the personality – physical, emotional, mental – work together to create you as an individual, but what of the Soul and the next of our Russian dolls? If you have no experience, awareness or even beliefs in the existence of such a 'body', how can you possibly get to know it or view the world through its eyes?

The answer lies in the world of imagination. Using this creative quality, the Rainbow Bridge between personality and Soul is forged. This takes place on the plane of mind, it being common to both, and it is the mental body that is closest to the Soul in our line-up of

Bridge Between Body and Soul

434

dolls. Now place your attention on the fourth doll, and, as before, imagine a world viewed through its eyes. This world compares to no other and, with the exception of the mind of the perceiver, lacks earthly origin. Picture a scene filled with light, its inhabitants made of the same substance as the world itself, where even the 'buildings' issue the promise of some vital ingredient to ensure awakening of the light within. Communication is beyond words, yet there is language. It is the *Language of Light* – symbol, image and geometric structure – so pregnant with possibilities it is tangible, so palpable you can almost touch it. It is the very essence of the air itself and leaves no doubt as to its meaning, for each and every being is imbibed with its frequency. Another quality soon demands recognition: Love. However, this is not a transient version of love such as that we experience in our dualistic earthly existence. This is Love beyond love, all-inclusive transpersonal Love. As a quality of the Soul, Love has as its foundation the all-embracing wisdom of an awakened mind, which at times, from our limited human perspective, can appear to be tough and to lack understanding. This could not be further from the truth. Sometimes difficult choices must be made in order for a higher purpose to be fulfilled; such choices are the ripened fruit sown from seeds of clarity and compassion.

As you continue to view the world of light through the eyes of the fourth doll, the Soul, another detail of profound significance becomes increasingly obvious: purpose. Beings of light, and there are many, of varying creed, race and colour, are performing their individual tasks with a strong sense of purpose. No one is greater or more important than another, each has an essential role to play, each is a crucial facet of the whole and each follows its course with an intrinsic sense of unity and direction. This purpose is otherwise called Divine Will and is the quintessential nature of Spirit, represented by the fifth and largest doll. There is very little to be said of the realm of Spirit. Like the Soul, it is light, but this is light that casts no shadow. Pure luminosity within which is purpose, whose intrinsic essence is to find form – be it human, planet, animal or galaxy – into which it may emanate its light. In short, anything you can perceive with your mind, feel with your heart or sense with your body is Spirit; Divine Will manifest in matter in its varying degrees of subtlety. The kingdom of nature is an obvious example of Spirit united with matter and offers explanation as to why we, as human beings, gain so much solace from being in its presence; a simple walk in the park holds the potential to work magic in terms of lifting our spirits. Many *Key of Light* contemplation cards feature images from Mother Nature, whilst the scripts impart her wisdom, encouraging you to engage with the natural intelligence inherent in this realm; each turn of a card serves to nurture your spirit, as does a stroll along a country lane.

Spirit

In summary

Five dolls, reduced to three, have now become a single doll containing all. This standalone doll illustrates the universality of Spirit; it appears there is only One, yet 'all' is within it. In answer to the title question, the *Way of Wholeness* lies in cultivating awareness of the many realms and frequencies of light that make up the totality of man, as has been described in the preceding pages. An important, and essential, part of this is to know how your thoughts and emotions influence the quality of your day-to-day life. It is no use denying they exist, blaming others or escaping into the realms of light and feeling ecstatically blissful if your life as a whole is a mess.

Know the process, **your** process, and understand your behavioural responses. Just as the mighty oak begins life as a tiny acorn, your journey into the realms of the Soul and Spirit begins with a single step. Given the right nutrients, such as those shared within these pages, there is no reason why you cannot become as the ancient oak. Together with courage, commitment and effort, they will help you to weather the storms of life as you walk a path only you can tread. Contemplation cards and guidebooks offered under the *Walk the Rainbow* umbrella serve as signposts or lights on a journey that might otherwise lack sustenance. They define the *Way of Wholeness* in such a way that each step you take is placed in the certain knowing that the 'pot of gold' at the end of the rainbow is your birthright; it is **you**, right here, right now, and you deserve to **be** it!

Building bridges

Bring our Russian dolls to mind again as we join a few dots. Following Esmerelda's revelation concerning bridge-building, it is worth taking a closer look to see how they tie in with esoteric teachings. The diagram opposite shows our three primary dolls – body, Soul and Spirit –

aligned vertically this time; the three smallest dolls – thoughts, feelings and physical body – as they apply to you as an individual maintain their original horizontal placement and are now illustrated by pictures. The image as a whole is sourced from authentic spiritual teachings concerning the Science of Light Manifestation[xxi] (also called the 'Science of the Antahkarana') and is the art of building the Rainbow Bridge between body and Soul, Spirit and matter. There are five threads of light linking the fundamental aspects of our nature, from the way we execute our daily life to full comprehension of the realms of Soul and Spirit. These threads have a specific purpose, dynamism and structure; nothing is random, all is divinely orchestrated and the diagram helps us to see this clearly, albeit simplistically considering the energy dynamics involved. We begin at the top and work downwards, mirroring Esmerelda's journey from the time she first ventured into the realms of light, "that she loved beyond all else", until the moment when she embraced her darkness to discover the "Real" as light in her ordinary life; her entire process to date is reflected in the fluid dynamics of this image.

The largest doll, Spirit, sits at the top of a column of light that proceeds in a straight line directly towards matter. It does not deviate; its sole purpose is to seek a form through which it may emanate its light, which in this case is a little girl watering flowers in an idyllic garden. This is the **life** thread, between Spirit and matter, and is anchored at the heart (shown in the diagram). All living beings on our planet are connected to Spirit in this way: insects, animals, mammals, cetaceans, amphibians, birds and, of course, human beings. The important thing to recognise is that it gives us life, in a physical sense, and is a natural function of being alive in a physical body. Whether or not you are aware of it, whether or not you believe in it, is irrelevant. It is the divine spark that breathes

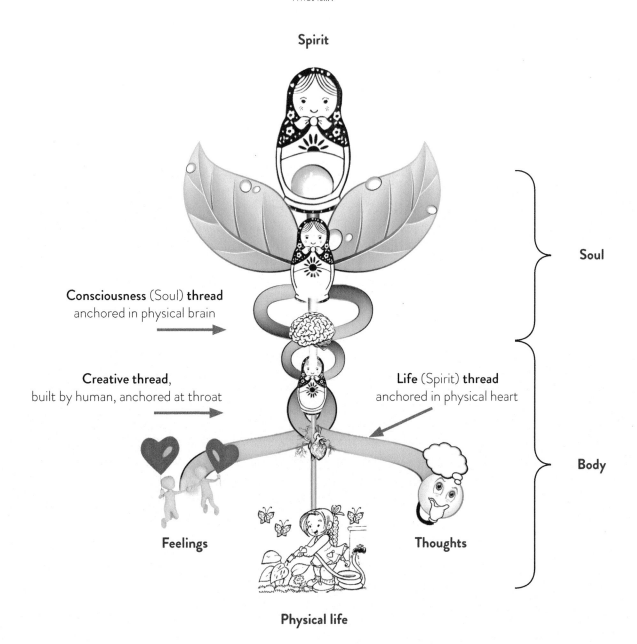

Spirit

Consciousness (Soul) thread
anchored in physical brain

Creative thread,
built by human, anchored at throat

Life (Spirit) thread
anchored in physical heart

Soul

Body

Feelings

Thoughts

Physical life

Building the Rainbow Bridge

Life *thread is the Divine spark that ignites in the heart to create life; it is severed at death.* **Consciousness**
thread (Soul) is anchored in at the brain and continues from life to life. **Creative** *thread (body), triple in nature,*
is anchored at the throat and constructed by the human through tending the 'Garden of the Soul'; unites with
the two primary threads, body/Soul and Soul/Spirit, to unify Spirit with matter.
N.B. *Diagram is in linear form but 'bridge-building' is an inner process, cyclic in nature, and unfolds in spirals.*

life into form, any form, and will remain intact until the moment arrives when it is time for the ultimate letting go – death to the physical body. There is, therefore, nothing for us to 'do' in order to enhance or develop this connection other than to 'live'. It is simply, just as it is.

However, as Esmerelda found out, 'allowing' is not quite as easy as it sounds. As human beings, we are as far removed from the natural rhythm and pulse of the spirit of life as is the earth from the far reaches of the known universe. We have lost our inherent connection to our sacred heritage, to the vital spark of divinity that gave us life, we have forgotten the vital part we play in balancing the natural environment and we have lost all true sense of who we really are. Remember nature **is** Spirit in matter. **We** are Spirit in matter; the thread of life is right before us, and **within** us, if we could only open our eyes and notice. Facets of the diamond featuring visions in nature help you to notice. They have an inherent relationship with all that is sacred in our planet, they **are** our natural world and they help you to rediscover the "light in the land", the source of so many "untold stories" in Esmerelda's adventure. On top of this, they help you to let go, to experience life as it is in each moment. They help you to **be** the thread that is life; in short, they help you to **live**.

Now return to the diagram. Notice how the two smaller dolls are linked by two spirals, as well as by a less clearly defined direct column of light that anchors the **consciousness** thread of the Soul to the brain of the physical 'body'. This link only becomes active when the third **creative** thread is diligently put together by the human being. A short visualisation using the diagram as a point of focus will help you to sense intuitively how these threads come together in the Rainbow Bridge; the mechanics of the process will be explained after.

Follow the spirals with your eyes, allow your imagination to visualise them as a continuous flow of lighted energy, where each rotation finds the consciousness thread, between body and Soul, becoming more and more evident. See it grow in definition until it matches the intensity of the life thread. Witness the links between body, Soul and Spirit merging to become one vibrant Rainbow Bridge of light. Finally, imagine the two smaller dolls, body and Soul, dissolving into the largest, Spirit, doll. It vibrates at such a rate that it too is absorbed... Spirit and matter are now one... the individual parts are no more... All that remains is a little girl, watering plants in an idyllic garden... Pause for a while... allow the full implication of this to be absorbed... be the child...

A Zen proverb is mentioned in Esmerelda's journey: "Before enlightenment, chop wood; after enlightenment, chop wood." The only difference between before and after is the consciousness of the one who chops wood; the child watering plants in her garden, having been through the systematic process of building the Rainbow Bridge, is based on the same principle.

This is all very well, but how do we build this bridge? Where do we begin? We have seen that the life thread pretty much takes care of itself, we just have to 'live', so which one do we choose next – consciousness or creative? If we return to the diagram, we will see that there is a definitive two-way relationship between them both. And this relationship is, quite simply, awareness; **to be aware is to be conscious**. As you can see, most of the 'activity' is centred on the lower part of the diagram. It is our daily life, our everyday relationships, together with our connection to the aspect of us, as yet beyond our comprehension, that demands our utmost attention at the outset. Honest personal reflection therefore builds **both** threads.

Before proceeding further, revisit the *Way of Wholeness* (p.432) and refresh your memory on the qualities of the three expressions of the

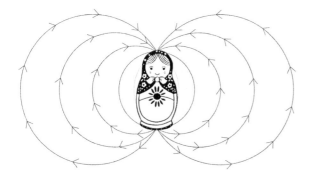

Figure 6 Energy Flow: As we give, so shall we receive

personality – mind, heart, and body. It is these aspects that make up the creative thread; they intertwine to complete the totality of who you are as an individual. When you are fully aware, in each moment, of these three aspects, you may be said to have realised **individual consciousness**; you know who you are, you know what makes you tick and, above all, you are **aware**; in such circumstances the creative thread is complete. Look at the 'body' doll on our Rainbow Bridge and you will see that the spiralling threads, originating from 'thoughts' and 'feelings', cross over at the throat before moving on to the Soul; the creative thread is anchored in at this point. When we are fully functional, it is from here that we communicate with the Soul and vice versa; we become a clear channel to express its wisdom with clarity and love. *Key of Light* cards are keys to the inner diamond and relate to personality transformation, stimulating your awareness of all conditions concerned with the creative thread; they help you to know yourself, inside out, as an individual, and they help you to talk to the Soul.

Figure 6 shows the movement of energy radiating around a central Russian doll. The point at which the doll is placed on the Rainbow Bridge is irrelevant as the message is the same: follow the arrows... whatever you project outwards – be it thoughts, words or deeds – will, at some point, come back to you; as you give, so shall you receive; you reap what you sow; what goes around comes around, etc., etc. These are all renowned tenets that align with sacred texts in accordance with universal Law. The figure is the same; its roots lie in physical science and the movement of energy is identical to that found around any object that is magnetic, including amongst a multitude of life forms, the human heart[xxii] and our very own planet.

The motive behind conscientiously building the creative thread is to behave like a magnet and attract 'light' qualities into our lives. Remember Esmerelda when she first 'woke up'? *In order to **live** the 'way of light', she had to travel far into the land, she had to reach out to those who inhabited its regions, who knew of its customs, who sang its song; she had to seek out those who were light.* She had to align with the Soul in order to **attract** its qualities into her life. *Light keys* within the inner diamond, relating to Soul expression, assist you in knowing light; they are the Soul in its own realm and are central to building both consciousness and creative threads; they teach you to be **aware** and they naturally draw light qualities towards you.

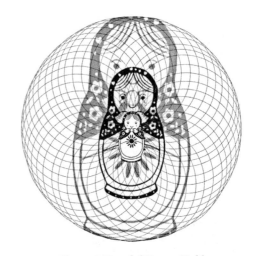

Figure 7 Toroidal Energy Field

Reflect on Esmerelda's journey. Use it as a guide to mirror your own process. She began in the *prison of her own undoing* and then realised how much she loved light. She used the *light in the land and others* to elevate her consciousness to a position where she could begin to remember who she really was: she found the light of the Soul. Then, and only then, she could revisit her darkness and hold it in a space of unconditional love – without fear. This is bridge-building. Each time you allow this process to unfold within you, you strengthen the link between personality and Soul; you intensify and give greater definition to the consciousness thread. Figure 7 takes the energy generated in Figure 6 and combines it with the outcome of our visualisation of the Rainbow Bridge. The result is an energy field, known as a torus, originating from our three Russian dolls; the Rainbow Bridge in its entirety is within, hidden from view. Symbolically, the diagram as a whole is... *the child watering plants in an idyllic garden...*

In a nutshell

1. The Rainbow Bridge is made up of five 'threads'.
2. Spirit – the life thread, *universal consciousness* – links Spirit with matter and is anchored at the heart in a human. It is terminated at physical death.
3. Soul – the consciousness thread, *group-consciousness* – links personality and Soul and is anchored at the head, or brain. It continues beyond death.
4. Human – creative thread, *individual consciousness* – is made up of three threads relating to thoughts, feelings and physical body. It is anchored through creative expression at the higher throat (alta-major chakra). It continues beyond death as biological karma.
5. The consciousness thread to the Soul only becomes active when the creative thread has been initiated by the human being.
6. These threads are not put together in a linear way – forging the Rainbow Bridge is an ongoing 'toroidal' process. 'Enlightenment' is just the beginning!
7. Use the diagram on p.437 as a map. **Know your place on the map** in your journey through life. Use the facets of the diamond as signposts to help you find your way.

A little bit of research...

Two 'systems' lie at the heart of *Walk the Rainbow*, as it pertains to this book – sacred geometry and the Science of the Seven Rays. Others are equal in value, such as the chakras and the endocrine and nervous systems, but they concern the expression of consciousness as it **interfaces** with the human being and do not refer to the core of **all** life, as we are exploring here. Sacred geometry and the Seven Rays are so integral to Esmerelda's, and your, journey that it is impossible to 'walk' with awareness and not be conscious of their presence; they are not only essential to this work, but also fundamental to the fabric of life itself. Let's look a little closer.

Every *Key of Light* card is infused with sacred symbolism, a large portion of images reveal geometric structure and the structure of the pack – 144 cards, 7+1 suits, the trinity, etc. – is inspired through the principles of Divine Architecture: sacred geometry. The Seven Rays not only are the rainbow through their innate psychologies, but they also constitute the fabric of life itself. Wisdom imparted through Esmerelda's story, suit titles and colours, card Soul alignment qualities and many of the visions have arisen as a result of contemplating these profound esoteric teachings.

Knowledge is not a substitute for experience, particularly when the essence and calling of material such as this is to awaken the light within; *Walk the Rainbow* is a breaking-down process not an adding on. Nevertheless, it feels appropriate to include some 'information' about the respective parts within each system, so the intellectual mind may gain some understanding of the 'parts' within the 'whole'. The following pages are therefore offered as a reference. Use them as a 'way in' – an introduction – to the respective teachings, and if you wish to research some more, refer to the bibliography at the end of the book.

What is sacred geometry?

Geometry, quite simply, is the structure of space. When you take this structure, or any structure that has geometry or number as its origin, and apply it to consciousness, it becomes sacred: sacred geometry. All living particles – whether atom, molecule, human, animal, earth or cosmos – has as its origin, and unfolds according to the principles of, sacred geometry. You have only to look around you, take a walk in nature, watch a

raindrop as it courts a puddle or even look closely at your own physical body, and you will wonder at the pure magic of divine proportion embedded within everything; nothing is exempt. So how did it all begin? What is the origin of space defined by boundaries that are non-existent? Perhaps a geometric story of creation will help us to understand.

Great Spirit abides as limitless light. It has no sense of 'self' or 'other', as it is All; All-Knowing, All-Seeing, All-Being. There is no concept of movement, as it has nothing relative to which to move; there is no up, no down, no gravity; there is no sense of separation or loss. In fact, there is no sense at all. There is nothing that isn't **it**. Except perhaps the experience of being nothing, of not knowing. Pause for a moment and reflect on how that might be. Wouldn't you begin to wonder what it might feel like to experience

Sacred Geometry – the Building Blocks of the Universe

Circle   *Vesica Piscis*   *Triquetra*   *Seed of Life*   *Divine Matrix*   *Fruit of Life*   *Metatron's Cube*

Five Platonic Solids
These are derived from Metatron's cube

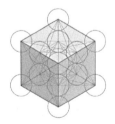    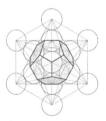

Cube   *Star Tetrahedron*   *Octahedron*   *Icosahedron*   *Dodecahedron*

that which you are not? There is a flip side to being everything! Great Spirit soon came see to it. However, as it was everything, it wasn't easy to create an area that was separate that it may experience isolation. So it created a space **within** itself and sent it to sleep. The sphere was born and all that lay within its boundaries was unconscious. As one sphere led to the birth of another, 3D reality, the world as we know it came into being. The rest, as they say, is **unconscious** history.

The remainder of this section is devoted to the **evolutionary** building blocks (platonic solids) and, as well as revealing the relationship and affinities they have to each other, shows how they may be applied to consciousness on a journey from separation to wholeness. When you know the beginning, you also know the end; understanding the process of unfoldment through geometric structure offers a direct route to integration where all your separate parts are called home. Remember, the first sphere was unconscious; you might call it the womb from which all else was birthed, so being in darkness need not necessarily be a 'bad' thing – quite the opposite! The cube and octahedron are 'duals' of each other, whilst the star tetrahedron is a dual of itself (two tetrahedrons facing in opposite directions). When platonic solids are dual, there is an inherent relationship between them. Let's explore this some more and find out why.

Stellation is a process whereby the vertices (corners) on each face of a solid are extracted to form a 'star' shape. For instance, when one square face of a cube is stellated, it creates a four sided pyramid; one triangular face of an octahedron creates a tetrahedron, etc. We will use this process to determine the relationship between each of these solids, starting with the lower geometries.

A stellated octahedron is a cube **and** a star tetrahedron; when turned on its side, the star tetrahedron is a cube! In daily life, stellation in lower geometries uses **control** to reinforce the personality 'box'. The resultant effects are clearly shown through the stellating progressions opposite, where if control or any other kind of manipulative behaviour is employed to make oneself feel more secure, the cycle is repeated over and over again to create an ever-expanding personality 'box'. Using this method, there is no way to progress from the octahedron to the icosahedron and thence to the higher geometries. Translating this into daily life, until a point of letting go and taking responsibility for one's own actions is reached, where the inner you – warts and all – is accepted for what it is, the process of box-building continues. Negative patterns of behaviour are repeatedly energised, belief systems are reinforced and 'control' is employed to manipulate yourself and others; it's otherwise known as life in sleep!

Duals equal symmetry

Edges of cube (12) = edges of octahedron
Faces of cube (6) = vertices of octahedron
Vertices of cube (8) = faces of octahedron
Smaller octahedron sits inside cube; all vertices touch each face of cube
Vertices of icosahedron (12) = faces of dodecahedron
Vertices of dodecahedron (20) = faces of icosahedron
Both icosahedron and dodecahedron = 30 edges
Edges of tetrahedron = 6
Edges of cube = 12 ⎫
Edges of octahedron = 12 ⎭ *= 30 icosahedron/dodecahedron 30 edges each*

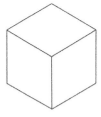

Cube

Star Tetrahedron

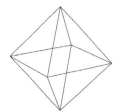

Octahedron

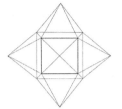

Stellated Cube

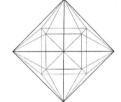

*Stellated Cube **is** an Octahedron*

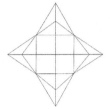

Stellated Octahedron

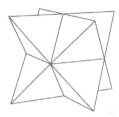

Star Tetrahedron/Cube

Icosahedron:
20 triangles

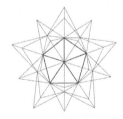

Stellated Icosahedron:
60 triangles

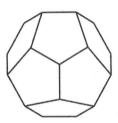

Dodecahedron:
12 pentagrams

Stellated Dodecahedron:
12 pentagonal pyramids,
60 triangles

The space between the lower and higher geometries may be referred to as the 'void'. It is the Great Unknown, and, as mentioned oftentimes, it is very useful to have a map or an inner compass when entering its territory. In geometry, this map is Metatron's cube, as it gives birth to all the platonic solids; the cube, icosahedron and octahedron being the only geometries to occupy it in its entirety. Now let's follow a similar process with the two higher geometries: the icosahedron and dodecahedron. These form the foundation of the Christ-Consciousness grid, with the **combined** stellated icosahedron and stellated dodecahedron being its full expression.

The dodecahedron forms around the 'points' of the stellated icosahedron which is then stellated to create the stellated dodecahedron; stellated icosahedron and dodecahedron sit **inside** the stellated dodecahedron. The full expression of the Christ-Consciousness grid, therefore, has 144 facets.

Stellated icosahedron	*60 triangles*
Dodecahedron	*12 pentagrams*
Stellated dodecahedron	*60 triangles*
	12 pentagonal pyramids

Total	*144*

Geometry as an expression of individual consciousness

For ease of reference, the following is tabulated alphabetically and details geometries with their inherent characteristics, associations – including *Key of Light* cards – and relationship to you and your journey as an individual in consciousness.

Cube

Keywords: Structure, boundaries, limitations
Affinity with: Star tetrahedron
Dual: Octahedron
Structure: 12 edges, 6 square faces, 3 of which meet at each of its 8 vertices
Element: Earth
Path: Evolution
***Key of Light* card:** *Celebration*

In a nutshell

Probably the most well-known and easily recognised and understood of the platonic solids is the cube. At first glance, it appears a solid and stable structure, but upon closer examination, particularly if it is built using straws, for instance, it is soon proved to be quite the opposite: it is unstable, collapses easily and cannot maintain its shape unless it is propped up by something external – a supporting hand, for instance. Try it and see. Appreciating these qualities is important when applying this geometry to consciousness. The cube is the structured, or personality, self

– the 'box' in which we live and experience life based upon our control and survival mechanisms. It defines our comfort zone – beliefs, stories, identity, etc. In short, all that is conducive to our unconscious sense of self is contained within this box we call 'me'; plenty of time and energy is devoted to keeping it propped up. But, of course, our 'me' box is founded upon falsehoods, so we have set ourselves an impossible task – unstable in both geometry and personal identity!

Stabilising the unstable

How do we stabilise our box? How do we feel safe in a world that doesn't meet our needs? How do we control an outside world we have absolutely no control over? The short answer is: we don't. The cube can only be stabilised from the inside; any other method simply creates a bigger **unconscious** box! We have to turn within and look at the constructs that make up our existence. If we strip back our beliefs, tear apart the story and relinquish control, what do we have left? At the very core of our being, who, or what, is the structured self?

Core Dualities: Six external faces of cube

When it comes down to it, if we expose the bare bones of our existence, all that we are, as an unconscious identity, comes down to **polarisation** of our three core dualities – inner child/adult, masculine/feminine and True Self/false self. Hard to believe, isn't it? But if you take some time to really consider this possibility, you will see that the war of opposites perpetuated inside has at its root these core duals. Understanding these underlying relationships, through mapping them to the faces of this basic geometry, can help us to see the box within which we create our reality. Knowing our box translates to inner peace and harmony in daily life, whatever its outer appearance. So how do we work with these core dualities, and how, in a practical 'living' sense, does knowing of their existence help us to move beyond the confines of the box in which we live? It may surprise you, but you don't actually 'move' anywhere, you don't 'banish' the box and neither do you 'raise your vibration' that it may vanish into thin air. Acceptance of what is, in the moment, is all that is required to bring the dualities home to each other. Collapse the cube, through releasing all resistance, and we return to the hexagon – divine matrix/Metatron's cube – from whence all life forms are birthed (see Metatron's cube diagram); a new way of being, in the form of stable 'higher' geometries

(octahedron, icosahedron and beyond), is birthed naturally as a result.

Finally, methods of stabilising the cube, and with it our false sense of self, set down above are not the only way. Cube to divine matrix/Metatron's cube offers the bigger-picture perspective, whereas affinity with the star tetrahedron shows the **inner process**; every polar opposite comes together through harmony within the three. How? A tetrahedron's basic component is an equilateral triangle, which, if reduced to linear form, has three axes.

Figure 8 shows the three points of a triangle, where X and Y are two opposites, or duals, and Z is the point of wholeness that is greater than the sum of its parts; the duals are in perfect harmony, not only with each other, but with the whole. Figure 9 is more in keeping with everyday life, where the vertical Z line not only

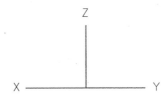

Figure 8 Three Points of Triangle in Harmony

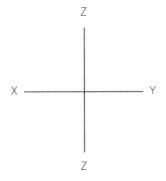

Figure 9 Extended Z Line: Divides the poles in two

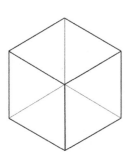

Cube: Six square faces

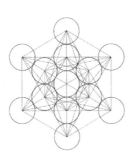

Collapsed Cube: Becomes Metatron's cube

intersects the horizontal, but also does a very good job of keeping the duals at odds with each other; it also illustrates, through the cross, the star tetrahedron's relationship with the cube. Remember, although giving the appearance of being solid and stable, the cube is, in fact, very unstable, constantly seeking **external** verification in order to prop itself up – the star tetrahedron stabilises it from the **inside**. Figures 8 and 9 show the relationship between these two geometries; when turned on its side, a star tetrahedron **is** a cube. Working with the dynamics of the triangle naturally balances and harmonises all opposing poles; a square or cross, quite literally, keeps them at arm's length where the only choices lie in resistance or surrender. Release resistance, collapse the Z line and, with nothing to keep them apart, the duals naturally come home to each other.

Dodecahedron

Keywords: Bliss, interdependence, the many and the One
Affinity with: Christ-Consciousness grid
Dual: Icosahedron
Structure: 30 edges, 12 pentagonal faces, 3 of which meet at each of its 20 vertices
Element: Ether
Path: Evolution
Key of Light cards: *Devotion Clarity, Devotion Compassion, Devotion Unity*

In a nutshell

Like the cube, the dodecahedron, in its lowest expression, is unstable and requires something external to itself to support it. Relative to consciousness, this translates as bliss and is particularly applicable to those on a spiritual quest. Look at it this way... Imagine a situation in which you are unhappy with your lot, your personal 'box' (cube) is filled with 'stuff' that

fails to bring any sense of satisfaction and you will do anything to plug the great void of emptiness you feel inside, but as you are now a spiritual person with a degree of awareness, the usual distractions also fail to bring any sense of peace inside, so what do you do? Enter the role of a spiritual retreat. Off you trot on the next stage of your journey, be it the latest meditation course, spiritual healing or sitting at the feet of an 'enlightened' guru. For a brief period in time, your life is transformed, you experience altered states of consciousness and, maybe for the first time, you become blissed out in the land of the Soul (dodecahedron). Reality hits home when you return to daily life where, after a relatively short period in time, something happens to burst your bliss bubble, and suddenly there you are back in your discontented box again. This cycle is repeated over and over again until you change the record and stop looking outside of yourself for something that can only be found within.

This marks a real beginning on an awakening journey. It marks a point when your greatest insight is to realise that enlightenment is a breaking-down process, a point where escapism, including bliss, is known to be the biggest distractor and a moment where you know, really know, the only one who can guide you on your way is you. Geometrically, the journey from hereon in is revealed through the dual to the dodecahedron, the icosahedron, a stable geometry whose root construction is 20 equilateral triangles. Triangles, as we well know, are perfect for harmonising polar opposites, for rising above conflicting dynamics (even those with more than two) and for integrating the seemingly impossible. The icosahedron, then, just like the cube/star tetrahedron dynamic, stabilises the dodeca from the inside; Christ-Consciousness, as has already been explained in the preceding chapters, is the end result.

Flower of life/divine matrix

Keywords: Completion, perfection, beauty
Affinity with: Seed of life/Metatron's cube,
all five platonic solids
Path: Involution
Key of Light **cards**: *Arcturus, Celestial Light,
Chrysalis, Flowering, Gnosis Intelligence,
Gnosis Purity, Gnosis Tranquillity, Inner Earth,
Stability, Starseed, Stewardship, Through
the Portal*

In a nutshell

The flower of life/divine matrix geometry is
the divine blueprint, absolute perfection in
geometric form – pure in shape and proportion.
It generates the fruit of life, as well as Metatron's
cube, and is parent to all five platonic solids;
it is 3D reality in geometric form. It has an
affinity with the first ray, yet its composition
– endless rounds of concentric circles – would
seem an antithesis to the essential nature of this
ray, which is dynamic and direct. Contemplation
of all these energies, however, shows there is a
synthetic unity in these dynamics. Remember,
the first emanates a will to exist and in that will
is purpose, Divine Purpose. The orchestrator
of perfection thus sets out its blueprint, as
intention, through the workings of the Universal
mind that it may be actualised as purpose within
the consciousness of each human being.

Icosahedron

Keywords: Focus, harmony, fluidity
Affinity with: Christ-Consciousness grid
Dual: Dodecahedron
Structure: 30 edges, 20 triangular faces,
5 of which meet at each of its 12 vertices
Element: Water
Path: Evolution
Key of Light **cards**: *Genesis Inception, Genesis
Manifestation*

In a nutshell

The relationship between the two higher
geometries has been explained above under
'Dodecahedron', we just need to fill in a few gaps
about the icosahedron to answer the why in how
it serves as stabiliser to its dual. This question is
easily answered when we take apart the geometric
construction of the Christ-Consciousness grid,
where the dodecahedron forms effortlessly
around its foundation as a result of stellating the
icosahedron (see p.443), but what does this mean
in relation to an inner journey? In a practical,
everyday-living sense, how do these principles
apply? And, if enlightenment really is a breaking-
down process, how is it that expansion into
Christ-Conscious awareness only occurs when
something is added – i.e. stellations?

The answer to all these questions can be
expressed in one word: surrender. When the ego
rises up to defend itself, turns a blind eye to its
beliefs and unconscious programs or fails to take
responsibility and projects everything outward
onto others, this is the time to go deep into the
heart and let go. Stripping back every last sense
of self until nothing remains is the breaking-
down process; expansion, as in the appearance
of the dodecahedron, is a natural result. In being
nothing, suddenly you are everything.

Lastly, the icosahedron is a feminine structure,
the most rounded of the platonic solids, and,
aside from the stellated dodecahedron, the
closest to a sphere; its element – water – is also
feminine. These are all qualities of an open
and loving heart, yet it is made up entirely of
straight lines – masculine and mind. In and
of itself, the icosahedron, then, is a perfect,
balanced representation of the heart-mind where
clear-seeing is married with compassionate
understanding. What better structure could there
be as foundation for the accumulation of wisdom
and ultimate realisation of Christ-Consciousness?

Metatron's cube

Keywords: Inter-dimensional gateway, manifestation.
Affinity with: Flower/fruit/seed of life, all platonic solids
Path: Involution
Key of Light **cards:** *Air, Cosmic Orchestra, Custodian, Earth, Fire, Fortitude, Omniscience, Raindance, Starseed, Water*

In a nutshell

Metatron's cube is made up of both circles and straight lines, with lines denoting masculine energy (mind) and circles, feminine (heart). It is also the geometry from which all five platonic solids (3D shapes – tetrahedron, cube, octahedron, icosahedron, dodecahedron) are derived. In other words, it is the gateway to third dimensional reality, yet it also carries the essence of unity through its integral structure: the circles of the fruit of life (p.441).

Octahedron

Keywords: Integration, balance, surrender
Affinity with: None
Dual: Cube
Structure: 12 edges, 8 triangular faces, 4 of which meet at each of its 6 vertices
Element: Air
Path: Evolution
Key of Light **card:** *Freedom*

In a nutshell

Sitting centre stage between the lower and higher geometries is the octahedron, another stable structure. Being made up of eight triangles and one square, it brings together architectures integral to both the cube and star tetrahedron, yet stands alone. Its structure is not arrived at through direct relationship to either of its 'lower' counterparts, only through return to,

and emergence from, Metatron's cube within the divine matrix. Herein lies a clue to its relationship with consciousness as it evolves through the awakening process: letting go. "Only as a child will you enter the kingdom of heaven" is a well-known phrase, but how often do we stand back and take, deep into our hearts, the full implication of its meaning. This is the gift that the octahedron brings. It **is** the child, and, through its affinity with the air element, it takes all that is natural, free and unfettered into your pure and innocent heart; it serves, quite literally, as a breath of fresh air to the Soul. As symbolic bridge between personality and Soul, matter and Spirit, the octahedron extends an invitation to take a leap of faith and play.

Seed of life

Keywords: Potential, New beginnings – "As you sow, so shall you reap"
Affinity with: torus
Path: Involution
Key of Light **cards:** *Arcturus, Becoming, Divine Darkness, Divine Inspiration, Earth, Gestation, Love, Messenger, Sacred Ceremony, Solar Angel, Spirit of Place, Stability, Starseed, Synchronicity, Through the Portal, Unconquered Sun, Whirlwind*

In a nutshell

The seed of life geometry, also known as the 'genesis pattern',[90] showing seven interlocking circles in perfect symmetry, reflects the wonder of the creative process, as well as illustrating natural order through its construction. It aligns with the sacral centre, for what better place to sow and nurture seeds than in the womb of physical creation? Each sphere within the seed of life connects to the septenate in all 'things': Seven Rays, seven chakras and all else that vibrates to the tune of seven, including notes on a musical scale.

---

[90] See glossary.

It forms the foundation for the Rainbow spheres of consciousness, as well as *Key of Light* suits, and is fundamental to understanding the nature of not only this work, but also of man himself.

Sphere/circle

Keywords: Inclusiveness, wholeness, unity
Affinity with: Spiral, wave
Path: Involution/evolution
Key of Light **cards**: *Arcturus, Becoming, Chrysalis, Divine Darkness, Divine Inspiration, Earth, Emergence, Gnosis Intelligence, Gnosis Purity, Gnosis Tranquillity, Messenger, Point of Light, Reception, Sacred Ceremony, Sanctuary, Secret Garden, Silent Night, Solar Angel, Stability, Starseed, Through the Portal, Wallington Wood*

In a nutshell

The sphere, as well as its 2D counterpart, the circle, has a fixed radius. It is the simplest and most perfect of forms and the ultimate in expression of unity, completeness and integrity. All points on the surface are equally accessible to the centre, from which they originate, whilst in an ordered construction of the universe they combine to mark its outset. It is at once the many and the One, conscious and unconscious, light and dark, but perhaps its most important characteristic is that of being a space within which all, or nothing, unfolds without judgement or condition; it simply is as it is, allowing everything within its embrace to express its essence without interference. Consider these qualities from a personal, human perspective and you have in this simple shape the perfect recipe for contemplating the mysterious unfolding of existence, your existence. Furthermore, as the mother of all forms, it implies a feminine quality and a natural propensity to love. What better conditions could there be for an open and vulnerable heart to embrace the light of its own true nature? The

sphere, therefore, is the essence of unconditional love and is beyond all systems whilst embracing them all; within its boundaries lies the Ultimate expressed as paradox – many in the form of one.

Spiral

Keywords: Growth, expansion and contraction, wisdom, love, continuity
Affinity with: Circle/sphere, wave
Path: Involution/evolution
Key of Light **cards**: *Brotherhood, Family of Light, Genesis Inception, Genesis Manifestation, Impulse, Inner Alchemy, Intelligence, Journey, Joy, Phone Home, Rainbow Bridge, Rebirth, Song of Freedom, Song of the Cycles, Song of the Soul, The Well, Timewarp, Transmission, Trust, Unicorn*

In a nutshell

The spiral is in intimate relation with the circle/sphere, not only in its construction (the circle has a fixed radius whereas the spiral's is variable), but also through its innate quality of love as an outpouring of Spirit in its Will to exist. Spirals are dynamic in nature and expand or contract according to the laws of divine proportion. Spirit is expressed by means of the golden ratio (phi) and cannot be replicated within the denser realms of matter, but nature approximates it very nicely by means of the Fibonacci sequence – 0, 1, 1, 2, 3, 5, 8, 13, etc. – a series of numbers that, when plotted on a graph, translates to a spiral. An Italian mathematician, Fibonacci, discovered through his observations that seeds, plants and even breeding rabbits followed a simple numerical sequence during their process of growth or reproduction. He recognised that all physical life evolved according to a certain formula: take the past, add it to the present and it creates the future, a perfect recipe for life, eh? The most obvious examples are nautilus shells, pine cones, ammonites and sunflowers, but look also to your physical body and notice the perfect relationship between the phalanges of your fingers, hand and elbow, leg and foot, etc. Aside from this, the spiral is the universal expression of our feeling nature, bringing the universal love of God to the realm of matter through interpersonal relationships and our inseparable bond with the kingdom of nature. No man is an island; the spiral is nature's gift to remind us of this.

Tetrahedron/star tetrahedron

Keywords: Alignment, change, integration, will
Affinity with: Cube
Dual: Tetrahedron is dual to itself (star-tetrahedron)
Structure: (tetrahedron) 6 edges, 4 triangular faces, 3 of which meet at each of its 4 vertices
Element: Fire
Path: Evolution
Key of Light cards: *Apocalypse Fire, Apocalypse Water, Furnace, Holographic Universe, Mystic Union, Will*

In a nutshell

The star tetrahedron is a stable geometry featuring two tetrahedrons (3D triangles); one sits upon the earth turning its attention towards Spirit, whilst the second, like an arrow, directs its force downwards into matter. As a whole, it facilitates the union of Spirit with matter. Consider carefully the implications of this all-embracing statement, for in order for spirit and matter to come together in harmony, **every** duality must also be a part of the integration process; the war of opposites must end. Another quality integral to this geometry is that concerning will; the fire of Spirit, with its propensity to ignite the will of the small self, eventually ensures all will return home to itself. However, in one who is unconscious, it serves to fuel the fire of desire towards self-serving ideals. Only when the lower will is offered in service to the higher may the duals come home to each

other, only then may the star tetrahedron fulfil its Divine Purpose in uniting Spirit with matter and only then may the real *Art of Synthesis* begin.

Torus

Keywords: Radiance, resonance, projection/integration
Affinity with: Seed of life
Path: Involution/evolution
Key of Light cards: *Alchemist, Cooperation, Enchantment, Family of Light, Father Time, Flowering, Inner Earth, Jubilation, New Earth, Ostara, Resting Place, Reverence, Silent Night, Weaver, Whirlwind, Woodhenge, World Tree*

In a nutshell

The torus is a doughnut-shape that continuously folds in on itself. Constructed using a 'ratcheting' effect with the seed of life as its base, it symbolises continuous evolution of consciousness and is, therefore, the dynamic force present at all chakras. The first shape to emerge out of the genesis pattern,[91] it governs many aspects of life, including the human heart with its seven muscles that form a torus. The torus is literally around all life forms, all atoms and all cosmic bodies such as planets, stars and galaxies.

Triquetra

Keywords: Change, trinity
Affinity with: Circle/sphere, spiral, vesica piscis
Path: Involution
Key of Light cards: *Enchantment, Integrity, Intelligence, Invitation, Love, Will, Wisdom Keeper*

In a nutshell

The triquetra is an ancient symbol consisting of three vesica piscis interlocked in an eternal arc. Hence, all symbolism relating to the vesica piscis may be applied to the triquetra. It is typically

---

[91] See glossary.

used to symbolise people or ideas occurring in groups of three. In Christian symbolism, it is the holy trinity: Father, Son and Holy Ghost. Its relevance within these pages refers to body, Soul and Spirit, as well as the aspects of divinity – Will, Love, Intelligence – gathered together prior to Esmerelda sounding the one note. In pagan symbolism it is the threefold nature of the Goddess: virgin, mother and crone. Setting aside particular traditions, the triquetra is the tripartite nature of the universe and is fundamental to understanding the greater and lesser cycles, our place within the cosmos and man's eternal quest to "know himself".

Vesica piscis
Keywords: Right relationship, mutual reception, light
Affinity with: Circle/sphere, spiral, triquetra
Path: Involution
Key of Light cards: *Becoming, Brotherhood, Celestial Light, Chrysalis, Divine Darkness, Divine Inspiration, Eye Eye, In Lak'ech, Mystic Union, Reception, Sanctuary, Secret Garden, Synchronicity, Wallington Wood*

In a nutshell
The vesica piscis is formed by the intersection of two circles or spheres whose centres exactly touch. This symbolic intersection represents the 'common ground', 'shared vision' or 'mutual understanding' between equal individuals, states of mind or ways of being. The shape of the human eye itself is a vesica piscis. The ratio of the axes of the form is the square root of three, alluding to the deepest nature of the triune, which cannot be adequately expressed by rational language alone. This same ratio is at one with the phi or Fibonacci spiral. Known as the geometric symbol for light, it is also the womb of creation and gives birth to all forms, including time.

Wave
Keywords: Infinite possibilities, vibration, light, sound
Affinity with: Circle/sphere, spiral
Path: Involution/evolution
Key of Light cards: None

In a nutshell
A circle halved creates two semicircles. Inverting one and setting both side by side results in a sine wave. This wave may take the form of sound, ripples in water, DNA strands or even vibrations in photon particles, creating visible light. Waves are the vertical and horizontal positions of a circle plotted out over time. This quality is really important to understand, for it reinforces its relationship with the circle, on a feeling level, as an agent of love. All vibration, as an expression of Spirit, is therefore an outpouring of love dispatched over time. Quantum physics states that before a particle is observed, it exists as a wave of infinite possibilities, so if you take into account the continuation of consciousness as it relates to life, death and subsequent rebirth, the wave of love carries the ultimate potential to transcend the bounds of both time and space for every single unit of consciousness. Put another way, vibration, as a wave of infinite possibilities, ensures that every human being, as a particle within consciousness, is assured of its return to Spirit; all that is required is to let go and allow the wave to do its work.

What are the Seven Rays?
If geometry is the structure of space, the Seven Rays are its fabric. Infiltrating all forms, inseparable from that which gave rise to the birth of 'all', they are the very substance of Spirit in its most pure expression. The Science of the Seven Rays in the writings of the Tibetan as set down in the works of Alice A. Bailey, is a vast, deep and very profound subject; it would take

a lifetime (at least) of research to gain even a tiny glimpse into the role cosmic relationships play in the life of an individual on planet earth. Every aspect – from the smallest atom to the great expanse of the universe as a whole; from the most crystallised expression of matter to the subtle realms of Soul and Spirit through planets and constellations; human, animal, vegetable and mineral kingdoms; thoughts, feelings, light and sound; countries and cities – falls under the influence of the Seven Rays and is governed by their inherent psychologies. As individuals, human beings are conditioned by five primary rays[xxiii] – Soul, personality, mental, emotional and physical – which, with the exception of the Soul, change with each incarnation. In short, 24 books of esoteric philosophy set down the inner workings of Soul and Spirit in their expression outwards through substance to create everyday reality – you and your daily life. The method by which these most refined vibrations of light are stepped down into matter, as the diagram below in some small part illustrates, is so inclusive in its totality that one cannot fail to stand back and wonder at its magnificence.

The Seven Rays, by virtue of the seven spheres of group-consciousnesses (see 'A Rainbow', p.45) and, by extension, seven suits in *Key of Light* cards, are an integral part of *Walk the Rainbow*, but this is merely the tip of the iceberg. Inspiration for many visions and card titles, as well as Soul alignment qualities, is rooted in the journey to integration such as that set down in these Ageless Wisdom teachings, where every detailed fragment of human consciousness – from separation to integration, matter to Spirit, personality to Soul – is revealed clearly and in precise detail, leaving no doubt in the mind of the aspirant as to the task that lies ahead should they wish to be awake. Esmerelda's journey from isolation in the place of shadows to the land of

light and her subsequent return to the world of form, her meeting with Thomas, the Mentor as a group-conscious expression of her inner teacher and the intricate unravelling of the deeper mysteries of subtle realms within the outer world of form have as their foundation many hours of contemplation following research into teachings expressed through these 24 books, therefore, nothing in this work is random or imagined; it is backed up by verifiable sources. However, it must be emphasised that as far as esoteric philosophy and the Seven Rays are concerned, the material laid down throughout the pages of this book is for the most part **subjective** in nature, arising, as has already been stated, through the author's research, contemplation and interpretation of esoteric philosophy over many years. It is by no means definitive and certainly not offered as an alternative authority to the writings of the Tibetan in the works of Alice A. Bailey. In this, there is no substitute for reading, researching and contemplating the original material.

With this in mind, information on the Seven Rays is included below. It is hoped it will serve as a reference guide for further reflection whilst also offering some insight into the original impulse inspiring *Walk the Rainbow*. Summaries of the rays ('In a Nutshell') are the author's, again derived through research and contemplation of her findings. Use it as a background to the Rainbow material – particularly when working with 'A Diamond', 'A Rainbow' and 'An Invitation' – then, if you feel inspired and wish to explore deeper, refer to the bibliography in the closing pages. Finally, the subjective expression of these ray energies, as seen through the eyes of Thomas and Esmerelda, is found in the chapter, 'A Rainbow', where each group-conscious expression reflects the Soul in manifestation. A simple diagram serves to illustrate how they come into existence.

Prism as a triangle of force
A triple vortex, arising as aspects
of Divinity, expresses outwards
through three constellations to
create the rainbow (every ray
has these essential qualities):
Will – Great Bear: 7 stars
Love – Sirius
Intelligence – Pleiades: 7 stars

The Seven Rays
Fractured light emerges from the
prism in the form of the rainbow
and is transmitted through twelve
constellations (see below)

Transformed by the (spiritual) sun

Seven Rays Transfigured
(spiritualised) through seven
sacred and five non-sacred
planets (see below)

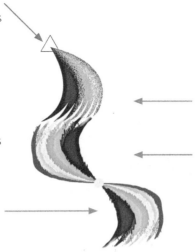

Ray 1	Ray 2	Ray 3	Ray 4	Ray 5	Ray 6	Ray 7
Aries	Gemini	Cancer	Taurus	Leo	Virgo	Aries
Leo	Virgo	Libra	Scorpio	Sagittarius	Sagittarius	Cancer
Capricorn	Piscis	Capricorn	Sagittarius	Aquarius	Piscis	Capricorn
Vulcan	**Jupiter**	**Saturn**	**Mercury**	**Venus**	**Neptune**	**Uranus**
Pluto	Sun	Earth	Moon		Mars	

The Seven Rays and their Cosmic Distributors: Adapted from: Soul Cycles of the Seven Rays[lxxiv]

Ray 1 – Will or Power (red or white)
Cosmic distributors: Aries, Leo, Capricorn,
Vulcan, Pluto[xxiv]
Rainbow sphere – seed thought: Will –
"Be the change"

In a nutshell
The first ray is the initial impulse that arises
through the most pure and primal of intentions:
the will to exist. However, it is far more than
bringing life to physical existence, it also
penetrates to the core of every life form it touches

to infuse all with purpose, Divine Purpose.
Direction is clear – "like an arrow", it moves from
source to form, with nothing, absolutely nothing,
able to arrest its force; as destroyer of worn-out
forms, it ignites power through fiery will. Non-
discriminatory in its expression, whether in one
who serves for the highest good of humanity or
is hell-bent on manifesting its own self-serving
agendas, its action is the same – fire![xxv] Two great
planetary destroyers – Vulcan and Pluto – ensure
old, worn-out forms are incinerated that the
beauty and light of the Divine may shine through.

This is Divine Will in action. As much as it forges its way deep into matter, destroying all in its wake, its ultimate expression is to raise that form once more to Spirit. Constellations mark the Soul's return to wholeness, where Aries comes forth "from the plane of mind to rule",[xxvi] Leo draws out the ego in all its glory until, upon opening its heart, it becomes the wise and compassionate leader and in Capricorn, sign of the initiate, life begins as a crocodile and personal ambition enslaves the Soul in earth (physical) and water (desire) until, as the mountain goat, it turns its attention towards the mountain top, emerging as the unicorn of God upon reaching the summit – pure and undefiled, equipped to serve.

Ray 2 – Love-Wisdom (indigo)

Cosmic distributors: Gemini, Virgo, Pisces, Jupiter, Sun (physical sun, heart of the sun, central spiritual sun)[xxvii]

Rainbow sphere – seed thought: Love – "Let go and let God"

In a nutshell

The underlying force governing our universe is love. It is the intuitive 'glue' that ensures, at some point in our evolutionary journey, that two will become one. The second ray, therefore, is concerned with how this all-pervasive, all-inclusive force is coalesced within a world whose foundation lies in separation.[xxviii] Personality, Soul and Spirit, as modes of human consciousness, determine the degree to which we respond with love to daily challenges. The personality is often self-centred and selective but, as the sacrificial lamb is crucified upon the cross of desire, Soul consciousness emerges; love for humanity as a whole, including personality, becomes its natural mode of expression. Spirit, as Love Divine, transcends all separates; nothing exists outside the pure vibration of love. Second-ray

constellations carry the essence of duality whilst holding the seeds of integration at their heart. Gemini, sign of the heavenly twins, is duality in its most pure expression and distributes the second ray alone.[xxix] In Pisces, as the personality swims against the tide of its higher nature, the clarion call of the Soul forces a reversal of the current; Christ transcendent is realised.[xxx] Virgo, as the "blended dual light", witnesses the birth of Christ-Consciousness within the human heart; mother and child, spirit and matter, are one.[xxxi] Vibrating at three distinct levels, the sun reflects body (physical sun), Soul (heart of sun) and Spirit (central spiritual sun) in one expression of light. Finally, as the largest planet in our solar system, Jupiter reigns supreme in the art of fusion; expansive, all-inclusive love seamlessly married with wisdom **is** the second ray.[xxxii]

Ray 3 – Active Intelligence (green)

Cosmic distributors: Cancer, Libra, Capricorn, Saturn, Earth[xxxiii]

Rainbow sphere – seed thought: Light – "To every season is a purpose"

In a nutshell

This is the ray of intelligent activity, the Universal mind of God, and takes the first outpouring of Spirit into the heart of matter through ordered intelligence. Infused with Love and Will, it ensures every appearance, whether human, animal, mineral or vegetable, is tuned to the rhythm of the great Cosmic metronome: Divine Will. Time and space come under its auspices, as do cycles of birth, life and death; planetary orbits, phases of the moon and creatures of land, sea and air owe their innate modus operandi to the intelligent activity of this ray. At its heart is the principle of balance, where polar opposites are brought to a point of unity in accordance with Cosmic Law; it **is** the middle path. In terms of human consciousness, it encompasses the full spectrum of life in physical form from the moment of incarnation through evolutionary growth to eventual rebirth into the realm of Spirit. Cancer,[xxxiv] is the 'gate in', where the spark of human life is received by the mother and nurtured by the family to instil a sense of belonging that 'tribal' traditions are followed throughout life. The mass consciousness of humanity, with its follow-the-crowd mentality, has its roots in this sign. In Capricorn,[xxxv] as the 'gate out', the 'mass conscious' individual, following many trials and tribulations, wakes up to the innate divinity within; the initiate is born. Saturn, Lord of Karma,[xxxvi] as "Dweller on the Threshold", ensures no stone is left unturned in exposing every cause through its resultant effects. Libra,[xxxvii] sign of balance, marks the turning point, the reversal of the wheel, where man turns his consciousness inwards to walk a middle path between the pairs of opposites. Earth,[xxxviii] is the third ray in matter, the realm of nature and the playground upon which all is worked out.

Ray 4 – Harmony through Conflict (yellow)

Cosmic distributors: Taurus, Scorpio, Sagittarius, Mercury, Moon[xxxix]
Rainbow sphere – seed thought: Beauty – "Empty and be filled"

In a nutshell
The fourth is the ray of humanity and, as well as marking man's propensity to polarise everything dual, it draws to the surface his interminable battle with himself. The symbol could not be clearer: two tetrahedrons pulling in opposing directions, symbolising the battlefield and endless war of divisive thought that defines 21st-century life on planet earth. In the end, unity must prevail. Everything about this ray, therefore,

points to the polarisation of core dualities, but of far more import to one who has turned his attention inwards is the glaring chasm between heart and mind, thought and feelings. Mercury and the moon, as planetary distributors, assist in bridging this gap, however all is not quite as it seems. The moon, although feminine in nature and thus attuned to feelings, is also the storehouse of the past, whilst Mercury, whose realm is that of the mind, is an accomplished messenger and thus admirably gifted to forge the bridge between thought and emotion, not by use of the intellect but through the higher intuitive faculties of the Soul. Scorpio,[xl] as the battle-scarred spiritual disciple, treads the "razor-edged" path deep into the abyss of his past. Emotional detritus is raised to the plane of mind where, as a phoenix risen from the ashes, the spiritual warrior emerges free forever from the chains of desire. Spiritual illumination is realised through its polar opposite, Taurus, light on the path[xli] and *Way of Beauty*. Sagittarius, a "beam of directed focussed light"[xlii] keeps the "eye of the bull" firmly fixed on the "Lighted Way" to assist the traveller as he sinks into the depths of his most vile nature. Finally, the fourth ray is also known as the ray of the Buddha; Gautama Buddha was born, died and attained enlightenment in the constellation, Taurus.

Ray 5 – Concrete Knowledge or Science (orange)

Cosmic distributors: Leo, Sagittarius, Aquarius, Venus[xliii]
Rainbow sphere – seed thought: Mind – "Every thought is a prayer"

In a nutshell
The fifth ray unites human being, the Soul and Spirit through the medium of mind; "three minds" - intellect (human), group (Soul) and

universal (Spirit) – are aligned, harmonised and integrated under the auspices of this ray. The plane of mind is the realm where the Soul resides. It is therefore an obvious ground upon which they may meet and emphasises why this ray is so important for the integration of body and Soul, Spirit and matter; it also shows clearly why the leading edge of the Aquarian age lies through development of the intellect using 'concrete' and 'scientific' methods; the only ray transmitted through the constellation Aquarius is the fifth.[xliv] Essentially, this ray is concerned with the middle principle, the Soul, so all distributors are imbibed with qualities to facilitate its union. Leo, as the "light of the Soul"[xlv] has surrendered its egotistical tendencies, expressed as the "will to rule" in the first ray, in favour of Soul purpose, which allows the "will to illumine" to come into its own.[xlvi] When the individual in Leo turns identification from personality to Soul, its polar opposite, Aquarius, comes into play; mind and heart unite in the group-conscious-aware world server. Sagittarius, as the higher mind, provides the single-pointed focus necessary to facilitate this orientation. Finally, Venus as sole planetary distributor, is the pure expression of the Universal mind – Spirit – and functions to transmute knowledge into wisdom. Consider the mind to be as a cloud veiling the sun: when it is seen and known for what it is, the clouds dissipate to reveal the light of love that is always there; the illumined mind of the Soul is able to shine through the dross of daily life.

Ray 6 – Devotion or Idealism (blue or rose)

Cosmic distributors: Virgo, Pisces, Sagittarius, Neptune, Mars[xlvii]

Rainbow sphere – seed thought: Truth – "The key is the door as is the vision reality"

In a nutshell

The sixth ray is love at its most polarised. At its depth, it bears witness to the most extreme expression of self-centred love, fraught with conditions that waft to and fro with the opinions of others. Transpersonal Love of the Divine is at its height when a compassionate heart is its only expression. On a global scale, extremes in polarity give rise to the religious fanatic on the one hand and, through the life of Christ, the world saviour on the other. Two constellations highlight the familiar story that is the life of Christ: Virgo,[xlviii] as Mother Mary, nurtures the Christ child until he is ready to begin his life of service; Pisces,[xlix] sign of the fishes, is not only indicative of the world saviour, but also of sacrifice and, ultimately, following death through crucifixion, sign of resurrection – Christ transcendent. The sixth ray epitomises the life of Christ and has dictated the consciousness of humanity for the past 2000 years; religious fanaticism, guru worship and blind idealism are all significant keynotes. However, although still in evidence to this day, the tide is turning. Sagittarius,[l] as the higher mind, rotates mass consciousness inwards where the light of the Soul awaits the devotee's unbridled service. Mars, the fiery aspirant, joins forces and harnesses its rage into fuel for the Soul. Neptune, lord of the waters, planet of illusion, is equally polarised but far more subtle than its fiery companion; addiction, particularly alcoholism, lies at its depths whilst the visionary, whose heart bathes in the waters of compassion, is its ultimate expression.

Ray 7 – Ceremonial Order or Magic (violet)

Cosmic distributors: Aries, Cancer, Capricorn, Uranus[li]

Rainbow sphere – seed thought: Order – "Beauty expressed outwards is life"

In a nutshell

The seventh ray, as the seed thought suggests, sees the most refined vibrations of Spirit abide in the heart of matter. That which began in Aries[lii] as a spark, an impulse to create, has found its way into the mass consciousness of humanity to arrive in Cancer,[liii] sign of the mother and the home; male, Spirit, has impregnated its feminine counterpart, matter, with its Will to exist. The home, of course, refers to the light of the Soul, whose essence is love, found within the heart of physicality; "I build a lighted house and therein dwell"[liv] is the perfect keynote for this sign. Its polar opposite, Capricorn,[lv] encourages 'the crab' to emerge from the safety of its shell and rise to the heights of worldly ambition. A moment of awakening subsequently sees the Capricorn initiate crumble to its knees when the false reality is recognised for what it is. The "lighted shadow" within then ascends the mountain top of spiritual realisation and is eventually liberated from the bounds of flesh to emerge as the world server in Aquarius. Uranus, sole distributor of this ray, is agent of this awakening. Most importantly, at this period in earth's history, the seventh ray heralds the emergence of the Aquarian age, era of the group, where conscious cooperation and the "will to good" are cornerstones to right human relationship. Two signs, although not distributors, are fundamental to this ray expression: Leo and Aquarius. The first follows Cancer on the great zodiacal wheel and leads the mass-conscious "crowd follower" to make its mark as an individual. Aquarius, ruled by Uranus, polar opposite of Leo and sign following Capricorn, marks the birth of the world server. All has come full circle, what began as a flame in a "lighted house" made its way to the height of self-serving individualism and then fell at the final gate to emerge as servant to the whole; Divine Will is expressed through ordered intelligence in matter.

What is Quantum Navigation, with Ronald L. Holt?

There is a part of us that is ever awake, always watching the small self that is having a human experience. This Big Self fully understands, from a bird's eye perspective, the complete picture of our many existences and why we choose the lives and challenges that we do in the here and now. This Big Self is our integrated consciousness that exists on the quantum level. It is outside of time and space and communicates constantly to us, but without verbal or intellectual language. It communicates from the quantum level, using the tools of metaphor, synchronicity, and emotional resonance in order to nudge us toward our unique awakening process. This is the **Quantum Navigator** *-- the aspect of the Big Self whose insights and guidance are filtered through the unconscious and the subconscious minds. When we become quiet inside, we can begin to hear and respond to this essential wisdom and insight that is born from the true essence of our consciousness.*

Imagine what it would be like to fully understand the messages given to you by your Quantum Navigator, especially when going through challenging times. And further imagine how profound it would be if you learned to communicate, beyond time, space, and language, back to the Navigator. The result is a profound integration between the conscious illusionary ego-self and the true you, or the Big Self that is the only you that truly exists.

Quantum Navigation *represents the next step in human evolution. This work requires us to go deep within ourselves into a very vulnerable and yet powerful place. It also requires us to see our own ego construct (without judgement) so we can understand the belief structures we have created for ourselves that keep us imprisoned. Like all authentic spiritual paths, it is a deep journey that is unique for each person and isn't a quick-fix. It isn't a surface-level practice, but it is available to any sincere practitioner who is ready for this step.*

Ronald L. Holt, Seed of Life Institute (2018)[lvi]

These few words, taken from Ronald Holt's website, are a mere tip of the iceberg and by no means reflect the sheer magnitude of transformation available to one who embarks, with sincerity, upon this awakening journey. If you slow down and **feel** the words he has written, you may touch upon their essence and therein find your Quantum Navigator, and then you will know, beyond doubt, that he has touched upon something so very profound and true it brooks no questioning. However, when I first heard about this, his latest work, I asked myself "Why is Ron doing inner child stuff?" The teaching and wisdom I had received from him for many years surely far surpassed anything that could be offered under this umbrella. Besides, I had done 'all that' years ago, hadn't I? How wrong could I be! I now realise that, as valuable as all this inner work had been, it merely scratched the surface, leaving many, many layers of under-processed belief systems and behavioural patterns to wreak unconscious havoc in my daily life; Quantum Navigation addressed these issues by making my darkness conscious. Several layers – core dualities (masculine/feminine, inner child/adult, True Self/false self), roots of the unconscious and diamond in the heart, for instance – he generously shares through a series of tutorial videos on his website.[lvii]

Many of the insights shared through Esmerelda's journey, particularly those concerning the shadow self, have as their source Quantum Navigation, under Ronald Holt's mentorship. Contemplations, teachings, inner dialogue with the Beloved and even visions have arisen as a result of my own journeys into the quantum realms of which he speaks. The still-small Voice in the Silence, when given space to be heard, allows wisdom from the depths of beyond to flow effortlessly into the world of form, bringing clarity where once there was none, but he is quite right when he states in paragraph two of his introduction, that you must "go deep within to a vulnerable, yet powerful place" before these ego constructs can be exposed and then seen for what they are. When integrated, a whole new panorama opens up in the consciousness of one who dares to enter the dark, and life, quite literally, is never the same again.

Walk the Rainbow, as has been shared many time times throughout the telling, has two systems underpinning the source of its esoteric knowledge; Quantum Navigation completes the picture. It is the subtle, essential ingredient, the river of authenticity that allows Truth to emerge from the shadows, claim its mastery and permit *Walk the Rainbow* to own its rightful place in **being** a *Way of Wholeness*.

What are the Universal Principles?

Hermeticism, from which these principles originate, is a system that is universal in origin and expression and is founded upon the wisdom of Thoth the Atlantean and Hermes Trismegistus (meaning thrice-born); in effect, these entities are one and same and said to be expressions of the Universal mind of God incarnate at different eras in earth's history. The common thread is that they serve as transmitters for the Word of God with writing, mathematics, science, geometry, magic, astrology and alchemy, to table but a few, attributed to their name. Texts in which their wisdom may be found are *The Emerald Tablets of Thoth the Atlantean*, reputed to be more than 30,000 years old, and *Corpus Hermeticum*, dated around 1460. The principles tabled below are sourced from the original 1908 version, *The Kybalion*.[lviii]

The important thing to grasp in relation to *Walk the Rainbow* is that these principles are not outdated or random. Not only do they form the foundation for many of the world's esoterica and occult traditions, including those set down in the Ageless Wisdom teachings, but once these principles are contemplated and applied to daily life, they open doors to the infinite, where its founding principle, "As Above, So Below", cannot fail to ignite this ancient maxim in you.

In summary, the word "principle" may be translated as "law", Cosmic Law, and as such these maxims are fundamental to the working out of the divine plan in matter, and that includes you, a human being and co-creator in existence within your everyday reality. The Universal Principles are included here that their infinite wisdom may be felt with each turn of a page or selection of a vision or whilst simply musing in nature. Finally, it is worth repeating: these principles are Laws; they **will** fulfil their purpose, as they have been doing since the beginning of time, whether you believe in them or not.

The Principle of Mentalism
All is mind: The Universe is Mental.

The Principle of Correspondence
As above, so below; as below, so above; As within, so without; as without, so within.

The Principle of Vibration
Nothing rests; Everything moves; Everything vibrates.

The Principle of Polarity
Everything is dual; Everything has its pair of opposites; Like and unlike are the same; Opposites are identical in nature, but differ in degree; Extremes meet; All truths are but half-truths; All paradoxes may be reconciled.

The Principle of Rhythm
Everything flows, out and in; Everything has its tides; All things rise and fall; The pendulum swing manifests in everything; The measure of the swing to the right is the measure of the swing to the left; Rhythm compensates.

The Principle of Cause and Effect
Every cause has its effect; Every effect has its cause; Everything happens according to law; Chance is but a name for law not recognised; There are many planes of causation, but nothing escapes the law.

The Principle of Gender
Gender is in everything; Everything has its masculine and feminine principles; Gender manifests on all planes.

Appendix 1
Practical Geometry

Inner vesica piscis

The geometries on the left show the vesica piscis in varying stages of inner expansion, beginning with two circles of common radius enclosed within a larger circle. Those on the right form the basic structures required – golden ratio cross, two tetrahedrons and hexagram, symbols for *Love, Beauty* and *Mind* respectively – to create the next level; they may be viewed as foundations for the manifestation of light.

Constructing the Inner Vesica Piscis: Stage 1 – Identification

Constructing the inner vesica piscis

Basic constructs are shown below, with detailed instructions following on the next page. Below, vertical and horizontal tetrahedrons form the foundation for constructing the inner vesica piscis, along with hexagrams; they are rotated 90° at each stage of inner expansion.

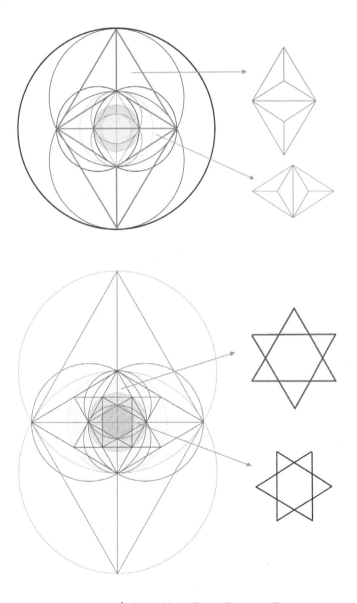

Constructing the Inner Vesica Piscis: Stage 2 – Extraction

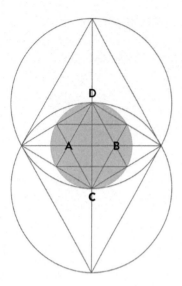 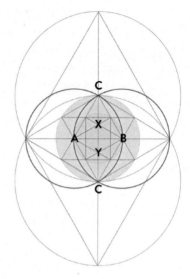

Constructing the Inner Vesica Piscis: Stage 3 – Journey inwards

Method

1. Draw two circles of equal radius to create a vesica piscis, ensuring the centre point of each circle touches the outer edge of the other.
2. Create the vertical tetrahedrons by connecting the salient points as shown in the diagram.
3. Draw a smaller circle within the 'eye' of the vesica piscis.
4. Create the first hexagram (six-pointed star) by joining the points where the inner circle intersects with the lines of the tetrahedrons.
5. Points A and B are the centre points used to create the next vesica piscis, with the radius being AC/BC as shown in second diagram.
6. Notice how the new vesica piscis is at 90° to the first. The inner circle can now be drawn, followed by a new hexagram
7. This process continues to infinity, with X and Y being the centre points of the next two circles.

Constructing a pentagon/pentagram within the vesica piscis

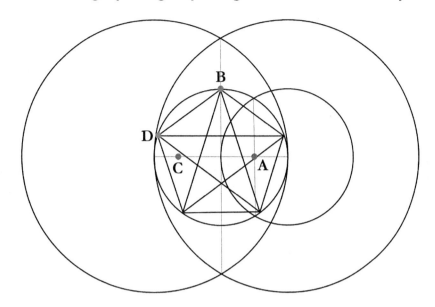

Method

1. Draw a large vesica piscis.
2. Draw a horizontal straight line to join the two circles, and then draw another vertically through the vesica piscis – this determines the centre point from where the next circle is drawn.
3. Draw a circle in the centre – the 'eyeball'.
4. Draw a small vesica piscis using same radius as the first small circle.
5. Draw a vertical line down the centre of new small vesica piscis to determine the centre point (as with the larger vesica piscis).
6. Set the compass point on position 'A' with the pencil on point 'B'.
7. Using the parameters AB, draw an arc to intersect the horizontal straight line at point 'C'.
8. Set a compass distance BC and place the point on position 'B'.
9. Draw an arc to intercept the circle at point 'D'.
10. Continue walking round the circle, keeping the same parameters BC/BD, until you reach point 'B' again – the circle has now been divided into five equal portions.
11. Join these points around the edge to create the pentagon. The star (pentagram) is created by joining the same points internally.
12. Once the pentagon/pentagram has been established, in a like manner to the hexagram, it is easy to keep drawing more stars within the original (see diagram overleaf). The process continues, spiralling inwards, ad infinitum.

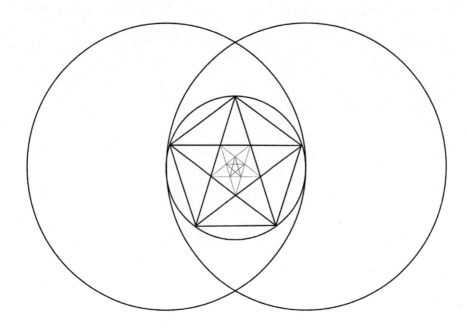

Vesica Piscis Journey Inwards: Pentagram within a pentagram ad infinitum

Appendix 2
Facets of the Diamond

Facets of the diamond
Co-creative families

As well as belonging to Rainbow spheres/*Key of Light* suits, easily identified by their colour, many visions/cards form an affinity with themed expressions or creative communities, alike in purpose; sacred geometry, for instance, is an obvious example. The following, then, is a means by which these groups may be explored within a wider context. Some are more obvious than others and, where necessary, additional information is included under the heading to assist in clarification. Use them as you intuit to deepen your understanding of themes or teachings relative to your chosen vision/card. Note that this list is not definitive: view it as a beginning; there may be many other visions/cards that would do equally well in these categories and some that you might intuit don't fit in at all – you're in the driving seat, you decide!

Sacred geometry

Involution
Spirit's descent into matter

Circle	*Love*	Rainbow
	Will	Rainbow
Vesica piscis	*Becoming*	Light/Green
	Raindance	Order/Violet
	Reception	Beauty/Yellow
	Sanctuary	Love/Indigo
	Secret Garden	Love/Indigo
	Synchronicity	Mind/Orange
	Wallington Wood	Light/Green
Triquetra	*Enchantment*	Light/Green
	Integrity	Light/Green
	Intelligence	Rainbow
	Invitation	Beauty/Yellow
	Love	Rainbow
	Will	Rainbow
	Wisdom Keeper	Mind/Orange
Seed of life	*Earth*	Beauty/Yellow
	Flowering	Love/Indigo
	Gestation	Beauty/Yellow
	Love	Rainbow
	Messenger	Light/Green
	Sacred Ceremony	Love/Indigo

	Solar Angel	Mind/Orange
	Spirit of Place	Light/Green
	Stability	Will/Red
	Starseed	Rainbow
	Synchronicity	Mind/Orange
	Touching Paradise	Light/Green
	Unconquered Sun	Light/Green
	Whirlwind	Order/Violet
Seed of life/tree of life	*Divine Darkness*	Light/Green
	Divine Inspiration	Light/Green
Seed of life/tree of life/vesica piscis	*Becoming*	Light/Green
Seed of life/flower of life	*Arcturus*	Order/Violet
	Through the Portal	Rainbow
Divine matrix	*Celestial Light*	Love/Indigo
	Chrysalis	Beauty/Yellow
	Gnosis Intelligence	Light/Green
	Gnosis Purity	Rainbow
	Gnosis Tranquillity	Will/Red
	Inner Earth	Rainbow
	Stability	Will/Red
	Starseed	Rainbow
Fruit of life/Metatron's cube	*Air*	Beauty/Yellow
	Cosmic Orchestra	Light/Green
	Custodian	Will/Red
	Earth	Beauty/Yellow
	Fire	Beauty/Yellow
	Fortitude	Order/Violet
	Omniscience	Mind/Orange
	Raindance	Order/Violet
	Starseed	Rainbow
	Water	Beauty/Yellow
Torus	*Air*	Beauty/Yellow
	Alchemist	Order/Violet
	Cooperation	Light/Green
	Enchantment	Light/Green
	Father Time	Rainbow
	Flowering	Love/Indigo
	Inner Earth	Rainbow
	Intelligence	Rainbow
	New Earth	Light/Green
	Ostara	Light/Green

	Resting Place	Rainbow
	Reverence	Beauty/Yellow
	Weaver	Mind/Orange
	Whirlwind	Order/Violet
	Will	Rainbow
	World Tree	Will/Red
Torus/triangle	*Silent Night*	Rainbow
	Love	Rainbow
	Will	Rainbow
Spiral	*Joy*	Truth/Blue
	Song of Freedom	Order/Violet
	Song of the Cycles	Order/Violet
	Song of the Soul	Order/Violet
	Trust	Truth/Blue

Evolution

Path of return

Cube	*Celebration*	Light/Green
Star tetrahedron	*Apocalypse Fire*	Will/Red
	Apocalypse Water	Truth/Blue
	Furnace	Will/Red
	Holographic Universe	Mind/Orange
	Mystic Union	Love/Indigo
	Will	Rainbow
Octahedron	*Freedom*	Love/Indigo
Icosahedron	*Genesis Inception*	Mind/Orange
	Genesis Manifestation	Order/Violet
Dodecahedron	*Devotion Clarity*	Truth/Blue
	Devotion Compassion	Truth/Blue

N.B. Alignment between cards/visions/facets and geometries are tabulated in three chapters, each with its focus on a particular aspect of their relationship.

'A Diamond' (p.107) – geometries are integral to the vision or are mentioned within contemplation or guidance.

'What is...?', 'Sacred geometry' (p.441) – focus is on the geometry whose essence may also, through contemplation, be found within a particular facet of the diamond.

'Facets of the diamond: Co-creative families' (p.468) – emphasis is on the group relationship in which individual facets may form a part.

Kingdom of nature

Nature is expressed in both subtle and physical existence, from Devas (angelic realm) through elemental and nature spirits to the four elements and the cyclic nature of the four seasons. Some species – spiders, birds, trees, etc. – are included here to shine a light on the co-dependent relationship between the kingdom of nature and human consciousness; sacred geometry is an important feature in many of them.

Devas		*Brilliance*	Rainbow
		Cooperation	Light/Green
		Reverence	Beauty/Yellow
		Touching Paradise	Light/Green
Four elements		*Air*	Beauty/Yellow
		Earth	Beauty/Yellow
		Fire	Beauty/Yellow
		Water	Beauty/Yellow
Four seasons	Spring	*Ostara*	Light/ Green
	Summer	*Woodhenge*	Light/Green
	Autumn	*Cosmic Orchestra*	Light/Green
	Winter	*Unconquered Sun*	Light/Green
Spider medicine		*Jubilation*	Order/Violet
		Multiverse	Mind/Orange
		Omniscience	Mind/Orange
		Timewarp	Mind/Orange
		Walk in the Park	Order/Violet
		Weaver	Mind/Orange
		Whirlwind	Order/Violet
		Wisdom Keeper	Mind/Orange
Crow medicine		*Alchemist*	Order/Violet
		Fortitude	Order/Violet
		Integrity	Light/Green
		Messenger	Light/Green
		New Earth	Light/Green
		Raindance	Love/Indigo
		Reception	Beauty/Yellow
		Sanctuary	Love/Indigo
		Stewardship	Order/Violet
Woodlands		*Custodian*	Will/Red
		Enchantment	Light/Green
		Stability	Will/Red
		Wallington Wood	Light/Green
		World Tree	Will/Red

Esoteric astrology

It is worth pointing out that few of the visions/cards tabulated here have traditional astrological imagery as their source. These alignments are based upon the author's knowing of visionary art and her innate knowing of esoteric astrology following years of research into the subject matter. Some, such as those aligned with Sirius, Uranus, Neptune and Pluto, for instance, have photos of the star/planet (courtesy of NASA) embedded within the layers; others are more intuitive and stimulate the essence of the alignment through the subtle senses (contemplations/guidance associated with each vision/card will assist in tuning into this).

Solar Logos		*The Well*	Will/Red
Sirius		*Holographic Universe*	Mind/Orange
		Mystic Union	Love/Indigo
		Through the Portal	Rainbow
Sun	Physical sun	*Flowering*	Love/Indigo
	Heart of sun	*Celestial Light*	Love/Indigo
	Central spiritual sun	*Unconquered Sun*	Light/Green
Moon		*Amygdala*	Beauty/Yellow
Vulcan		*Starseed*	Rainbow
Mercury		*Transmission*	Rainbow
Venus		*Inside Out*	Mind/Orange
Earth		*Inner Earth*	Rainbow
Mars		*Aspiration*	Truth/Blue
		Eureka!	Will/Red
Jupiter		*Fusion*	Love/Indigo
		Joy	Truth/Blue
Saturn		*Father Time*	Rainbow
Chiron		*Rainbow Bridge*	Order/Violet
Uranus		*Awakening*	Order/Violet
Neptune		*Illumination*	Truth/Blue
		Illusion	Truth/Blue
Pluto		*Shattering*	Will/Red
		Underworld	Will/Red
		Transcendence	Will/Red

Teachings

It may be said that every vision/card, or even each page, is a teaching in and of itself, but some fall into categories that allow deeper penetration of the subtle layers making up the constitution of man. The following are themed teachings and warrant many hours, days or even years of pondering to touch upon their essence and eventually come to the realisation that this essence is indeed you; they warrant time and space, and above all, a letting go of all you are not.

Consciousness/mind	*As Above, So Below*	Mind/Orange
	Awakening	Rainbow
	Bridge Across Forever	Mind/Orange
	Brotherhood	Order/Violet
	Conversion	Rainbow
	Dharmakaya	Truth/Blue
	Doorway	Mind/Orange
	Festival of Light	Order/Violet
	Fusion	Love/Indigo
	Guidance	Mind/Orange
	Holy Grail	Love/Indigo
	Impulse	Will/Red
	Initiation	Order/Violet
	Inside Out	Mind/Orange
	Materialisation	Mind/Orange
	Point of Light	Rainbow
	Sacred Ceremony	Love/Indigo
	Secret Garden	Love/Indigo
	Starseed	Rainbow
	Substance	Rainbow
	Sweet Surrender	Mind/Orange
	Transmission	Rainbow
	Way of Light	Beauty/Yellow
Imagination	*Rainbow Bridge*	Will/Red
	Resting Place	Rainbow
	Unicorn	Will/Red
Soul/Spirit	*Absorption*	Rainbow
	Blessing	Truth/Blue
	City of Light	Beauty/Yellow
	Family of Light	Mind/Orange
	Gathering	Beauty/Yellow
	Presence	Rainbow
	Solar Angel	Mind/Orange

Time		*Father Time*	Rainbow
		Spirit of Place	Light/Green
		Song of the Cycles	Order/Violet
		Synchronicity	Mind/Orange
		The Web	Light/Green
		Timewarp	Mind/Orange

Golden age

It could be argued this category fits into one of 'time', and the argument would be correct. However, the following visions/cards mark the outset of not only the Rainbow journey, but also the author's about-face from outer to inner. Therefore, their inspiration is her search for Truth. The golden age of Lemuria and Atlantis, extra-terrestrials, Buddhism and naturally many spiritual retreats that were part and parcel of the journey set the course of its trajectory; the most obvious reason for their alignment is the artwork of course, with almost every one being bathed in soft, golden light.

Atlantis		*Alien Nation*	Will/Red
		Burning Ground	Beauty/Yellow
		Follow the Crowd?	Truth/Blue
		Stillness	Will/Red
		Welcome	Order/Violet
Buddhism	Bodhisattva	*Creation*	Beauty/Yellow
	Emptiness	*Empty Vessel*	Love/Indigo
	Karma	*River of Souls*	Love/Indigo
Consciousness stream		*Chaos*	Beauty/Yellow
		Eye Eye	Love/Indigo
		Mind	Love/Indigo
Extra-terrestrials		*Alien Nation*	Will/Red
		Phone Home	Love/Indigo
Lemuria		*Emergence*	Love/Indigo
		Recognition	Mind/Orange

Shadowlands

The essence of shadow work, this category in many ways speaks for itself. Alongside the visions/cards tabulated below, it is well worth reading, and contemplating, the chapter "A Rainbow", especially *Beauty*, *Love*, *Light*, *Mind* and *Truth*, where you will find the 'how' in Esmerelda's black diamond and reference to Ronald L. Holt's Quantum Navigation, as well as the author's experience in delving into their mysteries. You might say they present signposts in a territory that doesn't even have a map!

Instinct	*Amygdala*	Beauty/Yellow
	Beauty and the Beast	Truth/Blue
Perception	*Appearances*	Beauty/Yellow
	Brick Wall	Love/Indigo
Unconscious	*Fortress*	Will/Red
	Headspace	Truth/Blue
	Roots	Truth/Blue
Psychic powers	*Alien Nation*	Will/Red
	Burning Ground	Beauty/Yellow
	Follow the Crowd?	Truth/Blue
	Journey	Will/Red
	Stillness	Will/Red
	Welcome	Order/Violet
Heart	*Guidance*	Mind/Orange
	Harmony	Beauty/Yellow
	In Lak'ech	Love/Indigo
	Quiescence	Love/Indigo
	Rudderless Boat	Truth/Blue
	Sacred Space	Truth/Blue
	Trust	Truth/Blue
	Way of Light	Beauty/Yellow
Change	*Inner Alchemy*	Order/Violet
	Rebirth	Truth/Blue

Facets of the diamond
Rainbow spheres/*Key of Light* suits

Visions aligned to Beauty

Air, Amygdala, Appearances, Burning Ground, Chaos, Chrysalis, City of Light, Creation, Earth, Fire, Gathering, Gestation, Harmony, Invitation, Reception, Reverence, Water, Way of Light

Visions aligned to Light

Becoming, Celebration, Cooperation, Cosmic Orchestra, Divine Darkness, Divine Inspiration, Enchantment, Gnosis Intelligence, Integrity, Messenger, New Earth, Ostara, Spirit of Place, The Web, Touching Paradise, Unconquered Sun, Wallington Wood, Woodhenge

Visions aligned to Love

Brick Wall, Celestial Light, Emergence, Empty Vessel, Eye Eye, Flowering, Freedom, Fusion, Holy Grail, In Lak'ech, Mind, Mystic Union, Phone Home, Quiescence, River of Souls, Sacred Ceremony, Sanctuary, Secret Garden

Visions aligned to Mind

As Above, So Below, Bridge Across Forever, Doorway, Family of Light, Genesis Inception, Guidance, Holographic Universe, Inside Out, Materialisation, Multiverse, Omniscience, Recognition, Solar Angel, Sweet Surrender, Synchronicity, Timewarp, Weaver, Wisdom Keeper

Visions aligned to Truth

Apocalypse Water, Aspiration, Beauty and the Beast, Blessing, Devotion Clarity, Devotion Compassion, Devotion Unity, Dharmakaya, Follow the Crowd?, Headspace, Illumination, Illusion, Joy, Rebirth, Roots, Rudderless Boat, Sacred Space, Trust

Visions aligned to Order

Alchemist, Arcturus, Awakening, Brotherhood, Festival of Light, Fortitude, Genesis Manifestation, Initiation, Inner Alchemy, Jubilation, Raindance, Song of Freedom, Song of the Cycles, Song of the Soul, Stewardship, Walk in the Park, Welcome, Whirlwind

Visions aligned to Rainbow

Absorption, Blank Canvas, Brilliance, Conversion, Father Time, Gnosis Purity, Inner Earth, Intelligence, Love, Point of Light, Presence, Resting Place, Silent Night, Through the Portal, Starseed, Substance, Transmission, Will

Visions aligned to Will

Alien Nation, Apocalypse Fire, Custodian, Eureka!, Fortress, Furnace, Gnosis Tranquillity, Impulse, Journey, Rainbow Bridge, Shattering, Stability, Stillness, The Well, Transcendence, Underworld, Unicorn, World Tree

Appendix 3
Glossary

Absolute – The All-Seeing, All-Knowing, All-Being, Unchangeable Source of existence. Called God in many of the world religions, Great Spirit amongst indigenous tribes and Brahman, the Creator, in Hindu.

Absorption – The way of 'return'. Absorption is the means by which a unit of consciousness assimilates within itself to co-create itself and so effect its 'return' to the primal Cause. Works in tandem with becoming, the condition in which outpouring, involutionary forces may be 'absorbed' in one who is on the evolutionary path of return.

Abyss – The Void, the Great Unknown, a term used to describe the space giving rise to 'unconscious' existence.

Anam Cara – Gaelic expression meaning Soul (Anam) friend (Cara), someone with whom you can share your innermost Self and with whom you are accepted as you are without judgement or censorship.

Ancient of Days – Another name for God. In the Book of Daniel (7:9), the term is used in the sense of God being eternal; in the Kabbalah, it is the unmanifested Godhead, the most primary and ancient source of creation; in Christianity, it is attributed to God the Father.[lix]

Ageless Wisdom – Profound esoteric teachings handed down from generation to generation describing how the universe came into existence, its modus operandi and humanity's place within it. Specifically, but not exclusively, those teachings set down in the works of Alice A. Bailey.

Antahkarana – 'Inner cause', originating from the Sanskrit, 'antar' – within – and 'karana' – meaning cause.

Asclepius Rod – Asclepius, son of Apollo, is the god of healing, taught not by his father (god of healing, truth and prophecy) but by the wise and gifted centaur, Chiron. He became so proficient in his art he was perceived as a threat by Zeus, who struck him down with a thunderbolt, fearing humanity might become immortal as a result of his ministrations. Apollo, however, pleaded his cause and Asclepius was raised to the stars to be immortalised as the serpent-bearer, Ophiuchus. The Asclepius Rod combines the snake, symbol of rebirth and fertility, with a rod and even to this day is a renowned symbol for healing – the World Health Organization logo being a well-known example. Often confused with the Caduceus (see below), it is important to remember that Asclepius Rod is always depicted with one black snake (also significant – see: Black Lilith), whereas the Caduceus has two intertwining snakes culminating in a pair of wings.

Becoming – Primal Cause in which consciousness may experience, and return all to, itself. See also: Absorption.

Black Lilith – Lilith, according to Hebrew legend, was the first wife of Adam. Fashioned from clay, as was Adam, she was created equal. Often portrayed as part snake and part female with wings, she was a power unto herself and refused to bow down to his (or God's) authority; differing sources see her banished from the Garden of Eden as punishment or departing of her own volition and taking command over the course of her own destiny. She became goddess of the night, mistress of chaos and antithesis to order, and was reputed to be mother to numerous demons as well as a killer of children – punishment, she believed, for the sins of their fathers.[lx] Lilith then, **is** First Female, an embodiment of the divine feminine, pure, undefiled, true to her innate nature and mistress to no one. Astrologically, she has three points in the heavens, the most used being 'Black Lilith', where its placement in a chart reveals a source of hidden power or inner strength but only once inner demons have been laid to rest. Her inclusion here is down to the rich symbology running through her legends and her intimate relationship with the shadow as told through the *tale of three snakes* in three visions – *Roots*, *Headspace* and *Fortress* – and, particularly, through the story of *First Female* ('A Rainbow', 'Sphere: Light').

Brahma, Vishnu, Shiva – Known as the Trimurti in Hindu mythology, these three deities are collectively responsible for the creation, preservation and destruction of the known universe. **Brahma** is the pure creative force and balancer of the two 'brothers' and serves as director. It is said that when Brahma wakes, all is created, and when he sleeps, all is destroyed; a day of Brahma is 4.32 billion years and a night equal in duration. **Vishnu** is the preserver and protector of the world, in him lies responsibility for humans and gods alike. Known to have ten incarnations, or Avatars, each being an evolutionary step up from the previous, he appears during times of great need; his first Avatar was a fish, Matsya, who appeared at the time of the great flood. Others included Krishna, eighth, who mentored Arjuna during his battle with himself, and Gautama Buddha as the ninth. The tenth and last Avatar, it is said, will appear at the end of the present age, the Kali Yuga, when humanity will face a breakdown of civilisation and loss of spiritual and moral values. Its destruction will herald a new 'golden' era.[lxi] The destroyer aspect of the Trimurti is attributed to **Shiva**, but this label belies the totality of his expression, for he can also be kind and protective. In him is both the aesthetic that has conquered his base desires and the god of fertility, in him is both dispenser and conqueror of death and in him is the place where all opposites are reconciled. As god of time, he is both weaver and destroyer of worlds, ordering the universe as Nataraja, Lord of the Dance, with one foot placed upon the back of a dwarf (symbolising ignorance) surrounded by a garland of wisdom flames.[lxii] The Trimurti, although not mentioned by name, features in the visions, *Shattering* (Shiva) and *Resting Place* (Vishnu), for instance; Brahma, less obvious, is more universal in its expression, being attributed to group process within eras of time.

Caduceus – Traditionally, the caduceus is attributed to the Greek god, Hermes (Roman – Mercury), who was not only messenger to the gods but also patron of travellers, herdsmen, invention and trade. Its tale is told in the Myth of Hermes, in which the god on bearing witness to two snakes fighting touched them with his rod, giving rise to peace between the warring reptiles. The symbol is thus two intertwining snakes facing each other around a central rod culminating in a pair of wings – in honour of the 'winged messenger'. Often erroneously assigned to healing (see: Asclepius Rod), the caduceus is more aptly represented as symbol for trade, commerce, writing and mathematics, etc., as well as one for peace and diplomacy. Its placement within the pages of *Walk the Rainbow*, however, has untold value in that not only does it reflect the dance of polarity, expressed as an enlightening journey through seven chakras, but it also illustrates the subtle forces at play when engaging with shadow-self dynamics.

Cause (primal) – Continuous outpouring force whose origin lies with Absolute.

Chakra – A Sanskrit word meaning a wheel or disc. Energy vortices centred on the spinal column, they are focal points for the reception and transmission of energies, rising from the base of the spine to the top of the head. There are seven major chakras (many more are placed at significant points around the body – the palms of the hands, for instance), six within the physical body, with the seventh positioned just above the crown at the top of the head. Aspects of consciousness from the most refined vibrations of light are thus able to interact with the physical body using two major physiological systems – endocrine and nervous systems – as disseminators; each one correlates with seven endocrine glands and an equal number of nerve plexuses at the location of each chakra. All senses, perceptions, states of awareness and experiences can be categorised by the energies being expressed through these centres. Thus, the chakras represent not only particular areas of the physical body but also aspects of consciousness. Good health, emotional stability, mental clarity and spiritual well-being are achieved by bringing all these energies into balance. The seven chakras thus serve as gateways between the unified consciousness of man (Soul and Spirit) and are placed at varying degrees of spiritual subtlety, with the crown, at the top, being connected with the Divine, and the base, at the bottom, with integration with matter; expressed outwardly as fractured or polarised consciousness.

Changeless – Term used in place of 'Absolute' to describe the same condition.

Christ-Consciousness – Union of bliss (heart) and emptiness (mind) in which a Self-realised being, awake to their innate divinity, has fused body, heart and Soul with Spirit.

Christ principle – Symbolic term meaning Absolute is present in everything.

Chronos – Greek god of time (Roman – Saturn). Many references to measured time have as their origin the name of this god – chronological, chronicle, synchronised, chronograph, etc.

Consciousness – Primal Cause giving rise to existence. May be coloured according to the realm, entity or reality through which it is expressed (universal, galactic, Christ, individual, group, etc.). See also: Absorption, Becoming, Cause.

Desire nature – Expression of the lower emotional nature where all focus is on 'me first', 'my wants and needs', etc., to the exclusion of all else.

Deva – Being of the angelic realms whose responsibility lies with the kingdom of nature.

Divine Architecture – expression of order and structure through the mind of God. Sacred geometry is a prime example.

Dweller on the Threshold – There comes a point on a spiritual journey where, despite the Herculean efforts already undertaken in bringing the personality to heel, realisation dawns that there is much still hidden beneath the shiny exterior presented to an outside world. Lurking in the shadows are lifetimes of thoughts, desires, instinctual behaviours, ancestral, racial and national sub-routines and ancient liabilities that combine to create a potent, *unconscious*, entity in its own right; this is the Dweller on the Threshold. When soul contact is sufficiently established, there comes a life where the highly developed personality becomes in itself the Dweller, battle for control of the outer form begins and in a blaze of glory, the lesser is obliterated by the greater. This is only possible when the personality, having given of itself to the Soul, recognises itself as the Dweller. The territory upon which the battle is enacted is known as the **burning ground** and comes into play at the threshold of every new advance – or, more to the point, every letting go, where the ashes of the past are as fuel for the burgeoning Spirit within. Lastly, the Dweller on the Threshold is seen in contrast to the Solar Angel (Soul) yet *both* must be cast aside, for energising either is to perpetuate a war of opposites.[lxiii]

Elemental essence – Evolved beings, Devas and elementals, inhabit the three kingdoms in nature and cooperate with the Plan of the Logos (see: Logos) in the scheme of evolution – mankind derives his perishable bodies (physical/etheric, emotional, mental) from this work. Their constitution is elemental essence, which is coloured according to the kingdom within which they live and have their being. In the higher mental plane, for instance, they make material to clothe abstract thoughts, in the lower mental plane, concrete thoughts and in the astral world, clothing of desires. Nature spirits are a part of this world, manifesting the plan on earth according to Divine Purpose expressed as the Logos.[lxiv] The important thing to grasp is that the fabric throughout the many planes of existence, in its essential essence, is impregnated with purpose in which the Deva beings serve as weavers.

Elysium – In Greek mythology Elysium was the paradise to which those Heroes whom the gods blessed with immortality were sent. Homer's writings describe the Elysian Plain as a place of perfect happiness at the ends of the earth. In the 21st century, it might be considered as heaven.

Esoteric – Inner or secret knowing ('eso', within)[lxv] often applied to ancient mystery schools (Pythagoras, for instance) to which a degree of 'inner' progress in a student will have been attained as a prerequisite to initiation.

Eternal thought – Thought, expressed through time, whose origin lies in consciousness.

Etheric – Subtle body, part of the human energy field or aura and closest to the physical body. Chakras are part of the etheric, as are meridians (etheric web/channels) used by acupuncturists to maintain healthy balance of the gross physical layers.

False lights – Broad-spectrum term used to describe the many pitfalls experienced whilst treading a spiritual path. False gurus, 'enlightened' masters, inner 'sparkles' such as 'divine' visitations, etc., and many other forms of paranormal activity are included under its banner. Awareness is the key, as is a clear-seeing, discerning eye. See also: Siddhis.

Feminine/masculine – The yin and yang of the universe as it expresses the principle of duality through gender. Every feminine has its masculine and every masculine, its feminine; each is one in expression, regardless of outward appearance.

First female – See: Black Lilith.

Genesis pattern – 'Seed of life' (seven circles) as a geometric blueprint, a 'seed', for the creation of the manifested universe. The biblical term, 'Genesis', refers to how God created the earth in six days, which correlates with six of the seven circles in the seed of life – the seventh circle is the 'One' consciousness. See also: 'What is...?', 'What is sacred geometry?', 'Seed of life'.

Great Dark – See: Great Unknown, Void.

Great Spirit – See: Absolute.

Great Unknown – Aspect of Absolute that expresses its polar opposite whilst remaining inseparable from itself.

Heart Sutra – The shortest yet most profound sutra (means 'thread') in Buddhism. Utilises clear-seeing to question the origin of every 'phenomenal' appearance to mind, regardless of its origin; a compassionate heart married with a pristine mind is a prerequisite to experiencing its unfolding wisdom.

Higher Self/Big Self – Terms used in many spiritual circles to mean the Soul.

Karma – A Sanskrit word, literally translated, which means 'action', originating from the root 'kri', meaning to act. Many years ago, a wise Buddhist teacher told the following story to illustrate how karmic principles played out over time. *A dog in a canyon believes it sees another dog in the distance so, feeling* *threatened, it barks. Of course, canyons are renowned for amplifying noise and returning it to the sender, so no surprise that the dog was infuriated when its opponent barked back. Naturally, it barked again – louder and with greater force – as did the other dog. How long the situation continued was determined by the dog who initiated the sequence of events by barking in the first place.*

At some point, the dog gives up and stops barking. This is a crucial time, for the echoes of its past actions are still 'out there' and will, without question, at some point return; the only variable is the timing. Being aware of thoughts, words and deeds in the present can at least put a stop to future echoes, known as karmic propensities, ripening when least expected. In 'Origin' (see 'A Rainbow', 'Sphere: Mind'), the character in the story suffers a vicious, unprovoked attack from 'out of nowhere', only to realise, after much soul-searching, that she was the cause. Her past actions had returned to her, in a like manner to the echoes of the barking dog, as an opportunity to elicit a different response.

Kingdoms – Specifically refers to kingdoms in nature – human, animal, vegetable or mineral – but also includes the kingdom of the Soul and Spirit.

Lighted Way – Term used to describe the spiritual path where the intention of the one who walks is to forge a bridge to the Soul/Higher Self.

Logos – Greek, meaning speech or word. The Logos is not an entity but an *expression* (sound/vibration) of an entity – the manifestation of the subjective, silent and Unknowable Absolute. A Solar Logos, for instance, would be the expression of Deity governing a solar system, with the sun being its physical manifestation.

Mahayana (Buddhism) – Translates to 'Great Vehicle', being the union of bliss and emptiness, expressed through two supreme beings, Avalokiteshvara, Bodhisattva of Compassion, and Prajnaparamita, the Blessed Mother, Buddha of transcendental wisdom. Mahayana Buddhism, then, is the 'great path' to enlightenment where these 'two wings' unite as the 'heart of wisdom' in one who seeks to attain. In this tradition, there are three Buddhic 'kayas', Trikaya, or ways of being: Dharmakaya, Truth body – essence, unmanifested and supreme state of Absolute; Sambhogakaya, enjoyment or Bliss body; Nirmanakaya, body of transformation (closest to the physical).[lxvi] Metaphors and stories in *Walk the Rainbow*, as well as facets of the diamond (*Dharmakaya* is an example) featuring emptiness and other such Buddhic qualities have as their inspiration teachings (and meditations) from this tradition.

Mantra – Rooted in the Sanskrit, 'manas', meaning mind, and 'tra', vehicle, mantra is an instrument of mind. Recited repeatedly as an aid to meditation and foundation for spiritual practice, either as sound, vibration or constructive thought-form, the practice may be likened to planting seeds in the garden of the Soul. Seed thoughts featured in *Walk the Rainbow* and *Key of Light* cards are set with the same intention.

Mentor – Group-conscious entity serving as the voice of Esmerelda's Higher Self or Soul.

Monad – Absolute expression of unity in the form of one. A Monad (there are many) is the highest spiritual essence attainable by the human and is the source of the creative spark giving rise to its existence from life to life.

Ouroboros – A snake or a dragon consuming its own tail is an alchemical symbol expressing the unity in all things, where the perpetual cycle of destruction, renewal and rebirth is actuated by consummation and transcendence of the past (eating of the tail).[lxvii] *Emergence* (p.185) is a prime example.

Planes of existence – The Constitution of Man, in the works of Alice A. Bailey, sets down Seven Planes of our Solar System, each having seven sub-planes, within which man, and his evolution in consciousness, is an integral part. It goes on to state that man's constitution is essentially threefold, being: the Monad (Spirit), the Ego (Higher Self or Soul) and the personality (lower self). Each of these threefold expressions is further coloured in three ways: **Monad** – Will or Power, Love-Wisdom, Active Intelligence; **Soul** – Spiritual Will, Intuition (Buddhi – the Christ principle), higher or abstract mind; **Personality** – mental body, emotional body, dense physical and etheric body. The evolutionary journey is one where the consciousness of an aspirant, and later disciple, is to bring the lower nature under the control of the higher through a series of initiations.[lxviii] Whilst not defining the Rainbow journey in such explicit terms, *Walk the Rainbow* nevertheless incorporates the principles laid down in these Ageless Wisdom teachings through its intention to integrate body, Soul and Spirit in such a way that service to the whole is paramount, not ego aggrandisement.

Primordial chaos – First movement within the Void, the cosmic womb of creation, which created the manifested world. It could also be said that, "the Spirit of God moved across the face of the waters," is a biblical representation of the same sentiment.

Real (the) – Used to distinguish from the unreal with 'Real' being the Absolute.

Sacred Female – Not the same as divine feminine. Sacred Female is one who has claimed her female heritage through taking ownership of her innate nature, including qualities of **both** masculine and feminine, and then embodying it. Her expression is female but, in Truth, she is without gender, being one with Spirit.

Sacred Seven – Seven Rainbow spheres express individual group-consciousness entities, as part of the geometric structure, seed of life.

Sacred Sound – Traditionally, especially in eastern philosophy, this is the universal sound, OM (AUM), a threefold note expressing Absolute perfection throughout the fabric of the Void-space. Esmerelda, in gathering together three aspects of Absolute – Will, Love, Intelligence – prior to sounding the one note, is the same principle.

Serpent – Expression of the divine feminine who often manifests in subtle, manipulative and seductive ways but whose Purpose in Divinity cannot be denied. Her ways are revealed through the *tale of three snakes* in three visions – *Roots*, *Headspace* and *Fortress* – as well as *Inner Alchemy*, and, particularly, through the story of *First Female* ('A Rainbow', 'Sphere: Light').

Science of Light Manifestation – Also called the 'Science of the Antahkarana'. Profound esoteric teachings detailing the steps involved in fusing a bridge between the personality and the Soul – the Rainbow Bridge – where 'light' as a fundamental expression of consciousness is its initiating cause.

Seed thought – See: Mantra.

Shadow – In analytical psychology, the shadow is either an unconscious aspect of the personality that the ego does not identify with or the entirety of the collective unconscious – in other words, the unknown. Jung, contrary to Freud, included both light and dark in his interpretation, as 'good' qualities may be equally denied, especially in those with low self-esteem, etc. If these aspects remain suppressed, Jung writes, the shadow is prone to psychological projection in which moral deficiency is 'projected' onto others.[lxix] Integration of the shadow, individual and, where it impacts upon the life, collective is fundamental to *Walk the Rainbow* – the story of Worthless Shadow (see 'A Rainbow', 'Sphere: Beauty') being a most obvious example.

Shangri-La – A remote, beautiful and imaginary place where life approaches perfection.[lxx]

Shining One – Angelic or Deva being (see: Deva). Also referred to as 'luminous being' in text.

Shiva – See: Brahma, Vishnu, Shiva.

Siddhis – Mystical powers, according to yogic tradition, can be cultivated and attained by means of specific spiritual practices, however, as Patanjali states, "these super-physical senses are obstacles to Samadhi [enlightenment] but are siddhis (powers or accomplishments) in the worldly pursuits."[lxxi] Inherent within the process of integrating personality with Soul is the natural arising of 'super senses', where the regular five senses are enhanced to such a degree that they render a person 'super-human' or a 'giant amongst men', at least to those who readily fall under the spell of such spiritual 'accomplishments'. An unfettered ego, whether in one with such powers or in those who feed upon them, is easily seduced when the 'Test of the Siddhis' makes its appearance, requiring much inner work, letting go and, above all, clear-seeing to see them for what they are and rise above their influence before claiming the ultimate in spiritual attainment. Patanjali makes this clear in his Sutra.

Solar Fire – This is the fire of mind. Deep and profound teachings reveal a breadth of understanding of the many expressions of mind as creator of reality, including: the nature of mind; mind as expressed through cosmic, systemic and human forms; thought and fire elementals; the Law of Attraction.[lxxii]

Soul-infused personality – Integrated way of being where personality expresses Soul qualities within the three worlds – mental, emotional, physical/etheric.

Superposition – Quantum state where two (or more) particles of matter exist in more than one place at the same time. Consciousness expresses this principle through it being, at one and the same time, individual and universal.

Thoth – Atlantean priest-king said to be an embodiment of the universal mind of God. Of particular interest to *Walk the Rainbow* are the Emerald Tablets of which the 'Key of Time' inspired Esmerelda's dialogue with her inner teacher on the relationship between sound and form (p.196).

Threefold note – See: Sacred Sound.

Triple triad – In the context of integration, this refers to the three qualities/ aspects of Spirit, Soul and body, being: Will, Love, Intelligence – Spirit; consciousness, intuition (Christ principle), abstract mind – Soul; and mental (intellect), emotional and physical/etheric – body.

Truth – Relative or Absolute is distinguished by the use of a capital letter. Absolute **T**ruth refers to Absolute and any aspect or word directly attributed to it – relative truth is dependent upon the perspective and beliefs of the one who is declaring 'something' to be 'true' but who lacks the bigger-picture awareness or wherewithal to qualify their findings.

Unmanifest – Pre-existent state prior to Absolute's expression outwards into substance.

Vishnu – See: Brahma, Vishnu, Shiva.

Void (the) – Space of infinite potential whose fabric is nothingness. See also: Great Unknown.

World game – 21st-century life with all its complexities, 'must have' commodities and self-centred, polarised attitudes, viewed from the perspective of the One consciousness, is referred to as the 'world game'.

Yoni – Sanskrit, meaning 'abode', 'source', 'womb' or 'vagina'. In Hinduism, it is the symbol of the goddess Shakti, consort of **Shiva**. The symbol is the **lingam**, which resembles a male phallus; together they represent the eternal process of creation and regeneration, the union of masculine and feminine principles and the totality of all existence.[lxxiii]

Zero – Absolute Zero is the space created before ever there was a spark, before primordial chaos initiated birth to existence and before an idea of unconsciousness had ever been sown as a seed.

ABOUT THE AUTHOR

Barbara Rose is a visionary artist, writer and researcher of Truth. An Air Traffic Controller for almost 30 years, she received her first wake-up call when the stress of the job began to have a detrimental effect on her mental health and physical well-being. She realised she had to change, and the only person who could do that was her. No more blaming others for **their** inadequacies; she had to take full responsibility and claim ownership of **her own** – easier said than done! Following more than one stress-induced breakdown, at the turn of the century she relinquished her profession, turned her attention inwards and began a journey of self-discovery, choosing tai chi, homeopathy and meditation as mediums to explore her inner landscape.

Following qualification some three years later, these became foundations not only for *her* journey, but also for those of others, through her classes, workshops, meditations and retreats. However, it was not to last. Inner change will at some point manifest as outer reality, alignment with the Soul inevitably means allowing its purpose to be paramount, rather than the will of the small, and even though she was at times dragged kicking and screaming against her wall of resistance to yet more change, she eventually gave in.

As one door closes another opens and if attention is paid to the possibilities available in each moment magic can happen; this is how it was for Barbara. As well as creating her first drawing, a series of synchronicities led her to the door of Flower of Life Research (now Seed of Life Institute) and the work of Ron and Lyssa Holt. Paralleling her explosion of creativity, advanced sacred geometry workshops and retreats became the order of the day, including meditating with dolphins in Mexico. Little did she know it at the time, but the seeds to *Walk the Rainbow* were sown in these early years. The time, however, was not quite ripe, and other avenues of creative expression found their voice first, including the publication of her first book, *Visions of Reality*. Shortly after its release, she entered the USA 'Best Books' awards, just for fun! You could have knocked her over with a feather when she was nominated as a finalist in the category 'Best New Non-Fiction' – she wasn't even sure she qualified as a writer, let alone a candidate worthy of consideration. It was a wonderful confidence booster, and over the space of a year she published three decks of contemplation cards.

Understanding as to their significance emerged during her *Walk the Rainbow* programme – a series of workshops and courses, spread over seven years, where Rainbow teachings could be shared and explored with others. More visions were birthed, the original 42 soon numbered 144 and inspiration for *Key of Light* cards was born. *Walk the Rainbow*, then, evolved naturally into its current form over a period of ten years, synthesising the best from her publishing past in the process. Questions from fellow travellers inspired her to dig deep into their substance to find answers; the fruit of her research being condensed into course handouts, which matured into the comprehensive guidebook you are holding today. The most magical and humbling experience during its evolution was that the recipients, through their own searching, were equal co-creators in its birthing. Such is the power of the universe in expressing purpose!

Barbara lives in North West England, leads a simple life in her personal Shangri-La and is perfectly happy whether walking her dog, playing with paint or words, being present in nature or sharing magical adventures with friends – real or imagined. Most of all, she is extremely grateful for life's many and varied blessings that have led her to such a space of enrichment.

RAINBOW EXPERIENCES

The following testimonials were received from *Walk the Rainbow* workshop participants or following one-on-one sessions with the author.

"Another truly amazing day with Barbara Rose... and the Walk the Rainbow, sacred geometry group... we have been deepening our understanding and experience of spirit, meditation, human evolution... cannot put into words, the depths are non-wordable!!! It's been an amazingly beautiful day..." L.H.

"Eternal gratitude for all your energy, wisdom and presence..." L.D.

"I must thank you for being so dedicated to your spiritual path by allowing all the ancient wisdom to permeate your whole being and allowing your creative spirit to present all that ancient wisdom in a format that is a lot easier for us to learn and benefit from. Please continue what you do so that others like me can benefit from the beauty of your soul. Thank you." L.S.

"...each gathering centres me back to a point of 'right belonging' and gives me thought for reflection and contemplation. It certainly has brought more awareness into my daily life and hopefully I can use the learning to enhance not only my life but those of others. Heartfelt thanks." B.W.

"... I DID IT... the seed of life from last week and I did it on my own, this morning. I feel positively euphoric... what a shift..." L.B

"Everyone really enjoyed your workshop, and your talk at the beginning was excellent, you presented some fairly complex material in a very accessible manner. BIG thank you! I personally got a lot from it, both the talk and the meditation, the implications of the cards I drew plus the meditation are still slowly unfolding for me as there are layers of meanings." A.M.

"Absolutely wonderful day yesterday Barbara, thank you for your time and effort, and for sharing your amazing work and knowledge. ♥ ♥ ♥" A.B

"Barbara is a very wise and gifted woman. Whenever I look at and meditate on her contemplation cards, they always make me feel so much better. Her one-on-one sessions are a life-changing and wonderful event, where she lovingly guides you in remembering your birthright. Thank you, Barbara. You are awesome!" L.B.

"Meditating on the contemplation cards with Barbara's guidance was both insightful and empowering, focusing on key issues which proved to be accurate and very relevant to what is happening for me at the present time. Barbara has helped me to see aspects of my life which need re-aligning and I can work on for my personal growth." S.R.

"What an amazing moment yesterday was for me, once I got home yesterday and opened my journal the words just poured out, I felt like a gifted tarot reader!" L.B.

"Thank you for giving me so much peace and inspiration at what was a very difficult time in my life. For the first time I am actually focusing on the positive light side of myself rather than the dark negative. I cannot believe how simple the switch has been... And your cards... what can I say? They are truly wonderful, inspirational and extremely powerful. They are a true enigma." L.S.

ACKNOWLEDGEMENTS

Rarely, if ever, is any creative work solely down to the efforts of one person. It is collaboration, a meeting of minds and skillsets, spread over the course of time and often, if subtle qualities are involved, without conscious knowing on the part of the collaborators. If such a work takes place over a number of years, as in the case of *Walk the Rainbow*, many of the original players or events can be lost to the annals of time. The following is my attempt at remembering some of the sparks that heralded the finished article. Some will be more obvious than others, many are embraced within the 'Appreciation' transcript at the beginning and more are given space within the main body of work. View the acknowledgements below as pieces of a jigsaw you might gather first – corners and edges – so the complete picture may be more easily assembled inside. Placement here does not render these players any more or less important than others – they are merely set out in their proper place.

Ron Holt is first and foremost on my list. His willingness to write a foreword, when writing by his own admission is not his forte, is testament to the honour he has bestowed both upon myself and *Walk the Rainbow*. He is a well-respected spiritual facilitator, meditation teacher and mentor to many (me included) of international standing, but it is his personal qualities I wish to acknowledge here. Over the years, he has shown me, simply through his presence and generosity of spirit, how to believe in myself. His openness and willingness to share his vulnerability has enabled me to embrace my own, and his depth of vision and clarity, whether related to Great Spirit or under-processed structures within the shadow self, has shone a light on the many, many aspects of my own being. As to *Walk the Rainbow*, his readiness to authenticate teachings revealed through Esmerelda's and Thomas' musings, when at times I've wondered that their magnitude might not be plausible, has made the writing of this book not only easier but more credible. Ron, from this little human's perspective and from the wider vision that is portrayed through these pages, I cannot thank you enough – you have enabled the vision to become a reality and for this I am and always will be **in**ternally grateful.

She has no recollection of the event but Lyssa Royal Holt, Ron's wife, is responsible for the title. A world-renowned channel for extra-terrestrial consciousness of many years' standing, she made the suggestion, "We must learn to walk the rainbow," during one of her workshop sessions. However, her inclusion here is not down to this alone. Having felt as an alien on a strange planet for most of my life, Lyssa reconnected me with my galactic heritage as a facet of my inner being. She has a way of presenting 'off-the-planet' realities in a way that makes them more real than what lies in the back yard – ordinary, grounded, life-affirming and believable. Several works of art included herein have as their inspiration realisations from her teachings. Gratitude just doesn't cut it but it's the only word I have to express how thankful I am. As a personality, she is fun, playful, insightful and human – pure joy to be with and she makes me laugh. Lyssa, I love you to the stars and back and I am so grateful they set a course for Scotland in the summer of 2007 that we may meet. From the bottom of my heart, I thank you for the gifts you share with us all, for the revelations, for the memories – for Italy and Glastonbury – and simply for being you – thank you, so much!

My meeting with Ron and Lyssa was down to the auspices of Flower of Life facilitator, Angela Morse. In Scotland 33 participants came together for what can only be described as a meeting of souls. A mere six days in duration yet the effects, friendships and soul connections have rippled throughout the fabric of the space-time continuum to echo its purpose through to this day. How could Angela not be included, being the instigator of an event of such magnitude? Furthermore, she wrote the foreword to my first book – *Visions of Reality* – facilitated her own workshops at my home in Preston and was instrumental in setting up a Rainbow group in Durham that these teachings could be explored. Ours was a co-creative partnership in which I considered it an honour to serve. Angela, bless you and thank you for giving of yourself so wholeheartedly to this work whilst honouring yourself in the process.

Thanks to my dear friends and soul companions, Chris Anders and Jon Corbett (Yogi Jon), for making this world a better place. Chris, from the moment we met in Thailand so very long ago, I knew you. Your gentle soul, the infinite wisdom that flows untainted through you and the child-like joy you share so spontaneously with others light my eyes with love. In you, I see me, and *through* you, I touch the profound. Every step of the Rainbow journey, you have been there, offering guidance and direction, gently encouraging me to continue – especially when I was stuck! Thank you for allowing profound teachings to flow uninhibited through you to grace these pages and for granting permission for your artwork to be published in this format. Most of all, I thank you for your friendship – honest, untainted, intimate, timeless – and for including me in your beautiful family – I love you all. New pathways, new adventures, expressed through one beautiful life – what more could we possibly wish for?

And Yogi Jon, you are as a mirror to the soul, a perfect reflection of all that is real in me. My karma barometer, who never fails to speak as the Soul would speak and who, without fail, recognises the infinite in me. Thank you for helping me to remember when, at times, I forget. Artist, musician, meditator, yogi – I love all that

is sacred in you and your commitment to love God, above all else. I love your love of nature, the beauty you see in a flower, the simple life you lead and how you always make time for our friendship. I give thanks for your honest feedback on this book and my artwork, especially the fairies; it has helped considerably in my growth as a 'real' artist, as well as a writer. The fun we have on our days out, our shared love of cats and frustration with herons and all else that is ordinary in our relationship can only be truly expressed in words such as these, "I am blessed indeed to have you call me friend, for you are Anam Cara – friend to the Soul."

Gratitude to Sheila Fish, who was there at the beginning when I was spiritually bereft, whose meditation classes offered a space where my inner being could be nourished and whose passion for all things 'Bailey' led me deeper into the 'blue' books. Friend, teacher, shadow and go-to resource for Alice A. Bailey-related material, I have treasured the many twists and turns in our relationship for many years. Too few words for two decades of experiences, nevertheless I remain grateful for all we share now, as we have always. Thank you S, you remain a treasured and much-loved friend.

And Gen Kelsang Pagpa, who on our first meeting taught me the meaning of wisdom and whose eyes filled with compassion when my seeker's heart was laid bare at his feet. My spiritual heritage was awakened the moment I walked through your door. In gifting me emptiness, the teachings you imparted, with such humility and humour, abide in my heart to this day and serve as a barometer to walk in Truth, always. Thank you Pagpa, the Spirit of Buddha shines through all you share and thenceforth into others, and I for one am filled with gratitude that it does.

I offer my sincere thanks to those who, oftentimes without knowing, have helped inspire my publishing journey. Liz Berry for remarking, "These would make a set of cards," whilst reflecting upon my doodles. Maureen Thomas for acknowledging the 'visionary' in me before it had ever entered my mind. Linda Strickland for 'getting it' – you've no idea how much this means! The Sanctuary of Healing, Blackburn, for being supportive of me and my creative offerings – from hosting art exhibitions and workshops to promoting my book, art and cards, they have always been a joy to deal with. In this regard, special thanks go to Julie, who always has a ready smile accompanied by a willingness to serve. And Bonnie Craig, editor, typesetter and designer, who, through her clear professionalism in attending to every detail, has elevated this book to a credible work of art; one I can be truly proud of. It is, however, her personal attributes that I have appreciated the most and wish to acknowledge here. I have loved her love of boundaries, her deadlines, her enthusiasm in engaging with material that must have, at times, seemed 'off the planet' and her openness in accepting that the impossible might just be possible. Furthermore, her suggestions, her willingness to embrace mine, and her tenacity in not letting me get away with anything has helped me to grow, not only as a writer but also as a person. Bonnie, I cannot thank you enough, you have turned what could have been a torturous process (for me) into an adventure, and it really has been a joy to walk alongside you on this Rainbow journey – thank you, so much, for participating body, heart and Soul, in its birthing.

This list would not be complete without mention of my brother, Peter Hage. Through his contacts in China he sourced, printed and shipped three sets of contemplation cards, marking the beginning of my self-publishing 'career' whilst giving me the confidence to 'go it alone' and trust in the outcome. Undertaken without complaint, at a time when he was maxed out with his own business, it was to me a labour of love. His interest in the visions, even though they are not "his cup of tea", has always been evidenced by the quiet, introspective attitude he employs whilst slowly turning the cards over in his hands before making pertinent suggestions. Words do not do justice to the feelings of gratitude, and love, I feel whilst acknowledging his worth to me. Thank you, Peter – you are one special person and it is an honour for me to acknowledge you as my brother in this way.

Above all else, I honour the Creative Spirit that runs through us all. Without it, this book would be a tome of empty pages and life, all life, would be meaningless.

Licences

Artwork p.29 'A Gift', 'Fairy' – 'Musical Sphere' designed by Harryarts/Freepik.

Artwork p.159 'A Diamond', 'Conversion' and 'The Word' – by Chris Anders.

Artwork p.437 'What is...?', 'Building Bridges', 'Building the Rainbow Bridge', 'Caduceus' graphic – © sunnymars www.fotosearch.com.

Galactic content in visions courtesy NASA: images.nasa.gov.

Quantum Navigation p.457 – shared with permission from Ronald Holt and the Seed of Life Institute.

BIBLIOGRAPHY

[i] Alice A. Bailey, *Education in the New Age* (New York: Lucis Trust, 1954) p.144

[ii] Alice A. Bailey, *Esoteric Psychology II* (New York: Lucis Trust, 1942) pp.21–22

[iii] *Ibid.* pp.36–39

[iv] Sogyal Rinpoche, *The Tibetan Book of Living and Dying*, edited by Patrick Gaffney and Andrew Harvey (Rider, 1992) pp.247–256

[v] Mary Bailey, *A Learning Experience* (New York: Lucis Trust, 1990) pp.50–51

[vi] Dr. Douglas Baker, *The Jewel in the Lotus* (Essenden, England: Douglas Baker, 1975) p.84

[vii] Phillip Lindsay, *Unveiling Genesis – Mysteries of the Rootraces and Cycles* (Australia: Apollo Publishing, 2017)

[viii] Lyssa Royal Holt, *The Prism of Lyra* (Scottsdale, AZ: Royal Priest Research, 1992) p.50

[ix] Lyssa Royal Holt, *The Prism of Lyra* (Scottsdale, AZ: Royal Priest Research, 1992)

[x] Phillip Lindsay, *Unveiling Genesis – Mysteries of the Rootraces and Cycles* (Australia: Apollo Publishing, 2017)

[xi] Doreal, *The Emerald Tablets of Thoth the Atlantean* (Nashville, TN: Source Books, 2002) pp.55–59

[xii] Phillip Lindsay, *Unveiling Genesis – Mysteries of the Rootraces and Cycles* (Australia: Apollo Publishing, 2017)

[xiii] Alice A. Bailey, *The Rays and Initiations* (New York: Lucis Publishing Company, 2002) pp.460–462

[xiv] Phillip Lindsay, *Unveiling Genesis – Mysteries of the Rootraces and Cycles* (Australia: Apollo Publishing, 2017)

[xv] "Hindu units of time" Wikipedia, 2021, https://en.wikipedia.org/wiki/Hindu_units_of_time Accessed 3 January 2022

[xvi] Arthur Cotterell and Rachel Storm, *The Ultimate Encyclopedia of Mythology* (London: Anness Publishing, 2003) p.356

[xvii] Paul Foster Case, *The Book of Tokens* (Los Angeles, CA: Builders of the Adytum, 1968) p.14

[xviii] Paul Foster Case, *The Book of Tokens* (Los Angeles, CA: Builders of the Adytum, 1968) p.14

[xix] Phillip Lindsay, *Unveiling Genesis – Mysteries of the Rootraces and Cycles* (Australia: Apollo Publishing, 2017)

[xx] "Rainbow" Encyclopaedia Britannica, 2021, www.britannica.com/science/rainbow-atmospheric-phenomenon Accessed 21 January 2022

[xxi] Alice A. Bailey, *The Rays and Initiations* (New York: Lucis Publishing Company, 2002) pp.444–452

[xxii] Drunvalo Melchizedek, *Living in the Heart* (Flagstaff, AZ: Light Technology Publishing, 2003) p.95

[xxiii] Alice A. Bailey, *The Seven Rays of Life* (New York: Lucis Publishing Company, 2003) p.205

xxiv Alice A. Bailey, *The Seven Rays of Life* (New York: Lucis Publishing Company, 2003) p.77

xxv Alice A. Bailey, *Esoteric Psychology I* (New York: Lucis Publishing Company, 2002) p.63

xxvi Alice A. Bailey, *Esoteric Astrology* (New York: Lucis Publishing Company, 1968) p.653

xxvii Alice A. Bailey, *The Seven Rays of* Life (New York: Lucis Publishing Company, 2003) p.77

xxviii Alice A. Bailey, *Esoteric Psychology I* (New York: Lucis Publishing Company, 2002) pp.65–67

xxix Alice A. Bailey, *Esoteric Astrology* (New York: Lucis Publishing Company, 1968) pp.343–370

xxx *Ibid.* p.115

xxxi *Ibid.* p.329

xxxii *Ibid.* p.167

xxxiii Alice A. Bailey, *The Seven Rays of Life* (New York: Lucis Publishing Company, 2003) p.77

xxxiv Alice A. Bailey, *Esoteric Astrology* (New York: Lucis Publishing Company, 1968) p.311

xxxv *Ibid.* p.153

xxxvi *Ibid.* p.164

xxxvii *Ibid.* p.226

xxxviii *Ibid.* p.12

xxxix Alice A. Bailey, *The Seven Rays of Life* (New York: Lucis Publishing Company, 2003) p.77

xl Alice A. Bailey, *Esoteric Astrology* (New York: Lucis Publishing Company, 1968) p.193

xli *Ibid.* p.329

xlii *Ibid.* p.330

xliii Alice A. Bailey, *The Seven Rays of Life* (New York: Lucis Publishing Company, 2003) p.77

xliv Alice A. Bailey, *Esoteric Astrology* (New York: Lucis Publishing Company, 1968) p.134

xlv *Ibid.* p.329

xlvi *Ibid.* p.289

xlvii Alice A. Bailey, *The Seven Rays of Life* (New York: Lucis Publishing Company, 2003) p.77

xlviii Alice A. Bailey, *Esoteric Astrology* (New York: Lucis Publishing Company, 1968) p.251

xlix *Ibid.* p.115

l *Ibid.* p.174

li Alice A. Bailey, *The Seven Rays of Life* (New York: Lucis Publishing Company, 2003) p.77

lii Alice A. Bailey, *Esoteric Astrology* (New York: Lucis Publishing Company, 1968) p.91

liii *Ibid.* p.312

liv *Ibid.* p.654

lv *Ibid.* p.153

lvi "Quantum navigation" 2018, www.quantumnavigation.net Accessed 3 January 2022

lvii "Quantum navigation library" 2018, www.quantumnavigation.net/quantum-navigation-videos.html Accessed 3 January 2022

lviii *The Kybalion: A Study of the Hermetic Philosophy of Ancient Egypt and Greece by Three Initiates. Published 1908.*

lix "Ancient of Days" Wikipedia, 2020, https://en.wikipedia.org/wiki/Ancient_of_Days

Accessed 3 January 2022

lx   Arthur Cotterell and Rachel Storm, *The Ultimate Encyclopedia of Mythology* (London: Anness Publishing, 2003) p.286, p.296

lxi   *Ibid*. pp.378–379

lxii   *Ibid*. pp.402–403

lxiii   Alice A. Bailey, *Esoteric Astrology* (New York: Lucis Publishing Company, 1968) p.207

lxiv   Dr. Douglas Baker, *The Jewel in the Lotus* (Essenden, England: Douglas Baker, 1975) pp.83–84

lxv   "Esoteric" Encyclopaedia Britannica, 2016, www.britannica.com/topic/esotericism Accessed 19 October 2021

lxvi   "Trikaya" Encyclopaedia Britannica, 2017, www.britannica.com/topic/trikaya Accessed 18 October 2021

lxvii   "Ouroboros" Encyclopaedia Britannica, 2020, www.britannica.com/topic/Ouroboros Accessed 20 October 2021

lxviii   Alice A. Bailey, *Initiation, Human and Solar* (New York: Lucis Publishing Company, 2008) pp.xiv–xv

lxix   "Shadow (psychology)" Wikipedia, 2021, https://en.wikipedia.org/wiki/Shadow_(psychology) Accessed 3 January 2022

lxx   "Shangri-la" Merriam-Webster, n.d., www.merriam-webster.com/dictionary/Shangri-la Accessed 20 October 2021

lxxi   Sri Swami Satchidananda, *The Yoga Sutras of Patanjali* (Buckingham, VA: Integral Yoga Publications, 2008) p.193

lxxii   Alice A. Bailey, *A Treatise on Cosmic Fire* (New York: Lucis Publishing Company, 2005) p.221

lxxiii   "Yoni" Encyclopaedia Britannica, 2018, www.britannica.com/topic/yoni Accessed 22 October 2021

lxxiv   Phillip Lindsay, *Soul Cycles of the Seven Rays* (Australia: Apollo Publishing, 2006) p.15

Walk the Rainbow

With Barbara Rose

New material, events and products, including signed copies of this book, and
Key of Light contemplation cards are offered through the author's website.
Please visit: **www.visionsofreality.co.uk**

Printed in Great Britain
by Amazon

13815067R00282